Community Corrections

Community Corrections

Elaine Gunnison
<small>SEATTLE UNIVERSITY</small>

CAROLINA ACADEMIC PRESS
Durham, North Carolina

Library of Congress Cataloging-in-Publication Data

Names: Gunnison, Elaine, author.
Title: Community corrections / Elaine Gunnison.
Description: Durham, North Carolina : Carolina Academic Press, [2017] |
    Includes bibliographical references and index.
Identifiers: LCCN 2017017158 | ISBN 9781611637557 (alk. paper)
Subjects: LCSH: Community-based corrections--Law and legislation. |
    Correctional law. | Alternatives to imprisonment. | Probation. | Parole. |
    Juvenile delinquents. | Ex-convicts--Rehabilitation. |
    Ex-convicts--Services for.
Classification: LCC K5516 .G86 2017 | DDC 364.6--dc23
LC record available at https://lccn.loc.gov/2017017158

e-ISBN 978-1-53100-535-1

Carolina Academic Press, LLC
700 Kent Street
Durham, North Carolina 27701
Telephone (919) 489-7486
Fax (919) 493-5668
www.cap-press.com

For the fantastic young men and terrific husband in my life
who make it so much fun: Daniel, Zachary, & Evan

For my parents: Walter and Jane

—*E. G.*

Contents

Acknowledgments

This book would not have been possible without the support of many individuals. First, and foremost, I must thank Carolina Academic Press for providing me with an opportunity to write this book. A special thanks to Beth Hall, the Acquisitions Editor, who approved this book project and TJ Smithers in the Production Department. Also, thanks to Laura Dewey who provided the index. Second, a very big thank you to Devan Duenas at Seattle University. Devan worked as my Research Assistant on this project, and he never let me down. He worked tirelessly on editing my chapters and formatting the book per required guidelines, and he single-handedly was responsible for all the instructor materials for the teacher's manual. He never missed a deadline I gave him, his work ethic and dedication to this project was amazing, and the work that he produced for this project was always at such a high caliber. I am very grateful and appreciative of his help on this project.

I would also like to thank the Dean's Office of the College of Arts and Sciences at Seattle University for their support. Additionally, I would like to thank my Criminal Justice Department colleagues and staff who have been so supportive throughout this project: Jackie Helfgott, Matthew Hickman, Stephen Rice, Peter Collins, William Parkin, David Connor, Kate Reynolds, and Devin MacKrell. Finally, I would like to thank my family, friends, and loved ones who cheered me along the way. Since I arrived at Seattle University in 2004, Jackie Helfgott has been an incredible mentor and friend. Thanks Jackie for all the lunches, coffee breaks, advice, and attempts to get me to move from a Type A to a Type A- personality. I am not there yet, but I am trying! I am also very thankful to my husband, Daniel, who has cheered me yet again on another book endeavor. Thanks Dan for always standing by my side, supporting me, and being the best friend ever. Of course, I am so thankful for my wonderful boys, Zachary and Evan. Both boys are smart, kind, loving, caring, athletic, talented, and hardworking, and I am so lucky to be their mom. Thanks boys for listening to my many discussions of content in this book on our bike rides and walks over the summer. I also cannot leave out thanks to my miniature dachshund, Snaps, who slept and snored next to me as I wrote this book. She is such an amazing dog! Another miniature dachshund, Paws, also helped as I completed this book. Paws is Evan's dog, and while he was away at school, Paws slept on my lap as I edited this book. I would also like to thank my many friends from graduate school (Lo Presser, Julie Kiernan-Coon, Lisa McCartan-Kim, Randy and Kati Pagulayan) and beyond (Katie and Paul Windle, the Collins family) for their encouragement. Last, but not least, I would like to thank my parents, Walter and Jane, for all their support. Thanks for all your phone calls, visits, and words of wisdom. Also, thanks for joining us on vacations in wonderful locations, allowing us all to be together and giving me the opportunity to de-stress over all the projects I am involved with.

Community Corrections

Chapter 1

Community Corrections: Historical Development & Current Trends

Student Learning Outcomes

After reading this chapter, you should be able to:

- Explain why a text on community corrections is important.
- Describe what is meant by the term "community corrections."
- Summarize the history of community corrections in the U.S., and describe how current economic conditions have impacted community corrections practices in the U.S.
- Describe reentry challenges faced by community corrections offenders.

Introduction

When most citizens in the United States think about formal punishment in the criminal justice system, their thoughts tend to gravitate towards prison initially, as many equate prison with punishment. This equation of prison with punishment may occur for several reasons. First, there may be a natural tendency to view prisons as the primary form of punishment in the U.S. given their visibility. Whether driving through a small town or on the freeway, there is a good chance that you have stumbled across a prison and have seen it with your own eyes. If you haven't had the opportunity to view a prison up close, you may have noticed signs while you were driving warning you not to pick up hitchhikers. Hence, the visibility of prisons may seep into the minds of citizens as the prevailing form of punishment in society more so than other correctional punishments. Another reason that prisons may be equated with punishment may be due to the role of the media. After all, the media does a terrific job of highlighting crimes in the U.S.—particularly violent ones. The media will select certain cases to focus on and spoon feed the public every element of the crime and ensuing criminal trial for that crime from the very beginning of the trial to the final sentence. If the final outcome of the case is a prison sentence, then the punishment of prison gets further etched in the minds of citizens, who again, often erroneously infer that prison is the most common sentence. Whatever the actual reason may be for the linking of prison with punishment, citizens tend to overlook other forms of punishment that are found in their communities—specifically community corrections sentences. In fact, community corrections sentences account for the largest number of offenders sentenced in the U.S.

When citizens do think about community corrections sentences, it may be due to the media highlighting a famous offender who is being considered to serve a community corrections sentence, such as parole. Charles Manson, who was convicted of seven murders that happened during a 1969 killing spree in Los Angeles, California, is one infamous offender whose name surfaces in the media whenever he is considered for parole release (Ng, 2012). Manson, the leader of a cult in the 1960s, rallied his cult members to carry out these seven murders under his direction. While these murders would certainly create outrage in any community, the manner in which his followers carried out the killings—by stabbing the victims repeatedly with knives and writing "pigs" on the walls of the homes of the victims' blood—created outrage and mortified the community of Los Angeles (Bugliosi & Gentry, 1974). Originally sentenced to death, his death sentence was later commuted to a life sentence with the possibility of parole due to a 1972 Supreme Court ruling whereby the death penalty was deemed unconstitutional, and thus, banned (Ng, 2012). Since Manson is now eligible for parole, he is still granted a parole board hearing when he is deemed eligible to have one per state guidelines. Whenever word of Manson's parole board hearing gets out, there is often a media firestorm surrounding the potential parole sentence, which usually coincides with public outcry. Despite parole now being an option for Manson, he has been denied parole on over one dozen occasions (Ng, 2012). After being denied parole yet again in 2012, his next parole board hearing has been scheduled for the year 2027 (Martinez, 2012).

For other instances of when community corrections sentences may come to the minds of citizens, it may be due to the media publicizing a case whereby a rogue community corrections offender committed a crime against an innocent community member. One such community corrections case that garnered national media attention and brought utter outrage against the parole process is the case of Phillip Garrido in the state of California. Garrido, a paroled sex offender, kidnapped 11-year-old Jaycee Dugard in 1991 in California (Martinez, 2011). He managed to kidnap Dugard, with this assistance of his wife Nancy, while he was on parole. He subsequently held her captive in his backyard for 18 years, during which time he raped Dugard and fathered her two children, all while on parole (Martinez, 2011). This fact led to quite a bit of outrage against his parole officers. That is, citizens wondered what exactly his parole officers were doing and why they hadn't discovered Dugard in Garrido's backyard much earlier—especially since parole officers can search a parolee's residence without a search warrant. Nancy assisted in holding Dugard captive as well, even during a period of time when Garrido was sent back to a federal prison to serve a five-month prison sentence for violating a condition of his parole (Martinez, 2009). Subsequently, in 2010, the state of California awarded Dugard and her family a $20 million settlement due to negligence by the Department of Corrections and Rehabilitation (La Ganga & Goldmacher, 2010). Moreover, in

2011, Garrido was sentenced to a 431 years to life prison sentence, and his wife was sentenced to a 36 years to life sentence (Martinez, 2011).

This chapter offers an overview of the book, including providing the reader with a definition and an understanding of what is meant by the term "community corrections." Additionally, this chapter will provide the reader with a historical overview of the development of community corrections in the United States. Further, this chapter will discuss the current trends within community corrections in terms of the number supervised, expansion of particular community corrections programs (e.g., probation, parole, day reporting) in recent years in both urban and rural communities, how the current state of the economy has contributed to growth and/or problems within community corrections, and the challenges community corrections offenders face during reentry.

Reasons for Focus on Community Corrections

As mentioned earlier, when most citizens think about the correctional system, their thoughts often gravitate towards prisons, as prisons, given their visibility, seemed to be most equated with punishment. However, thinking of the correctional system as being solely comprised of prison operations is narrow minded, as corrections encompasses many distinct forms of punishments—including community corrections. **Community corrections** refers to the range of formal criminal justice punishments that are carried out in the community (i.e., outside prison walls). You are likely familiar with some forms of community corrections sentences already such as probation or parole—particularly when celebrities such as Justin Bieber end up serving such a sentence (D'Zurilla, 2015). Given your knowledge or awareness about community corrections sentences, you might be wondering why there is even a need for such a text on the topic. Perhaps the more important question may be why wouldn't there be a distinct text for community corrections?

Although the media portrays prison as the more common corrections punishment, this is certainly not the case. Reflect for a moment on movies and current television shows that you may have watched that feature correctional punishments. It may be the case that you thought about classic movies depicting prison such as *The Shawshank Redemption*, starring Tim Robbins and Morgan Freeman, or the recent comedy *Get Hard*, starring Will Ferrell and Kevin Hart. Additionally, television shows such as *LockUp* featured on MSNBC or *Prison Break* that aired on Fox or even perhaps the series *Orange Is the New Black*, airing on Netflix, might have come to your mind when you reflected on shows that feature corrections. What all these media depictions of corrections have in common is that they feature prisons, thus, it should certainly come as no surprise that the public may more readily adopt the idea that when it comes to correctional punishments in the U.S., the chief punishment is prison. However, the adoption of such an idea could not be further from the truth, as millions more individuals are serving community corrections than the number of all individuals serving time in state and federal prisons and in jails combined.

You might be surprised to learn that much of our knowledge of community corrections has emerged from researchers only in the past several decades. Wait, how can that be? To fully grasp why our knowledge of community corrections has been limited, we first have to examine why the study of community corrections was placed on the backburner. Within the field of **corrections**, the study of correctional systems, practices, and policy, the focus of researchers was on examining prisons — specifically prisoner subculture and institutional behavior. Since prisons were first established in the U.S. in the late 1700s and community corrections sentences emerged in the late 1800s and throughout the 1900s, it seems to make sense that much of the focus of researchers would be on examining prisons in some capacity. Thus, many of the early books and writings about corrections were focused on prisons. Although textbooks in the field have evolved over time to integrate community corrections topics, many researchers argue that the inclusion of such discussions is still limited. Given the oversight of community corrections topics in texts about prison or community corrections texts that focus on probation and/or parole, this book devotes a detailed exploration into all aspects of community corrections, moving beyond traditional probation and/or parole topics.

Apart from providing a book specifically on community corrections, courses on the topic are critical. Reflect on your career goals. Do they include working at all with offenders in some capacity (i.e., either through arrest while working as a law enforcement officer or in a supervisory capacity while working as a community corrections officer)? If so, it is critical that you understand the population that you likely will be working with. By acquiring knowledge of community corrections and issues impacting this specific area of corrections, it will greatly improve your preparation for professions throughout the criminal justice system. Besides the acquisition of knowledge of various problems and issues in community corrections, you will be able to articulate the steps that you and others may need to make in order to ameliorate or eliminate these problems through the use of **policy implications**. Policy implications refer to policies that can be implemented to combat a social problem. In the future, you may find yourself working in the criminal justice system and will need to suggest policies to help the population you may be working with. Today, it is not enough to recognize that a problem exists in the criminal justice system, and think that the problem is unfortunate or that you are powerless to make a difference. Rather, there are many ways in which you can get involved in some form of activism on the topic, whether it is through knowledge dissemination to the public or more formal forms of activism such as establishing a grassroots campaign to change a law or institute a policy.

With a burgeoning number of community corrections sentences in society today, examining issues within this field has become increasingly important (see Text Box 1.1). With millions of community corrections offenders living in our society, it has become increasingly important to understand these offenders and determine how best to help this population. These offenders are driving on the same roads you and I drive on, shopping at the same stores, and perhaps are sipping coffee near you at your local coffee shop. If they are not already among us, they will likely be released from prison back into society. Thus, what happens to them before, during, and after the completion of a community corrections sentence may impact you in small or large ways — or perhaps ways in which you will never know. Community corrections offenders are worthy of our attention. Only by understanding the nature of their backgrounds and experiences can we work toward enacting policies and laws to assist them and, hopefully, foster their successful reintegration into society. Thus, the question today should not be why is it important to examine the community corrections system, but rather why would it *not* be important to examine the community corrections system?

Text Box 1.1: Community Corrections Across the World

The topic of community corrections is an important one across the globe. In 2013, the first World Congress on Probation took place in London (Confederation of European Probation, 2015). Two years later, a second World Congress meeting took place in Los Angeles (Confederation of European Probation, 2015). At the second World Congress meeting, the focus was not only on probation but on all aspects of community corrections, thus, the meeting was formally called the World Congress on Community Corrections. According to the Confederation of European Probation (2015), "The purpose of the World Congress was to bring together community corrections leadership professionals from all corners of the world to share effective practices, promising initiatives and challenges faced in providing services to those being supervised by justice systems." The two-day event included twelve distinct workshops tackling issues such as mental illness, reentry, and other community corrections issues for offenders in countries such as the U.S., England, Wales, Japan, the Netherlands, South Korea, Taiwan, and East Africa (Confederation of European Probation, 2015). This event was considered to be a major success, and it demonstrates that many are committed to community corrections throughout the world. Further, the success of this event has resulted in another World Congress meeting which will take place in Japan in 2017.

Brief History of Community Corrections and Trends

In the 1700s, U.S. jails were rarely used, particularly for punishment, as most punishments that convicted offenders received were corporal in nature (Barnes, 1921). For the most part, jails were utilized as holding places until corporal punishments could be carried out. Examples of corporal punishments during this era include: placing offenders in stocks to be put on display for public mockery; tying offenders to a whipping post where they could be beaten; branding offenders with some sort of sign or symbol denoting their status as an offender; or even conducting amputations on offenders (e.g., tongues, limbs) (Leighton, 2005). It wasn't until the late 1700s that a shift in punishment philosophies led to the abandonment of corporal punishment (Barnes, 1921). This change in punishment philosophies, away from corporal punishments, laid the groundwork for the implementation of penitentiaries, or prisons, as the new and preferred punishment method (Barnes, 1921).

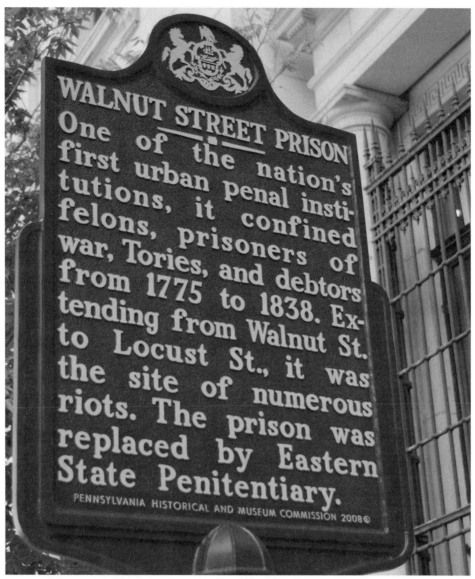

Image 1. A sign at the entrance explaining the history of the Walnut Street Prison in Philadelphia. ©
iStock.com/RiverNorthPhotography.

The foundation of corrections in the U.S. was established in Philadelphia during
1790 with the inception of the Walnut Street Jail, the first correctional facility in the
U.S. to be used for punishment (Skidmore, 1948). It is with this establishment that
prisons began to be equated with punishment and subsequent prisons were implemented across the U.S. throughout the 1800s. The shift towards the development of
community corrections began in Boston during the 1840s with the development and
implementation of **probation**, a sentence served in the community in lieu of incarceration (Lindner, 2007). When probation was first implemented, it was not well received. It took another 30 years before probation caught on as a possible alternative

community corrections sentence to prison and over 100 years before it was utilized across the nation (Petersilia, 1998). Similar to probation, **parole**, a sentence served in the community following an incarceration term, was first implemented in the U.S. in the 1870s and was established as a sentence in all states and the federal correctional systems about 80 years later (Hinkle & Whitmarsh, 2014; O'Toole, 2006). Both probation and parole sentences dominated as the primary forms of community corrections sentences until the 1970s, with each community corrections sentence being founded on the ideal of rehabilitation. That is, offenders would be permitted to serve these sentences in conjunction with participating in rehabilitative programs (e.g., work training, therapy).

During the 1970s, a bit of a backlash in corrections against the use of both probation and parole sentences occurred, resulting in the decreased use of these sentences. One reason both community corrections sentences fell out of favor was due to the shifting ideology of punishment, which moved from a rehabilitative ideal to a crime control model that stressed harsh punishments rather than reform. With the shift in ideology, probation and parole were now viewed as too lenient of sentences and incongruent with the crime control philosophy of punishment. Another reason these sanctions were falling out of favor was due to media coverage sensationalizing them. For instance, the case of Willie Horton in Massachusetts, a first-degree murderer released from prison for a weekend as part of rehabilitation program known as the prison furlough program, caused intense public backlash against this community corrections release option. When Willie Horton was released in 1986 for his rehabilitative furlough, he did not return but rather he physically and sexually assaulted a young couple (Anderson, 1995). Publication of his release and subsequent crime spree in the media sparked outrage by the public and politicians, which resulted in not only the closing of the furlough program in 1988, but also put intense focus on whether probation or parole sentences should continue to be used. In the case of parole, some states actually abolished this community corrections sentence altogether (Seiter & Kadela, 2003). Thus, many criminal justice policymakers began to develop other alternative community corrections sanctions that would not only be more harsh but also would enhance community safety.

Between the 1970s and the 1990s, both the state and federal governments began to shift their funding from rehabilitation and funnel it instead to crime prevention (e.g., policing of hot spots, enhanced surveillance) and other forms of deterrent punishments, known as intermediate sanctions, which are sentences that are alternatives to probation such as house arrest (Seiter & Kadela, 2003). **Intermediate sanctions** have been defined as "a punishment option that is considered on a continuum to fall between traditional probation and traditional incarceration" (U.S. Department of Justice, 1990, p. 3). The implementation and proliferation of intermediate sanctions has caused the field of community corrections to greatly expand.

Without a doubt, the numbers of individuals serving community corrections has grown exponentially over the past several decades. There are approximately 5 million individuals serving probation and parole sentences in the U.S. today (Kaeble et al.,

2016). This number far surpasses the 1.9 million total of those incarcerated in the U.S. in both prisons and jails today (Kaeble et al., 2016). While there have been some dips and fluctuations in numbers of individuals under correctional supervision (i.e., prison, jail, probation, and parole) throughout the 2000s, with 2008 being the year with the highest levels of individuals under correctional supervision, overall, the trends have predominately ticked upward over the past three decades (Glaze & Kaeble, 2014). Most recently, the use of incarceration has decreased as correctional administrators, strapped with shrinking budgets, looked to alternative and cheaper forms of supervision (Scott-Hayward, 2009).

Correctional administrators walk a tightrope as they try to balance community safety and foster offender reentry success while facing cutbacks to their budgets. The cuts to the budgets of departments of corrections are a national problem (Scott-Hayward, 2009). In fact, the cuts have been so severe the Vera Institute of Justice labeled the problem as a "fiscal crisis in corrections" (Scott-Hayward, 2009, p. 1). This fiscal crisis in corrections has greatly impacted prison operations, which are always much higher in cost than community corrections alternatives. Thus, the economy plays a large role in determining how community corrections may operate in the U.S. In Alabama, for example, budget cuts have left correctional administrators scrambling for cheaper forms of correctional supervision, which has resulted in the increased use of community corrections sentences—specifically probation and parole (Chandler, 2015). Therefore, it should come as no surprise that while the use of incarceration dipped in 2014, the use of parole actually increased during this time—likely due to fiscal constraints (Kaeble et al., 2016). Additionally, some prison administrators may want to increase the use of parole if their facilities are overcrowded. In California, for example, the $20 billion state budget deficit, of which 11% is devoted to prisons and overcrowded prisons in the state, resulted in more offenders being released from prison to serve parole sentences (Archibold, 2010). Further, the state revamped its laws in regards to parole violations in an effort to curb those offenders, who violate minor parole conditions, from being returned to prison as punishment for those minor violations (Archibold, 2010).

Of course, above the approximate 5 million figure of those serving probation and parole sentences, there are many more individuals serving other forms of intermediate sanctions in the community such as house arrest, work release centers, and day reporting centers. Since no formal record keeping is obtained at the national level, it is difficult to generate any exact figure. However, given the fact that there are over half a dozen intermediate sanctions in use across the nation in all jurisdictions, it would not be a far stretch to state that there are likely another 1 million individuals serving community corrections sentences above and beyond probation and parole.

With correctional administrators utilizing community corrections sentences at increasing rates, the public appears to be tolerating the approximately 6 million offenders serving such sentences. However, the public appears to support such sanctions to a point. That is, if these offenders commit crimes while serving these sanctions, the community becomes outraged—often fueled by media coverage. In 2002, Elizabeth Smart was abducted from her bedroom in the middle of the night in Salt Lake City, Utah, and her case drew national media attention and scrutiny. The police focused their attention on Richard Ricci, a parolee, who had been hired as a handyman by the Smart family as the main suspect (Manson, 2005). A media circus enveloped Ricci as he seemed to "fit" the profile. To the media and the public, Ricci was another example of a parolee who could not reintegrate successfully into society following his prison sentence and harmed an innocent community member. However, Ricci refused to confess to the crime, maintained his innocence, and ultimately died from a brain hemorrhage in jail a few weeks later. Ultimately, Smart was found nine months later alive in the custody of Brian Mitchell and Wanda Barzee (his wife)—her kidnappers. Ricci's case is an example of a concern, and sometimes suspicion, that the public has with parolees serving sentences in their communities.

Community Corrections and Reentry

While the increased use of community corrections sentences might be viewed as a positive, the result in Alabama has been the siphoning off of funds to assist offenders in various rehabilitation programs during their incarceration terms and shifting monies to hire more probation and parole officers (Chandler, 2015). Although the state of Alabama will boost their community corrections populations, this outcome is not necessarily a win for offenders. For instance, those offenders who were serving prison sentences before being released early to serve parole sentences are likely at a greater disadvantage during their reentry into society. If prison rehabilitation programs were removed or reduced to pay for community corrections sentences, then these offenders are being released into society even less equipped to possibly be able to successfully reenter society. Offenders released from prison to serve community corrections sentences, such as parole, face almost unsurmountable odds during reentry, such as difficulties in obtaining housing and employment, family reunification problems, coping with drug and/or alcohol addictions, and overcoming discrimination and stigmatization (Gunnison & Helfgott, 2013). Thus, if prison rehabilitation programming is cut, then it shouldn't be expected that these offenders will have successful parole outcomes. Think about it, could you reintegrate back into society on a parole sentence with $40 given to you by the prison at release, with no job, limited education, no previous legal work history, no home to return to, and no friends or family to support you? Yet, society expects parolees to be successful in the face of these obstacles, and, if they can't be, the public often demands further punishment, whether it be further incarceration or the loss of civil rights (e.g., voting).

Image 2. © iStockphoto.com/AVNphotolab.

Another obstacle for community corrections offenders during reentry is that they are also saddled with supervision costs for their sentence—an additional form of punishment. These fees, known as **legal financial obligations (LFOs)**, are collected from community corrections offenders help to subsidize the cost of probation and parole, for instance, and save taxpayers money (Peterson, 2012). Essentially, the fiscal constraints experienced by the state end up shifting from the state to the offender (see Text Box 1.2). However, such fees place an additional burden on those who are already struggling to reenter society—for any offender serving a community corrections sentence. The Washington State Supreme Court has stated that the LFO system " 'carries problematic consequences' for poor offenders, and can impede their ability to re-enter society and can contribute to recidivism" (Carter, 2015).

Text Box 1.2: The Reality of LFOs in Florida

Diller (2010, pp. 1–2), with the Brennan Center for Justice investigated LFOs in Florida, and the following points are key findings directly adapted here from their report:

1. **Florida increasingly relies on fees to finance core government functions.** The legislature has added more than 20 new categories of legal financial obligations ("LFOs") to the criminal justice process since 1996. The state has acted without considering the effects of the new LFOs and without examining whether cumulative debt promotes recidivism or otherwise hinders reentry into society for those convicted of crimes.

2. **The legislature has eliminated exemptions for the indigent, thus demanding revenue from a population unable to afford payment.** Florida ignores inability to pay when imposing LFOs, considers inability to pay in theory, when collecting LFOs, but bypasses the requirement in practice. For example, Florida law permits the indigent to pay off debt through community service, but most courts have no such programs.

3. **Despite rising pressure to collect fees, little attention is paid to the costs of collection.** As courts become more reliant on fee revenue, clerks' offices are, increasingly, under pressure to step up the collections process. Yet, state performance standards only look at one side of the ledger—the revenue raised—and fail to assess the costs and consequences of collection efforts. Some counties also incur hidden costs in budgets for sheriffs, local jails, and clerk operations.

4. **The current fee system creates a self-perpetuating cycle of debt for persons re-entering society after incarceration.** Fee amounts are often unpayable on limited budgets. Missed payments prompt additional fees and create a mounting debt cycle.

5. **Collection practices in some counties create a new form of debtors' prison.** In some counties, courts arrest individuals who miss court dates scheduled to discuss LFO debt, disrupting lives and employment. This practice resulted in more than 800 arrests and more than 20,000 hours of jail time in Leon County alone in one year. The arrests and nights spent in already overcrowded local jails cost the public money.

6. **Florida routinely suspends driver's licenses for failure to make payments,** a practice that sets the debtor up for a vicious cycle of "driving with a suspended license" convictions.

7. **Florida allows private debt collection firms to add up to a 40 percent surcharge on unpaid court debt.** Recent legislation requires courts to refer outstanding debt to collection agencies, which can add up to a 40 percent surcharge on existing debt.

While community corrections offenders face a myriad of struggles on a daily basis to successfully reenter society, correctional administrators and the public are perhaps predominately concerned with community safety during the reentry process. With the increase in community corrections sentences being utilized, including for those offenders convicted of violent offenses, such as sex offenses, community safety is definitely at the forefront of discussion. For specialized community corrections offenders, such as sex offenders, successful reentry is a particularly evasive goal. Sex offenders, for instance, face the same basic reentry struggles as other community corrections offenders, but they do experience additional hurdles in their transition, such as being required to pay for court-ordered treatment. Additionally, sex offenders experience enhanced stigmatization from the community due to the nature of their conviction. The stigmatization they experience is often due to fear by the community—that is, they are concerned for their safety. Given the concerns for community safety, correctional administrators often place pressure on community corrections officers (CCOs). CCOs are often expected to help offenders in their reentry while also maintaining strict surveillance of their clients. If a client of a CCO commits a crime while under the community corrections sentence, typically the next person deemed at fault, apart from the offender, is the CCO. Thus, CCOs are attempting to carry out their duties that will help their clients, protect their community, and abide by strict standards. This is a rather tough position to be in, and makes the role of a CCO increasingly challenging.

Outline of Text

This book seeks to fill a gap in current community corrections texts by providing an overview of all forms of community corrections sentences as well as through the inclusion of such topics as offender reentry and community corrections officers that are often not a part of such texts. In Chapter 1, a brief overview of the historical and contemporary perspectives on community corrections was provided. In Chapter 2, a discussion of offender classification through the use of various risk and needs assessment tools will be provided. A profile of community corrections offenders and specialized populations is presented in Chapter 3. Chapters 4, 5, and 6 provide a detailed historical overview and exploration into trends, and the effectiveness of key community correction sentences: probation, intermediate sanctions, and parole. Chapter 7 examines juvenile community corrections offenders—a topic often overlooked in discussions of community corrections offenders. In Chapter 8, a detailed examination into offender reentry is provided. All too often, reentry is thought of as being applicable to those coming out of prison—particularly parole. However, *all* community corrections offenders are reentering society in some capacity. Chapter 9 provides an examination into promising reentry interventions. Chapter 10 provides discussion on the revocation of probation and parole—that is, the process that occurs when successful reentry fails. Chapter 11 examines the role that community corrections officers have in assisting their clients and the challenges they face on the job. Chapter 12 presents information as to rights that community corrections offenders lose due to their conviction. Finally, in Chapter 13, a glimpse into the future trends in community corrections, including the steps that are currently being taken or need to be implemented to assist both offenders and practitioners within community corrections, is provided.

Key Terms

Community corrections

Corrections

Intermediate sanctions

Legal financial obligations (LFOs)

Parole

Policy implications

Probation

Discussion Questions

1. Research the number of community corrections sentences in your state over the past five years. Additionally, research the use of incarceration in your state over the past five years. What trends do you notice? Are community corrections sentences increasing?

2. Review news articles and research community corrections issues in your state. What are the most pressing problems or issues for these offenders in your state?

Are there forthcoming policy changes that will impact these offenders? If so, what are the policy changes and which community corrections offenders will benefit?

3. Attend a neighborhood community meeting and get a sense of what issues in regards to crimes are of concern to residents. Are community corrections offenders of concern? If so, in what way? Ask community members how they feel about community corrections sentences. Are they supportive?

4. What policies do you think hinder community corrections offenders in the nation as well as in your state? Are there any policies that you think should be implemented to help these offenders? Why?

References

Anderson, D. C. (1995). *Crime and the politics of hysteria: How the Willie Horton story changed American justice.* New York, NY: Random House.

Archibold, R. C. (2010, March 23). California, in financial crisis, opens prison doors. *The New York Times.* Retrieved from http://www.nytimes.com/2010/03/24/us/24 calprisons.html?_r=0.

Barnes, H. E. (1921). The historical origin of the prison system in America. *Criminal Law & Criminology, 12,* 35–60.

Bugliosi, V., & Gentry, C. (1974). *Helter skelter.* New York, NY: W.W. Norton & Company.

Carter, M. (2015, March 13). Poor offenders must be asked if they can afford to pay fines, state Supreme Court says. *The Seattle Times.* Retrieved from http://www. seattletimes.com/seattle-news/crime/state-supreme-court-says-judge-must-ask-if-defendant-can-afford-fine/.

Chandler, K. (2015, September 7). Budget cuts threaten prison reform efforts. *Washington Times.* Retrieved from http://www.washingtontimes.com/news/2015/sep/7/budget-cuts-threaten-prison-reform-effort/.

Confederation of European Probation. (2015). *World Congress on community corrections.* Retrieved from http://cep-probation.org/recap-of-the-world-congress-on-community-corrections/.

Diller, R. (2010). *The hidden costs of Florida's criminal justice fees.* New York: Brennan Center for Justice.

D'Zurilla, C. (2015, December 14). Justin Bieber reported to be off formal probation in egging case. *Los Angeles Times.* Retrieved from http://www.latimes.com/entertainment/gossip/la-et-mg-justin-bieber-off-formal-probation-egging-vandalism-20151102-story.html.

Glaze, L. E., & Kaeble, D. (2014). *Correctional populations in the United States, 2013.* Washington, DC: U.S. Department of Justice. Retrieved from http://www.bjs.gov/content/pub/pdf/cpus13.pdf.

Gunnison, E., & Helfgott, J. B. (2013). *Offender reentry: Beyond crime and punishment.* Boulder, CO: Lynne Rienner.

Herberman, E. J., & Bonczar, T. P. (2014). *Probation and parole in the United States, 2013.* Washington, DC: U.S. Department of Justice. Retrieved from http://www.bjs.gov/content/pub/pdf/ppus13.pdf.

Hinkle, W., & Whitmarsh, B. (2014). *Elmira reformatory.* Charleston, SC: Arcadia Publishing.

Kaeble, D., Glaze, L., Tsoutis, A., & Minton, T. (2016). *Correctional populations in the United States, 2014.* Washington, DC: U.S. Department of Justice.

La Ganga, M. L., & Goldmacher, S. (2010, July 2). Jaycee Lee Dugard's family will receive $20 million from California. *Los Angeles Times.* Retrieved from http://articles.latimes.com/2010/jul/02/local/la-me-0702-dugard-settlement-20100702.

Leighton, P. (2005). Corporal punishment. In M. Bosworth (Ed.), *Encyclopedia of prisons and correctional facilities* (pp. 182–185). Thousand Oaks, CA: Sage.

Lindner, C. (2007). Thacher, Augustus, and Hill: The path to statutory probation in the United States and England. *Federal Probation, 71*(3), 36–41.

Manson, P. (2005, April 16). Ricci widow sues over accusations. *Salt Lake Tribune.* Retrieved from http://archive.sltrib.com/story.php?ref=/utah/ci_2664014.

Martinez, E. (2009, August 31). Nancy Garrido: "The real monster" in the Jaycee Lee Dugard kidnapping? CBS News. Retrieved from http://www.cbsnews.com/news/nancy-garrido-the-real-monster-in-the-jaycee-lee-dugard-kidnapping/.

Martinez, M. (2011, June 2). Phillip Garrido sentenced in the Jaycee Dugard kidnapping. CNN. Retrieved from http://www.cnn.com/2011/CRIME/06/02/california.garridos.sentencing/.

Martinez, M. (2012, June 2). Charles Manson denied parole, with next parole hearing set for 2027. CNN. Retrieved from http://www.cnn.com/2012/04/11/justice/california-charles-manson/.

Ng, C. (2012, April 11). Charles Manson denied parole after saying he is a 'very dangerous man.' ABC News. Retrieved from http://abcnews.go.com/US/charles-manson-denied-parole-dangerous-man/story?id=16111128.

O'Toole, S. (2006). *The history of Australian corrections.* Australia: University of New South Wales Press.

Petersila, J. (1998). *Probation in the United States: Part 1.* American Probation and Parole Association. Retrieved from http://www.appa-net.org/eweb/Resources/PPPSW_2013/docs/sp98pers30.pdf.

Scott-Hayward, C. S. (2009). *The fiscal crisis in corrections: Rethinking policies and practices.* New York: Vera Institute of Justice.

Seiter, R., & Kadela, K. (2003). Prisoner reentry: What works, what does not, and what is promising. *Crime and Delinquency, 49*(3), 360–388. doi: 10.1177/001112 8703049003002.

Skidmore, R. A. (1948). Penological pioneering in the Walnut Street Jail, 1789–1799. *Criminal Law & Criminology, 39*, 167–180.

U.S. Department of Justice. (1990). *Survey of intermediate sanctions.* Washington, DC: U.S. Government Printing Office.

Chapter 2

Assessment: Offenders' Placement in the System

Student Learning Outcomes

After reading this chapter, you should be able to:

- Describe the process of classification.
- Identify and explain the various risk and needs assessment instruments that are utilized in the criminal justice system.
- Summarize the strengths and weaknesses of assessment tools.

Introduction

Most people probably don't give a lot of thought to the role of classification when it comes to offenders. Sure, many in society are familiar with the idea that prisons operate at minimum, medium, or maximum (and sometimes hybrid) classification levels. Perhaps, some even think about classification when it comes to sex offenders and understand that a classified Level 3 sex offender is much more serious of an offender than a Level 1 sex offender. However, most probably don't think about the process that informs classification, a process commonly referred to as assessment. One might be surprised to learn that assessment is utilized throughout the criminal justice system, and its importance in the criminal justice system cannot be overstated. The proper assessment and classification of offenders can result in both increased public safety as well as meeting the needs of offenders. The case of Curtis Thompson, a serial rapist and murderer in Seattle, is a prime example of what can occur if assessment tools are not adequately constructed to capture actual risk levels (i.e., they are flawed) or those who interpret the assessment tools do so incorrectly. In 2003, Thompson was released from prison after serving an eighteen-year prison sentence for raping three women (Pulkkinen, 2009). Before he was released, a jury in Washington State had to decide whether Thompson should be civilly committed to the Special Commitment Center at McNeil Island—a prison for sex offenders whereby release from this institution is granted to offenders only after they pose no threat to those in society. Thus, civil commitment is a special type of confinement that offenders can receive after completing the sentence for crimes they were convicted of and prior to the commission of a new crime. At the civil commitment trial, one forensic psychologist testified that, using a ten-question assessment tool called the Static-99, Thompson was "more likely than not" to re-offend (Willmsen, 2012). The psychologist stated that the Static-99 did not capture other factors that would push Thompson's classification into the higher level category of recidivism, and noted that, in her opinion, Thompson was a sexual sadist (Willmsen, 2012). However, another psychologist testified and argued that Thompson, whom he interviewed for two hours, was not a sadist and would not be a danger to society (Willmsen, 2012). Unfortunately, the testimony of the second psychologist was compelling, and the jury decided against civil commitment. Not even one year after his release, Thompson had sexually assaulted four women in Seattle and murdered one (Pulkkinen, 2009; Willmsen, 2012). Thompson was later convicted of the rapes and murder (Komo Staff, 2009; Pulkkinen, 2009).

Besides helping to protect society, classification tools can also help offenders. If classification and assessment instruments can accurately capture the needs that offenders have, correctional administrators can better assist the offenders in getting their needs met to foster successful reentry (Gunnison & Helfgott, 2013). For instance, ex-offender Kimberly Mays was arrested almost 50 times due to a cocaine addiction and lost custody of her nine children (Large, 2009). In 2004, she was arrested and charged with jumping bail and possession of a controlled substance — she was also three months pregnant (Large, 2009). While she had received treatment for her addiction in the past, it did not stick. Facing a five-year prison sentence and the loss of her tenth child to Child Protective Services, she made the decision to seek treatment for her addiction (Post-Prison Education Program, 2015). Her option of pursuing treatment was surely informed by results from the various assessments that were given to her throughout the years noting that her addiction was a significant contributor to her offending. Mays has turned her life around, regained custody of some of her children, and has completed both a bachelor's and a master's degree (Large, 2009). Proper assessment of Mays' risk and needs factors were crucial to helping her succeed.

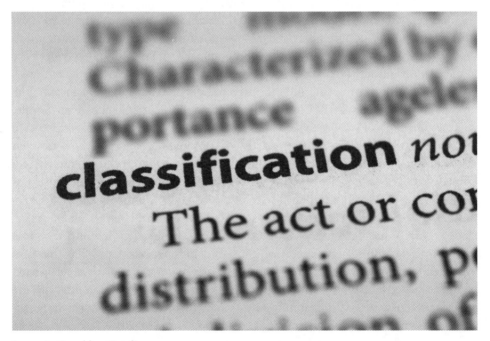

Image 3. © egokhan/Fotolia.

This chapter will provide an explanation of how offenders are selected for various types of community corrections sentences. Of course, classification is key to matching offenders to appropriate sentences. This is achieved through various risk and needs assessment tools. Thus, this chapter will provide a history of the assessment tools as well as an overview of various assessment tools that are utilized in the criminal justice system from pre-trial to post-trial. Additionally, how these assessments assist community corrections officers in the writing of presentence investigation reports will also be covered in this chapter. Finally, recommendations are provided for the use of assessments in the future.

Assessment

In the criminal justice system, an individual undergoes assessment at the pre-trial and conviction stages in order to determine his/her appropriate classification level. **Classification** refers to the procedure whereby the risk and needs factors of the offender are identified and an appropriate supervision plan is recommended. In the case of community corrections, pre-trial and convicted offenders will be serving their sentences in society, thus, it is imperative for probation and parole officers to understand what risk and needs factors their clients have. Over the last 100 years in corrections, assessments have evolved and changed quite a bit, with some scholars noting that there are now four generations of assessments (Bonta, Andrews, & Wormith, 2006) and even a "self-proclaimed fifth generation" assessment instrument (Shaffer, Kelly, & Lieberman, 2011, p. 170).

Historical Overview of Assessments

Historically, assessment of an offender's risk levels and needs were based on the professional opinions of those in the criminal justice system such as parole board members or probation and parole officers (Bonta et al., 2006; National Parole Resource Center, 2014). These subjective assessments are considered first-generation assessments. One of the chief problems with these early assessments is that they were based on professional judgement, or "gut feelings," which were prone to bias or error (Latessa, 2003–2004). After all, given the complexity of human nature, it is difficult to assess an individual based on his/her case file and determine the exact likelihood that the individual will re-offend. If the professional assessor harbors a personal bias towards the offender, this may cloud his/her judgement, resulting in the overemphasizing or underemphasizing of information that is pertinent to prediction (Latessa, 2003–2004). While subjective assessments have not been completely abandoned, today's correctional administrators primarily rely on more empirically based, or objective, assessments. An example of a risk assessment tool that is currently utilized that includes a subjective assessment component, along with objective components, is the HCR-20. The HCR-20, developed in the 1990s, is a violence risk assessment tool with 20 items that cover three main categories: (1) historical; (2) clinical; and (3)

Image 4. © tashatuvango/Fotolia.

risk management (Douglas et al., 2014). It is in the second category, clinical, whereby the offender is assessed by a mental health professional via a clinical interview. During the interview, the mental health professional is assessing the offender on recent problems of: insight, violent ideation, active symptoms of major mental illness, instability, and responsiveness to treatment (Douglas et al., 2014). Thus, the HCR-20 is a modern example of a risk assessment tool that includes the historical subjective component, as subjective assessments on their own have been abandoned.

Given the many shortcomings of purely subjective assessments early on in corrections, scholars began to examine more objective methods to classify and assess offenders. During the 1920s, second-generation assessments began to emerge (National Parole Resource Center, 2014). These second-generation assessments were purely risk assessments. **Risk assessments** attempt to determine the offender's risk, or propensity, to re-offend. For the most part, these early risk assessments were atheoretical and relied mostly on **static factors**, or unchangeable factors such as the number of arrests or convictions (Bonta et al., 2006; National Parole Resource Center, 2014). In 1928, Bruce, Burgess, and Harno published the first parole prediction instrument which was a 22-factor tool that was comprised primarily of static factors (e.g., nature of the offense, age at time of parole, residency status, and even psychiatric prognosis). The assessment tool was later referred to as the "Burgess method" and "Burgess scale," and it was empirically validated and adopted by states nationwide (Harcourt, 2006; Latessa, 2003–2004).

By the 1960s and through the 1970s, three additional risk assessment scales were implemented across the nation and in Canada: (1) the Base Expectancy Score (BES) in California; (2) the Salient Factor Score (SFS) in the federal system; and (3) the General Statistical Information on Recidivism (GSIR) in Canada (Bonta, Harman, Hann, & Cormier, 1996; Simon, 1993). All three assessment tools were a bit different in terms of the number of items that were assessed in the scale. For instance, the SFS was based on six items while the GSIR was based on 15 items (see Text Box 2.1) (Correctional Service Canada, 2015; Simon, 1993). Despite these differences, all three assessment tools were similar in construction as they were just based on static risk

Text Box 2.1: General Statistical Information on Recidivism (GSIR Scale)

General Statistical Information on Recidivism (GSIR Scale)
1. Current Offence
2. Age at Admission
3. Previous Incarceration
4. Revocation or Forfeiture
5. Act of Escape
6. Security Classification
7. Age at First Adult Conviction
8. Previous Convictions of Assault
9. Marital Status at Most Recent Admission
10. Interval at Risk since Last Offence
11. Number of Dependents at Most Recent Admission
12. Current Total Aggregate Sentence
13. Previous Convictions for Sex Offences
14. Previous Convictions for Break and Enter
15. Employment Status at Arrest

Source: Correctional Service Canada. (2015). *Forum on corrections research.* Retrieved from http://www.csc-scc.gc.ca/research/forum/e091/e091a-eng.shtml.

factors. Additionally, the interpretation of the scores on the assessment instrument was similar, whereby the higher the score on the items assessed, the lower the likelihood the offender would recidivate. A more recent 10-item risk assessment tool designed for adult male sex offenders emerged in 1999 known as the Static-99 (see Text Box 2.2) (Hanson & Thornton, 1999). This is the same tool utilized to assess Curtis Thompson as mentioned at the beginning of this chapter. While some of the second-generation assessment tools were found to be predictive and valid, scholars pushed for further refinement of these instruments, and assessment development moved into the third-generation phase.

Text Box 2.2: International Assessment: Static-99

The importance of assessment tools being utilized in the criminal justice has not gone unnoticed by international scholars, and, in fact, many popular assessments tools were developed by researchers outside of the United States. In the case of the Static-99, the assessment tool was developed by international scholars from Canada and Great Britain (Rettenberger & Eher, 2006). While the Static-99 has been found to be a valid risk assessment instrument for predicting sex offender recidivism, much of the research assessing the validity of the instrument had been conducted on offenders from North America and some countries in

Europe (Rettenberger & Eher, 2006). For instance, the Static-99 was found to be a valid predictor of sex offenders in Sweden; other researchers have found that its predictive accuracy may vary among ethnic groups (see Långström, 2004). In an effort to determine if the Static-99 was a valid assessment tool for German-speaking offenders, Rettenberger and Eher (2006, p. 1) first translated the Static-99 and then "adapted the instrument and the manual to the forensic context in Germany and Austria." Afterwards, the researchers sought to determine if the Static-99 was a valid predictor of recidivism for sex offenders. Utilizing a sample of Austrian sex offenders in their attempts to determine the predictive accuracy of the adapted German Static-99, Rettenberger and Eher (2006) found that the adapted German Static-99 did accurately predict sex offender recidivism. More research into international application of this assessment tool in other non-European countries is needed.

In the third-generation assessment phase occurring in the 1980s and 1990s, further development and implementation of new assessment instruments arose moving assessment tools beyond the mere inclusion of static factors as predictors. In fact, many of the new assessment tools that emerged included theoretically informed dynamic factors in addition to the static factor predictors (Andrews & Bonta, 1995). **Dynamic factors** are factors that are changeable through some form of intervention such as alcohol and drug use, marital problems, education level, skills level, or moral reasoning. These dynamic factors are empirically associated with criminal behavior and recidivism and, thus, they are often referred to as **criminogenic needs** (Andrews & Bonta, 1995). Given the inclusion of both risk and needs factors, many of the third-generation assessment tools were referred to as "risk-need" assessments (Andrews & Bonta, 1995). These new risk-needs assessments assisted correctional administrators and probation and parole officers in orienting clients to appropriate interventions tailored specifically to them (Bonta & Andrews, 2007). Additionally, these new tools assisted corrections personnel in assessing whether various programs and interventions that the offender was participating in were effective for that offender and assisted in the creation of strategic supervision plans for the offender (Bonta & Andrews, 2007).

One of the most well-known and widely implemented third-generation assessment tools that included both static and dynamic factors was the Level of Service Inventory-Revised (LSI-R) put forth in 1995 as a revision to its predecessor, the Level of Service Inventory (LSI) which was developed in 1982 (Andrews & Bonta, 1995; Roesch, Zapf, & Hart, 2010). The LSI-R is a risk-needs assessment tool comprised of 54 items covering ten criminogenic domains (i.e., criminal history, education/employment, financial, family/marital relationships, accommodations, leisure and recreation, companions, alcohol and drug use, emotional health, and attitudes/orientations) (Andrews & Bonta, 1995). Since the LSI-R is additive in nature, higher scores correlate with a higher propensity to re-offend, and offenders are categorized, or classified, as low, moderate, or high risk. The LSI-R is extensively used in correctional agencies across the nation, although some states have discontinued its use and have developed their own instruments. Washington State is an example of one state that is no longer using the LSI-R and replaced it with two new distinct instruments: the WA DOC Static Risk Level Tool and the WA DOC Offender Needs Assessment Tool (Baronoski & Drake, 2007; Drake, 2014). For female offenders, WA DOC is now using the Women's Risk and Needs Assessment (WRNA). More recently, a new combined risk-needs assessment tool called STRONG-R is expected to roll out in Washington State in 2017 (Drake, 2014).

Despite the success of third-generation assessment tools, assessment practices continued to improve and evolve, spawning fourth-generation assessment instruments in the 1990s and 2000s. Fourth-generation assessment tools are much more comprehensive than their predecessors as they measure risks and needs at intake, or where the offender enters the criminal justice system such as pre-trial, through case closure, or disposition of the case (e.g., the offender completes a probation sentence). Besides measuring risk and needs, these assessments also measure responsivity. **Responsivity** refers to the utilization of programming, preferably cognitive-behavioral and social learning approaches that are individually tailored to the needs and abilities of the offender (Andrews & Bonta, 1994). Examples of fourth-generation assessment tools include the Level of Service/Case Management Inventory (LS/CMI), the Women's Risk and Needs Assessment (WRNA), and the Correctional Offender Management Profiling for Alternative Sanctions (COMPAS). The LS/CMI, a revision to the LSI-R, emerged in 2004 as a risk/needs/responsivity (RNR) assessment tool for male and female offenders aged 16 and older that assists in treatment and management of offenders in the criminal justice system (Andrews, Bonta, & Wormith, 2004). While the LS/CMI has been implemented widely in the United States and in Canada and is considered the "gold standard" of offender assessment, it is not without its criticisms, including the ignoring of some risk factors (e.g., mental disorders) and that it's most predictive for adult male offenders (Roesch et al., 2010). COMPAS is an improvement over its predecessor, the LSI-R, in that it includes constructs from more theoretical traditions, additional criminogenic factors, and uses "more advanced statistical methods for predictive modeling and classification" (Brennan, Dietrich, & Ehret, 2009, p. 23).

Most recently, a touted fifth-generation assessment tool developed in 2005, known as the Risk Management System (RMS), attempts to overcome the limitations, such as generalizability, of earlier assessment tools (Modeling Solutions, 2005; Shaffer et al., 2011). The RMS "is a risk analysis system designed for corrections professionals by corrections professionals. It takes information about an offender typically collected by a correctional officer and applies an advanced mathematical approach called Example-based Modeling (EBM) to the information collected. RMS uses EBM to generate a risk estimate for a given offender based upon the pattern of risk factors the offender possesses" (Modeling Solutions, 2005, p. 3). Essentially, "EBM identifies historical offenders most similar to an offender's risk factor pattern for whom we have behavioral outcomes and builds a modeled simulation of what might be expected for a given risk factor pattern (i.e., whether the pattern is most associated with a recidivist or a nonrecidivist)"—or a high- or low-risk offender (Modeling Solutions, 2005, p. 8). This 65-item assessment tool covering the categories of needs, risk (i.e., dynamic and static), mental health, and other external factors (e.g., external resources, stressors, and living arrangement) classifies offenders as either low or high risk for recidivism or violence (Shaffer et al., 2011). Thus, the RMS only seeks to classify offenders into two categories which is very distinct from other assessment tools in use. To date, there has been only one empirical investigation into this unique instrument, and, in that investigation, researchers found that it is valid but categorized more offenders (70%) as low risk (Shaffer et al., 2011). Clearly, more research on RMS is needed. It appears that the RMS has not been widely implemented in the correctional system, perhaps due to its shortcomings with the inclusion of only two risk categories, and its proclamation of being a fifth-generation assessment tool needs greater scrutiny and investigation and remains to be seen.

Types of Assessments

Besides the aforementioned assessment tools, there are many other assessment instruments in use across the nation. It is beyond the scope of this book to identify and delve into an explanation of every one that is in use. The following sections provide a detailed examination of some of the main assessment tools that are used in the state and federal criminal justice system that aid in the classification and assessment of offenders at pre-trial and post-sentencing.

Pre-Trial Assessment Tools

The first implementation of pre-trial risk assessment, at the state level, arose out of bail reform in New York City in 1961 (Mamalian, 2011). The classic Vera Institute of Justice experiment, referred to as the **Manhattan Bail Project**, sought to determine which offenders should be released, pre-trial, from jail without the use of monetary bail based on a point scale (Mamalian, 2011). This point scale, which included items tapping community ties, would provide an objective assessment for judges as to whether releasing the offender on their own word that they would appear, or **Release on Recognizance (ROR)**, would be a good "risk" decision—that is, whether the offender be likely to appear in court when summoned for trial (McElroy, 2011). Results from evaluations of the experiment demonstrated that release based on the point-scale was effective in making bail release decisions as most offenders released on ROR returned to court when summoned (McElroy, 2011). Additionally, results of the research investigations garnered much attention nationwide, resulting in a focus of the importance and utilization of pre-trial risk assessments (McElroy, 2011). Subsequently, pre-trial assessments have been implemented across the nation in many jurisdictions—however, not all (Mamalian, 2011; McElroy, 2011).

Both the American Bar Association (ABA) and the National Association of Pretrial Services Agencies (NAPSA) have issued standards that pre-trial risk assessment should be utilized in determining risk and that the assessment should be objective rather than subjective in nature (Pretrial Justice Institute, 2009). In a 2009 survey of pre-trial agencies across the nation, a total of approximately 300 jurisdictions were identified as offering pre-trial services (Pretrial Justice Institute, 2009). Upon further inspection of the 171 agencies that responded to the survey, the Pretrial Justice Institute (2009) noted that only 10% of those agencies did not use any form of risk assessment.

Text Box 2.3: Pre-Trial Agencies' Utilization of Additional Assessments for Specific Populations

Populations Assessed	N = 151
Substance abuse	42%
Mental health	27%
Domestic violence	13%
Women	5%
Juveniles charged as adults	5%
Other	4%
None	50%

Source: Pretrial Justice Institute. (2009). *2009 Survey of pretrial services programs.* Retrieved from http://www.pretrial.org/download/pji-reports/new-PJI%202009%20Survey%20of%20 Pretrial%20Services%20Programs.pdf.

Of those agencies that utilized risk assessments, the Pretrial Justice Institute (2009, p. 36) reported that "the percentage of pretrial programs that rely exclusively on subjective criteria has decreased from 34% in 2001 to 12% in 2009. There has been a large increase in the percentage of pretrial programs that use a combination of objective and subjective criteria in risk assessment, up from 42% in 2001 to 64% in 2009." Additionally, most of the pre-trial agencies utilize similar risk factors in their assessments such as prior record, age, employment status, and drug and/or alcohol use (Pretrial Justice Institute, 2009). Further, some agencies report the use of additional risk assessment instruments for specialized populations (e.g., substance abuse offenders) (see Text Box 2.3) (Pretrial Justice Institute, 2009). While the use of risk assessments for pre-trial decisions is encouraging, it should be noted that about 48% of agencies in the study have not validated their instruments, or assessed whether their instruments are accurately and appropriately measuring risk (Pretrial Justice Institute, 2009).

Several states, such as Illinois, Ohio, Kentucky, and Virginia, have developed pre-trial risk assessments that have been implemented by agencies in as early as 2003 and most recently in 2010 (Cooprider, 2009; Mamalian, 2011). In all four states, each of these assessment tools has been validated. For instance, in 2003, the Virginia Pretrial Risk Assessment Instrument (VPRAI) was implemented to assess a defendant's risk of new arrest and failing to appear in court (Virginia Department of Criminal Justice Services, 2015). Adapting from Virginia's model, in 2006, the first pre-trial risk assessment was implemented in Lake County, Illinois, known as the Lake County Pretrial Risk Assessment Instrument (LCPRA) to assist in bond decisions as well as case supervision of clients as low, medium, or high risk (Cooprider, 2009). Further, in 2009, the Ohio Risk Assessment System-Pretrial Assessment Tool (ORAS-PAT) was developed and contains seven items, tapping criminal history, employment, residential stability, and substance abuse (see Text Box 2.4) (Latessa et al., 2009). Scores on the PAT range from 0–9 with scores of 6 or greater indicating a high risk of new arrest or failure to appear (Latessa et al., 2009). Although subjective discretion is not an inclusive part of the assessment tool, the creators of the ORAS-PAT recognize that professional insight and judgement to override the assessment in select circumstances may be necessary (Latessa et al., 2009). Thus, the ORAS-PAT allows criminal justice personnel to override the recommendation and state reasons as well as indicate areas of concerns regarding the client.

Text Box 2.4: Ohio Risk Assessment System — Pretrial Assessment Tool (ORAS-PAT)

Name: _____   Date of Assessment: _____

Case#: _____   Name of Assessor: _____

Pretrial Items   **Verified**

1.1 Age at First Arrest
    0 = 33 or older
    1 = Under 33

1.2 Number of Failure-to-Appear Warrants Past 24 Months
    0 = None
    1 = One Warrant for FTA
    2 = Two or More FTA

1.3 Three or More Prior Jail Incarcerations
    0 = No
    1 = Yes

1.4 Employed at the Time of Arrest
    0 = Yes, Full-time
    1 = Yes, Part-time
    2 = Not Employed

1.5 Residential Stability
    0 = Lived at current residence past six months
    1 = Not lived at same residence

1.6 Illegal Drug Use during Past Six Months
    0 = No
    1 = Yes

1.7 Severe Drug Use Problem
    0 = No
    1 = Yes

Total Score:

Scores	Rating	% of Failures	% of Failures to Appear	% of New Arrest
0–2	Low	5%	5%	0%
3–5	Moderate	18%	12%	7%
6+	High	29%	15%	17%

Please State Reason if Professional Override:

Other Areas of Concern. Check all that Apply:
_____ Low Intelligence*
_____ Physical Handicap
_____ Reading and Writing Limitations*

_____ Mental Health Issues*
_____ No Desire to Change/Participate in Programs*
_____ Transportation
_____ Child Care
_____ Language
_____ Ethnicity
_____ Cultural Barriers
_____ History of Abuse/Neglect
_____ Interpersonal Anxiety
_____ Other: _____

* If these items are checked it is strongly recommended that further assessment be conducted to determine level or severity.

Source: Latessa, E., Smith, P., Lemke, R., Makarios, M., & Lowenkamp, C. (2009). Creation and validation of the Ohio Risk Assessment System: Final report. Cincinnati, OH: University of Cincinnati. Retrieved from http://www.ocjs.ohio.gov/ORAS_FinalReport.pdf.

Besides the few states that have made an earnest effort to develop and validate their own pre-trial risk assessments, the federal system, in an effort to make decisions based on empirical evidence, or **evidence-based practices,** has also recently developed their own valid pre-trial assessment tool known as the Pre-trial Risk Assessment Instrument (PTRA) in 2009, and it was re-validated in 2012 (see Text Box 2.5) (Cadigan, 2009; Cadigan, Johnson, & Lowenkamp, 2012; Lowenkamp & Whetzel, 2009; Pretrial Justice Institute, 2010). By 2011, the PTRA was implemented in all 93 federal districts (Cadigan et al., 2012). As described by Cadigan and colleagues (2012, p. 5), "the PTRA tool is an objective, actuarial instrument that provides a consistent and valid method of predicting risk of failure-to-appear, new criminal arrest, and technical violations that lead to revocation while on pretrial release. The instrument contains 11 scored and 9 unscored items." The scored factors include the number of felony convictions, prior failure to appears, pending felonies or misdemeanors, current offense, employment, age, substance abuse, citizenship, educational level, and residence (Cadigan et al., 2012; Pretrial Justice Institute, 2010). For the PTRA, items are added resulting in five risk categories ranging from Category 1 to Category 5, whereby Category 5 (scored as 11+) represents the highest risk level for new arrests, failure to appears, and technical violations (Pretrial Justice Institute, 2010; VanNostrand & Keebler, 2009).

As far as the unscored PTRA items, they include alcohol use and various questions tapping foreign ties, travel, and financial interests. In 2012, Cadigan et al. (2012, p. 11) examined the both the PTRA scored and unscored items. The researchers found that the scored PTRA items provided "adequate predictive validity" while the unscored PTRA items did not enhance predictive ability. Therefore, the researchers recommended against the unscored items being added to the PTRA if the tool is further revised (Cadigan et al., 2012).

Overall, pre-trial risk assessments tools are relatively new in the corrections system at both the state and federal level. Given their inclusion of static risk factors only, these assessment instruments can be classified as second-generation tools. The next section examines assessment tools that are utilized after conviction, or post-trial.

Text Box 2.5: Federal Pre-Trial Risk Assessment Instrument (PTRA)

Defendant's Name: _____	Date of Assessment: _____
PACTS#:	Officer: _____
	District: _____
1.0 Criminal History & Current Offense:	

1.1 Number of felony convictions
  0 = None
  1 = One to four
  2 = Five or more	

1.2 Prior FTAs
  0 = None
  1 = One
  2 = Two or more	

1.3 Pending felonies or misdemeanors
  0 = None
  1 = One or more	

1.4 Current offense type
  0 = Theft/fraud, violent, other
  1 = Drug, firearms, or immigration	

1.5 Offense Class
  0 = Misdemeanor
  1 = Felony	

1.6 Age at interview
  0 = 47 or above
  1 = 27 to 46
  2 = 26 or younger	

Total Criminal History:	
2.0 Other Factors:	

2.1 Highest education
  0 = College degree
  1 = High school degree, vocational,
     some college
  2 = Less than high school or GED	

2.2 Employment status (Circle
  appropriate item and record score)
  0 = Employed full-time
  0 = Employed part-time
  0 = Disabled and receiving benefits
  1 = Student/homemaker
  1 = Unemployed
  1 = Retired, able to work	

2.3 Residence
  0 = Own/purchasing
  1 = Rent, no contribution, other, no
     place to live	

2.4 Current Drug Problems
    1 = Yes
    0 = No	

2.5 Current Alcohol Problems
    A = Yes
    B = No	

2.6 Citizenship Status
    0 = U.S. Citizen
    1 = Legal or illegal alien	

2.7 Foreign Ties
    A = Yes
    B = No	

2.7 (A) Does the defendant have any of
        the following ties to a foreign
        country?
    A = Yes
    B = No
 	
Circle all that apply
    Family (parents, siblings, cousins, etc.)
    Spouse
    Children
    Significant other
    Business relations
    Friends
    Other
    No foreign ties
 	
If Yes, what country or countries?	

2.7 (B) Does the defendant maintain
        contact with any individual in
        question 2.7(A)?
    A = Yes
    B = No	

2.7 (C) Is the defendant a citizen or
        resident of a foreign country? If
        Yes, which country or countries?
        (Please indicate what country.)
    A = Yes
    B = No	

2.7 (D) Does the defendant possess a valid
        or expired passport (either U.S. or
        foreign?)
    A = Yes
    B = No	

2.7 (E) Does the defendant have any
        financial interests (such as,
        property, bank accounts, etc.)
        outside of the U.S.?
    A = Yes
    B = No	

2.7 (F) Has the defendant traveled outside of the U.S.? A = Yes B = No **Circle appropriate item below:** Within the past 1–5 years Within the past 6–10 years No foreign travel	
2.7 (G) Was the travel in 2.7(F) for any of the following? A = Yes B = No **Circle appropriate item below:** A = Pleasure B = Business C = Both D = Not applicable	
Total Other:	
Total Score: [Items 1.1–2.7(G)]	

Risk Category	Risk Score
Category 1	0–4
Category 2	5–6
Category 3	7–8
Category 4	9–10
Category 5	11+

Source: Pretrial Justice Institute. (2010). *Federal Pretrial Risk Assessment Instrument.* Retrieved from http://www.pretrial.org/download/risk-assessment/Federal%20Pretrial%20Risk%20Assessment%20Instrument%20(2010).pdf.

Post-Trial Assessment Tools

As mentioned earlier in this chapter, the Level of Service Inventory-Revised (LSI-R), developed in 1995, is a 54-item risk/needs assessment tool that includes both static and dynamic risk factors and is utilized in case classification post-conviction (Andrews & Bonta, 1995). The LSI-R has become the standard assessment tool in corrections for identifying risk and needs and is used in more than 900 state correctional agencies (Flores et al., 2006; Lowenkamp, Lovins, & Latessa, 2009). The LSI-R is used by correctional administrators in assessing the risk level of probationers or which offenders should be granted early release from prison. Additionally, it is used in mapping the program treatment for the offender serving a community corrections sentence.

Although the LSI-R has been found to be a reliable and valid measure in terms of predicting a wide range of criminal offenses, from drug offenses to sex offenses, (Gendreau, Little, & Goggin, 1996; Hollin & Palmer, 2003; Kelly & Welsh, 2008; Labrecque et al., 2014; Lowenkamp et al., 2009; Manchak, Skeem, & Douglas, 2008; Simourd & Malcolm, 1998; Vose, Cullen, & Smith, 2008; Vose, Smith, & Cullen, 2013), it has received some criticism. For instance, some researchers have claimed that the tool may have better predictive validity for males than for females (Holtfreter & Cupp, 2007; Reisig et al., 2006). Holtfreter and Cupp (2007) reviewed 41 published articles on the LSI-R for female offenders and found that the validation of the instrument for female offenders was often based on non-representative samples of female offenders. Other researchers have asserted that the LSI-R may be predictive of recidivism for aboriginal offenders, but its predictive capabilities for this group are sometimes inaccurate (Wilson & Guiterrez, 2014). Additionally, subsequent researchers have noted that the predictive ability of the LSI-R may differ based on an offender's race or ethnicity (Chenane et al., 2015; Fass et al., 2008; Sclager & Simourd, 2007). Overall, the LSI-R is considered to be a valid predictive tool for offenders (Vose et al., 2013). In 2004, the LSI-R was revised to the Level of Service-Case Management Inventory (LS-CMI); it offers improvement over the traditional LSI-R in that it "provides a gender-informed RNR [risk/needs/responsivity] assessment with proven validity for female offenders" (Andrews, Bonta, & Wormith, 2008, p. 2).

Other states, such as Ohio, have discontinued use of the LSI-R in favor of other assessment tools such as the Ohio Risk Assessment System, the Community Supervision Tool (ORAS-CST), the Community Supervision Screening Tool (ORAS-CSST), and the Reentry Tool (ORAS-RT) (see Text Box 2.6) (Latessa et al., 2011). Each of these assessment tools offer probation and parole officers the opportunity to assess offenders at the time of conviction, during the community corrections sentence, and prior to release from prison in the community. Given that these assessment tools are tapping different points in the offender career, they each contain both similar and distinct items. For instance, each assessment tool contains items on criminal history and substance use, but differ on the inclusion of such items as neighborhood problems and peer associations (Latessa et al., 2011). Additionally, all assessment items allow for professional override.

Text Box 2.6: Ohio Risk Assessment System — Reentry Tool (ORAS-RT)

Name: _____   Date of Assessment: _____

Case#: _____   Name of Assessor: _____

Age at Time of Assessment
     0 = 24+
     1 = 18–23

1.0 Criminal History

1.1 Most Serious Arrest under Age 18
     0 = None
     1 = Yes, Misdemeanor
     2 = Yes, Felony

1.2 Age at First Arrest or Charge
     0 = 26+
     1 = 16–25
     2 = 15 or younger

1.3 Prior Commitment as a Juvenile to Department of Youth Services
    0 = No
    1 = Yes

1.4 Current Offense Drug Related
    0 = No
    1 = Yes

1.5 Number of Prior Adult Felony Convictions
    0 = None
    1 = One
    2 = Two or More

1.6 Number of Prior Adult Commitments to Prison
    0 = None
    1 = One
    2 = Two or More

1.7 Ever Received Official Infraction for Violence While Incarcerated as an Adult
    0 = No
    1 = Yes

1.8 Ever Absconded from Community Supervision as an Adult
    0 = No
    1 = Yes

Total Score in Criminal History:

2.0 Social Bonds

2.1 Ever Suspended or Expelled from School
    0 = No
    1 = Yes

2.2 Employed at the Time of Arrest
    0 = No
    1 = Yes

2.3 Ever Quit a Job Prior to Having Another One
    0 = No
    1 = Yes

2.4 Marital Status
    0 = Married or Cohabitating with a Significant Other
    1 = Single, Married but Separated, Divorced, or Widowed

Total Score in Social Bonds:

3.0 Criminal Attitudes and Behavioral Patterns

3.1 Criminal Pride
    0 = No Pride in Criminal Behavior
    1 = Some Pride in Criminal Behavior
    2 = A Lot of Pride in Criminal Behavior

3.2 Believes that It Is Possible to Overcome Past
    0 = No
    1 = Yes

3.3 Uses Anger to Intimidate Others
    0 = No
    1 = Yes

3.4 Walks Away from a Fight
    0 = Yes
    1 = Sometimes
    2 = Rarely

3.5 Problem Solving Ability
- 0 = Good
- 1 = Poor

3.6 Expresses Concern about Other's Misfortunes
- 0 = Concerned about Others
- 1 = Limited Concern
- 2 = No Real Concern for Others

3.7 Believes in "Do Unto Others Before They Do Unto You"
- 0 = Disagree
- 1 = Sometimes
- 2 = Agree

Total Score for Criminal Attitudes and Behavioral Patterns:

Risk Categories for Males			Risk Categories for Females		
Scores	Rating	Percent of Failures	Scores	Rating	Percent of Failures
0–9	Low	21%	0–10	Low	6.5%
10–15	Moderate	50%	11–14	Moderate	44%
17+	High	64%	15+	High	56%

Domain Levels

1.0 Criminal History

	Score	Failure
_____	Low (0–3)	23%
	Med (4–6)	45%
	High (7–12)	65%

2.0 Social Bonds

	Score	Failure
_____	Low (0–3)	32%
	Med (4–5)	45%
	High (6–7)	62%

3.0 Criminal Attitudes and Behavioral Patterns

	Score	Failure
_____	Low (0–2)	30%
	Med (3–5)	51%
	High (6–11)	58%

Professional Override:

Reasons for Override
(note overrides should not be based solely on offense)

Other Areas of Concern. Check all that Apply:
- _____ Low Intelligence*
- _____ Physical Handicap
- _____ Reading and Writing Limitations*
- _____ Mental Health Issues*
- _____ No Desire to Change/Participate in Programs*
- _____ Language
- _____ Childcare
- _____ Transportation
- _____ Ethnicity
- _____ Cultural Barriers
- _____ History of Abuse/Neglect
- _____ Interpersonal Anxiety
- _____ Other: _____

* If these items are checked it is strongly recommended that further assessment be conducted to determine level or severity.

Source: Latessa, E., Smith, P., Lemke, R., Makarios, M., & Lowenkamp, C. (2009). *Creation and validation of the Ohio Risk Assessment System: Final report.* Cincinnati, OH: University of Cincinnati. Retrieved from http://www.ocjs.ohio.gov/ORAS_FinalReport.pdf.

At the federal level, risk assessment tools are not new to the federal system as they were first used in some capacity in 1923 (U.S. Courts, 2011). Since their early inception, assessment was still very much a part of the federal system. In the 1970s, for example, federal policy required probation officers to classify offenders into supervision categories based on their risk, resulting in many agencies using a myriad of risk assessment tools (U.S. Courts, 2011). By 1982, there were more than two dozen probation or parole risk assessment tools in use across the federal system, such as the California BE16A (Modified), the Revised Oregon Model, the Salient Factor Score (SFS), and the U.S.D.C. 75 scale (U.S. Courts, 2011). The U.S.D.C. 75 scale, for instance, which assessed probation risk as poor, good, or excellent, was based on five main items: age, arrest-free period, prior arrests, opiate usage, and employment (Eaglin & Lombard, 1982). Interestingly, the scale allowed for professional override to the use of the tool stating, "If the client has a high school degree (exclude GED) and no history of opiate abuse, check the box to the right, ignore items A through E[assessment questions], and place the client in the excellent-risk category. Otherwise use items A through E to determine the rating" (Eaglin & Lombard, 1982, p. 76). After several empirical investigations of these four aforementioned tools, the U.S.D.C. 75 scale was selected to be implemented nationally for probation due to its potential accuracy in the prediction of risk and was renamed the Risk Prediction Scale 80 (RPS-80) (Eaglin & Lombard, 1982; U.S. Courts, 2011). This result may not be all that surprising when you consider the fact that the BE16A and SFS were developed based on samples of state and federal *parole* offenders, thus, their predictive accuracy for *probationers* would not be expected to be high (Eaglin & Lombard, 1982). Additionally, the SFS was utilized at the national level to access risk for paroled offenders (U.S. Courts, 2011). However, by the early 1990s both the RPS-80 and SFS were abandoned when a more reliable risk assessment tool named the Risk Prediction Index (RPI) was developed for use for probation offenders (U.S. Courts, 2011). By the mid-2000s, probation policymakers had grown weary of the RPI due to its reliance on static risk factors, and they explored the use of other risk assessment tools such as COMPAS — a computerized risk assessment tool (U.S. Courts, 2011). Ultimately unsatisfied with the various assessment tools available, the federal probation system decided to develop its own risk/needs assessment instrument in 2009 called the Federal Post Conviction Risk Assessment (PCRA), and this tool was implemented in the federal probation system in 2010 (Alexander, Whitley, & Bersch, 2014).

The PCRA is a risk/needs/responsivity assessment tool that consists of two sections (e.g., Officer Assessment and Offender Self-Assessment) and is comprised of 14 scored (based only on Officer Assessment) and 41 unscored scored items (U.S. Courts, 2011). In terms of the scored items included on the PCRA, the assessment taps seven domains: (1) criminal history, (2) education/employment, (3) substance abuse, (4) social networks, (5) cognitions (e.g., antisocial thinking patterns), (6) other (e.g., housing, finances), and (7) responsivity factors (Alexander et al., 2014; U.S. Courts, 2011). Offenders are classified into four risk categories: (1) low, (2) low-moderate, (3) medium, and (4) high (Alexander et al., 2014; Johnson et al., 2011). Investigations of its effectiveness have yielded positive results, as the PCRA has been deemed to be valid tool that accurately predicts risk (Cohen & Whetzel, 2014; Johnson et al., 2011; Lowenkamp et al., 2012).

Since the 1970s, the standard risk assessment instrument that has been utilized to assess parole risk upon release has been the Salient Factor Score (SFS) (Hoffman, 1994). Over the years, the instrument has undergone some revisions and is now referred to as the Salient Factor Score 98 (SFS 98) (U.S. Parole Commission, 2015). The SFS 98 consists of six static factors that tap: (1) prior convictions/adjudications, (2) prior commitments of more than 30 days, (3) age at current offense/prior commitments, (4) recent commitment-free period, (5) probation/parole/confinement/ escape status violator this time, and (6) older offenders (U.S. Parole Commission, 2015). Scores on the SFS 98 range from 0 to 10, and the scores offer the following risk categories of parole: poor (scores 0–3); fair (scores 4–5); good (scores 6–7); and very good (scores 8–10) (U.S. Parole Commission, 2015). Andrews & Bonta (2015) report that the SFS has performed satisfactorily in predicting outcomes. In 2013, the U.S. Parole Commission reported that it is planning to develop risk assessment instruments that target high-risk offender groups (e.g., those convicted of gang, sex, gun-related, and domestic violence offenses) for increased supervision on release. Thus, there may be some changes in the works for assessment tools utilized in federal parole release decisions in the near future.

Presentence Investigation Reports

Traditionally utilized as a sentencing tool, presentence investigation reports assist in not only proper classification of offenders but also aid in release decisions (Center on Juvenile and Criminal Justice, 2015). **Presentence investigation reports** (PSI) are reports that contain a history of information on an offender, including information on his/her case, criminal history, prior arrests, prior convictions, employment status and history, residency status, mental health status, financial status, family history and relationships, victim impact, and a recommended sentence (Walsh, 2001). PSIs are prepared by probation officers after an offender is found guilty, and these reports guide the judge in making decisions as to whether the offender may be eligible for various community corrections sanctions, such as probation, or should be sentenced to prison. The probation officer prepares the PSI after careful review of the case records as well as an interviews with the offender, employers, and family members. Additionally, the probation officer carefully reviews the risk factors for the offender and the needs of the offender with the assistance of data from pre-trial risk/needs assessment tools or mental health assessments that the offender may have undergone pre-trial to assist in crafting the recommended sentence. Besides the recommended sentence, the probation officer will also suggest specific correctional programming that addresses the needs of the offender such as drug and/or alcohol treatment— such recommendations stem from information gleaned from risk/needs assessments. Although PSI reports are utilized post-conviction, these reports follow the offender through their journey in the criminal justice system. For example, a parole board will also re-review the PSI report for an offender in addition to reviewing outcomes from risk/needs assessments and institutional disciplinary reports to assist in their release decision. Thus, risk/needs assessments play a vital role in shaping sentencing outcomes and treatment plans in PSI reports.

Guidelines and Points to Consider in Assessment

Assessment tools to enhance public safety, ensure fairness, and improve offender reintegration have widespread use and implementation throughout state and federal community corrections (Latessa, 2015; Milgram et al., 2015). As these assessment tools continue to evolve from fourth-generation assessments to the touted "fifth-generation" assessments, there are guidelines that should be followed such as (1) actuarial risk items should be included as part of the tool; (2) tools should be valid; (3) tools should be relevant to criminal behavior; (4) tools should be constructed from theory; (5) tools should include many factors, or items, that are related to criminal behavior; (6) tools should assess criminogenic needs; (7) tools should limit the inclusion of personality and cognitive tests to the assessment of responsivity; (8) assessors should use different methods when conducting assessments (e.g., interview or paper and pencil tests to reduce error); and (9) assessors should utilize assessments professionally and with good intentions (Bonta, 2002). While parsimony is often sought, Latessa and Lovins (2010) note that there are some important points to consider with assessment. For instance, Latessa and Lovins (2010) caution that there is no one-size-fits-all assessment tool, thus there is a need for different assessment tools at different points in the criminal justice system and for distinct groups of offenders (e.g., sex offenders). The scholars further note that assessment is not a one-time event; assessment can guide decisions but professional discretion is important and still needed; assessment tools should be validated on the population that they are to be used on; assessments should be conducted more frequently on higher risk offenders; and staff should be trained on the importance of assessments in addition to the actual procedures of administration. Additionally, the researchers caution that there could be resistance by employees in agencies in the use of assessment tools (Latessa & Lovins, 2010). It could be the case that employees are skeptical of the utility and validity of the tools or are concerned that the tools will somehow override their professional judgement. If practitioners do not understand the utility of these instruments, they may choose not to utilize such tools as required or utilize them haphazardly (Miller & Mahoney, 2013). Thus, it is important to properly onboard employees about the necessity and benefits in the use of assessments and to involve the appropriate stakeholders in a formal discussion if currently used assessments in their respective agencies will be revised or discontinued for a better model.

Conclusion

It is clear that both state and federal community corrections agencies recognize the importance of assessment and have adopted assessment tools at various stages in the criminal justice system (i.e., pre-trial, post-trial, and post-release) as a means to help offenders, reduce bias, and enhance public safety. While there are numerous assessment tools in use, researchers continue to explore their validity and reliability with various correctional populations. To date, there are many assessment tools that are in use that have good predictive ability of offender risk and are capable of accurately assessing the needs of an offender. In particular, researchers agree that those assessments that tap risk, needs, and responsivity will have the greatest ability to protect the public and help the offender. With their increasing implementation and empirical scrutiny, assessment tools will have a permanent place in corrections.

Key Terms

Classification

Criminogenic Needs

Dynamic Factors

Manhattan Bail Project

Presentence investigation reports

Release on Recognizance

Responsivity

Risk Assessments

Static Factors

Discussion Questions

1. Research the various assessment tools being utilized by local and state community corrections agencies your state. Are county community corrections offices using similar assessment tools to the state's?

2. Once you have located 2–3 different assessment tools in your state, carefully review them. Do they share any similarities and/or differences? Can you provide a few critical critiques of these assessment? That is, would you change anything about the current assessment tool? Why or why not?

3. Interview a community corrections officer at the local or state level regarding assessments. How does he/she feel about the assessments utilized? Are there any problems with the current assessments being utilized or the process by which they are administered? What recommendations for improvements does the officer have regarding the tool? Why?

4. Since the U.S. Parole Commission may be developing a new instrument for release decisions for higher risk offender groups, design an assessment instrument for one of these higher risk groups.

References

Alexander, M., Whitley, B., & Bersch, C. (2014). Driving evidence-based supervision to the next level: Utilizing PCRA, "drivers," and effective supervision techniques. *Federal Probation, 78*(3), 2–8.

Andrews, D. A., & Bonta, J. (1994). *The psychology of criminal conduct.* Cincinnati, OH: Anderson Publishing Co.

Andrews, D. A., & Bonta, J. (1995). *The Level of Service Inventory-Revised.* Toronto, Canada: Multi-Health Systems.

Andrews, D. A., & Bonta, J. (2015). *The psychology of criminal conduct* (5th ed.). Cincinnati, OH: Anderson Publishing Co.

Andrews, D. A., Bonta, J., & Wormith, J. S. (2004). *LS/CMI: Level of service/case management inventory.* Toronto, Canada: Multi-Health Systems.

Barnoski, R., & Drake, E. (2007). *Washington's Offender Accountability Act: Department of Corrections' Static Risk Instrument.* Olympia, WA: Washington State Institute for Public Policy.

Bonta, J. (2002). Offender risk assessment: Guidelines for selection and use. *Criminal Justice & Behavior, 29*(4), 355–379. doi: 10.1177/0093854802029004002.

Bonta, J., & Andrews, D. A. (2007). *Risk-need-responsivity model for offender assessment and rehabilitation 2007–06.* Retrieved from http://www.pbpp.pa.gov/Information/Documents/Research/EBP7.pdf.

Bonta, J., Andrews, D., & Wormith, J. S. (2006). The recent past and near future of risk and/or need assessment. *Crime & Delinquency, 52*(1), 7–27. doi: 10.1177/0011128705281756.

Bonta, J., Harman, W. G., Hann, R. G., & Cormier, R. B. (1996). The prediction of recidivism among federally sentenced offenders: A re-validation of the SIR scale. *Canadian Journal of Criminology, 38*, 61–79.

Brennan, T., Dietrich, W., & Ehret, B. (2009). Evaluating the predictive validity of the COMPAS risk and needs assessment system. *Criminal Justice & Behavior, 36*(1), 21–40. doi: 10.1177/0093854808326545.

Bruce, A. A., Burgess, E. W., & Harno, A. (1928). A study of the indeterminate sentence and parole in the state of Illinois. *Journal of the American Institute of Criminal Law and Criminology, 19*(1, part 2), 1–306.

Cadigan, T. P. (2009). Implementing evidence-based practices in federal pretrial services. *Federal Probation, 73*(2), 30–32.

Cadigan, T. P., Johnson, J. L., & Lowenkamp, C. T. (2012). The re-validation of the federal pretrial services risk assessment (PTRA). *Federal Probation, 76*(2), 3–9.

Center on Juvenile and Criminal Justice. (2015). *The history of the pre-sentence investigation report.* Retrieved from http://www.cjcj.org/uploads/cjcj/documents/the_history.pdf.

Chenane, J. L., Brennan, P. K., Steiner, B., & Ellison, J. M. (2015). Racial and ethnic differences in the predictive validity of the Level of Service Inventory-Revised among prison inmates. *Criminal Justice & Behavior, 42*(3), 286–303. doi: 10.1177/0093854814548195.

Cohen, T. H., & Whetzel, J. (2014). The neglected "r"—responsivity and the federal offender. *Federal Probation, 78*(2), 11–18.

Cooprider, K. (2009). Pretrial risk assessment and case classification: A case study. *Federal Probation, 73*(1), 12–15.

Correctional Service Canada. (2015). *Forum on corrections research.* Retrieved from http://www.csc-scc.gc.ca/research/forum/e091/e091a-eng.shtml.

Douglas, K. S., Hart, S. D., Webster, C. D., Belfrage, H., Guy, L. S., & Wilson, C. M. (2014). Historical-Clinical-Risk Management-20, version 3 (HCR-20V3): Development and overview. *International Journal of Forensic Mental Health, 13,* 93–108. doi: 10.1080/14999013.2014.906519.

Drake, E. (2014). *Predicting criminal recidivism: A systematic review of offender risk assessments in Washington State.* Olympia, WA: Washington State Institute for Public Policy.

Eaglin, J. B., & Lombard, P. A. (1982). *A validation and comparative evaluation of four predictive devices for classifying federal probation caseloads.* Federal Judicial Center. Retrieved from http://www.fjc.gov/public/pdf.nsf/lookup/clssprob.pdf/$file/clssprob.pdf.

Fass, T. L., Heilbrun, K., DeMatteo, D., & Fretz, R. (2008). The LSI-R and the COM-PAS: Validation data on two risk-needs tools. *Criminal Justice & Behavior, 35*(9), 1095–1108. doi: 10.1177/0093854808320497.

Flores, A. W., Lowenkamp, C. T., Holsinger, A. M., & Latessa, E. J. (2006). Predicting outcome with the Level of Service Inventory-Revised: The importance of implementation integrity. *Journal of Criminal Justice, 34*(5), 523–529. doi: 10.1016/j.jcrimjus.2006.09.007.

Gendreau, P., Little, T., & Goggin, C. (1996). A meta-analysis of the predictors of adult offender recidivism: What works! *Criminology, 34*(4), 575–607. 10.1111/j.1745-9125.1996.tb01220.x

Gunnison, E., & Helfgott, J. B. (2013). *Offender reentry: Beyond crime and punishment.* Boulder, CO: Lynne Rienner.

Hanson, R. K., & Thornton, D. (1999). *Static-99: Improving actuarial risk assessments for sex offenders.* Ottawa: Department of the Solicitor General of Canada.

Harcourt, B. E. (2006). *Against prediction: Punishing and policing in an actuarial age.* Chicago, IL: University of Chicago Press.

Hoffman, P. B. (1994). Twenty years of operational use of a risk prediction instrument: The United States Parole Commission's Salient Factor Score. *Journal of Criminal Justice, 22*(6), 477–494. doi: 10.1016/0047-2352(94)90090-6.

Hollin, C. R., & Palmer, E. J. (2003). Level of Service Inventory-Revised profiles of violent and nonviolent prisoners. *Journal of Interpersonal Violence, 18*(9), 1075–1086. doi: 10.1177/0886260503254514.

Holtfreter, K., & Cupp, R. (2007). Gender and risk assessment: The empirical status of the LSI-R for women. *Journal of Contemporary Criminal Justice, 23*(4), 363–382. doi: 10.1177/1043986207309436.

Johnson, J. L., Lowenkamp, C. T., VanBenschoten, S. W., & Robinson, C. R. (2011). The construction and validation of the Federal Post Conviction Risk Assessment (PCRA). *Federal Probation, 75*(2), 16–29.

Kelly, C. E., & Welsh, W. N. (2008). The predictive validity of the Level of Service Inventory-Revised for drug-involved offenders. *Criminal Justice and Behavior, 35*(7), 819–831. doi: 10.1177/0093854808316642.

Komo Staff. (May 27, 2009). Serial rapist found guilty in 2004 murder of Seattle woman. *Komo News.* Retrieved from http://www.komonews.com/news/462768 72.html.

Labrecque, R. M., Smith, P., Lovins, B. K., & Latessa, E. J. (2014). The importance of reassessment: How changes in the LSI-R risk score can improve the prediction of recidivism. *Journal of Offender Rehabilitation, 53*(2), 116–128. doi: 10.1080/ 10509674.2013.868389.

Långström, N. (2004). Accuracy of actuarial procedures for assessment of sexual offender recidivism risk may vary across ethnicity. *Sexual Abuse: A Journal of Research and Treatment, 16*(2), 107–120. doi: 10.1023/ B:SEBU.0000023060.61402.07.

Large, J. (June 22, 2009). An ugly side of life redeemed. *The Seattle Times.* Retrieved from http://www.seattletimes.com/seattle-news/an-ugly-side-of-life-redeemed/.

Latessa, E. (2003–2004). Best practices of classification and assessment. *Journal of Community Corrections, Winter,* 4–6, 27–30.

Latessa, E. J. (2015). Taking risk assessment to the next step. *Criminology & Public Policy, 14*(1), 67–69. doi: 10.1111/1745-9133.12120.

Latessa, E. J., & Lovins, B. (2010). The role of offender risk assessment: A policy maker guide. *Victims & Offenders, 5*(3), 203–219. doi: 10.1080/15564886.2010.485900.

Latessa, E., Smith, P., Lemke, R., Makarios, M., & Lowenkamp, C. (2009). *Creation and validation of the Ohio Risk Assessment System: Final report.* Cincinnati, OH: University of Cincinnati. Retrieved from http://www.ocjs.ohio.gov/ORAS_Final-lReport.pdf.

Lowenkamp, C. T., Johnson, J. L., Holsinger, A. M., VanBenschoten, S. W., & Robinson, C. R. (2012). The Federal Post Conviction Risk Assessment (PCRA): A construction and validation study. *Psychological Services*. Advance online publication. doi: 10.1037/a0030343.

Lowenkamp, C. T., Lovins, B., & Latessa, E. J. (2009). Validating the Level of Service Inventory-Revised and the Level of Service Inventory Screening Version with a sample of probationers. *Prison Journal, 89*(2), 192–204. doi: 10.1177/003288550 9334755.

Lowenkamp, C. T., & Whetzel, J. (2009). The development of an actuarial risk assessment instrument for U.S. pretrial services. *Federal Probation, 73*(2), 33–36.

Mamalian, C. A. (2011). *State of the science of pretrial risk assessment*. Washington, DC: Pre-trial Justice Institute, U.S. Department of Justice.

Manchak, S., Skeem, J., & Douglas, K. (2008). Utility of the Revised Level of Service Inventory (LSI-R) in predicting recidivism after long-term incarceration. *Law & Human Behavior, 32*(6), 477–488. doi: 10.1007/s10979-007-9118-4.

McElroy, J. E. (2011). Introduction to the Manhattan Bail Project. *Federal Sentencing Reporter, 24*(1), 8–9. doi: 10.1525/fsr.2011.24.1.8.

Milgram, A., Holsinger, A. M., Vannostrand, M., & Alsdorf, M. W. (2015). Pretrial risk assessment: Improving public safety and fairness in pretrial decision making. *Federal Sentencing Reporter, 27*(4), 216–221. doi: 10.1525/fsr.2015.27.4.216.

Miller, J., & Maloney, C. (2013). Practitioner compliance with risk/needs assessment tools: A theoretical and empirical assessment. *Criminal Justice & Behavior, 40*(7), 716–736. doi: 10.1177/0093854812468883.

Modeling Solutions, LLC. (2005). *Risk management system: A user's manual*. Retrieved from http://www.modelingsolutions.com/pdf/RMS_Users_Manual.pdf.

National Parole Resource Center. (2014). *Use of valid actuarial assessments of risks and needs*. Retrieved from http://nationalparoleresourcecenter.org/action-guide-use-of-valid-actuarial-assessments-of-risks-and-needs/history-of-risk-and-needs-assessment-tools.htm.

Post-Prison Education Program. (2015). *Success story: Kimberly*. Retrieved from http://postprisonedu.org/pages/135/success-story-kimberly/.

Pretrial Justice Institute. (2009). *2009 Survey of pretrial services programs*. Retrieved from http://www.pretrial.org/download/pji-reports/new-PJI%202009%20Survey %20of%20Pretrial%20Services%20Programs.pdf.

Pretrial Justice Institute. (2010). *Federal Pretrial Risk Assessment Instrument*. Retrieved from http://www.pretrial.org/download/risk-assessment/Federal%20Pretrial%20 Risk%20Assessment%20Instrument%20(2010).pdf.

Pulkkinen, L. (March 23, 2009). Curtis Thompson gets life for rape; murder trial awaits. *The Seattle Post Intelligencer*. Retrieved from http://www.seattlepi.com/local/article/Curtis-Thompson-gets-life-for-rape-murder-trial-1302817.php.

Reisig, M. D., Holtfreter, K., & Morash, M. (2006). Assessing recidivism risk across female pathways to crime. *Justice Quarterly, 23*(3), 384–405. doi: 10.1177/0093854809334076.

Rettenberger, M., & Eher, R. (2006). Actuarial assessment of sex offender recidivism risk: A validation of the German version of the Static-99. *Sex Offender Treatment, 1*(3), 1–11.

Roesch, R., Zapf, P. A., & Hart, S. D. (2010). *Forensic psychology and the law.* Hoboken, NJ: John Wiley & Sons.

Schlager, M. D., & Simourd, D. J. (2007). Validity of the Level of Service Inventory-Revised (LSI-R) among African American and Hispanic male offenders. *Criminal Justice & Behavior, 34*(4), 545–554. doi: 10.1177/0093854806296039.

Shaffer, D. K., Kelly, B., & Lieberman, J. D. (2011). An exemplar-based approach to risk assessment: Validating the Risk Management Systems Instrument. *Criminal Justice Policy Review, 22*(2), 167–186. doi: 10.1177/0887403410372989.

Simon, J. (1993). *Poor discipline.* Chicago, IL: University of Chicago Press.

Simourd, D., & Malcolm, P. B. (1998). Reliability and validity of the Level of Service Inventory-Revised among federally incarcerated sex offenders. *Journal of Interpersonal Violence, 13*(2), 261–274. doi: 10.1177/088626098013002006.

U.S. Courts. (2011, September). *An overview of the federal post conviction risk assessment.* Administrative Office of the United States Courts Office of Probation and Pretrial Services. Retrieved from http://www.ussc.gov/sites/default/files/pdf/training/annual-national-training-seminar/2014/PCRA_2011.pdf.

U.S. Parole Commission. (2013). *FY 2014 performance budget: Congressional submission.* Washington, DC: U.S. Department of Justice. Retrieved from http://www.justice.gov/sites/default/files/jmd/legacy/2014/07/23/uspc-justification.pdf.

U.S. Parole Commission. (2015). *Rules and procedures manual.* Washington, DC: U.S. Department of Justice. Retrieved from http://www.justice.gov/sites/default/files/uspc/legacy/2011/12/30/uspc-manual111507.pdf.

VanNostrand, M., & Keebler, G. (2009). Pretrial risk assessment in the federal court. *Federal Probation, 73*(2), 3–29.

Virginia Department of Criminal Justice Services. (2015). *Virginia pretrial risk assessment instrument training.* Retrieved from https://www.dcjs.virginia.gov/corrections/documents/vpraiManual.pdf.

Vose, B., Cullen, F. T., & Smith, P. (2008). The empirical status of the Level of Service Inventory. *Federal Probation, 72*(3), 22–29.

Vose, B., Smith, P., & Cullen, F. T. (2013). Predictive validity and the impact of change in total LSI-R score on recidivism. *Criminal Justice & Behavior, 40*(12), 1383–1396. doi: 10.1177/0093854813508916.

Walsh, A. (2001). Presentence investigation report (PSI). In A. Walsh (Ed.) *Correctional assessment, casework, and counseling* (pp. 97–120). Lantham, MD: American Correctional Association.

Willmsen, C. (2012, January 23). Swayed by a psychologist, jury frees 'monster' who attacks again. *The Seattle Times*. Retrieved from http://www.seattletimes.com/seattle-news/swayed-by-a-psychologist-jury-frees-monster-who-attacks-again/.

Wilson, H. A., & Gutierrez, L. (2014). Does one size fit all?: A meta-analysis examining the predictive ability of the Level of Service Inventory (LSI) with aboriginal offenders. *Criminal Justice & Behavior, 41*(2), 196–219. doi: 10.1177/009385481 3500958.

Chapter 3

Profile of Community Corrections Offenders and Specialized Populations

Student Learning Outcomes

After reading this chapter, you should be able to:

- Describe the offenders serving community corrections sentences.
- Explain who are the specialized offender populations and their needs.
- Summarize the complexities faced by specialized offender populations.

Introduction

It was supposed to be a fun-filled New Year's Eve celebration for Shannon Harps in Seattle in 2007. She had plans to have dinner with friends to celebrate and quickly left her condominium to stop at a store to purchase a few items for the dinner (Castro, 2008). Sadly, Harps never made it the celebration. As she returned to her building from shopping, she was fatally attacked and stabbed outside the entrance to her building (Castro, 2008). Her neighbors heard her screams and rushed to assist her, but it was too late—Harps was dead (Castro, 2008). The killing rattled Harps' community, and her friends and family were bewildered, wondering who could have done this to her as she had no enemies. This attack on Harps was merely random. It did not take long for police to identify a suspect, and they arrested a man named James Anthony Williams (Martin & Singer, 2008). Williams had been released from prison in 2006 after serving a lengthy sentence for assault (Martin & Singer, 2008). Upon his release, he was placed under supervision of a community corrections officer who noted that Williams, a diagnosed paranoid schizophrenic, was deteriorating mentally due to his failure to take his prescribed medications. Apparently, Williams was threatening to kill the officer as well as his mental healthcare providers (Martin & Singer, 2008). His erratic behavior and violent thoughts lead to Williams being labeled as one of the 70 most dangerous mentally ill offenders in King County (Martin & Singer, 2008). A mere three months before Harps' death, William had been convicted of threatening to kill his landlord. In this case, the judge was concerned about Williams and suggested commitment to a mental health hospital, but mental health evaluators deemed that

Williams did not meet the threshold for involuntary commitment (Martin & Singer, 2008). Ultimately, Williams was convicted for the killing of Harps and sentenced to a 35-year prison term (Sullivan, 2009). This unfortunate case highlights one type of offender, the mentally ill offender, who is under community corrections supervision and what can occur if the needs of the offender are not met.

For other offenders sentenced to community supervision, they may experience victimization by community members—particularly if they are sex offenders. In 2015, a Wisconsin man was arrested for arson after he was caught via video surveillance setting a home ablaze in his neighborhood (Golgowski, 2015). Apparently, this was not his first attempt to burn the home down, as he attempted to do so just three months earlier (Golgowski, 2015). The Wisconsin man was upset that a convicted child sex offender was planning to move into the home and wanted to thwart his attempts at relocation. Sometimes, the acts of victimization against sex offenders can extend beyond property damage. For example, in 2005, in Bellingham, Washington, a man impersonating an FBI agent went to the home of two registered sex offenders and warned them that they were on a "hit list" (Martin & O'Hagan, 2005). The two men were later found dead (Martin & O'Hagan, 2005). A few months later, the perpetrator called 911 and confessed to the crimes. He had located the sex offenders through the Whatcom County Sheriff's Office sex offender website (Marshall, 2005). While both of these cases are extreme, they highlight some of the difficulties that offenders can experience as they attempt to reintegrate back into their communities.

This chapter will provide an overview of the number and types of offenders that are under various community corrections sentences. Special attention will be made to highlight the age, race/ethnicity, and gender for those serving various community corrections sentences. Further, community corrections sentences can add a difficult layer of complexity for sex offenders, mentally ill offenders, offenders with drug and/or alcohol addictions, domestic violence offenders, and female offenders. The difficulties that these offenders experience will be discussed.

Offenders under Community Supervision

Offenders under community supervision are everywhere—on every block, in every store, and perhaps sipping a cup of coffee right next to you at your local coffee shop. Pinpointing the exact numbers of those offenders serving community corrections sentences is difficult. Statisticians are able to estimate that one in every thirty-four people in the United States is under some form of correctional supervision (Glaze & Parks, 2012). However, this statistic does not provide the exact count of offenders under supervision. Thus, it is necessary to dig a bit deeper to examine the number of offenders serving various forms of community corrections sentences where possible, as the data is often limited.

When examining the statistics for probationers and parolees, it is clear that there are millions of offenders under community corrections supervision. According to the most recent statistics, in 2014, approximately 3.9 million adults are serving state and federal **probation** sentences—sentences served in the community in lieu of incarceration (Herberman & Bonczar, 2014). Offenders serving **parole** sentences, those serving community sentences following an incarceration term, represent a much smaller number with approximately 856,000 adults on state and federal parole in 2014 (Kaeble et al., 2016). However, those figures alone do not give an accurate picture of the number of offenders who are serving other forms of community corrections sentences (e.g., work release, boot camps, or halfway houses). Annual national figures do not exist for those offenders serving alternative community corrections sentences, resulting in the reliance of older data to provide some sense of the figures. At the state level, an estimated 21,000 adult offenders went through boot camp programs in the year 2000 (Camp and Camp, 2000). In addition, in 2000, approximately 40,000 adult offenders were serving work release sentences, and 8,700 were participating in day-reporting center programs (Camp and Camp, 2000). Despite the limited data on offenders serving community corrections sentences other than probation and parole, it is safe to state that there are well over 4.7 million offenders under some form of community correctional supervision. Given the shortcomings in national data for all offenders under all types of community correctional supervision, the following sections will highlight the demographic information for offenders on probation and parole only.

Gender

Who are these approximate 5 million plus offenders under probation and parole supervision? Most of the individuals reentering society are male. This is perhaps not surprising given that more males are arrested for involvement in crime than females and more males are also incarcerated, at both the state and federal levels, than females (Carson, 2015; FBI, 2014). Of the approximately 3.9 million offenders on probation in 2014, 75 percent were male (Kaeble, Maruschak, & Bonczar, 2015). When examining the gender of the approximately 856,000 offenders who were on parole in 2014, the numbers are similar to probation. Specifically, 88 percent of parolees in 2014 were male with females accounting for less than 100,000 state and federal parolees of the 856,000 parolees nationwide (Kaeble et al., 2015). Thus, men represent a higher proportion of individuals who are transitioning into society from prison and parole sentences as well as reentering society through the serving of probation sentences.

Race

Racial disparity and discrimination, from arrest to sentencing, have plagued minorities in the United States—particularly African Americans (Walker, Spohn, & DeLone, 2007). Thus, it is important to examine whether certain races and ethnicities are more or less likely to be placed on the community corrections sentences of probation and parole. In the case of the race of probationers in 2014, Caucasians represented the highest number at both the federal and state level at approximately 54 percent (Kaeble et al., 2015). Kaeble et al. (2015) further report the following approximated percentages for federal and state probationers: 30 percent African American; 13 percent Hispanic/Latino; 1 percent American Indian/Alaska Native; and 1 percent Native Hawaiian/Pacific Islander. When examining the race of the approximately 856,000 offenders who were on parole in 2014, one finds similar percentages to those on probation. Specifically, Caucasians represented the highest percentages at both the federal and state level at approximately 43 percent (Kaeble et al., 2015). The researchers further report the following approximated numbers for federal and state parolees: 39 percent African American; 16 percent Hispanic/Latino; 1 percent American Indian/Alaska Native; and 1 percent Native Hawaiian/other Pacific Islander (Kaeble et al., 2015).

At the surface, the percentages reported tell an interesting story. On one hand, the percentages of Caucasians receiving the above-mentioned community corrections sentences is lower. Thus, it would appear that racial disparity is not at play as Caucasians are more likely to receive these sentences. On the other hand, however, with other minority groups being less likely to receive such sentences, the question of racial disparity and discrimination quickly arises. At the probation level, for instance, if Caucasians are more likely to receive probation sentences, does this mean that other minority groups are more likely to receive alterative punishments such as jail or prison? It very well could be the case given that a disproportionate number of those incarcerated in jails and prisons are members of a minority—particularly African American (Carson, 2015). Moreover, with more Caucasians receiving parole, does this mean that other minority groups are less likely to be released on parole? Again, this could be the case given the reports of racial disparity that occurs with parole decisions (Huebner & Bynum, 2006).

Age

No national statistics are kept on the average age of those serving community corrections sentences each year. Despite the gaps in data, there are some trends in age that have been reported for probationers and parolees that can be gleaned from the utilizing of existing, yet older, data. For probationers in 1995, the majority were between the ages of 18 and 44 with offenders ages 25–34 years old accounting for the highest percentage of probationers (Bonczar, 1997). In regards to parolees, in 1999, those most likely to be paroled in the state correctional system were between the ages of 18 and 39 (Hughes & Wilson, 2002). However, the average age for parolees is trending towards being older. For instance, the average age of parolees in 1999 was 34 years of age, up from 31 years of age in 1990 (Hughes & Wilson, 2002). Unfortunately, current data has not been released on the age of parolees today to provide a better picture of their ages now. Although a gap in this data exists, we may expect that (1) a wider range of ages of prisoners are being released on parole given fiscal constraints that states are facing; or (2) those paroled may indeed continue to be trending towards the older age ranges given the focus on the crime control, or "get tough on crime" model, whereby the public demands that offender be locked up and punished for lengthy periods. More recent research suggests that the age of release for parole may be dependent on the type of crime an offender has committed. For instance, Huebner and Bynum (2006) found that sex offenders who were older were less likely to be granted parole. Clearly, more research is needed to ascertain the current age trends for both probationers and parolees as well as for other offenders serving other community corrections sentences.

Offenders Serving Community Corrections Sentences: Specialized Groups

Without a doubt, offenders serving community corrections sentences encounter many challenges and difficulties. After all, they are expected to abide by court-imposed conditions while at the same time to successfully reintegrate back into society. For some offender groups, complying with conditions and reentering society is fraught with complexities. The next sections discuss specialized offender groups and the many challenges they face.

Sex Offenders

Sex offenders are perhaps one of the most feared groups of offenders in society due to the crimes they committed and concerns about their recidivism rates. Because of the community fear and concerns about sex offenders' ability to successfully reintegrate, this offender group often experiences an enhanced level of stigmatization. Clearly, much of the stigmatization that sex offenders face is from the requirement that they register as sex offender due to the enactment of the several pieces of legislation in the 1990s. Until 1994, only five states required sex offenders to register with local law enforcement agencies where they resided (Cochrane & Kennedy, 2010). However, that quickly changed with the passage of the **Jacob Wetterling Crimes Against Children and Sexually Violent Offender Act** in 1994 (Cochrane & Kennedy, 2010). In 1989, Jacob Wetterling, 11-years-old, was abducted by a masked gunman as he and his friends left a convenience store in Minnesota (Forliti, 2010). His case garnered national attention, which resulted in the 1994 legislation requiring states to track offenders for at least 10 years or for life if the offender had been convicted of a violent sex crime (Forliti, 2010; Office of Justice Programs, 2015). At the time of his abduction, it was suspected that a sex offender was responsible for his disappearance. Sadly, Wetterling's remains were found in 2016, and a sex offender confessed to the crime (Wootson, 2016). Coincidentally, another tragic case further expanded sex offender tracking in 1994. Megan Kanka, a 7-year-old girl, was raped and murdered in New Jersey in 1994 by a sex offender who lived across the street (Filler, 2001). Her parents and the community had no knowledge that a sex offender was residing in their neighborhood. Subsequently, New Jersey passed a law called "**Megan's Law,**" which required community notification of registered sex offenders (Cochrane & Kennedy, 2010). Two years later, in 1996, the federal government amended the Wetterling Act and mandated that states implement community notification programs (Cochrane & Kennedy, 2010). To encourage state adoption of sex offender registration and community notification, the federal government provided financial incentives to states resulting in all 50 states adopting and/or amending existing sex offender registration laws (Cochrane & Kennedy, 2010). For example, some states, such as Massachusetts, began to classify sex offenders into three categories: Level 1; Level 2; and Level 3. Level 1 offenders were considered the least dangerous or serious sex offenders while Level 3 offenders were considered the most serious sex offenders, and this group is much more likely to recidivate than Level 1 or Level 2 sex offenders (Tennen, 2014). In other states, sex offenders were classified into Tier 1, Tier 2, and Tier 3 categories, which mirrored the risk classification levels used in other states. Besides classifying offenders, states began to disseminate information about the offenders' status as a sex offender to the community through various forms of communication (e.g., newspaper ads, clothing labels) (Presser & Gunnison, 1999). This communication of sex offender status is unique to the United States, as in other European countries, such as the United Kingdom (U.K.), that require sex offenders to register, do not permit community notification (Hynes, 2013).

The concern regarding sex offenders has continued to expand. Most recently, the federal government passed the **Adam Walsh Child Protection and Safety Act** in 2006. Adam Walsh was a six-year-old boy who was abducted from a Sears store in 1981 in Florida and was later found murdered (Almanzar, 2008). His father, John Walsh, enraged by the brutality of losing his son, became an international crime fighter and has pushed for tougher laws and punishments for offenders. You may be familiar with John Walsh as he hosted the popular *America's Most Wanted* television show for over two decades. Thus, John Walsh pushed for the act in honor of his son's memory to better track sex offenders and keep children safe. Title 1 of this act is now known as the **Sex Offender Registration and Notification Act** (SORNA). One result of this legislation was the standard classification of sex offenders from Level 1, 2, and 3 to Tier 1, 2, and 3 respectively. Additionally, the legislation specified the length of time a sex offender was to be kept on the registry. The Office of Justice Programs (2015) explains that "SORNA specifies the minimum required duration of sex offender registration for Tier I sex offenders to be 15 years, for Tier II sex offenders to be 25 years, and for Tier III sex offenders to register for life. The registration period begins to run upon release from custody for a sex offender sentenced to incarceration for the registration offense, or in the case of non-incarcerated sex offenders, at the time of sentencing for the sex offense." Additionally, the act established a national sex offender registry database on the Internet, known as the Dru Sjodin National Sex Offender Public Website (NSOPW), which was named after a murder victim of a Level 3 sex offender, and it also implemented lengthier prison sentences for those offenders who failed to register or update their information (Cochrane & Kennedy, 2010). Estimates are that approximately 800,000 offenders are currently registered as sex offenders in the United States (Sanburn, 2014).

Have such laws impacted sex offenders' self-concept? Apparently, this law may have. Research has revealed that sex offenders who accept the label of "sex offender" may actually be more prone to recidivism (Marino, 2009). Thus, the sex offender label can be particularly stigmatizing to an individual's self-concept for some offenders. This law has also resulted in acts of violence against sex offenders or significant damage to their property. With SORNA in place, community members can conduct a simple online search to see if a sex offender is residing in their community. Their identification as a sex offender can lead to further stigmatization in their communities that they are residing in. As previously mentioned, in 2015, a Wisconsin man was arrested for arson after he attempted to burn down a home that a sex-offender was to move into (Golgowski, 2015). For many sex offenders, SORNA has also inhibited not only their housing options but their employment opportunities as well.

For any offender who entered the criminal justice system without stable housing or housing at all, housing becomes a very critical element if they are sentenced, or released, to a community corrections sentence that requires they serve their sentence at their residence (e.g., probation, parole, house arrest) (Gunnison & Helfgott, 2013). Housing is such an obstacle for offenders that Roman and Travis (2006, p. 389) suggest that the question for these offenders quickly becomes "Where will I sleep tomorrow?" For sex offenders, acquisition of appropriate housing is particularly difficult. Many landlords are reluctant to rent to ex-offenders due to their fear for community safety or losing current tenants who may become fearful of being a neighbor to an ex-offender (Clark, 2007; Harding & Harding, 2006; Helfgott, 1997).

Registered sex offenders in particular face this obstacle, not only from potential landlords but also from the authorities themselves as many states have passed legislation that further restricts their residency (i.e., not near schools, day cares, playgrounds, and parks) (Barnes, Dukes, Tewksbury, & De Troye, 2009; Chajewski & Mercado, 2009; Grubesic, Murray, & Mack, 2011). Unfortunately, sex offenders often do not have a full understanding of their residency restrictions (Tewksbury & Copes, 2013). These residency restrictions for sex offenders limit their access to affordable housing options (Levenson & Hern, 2007). Stromberg (2007, p. 20) refers to this group as being "locked up, then locked out," since sex offenders are excluded from many housing options due to fear for community safety. In a case study of ex-offenders in Florida, researchers found "that housing options for registered sex offenders within urban residential areas are limited to only 5% of potentially available parcels and that bus stop restrictions impact the amount of livable area the most, followed by daycares, schools, parks, and attractions. The limited options to establish residency exist mostly in low-density rural areas" (Zandbergen & Hart, 2006, p. 1). Thus, sex offenders may be pushed out to rural communities, which pose their own unique challenges for successful reintegration (see Wodahl, 2006). Within the state of Florida, which has some of the most stringent laws regarding residency for sex offenders, a new community of sex offenders has flourished known as *Miracle Village* (Sanburn, 2014). Located in a secluded,

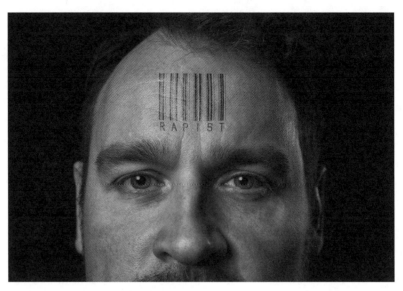

Image 5. © iStockphoto.com/StockFinland.

non-populated area in Florida situated among sugarcane fields, Miracle Village is a community where about 150 sex offenders are able to reside (Sanburn, 2014). Within this community, offenders receive support as they attempt to transition back into their communities.

While it is well known that sex offenders will face such stigmatization and abuse, what is often not known is the impact their status has on their family members. Results from the research revealed that the children of the registered sex offenders were treated differently at school or by peers and also experienced stigmatization due to their parents' status (Levenson & Tewksbury, 2009). In a study examining the impact of sex offender registration laws on family members, Levenson and Tewksbury (2009) found that family members experienced employment limitations, housing disruption, and sometimes threats, harassment, or property damage due to their association with a registered sex offender. Thus, their offender status has far-reaching collateral consequences and can disrupt their efforts at family reunification. This fact can certainly be a source of frustration for sex offenders.

Further complicating the ability of sex offenders to abide by the conditions of their community corrections sentence is the fact that they are mandated to undergo treatment. If they cannot pay for their treatment, they are in violation of their conditions of release and may be returned to jail/prison. For female sex offenders, obtaining treatment is especially needed, not to just curb future offending behavior but to also address their own victimization backgrounds, which could be a contributing factor to their offending. Goldhill (2013) noted that female sex offenders are almost four times more likely than male sex offenders to have experienced sexual abuse as a child. Thus, sex offenders are required to undergo treatment and burdened with the costs of obtaining treatment while, at the same time, struggling to find housing and employment, which is severely limited due to their status as sex offenders. Employers are often hesitant to hire ex-offenders in general and their status as "sex offenders" further stymies their ability to obtain gainful employment (LeBel, 2012).

Mentally Ill Offenders

Within the entire criminal justice system, mental health is a huge issue calling some to note that the criminal justice system is plagued by a "mental health crisis." Part of the current problem stems from well-intentioned federal legislation that was passed in the 1960s that led to decreased services for those with mental health problems. In 1963, the **Community Mental Health Centers Act** was signed into law, the provisions of which led to the deinstitutionalization of the mentally ill, removing them from in-residence treatment centers to community-based treatment programs (Solomon et al., 2008). This legislation clearly reduced the level of abuse that many individuals were facing in institutions, but, by shifting the care to community-based treatment facilities, it created the opportunity for gaps in care for those with mental health issues as their level of supervision was reduced. With this reduction in supervision, many mentally ill offenders residing in the community could freely exhibit behaviors out and in the open that put them at risk for police intervention (e.g., public urination, threatening behavior towards community members). It was during this era that the gradual assimilation of mentally ill offenders into the criminal justice system began. Further, the federal court decision of *Wyatt v. Stickney* in 1972 stated that mentally ill and mentally retarded individuals have a constitutional right to a minimum level of care and treatment in institutions. With the new requirement in place, some states began to release residents to community-based treatment facilities as the cost of providing minimum services (i.e., treatment and staffing) to those residents within the institution were cost prohibitive (Perez, Leifman, & Estrada, 2003). However, these new outpatient services were extremely inadequate. Perez et al. explain (2003, p. 63), "Unfortunately, many states saw deinstitutionalization as an opportunity to save money rather than an opportunity to improve their mental health services. States closed down hospitals condemned for failure to meet the minimum constitutional standards of care for people with mental illnesses, but they did not use the money saved to develop community-based outpatient treatment centers or much-needed social services. The result has been nothing short of disaster."

The impact of deinstitutionalization has resulted in many mentally ill individuals being shifted from state hospitals to becoming ensnared in the criminal justice system. According to the National Association of State Mental Health Program Directors Research Institute (2000), more than 300,000 individuals with mental illness are incarcerated in jails. Crayton and colleagues (2010) report that approximately 24 percent of those incarcerated in jails show symptomatic evidence of mental illness. Persons with mental illness are overrepresented in jails and prisons, with 6–8 percent having

Image 6. © Mikael Damkier/Fotolia.

a serious mental illness in state prisons, 7.2 percent in jails, and many more that have had contact with the criminal justice system but were not incarcerated (National Alliance on Mental Illness, 2008). Davis and Pacchiana (2004) report that the prevalence of schizophrenia and bipolar disorder are about one to five times greater in the prison population than the general population. Thus, it is clear that a high percentage of those that are incarcerated suffer from mental illness, which is an artifact of the de-institutionalization movement. On the community corrections side, Slate et al. (2003) report that approximately 16% of probationers and 5–10% of parolees suffer from mental illness.

Over the past few decades, additional policy changes in the criminal justice system have resulted in those with mental illnesses being even more likely to enter into the criminal justice system and also become ensnared in it (Lurigio & Swartz, 2000). With correctional administrators unable to offer comprehensive services to those suffering from such problems due to budgetary constraints, the mental health problems for mentally ill incarcerated individuals often worsen. With deteriorating mental health disorders, many sufferers act out during their incarceration terms and wind up accruing numerous disciplinary infractions, which only extend their stay in the correctional system (Kondo, 2000). Further complicating successful reentry for those incarcerated with mental illness is often inadequate transition planning when they are released from jail or prison (Osher, Steadman, & Barr, 2003). These offenders need a wide range of available services that will meet their needs during reentry. Unfortunately, the lack of adequate transition planning for this group increases their likelihood of recidivating. Some researchers have found recidivism rates as high as 70 percent for those ex-offenders with mental illnesses returning to their communities after incarceration (Ventura et al., 1998).

Mental health issues are indeed a challenge for many ex-offenders attempting to reenter society (see Text Box 3.1). Travis, Solomon, and Waul (2001) report that approximately 16 percent of all ex-offenders have a diagnosable mental disorder. For many ex-offenders, mental health problems are not isolated but are experienced in tandem with other problems such as substance abuse. The mental health problems also cross over and present challenges for ex-offenders in other areas of their reentry, such as obtaining employment, finding housing, and reestablishing family connections (Fontaine, Roman, & Burt, 2010). Thus, mental health problems often inhibit ex-offenders' ability to made strides toward success since these problems impact other aspects of their reentry.

Text Box 3.1: Mental Health of Offenders: Canada

The concern over the mental health of offenders is not isolated to the United States. Other countries, such as Canada, are also struggling to meet the needs of mentally ill offenders (Simpson, McMaster, & Cohen, 2013). Similar to incarcerated offenders in the United States, the rates of serious mentally ill persons incarcerated in Canada are almost three times higher than the mental illness rates in the general, non-incarcerated population (Simpson et al., 2013). In Canada, each province establishes its own policies and legislation to reasonably meet the mental health needs of incarcerated offenders. This has resulted in some disparity of care across the provinces, and budget woes have also plagued the ability of various institutions to offer comprehensive treatment for offenders and post-release (Simpson et al., 2013). Without comprehensive mental health treatment, offenders, upon release, will ultimately have difficulties in reintegrating successfully. Additionally, without strong mental health support post-release, such as in the form of wrap-around services, released mentally ill offenders are likely to continue to struggle and recidivism is a very strong possibility.

Substance Abuse Offenders

Previous research has established a link between substance use and criminal involvement (Anglin & Perrochet, 1998; Inciardi, 1992; Inciardi et al., 1997; MacCoun & Reuter, 2001). In fact, drug and alcohol use is both a contributor to the onset of criminality for both males and females as well as a factor contributing to future criminality (Belknap, 2007; Olson et al., 2003). Solomon and colleagues (2008, p. 32) state that "more than two-thirds (68 percent) of all jail inmates meet the criteria for substance abuse or dependence, as defined by the *Diagnostic and Statistical Manual of Mental Disorders*, fourth edition. In comparison, only nine percent of the U.S. population abuse or are dependent on drugs or alcohol." Other researchers have reported that, in general, up to 75% of all ex-offenders have a history of substance abuse or addiction (Travis et al., 2001).

Image 7. © stocksolutions/Fotolia.

Research has uncovered that ex-offenders who participate in treatment while in-carcerated and community-based substance abuse programs after release have lower levels of substance use and lower rates of recidivism (Jannetta, Dodd, & Elderbroom, 2011; Miller & Miller, 2010; Visher & Courtney, 2007; Zhang, Roberts, & Callanan, 2006). However, oftentimes offenders may not participate in drug/alcohol treatment programs while incarcerated — this is especially true for jail inmates (Solomon et al., 2008). Part of this problem may stem from the fact that "less than one-fifth of convicted jail inmates who meet the criteria for abuse or dependence receive formal treatment or other programs after admission to jail" (Crayton et al., 2010, p. 21). The lack of access to formal substance abuse programs for jail inmates may also stem from budget cuts to state correctional budgets (Scott-Hayward, 2009). That is, given the cost of offering such treatment programs and the transiency of the jail populations, correctional administrators, when faced with making cuts, may decide to first cut jail programs. Further complicating the reentry for jail inmates suffering from substance abuse issues who were fortunate to have received treatment is the length of time they were able to participate in treatment. The length of time an ex-offender has spent in treatment appears to be a significant factor in reentry success. Researchers have found that the longer the time that offenders participate in treat-ment, the likelihood of these offenders committing future crimes is reduced (Lewis & Ross, 1994; Simpson, Joe, & Brown, 1997). Simpson and colleagues (1999) report that those with severe substance abuse problems have better success following 90 days of treatment.

Ex-offenders with substance abuse histories (the majority of the ex-offender population) making the transition from incarceration to the community are in the precarious position of having to manage extraordinary stressors without engaging in old habits of substance use and abuse as a way to manage everyday stressors and problems in living (Brazzell & La Vigne, 2009). Substance abuse problems often interfere with an ex-offender's ability to obtain or maintain employment (Heinrich, 2000). Additionally, many substance abuse offenders suffer from co-occurring disorders, such as mental illness, which can further complicate their ability to effectively meet the conditions of release (e.g., finding housing and employment) (Hammet, Roberts, & Kennedy, 2001).

It is important to note that not all ex-offenders have access to community-based treatment programs upon release from incarceration (Crayton et al., 2010; Thompson, 2004). Crayton and colleagues (2010, p. 21) explain that "lack of insurance, conviction-based bans on receiving public assistance, or the lack of available treatment can create substantial barriers to post-release substance abuse treatment." Without access to formal treatment, these offenders may come to rely on their parole officer, for example, for assistance (Thompson, 2004). It may very well be that the community corrections officer is the only pro-social individual in the life of the ex-offender, and thus, the ex-offender really must rely on his/her parole officer for support and guidance. Unfortunately, community corrections officers generally have a large client caseload and are not trained treatment providers, which clearly inhibits their ability to navigate ex-offenders to the pathway of recovery from addiction or abstinence from drug and/or alcohol consumption. With community-based substance abuse programs being unreachable or unattainable for many ex-offenders, many researchers have found that these offenders will continue consuming drugs and/or alcohol upon release.

Substance abuse addiction is a struggle for many offenders sentenced directly to community corrections sentences such as probation and those sentenced to incarceration terms. Without adequate treatment while incarcerated or in the community, the journey to successful reentry is fraught with many obstacles. Formerly addicted ex-offenders trying to reintegrate successfully into their communities are prone to relapse and are in need of services and continued services post-supervision. Without their substance abuse issues being met as well as other needs being met, such as co-occurring mental health disorders, then ex-offenders will have great difficulties in meeting the bare minimum requirements of release (e.g., housing and employment) and are not likely to reintegrate successfully.

Domestic Violence Offenders

With the passage of mandatory and preferred arrest laws in many states for perpetrators of domestic violence beginning in the 1970s, there has been an increase in intimate partner violence arrest rates for both men *and* women (Hirschel, Buzawa, Pattavina, & Faggiani, 2007). One reason why women are experiencing an increase in their arrests rates for intimate partner violence may be due to law enforcement officers arresting both parties involved in a domestic violence incident (Hirschel et al., 2007). Despite this trend, men are predominately more likely to be the perpetrators of intimate partner violence. The increase in the arrests as well as prosecution has resulted in more domestic violence offenders being convicted and sentenced to community corrections sentences such as probation. For other domestic violence offenders, their crime may result in an incarceration sentence followed by release to parole. Researchers have examined re-arrest for both domestic and nondomestic violence offenses and have found recidivism rates to be high. For instance, in an examination of approximately 300 domestic violence offenders who were followed over a 10-year period, Richards et al. (2014) found that almost half of the offenders were rearrested. Thus, it appears that appropriate treatment may be critical for domestic violence offenders to be able to reintegrate successfully.

Historically, the approach to treating domestic violence offenders was to implement a similar treatment plan for all offenders. For instance, a similar treatment plan (e.g., anger-management programming, cognitive-behavioral therapy, group counseling) over a fixed period of time was instituted for all domestic violence offenders. One chief problem with the one-size-fits-all programming approach for domestic violence offenders is the fact that research has emerged that domestic violence offenders are not all the same — that is they are a heterogeneous group (Gover, Richards, & Tomsich, 2015). Cavanaugh and Gelles (2005) report that there are three types of batterers: low, moderate, and high-risk offenders. Additionally, the researchers note that despite the notion that male batterers move from being low to high-risk offenders over time, this idea has not been empirically supported (Cavanaugh & Gelles, 2005). Since not all domestic violence offenders are the same, then similar court-mandated treatment for all offenders is not likely to be effective. The researchers found in their evaluation that interventions designed to address the needs of specific domestic violence offenders can be effective (Cavanaugh & Gelles, 2005). Without specifically designed treatment for domestic violence offenders based on their needs and risk factors, Cavanaugh & Gelles (2005) caution that interventions will likely not be effective and the safety of the victim may be compromised.

One state that has taken steps to address the needs of domestic violent offenders based on their risk level is Colorado (Gover et al., 2015). Traditionally, domestic violence offenders were all required to be provided with the same treatment over a 36-week treatment period (Gover et al., 2015). However, in 2010, the state implemented a new Domestic Violence Risk and Needs Assessment Tool (DVRNA), whereby offenders could be assessed as to their needs and risk factors, their risk level established (i.e., A, B, or C with C level offenders being most at risk for recidivism), and specific interventions developed based on their needs and risk level (Gover et al., 2015). As shown in Text Box 3.2, the DVRNA instrument contains 14 static and dynamic risk factors which assist in identifying the appropriate level of treatment for the offender.

Text Box 3.2: Colorado's DVRNA Risk Factor Domains

- Prior domestic violence related incidents
- Drug/alcohol abuse*
- Mental health issues*
- Use and/or threatened use of weapons in current or past offense, or access to firearms*
- Suicidal/homicidal*
- Criminal history (non-domestic violence related)*
- Obsession with the victim
- Safety concerns
- Violence toward family members, including child abuse
- Attitudes that condone or support partner assault
- Prior completed or non-completed domestic violence offender treatment
- Involvement with people who have a pro-criminal influence
- Separated from victim within last six months
- Unemployed

* Denotes significant/critical risk factor resulting in automatic placement in treatment intensity level B or C.

Source: Adapted directly, p. 3 from Gover, A. R., Richards, T. N., & Tomsich, E. A. (2015). *Colorado's innovative response to domestic violence offender treatment: Current achievements and recommendations for the future: A Buechner crime briefing.* Denver, CO: University of Colorado, Denver.

Gover et al. (2015) evaluated approximately 3,300 domestic violence offenders in Colorado who were court ordered to complete treatment utilizing the new DVRNA assessment tool. The researchers found that most offenders were classified as higher (C) or moderate risk (B). Interestingly, once the offenders were placed into a treatment plan based on their risk level, they could move between levels of treatment plans at any time during treatment delivery. That is, an offender classified as a C who made good progress during treatment, could be moved into a lower level treatment plan (A or B) based on their outstanding needs and risk factors. Additionally, time in treatment was not designated, meaning that offenders were discharged from treatment "when they have met all required competencies and conditions of their treatment plan and offender contract" (Gover et al., 2015, p. 5). Upon examination of average time spent in treatment, the researchers found that level A offenders spent 12 weeks in treatment, level B offenders spent 35 weeks in treatment, and level C offenders spent 37 weeks in treatment. In terms of which offenders were most likely to complete the treatment plans successfully as required, the researchers found that offenders placed in level A treatment plans were the most likely to complete it successfully, followed by offenders placed on level B and level C treatment plans. The researchers did not examine recidivism rates for these groups to determine treatment outcomes. However, the researchers interviewed treatment providers and community corrections officers about their perspectives as to what makes for "successful treatment." The majority of those interviewed identified that accountability was a critical skill for the offender to have acquired upon completion of the program. Probation officers, for instance, carefully examined whether their clients exhibited accountability for their actions. Gover et al. (2015, p. 9) reported that one probation officer looked for 'High accountability for what happened. It has to be in the eyes of myself and the therapist, more the therapist than me, something genuine,' while another probation officer prioritized, 'Ownership, and they're making amends with the victims involved. Not just the direct victim, but the community....' Another probation officer closely reviewed offender writing assignments, such as letters of accountability or personal change plans, stating, '... when they write that, I think you can really get a feel for their empathy and their accountability for their actions so it's helpful and validating that treatment's working when you see them take accountability.'

While often not thought of as a specialized group serving community corrections sentences, domestic violence offenders are indeed a group in need of attention—especially since no man or woman should be a victim of domestic assaults. With historic programming plans that sought to treat all domestic offenders the same with common treatment plans (e.g., anger management or cognitive-behavioral programming), it has now become clear that domestic violence offenders are in need of more expansive programming options. Ideally, flexible programming that meets the needs of these offenders and perhaps continued services post-supervision are the best measures to assist domestic violence offenders and reduce their likelihood of future assaultive behaviors.

Female Offenders

While men represent a higher proportion of those serving community corrections sentences, it should be noted that female offenders serving parole sentences experience quite a number of difficulties—often even more complex than those experienced by their male counterparts. It is true that female parolees, similar to their male parolee counterparts, have difficulties in acquiring housing and employment—a challenge for virtually all parolees (Gunnison & Helfgott, 2013). Despite this similarity between female and male parolees, female paroles experience other unique and significant challenges. One significant challenge the female parolees face during reentry is regaining their role as a mother and balancing the role of motherhood with other reentry demands. Since a greater number of incarcerated women are mothers and resided with their children prior to incarceration than males, female parolees are often very concerned and motivated to be reunited with their children (Richie, 2001). However, regaining custody is difficult due to legal obstacles (Mapson, 2013). The passage of the **Adoption and Safe Families Act** in 1997 may make it impossible for female parolees to regain custody of their children. One provision of the act requires termination of parental rights for children who have been in foster care for at least 15 months (Petersilia, 2003). Clearly, those women who have served lengthy prison sentences may have lost their children to the foster care system given this provision, especially since women who are incarcerated are more likely to have their children placed in foster care system when they are sentenced to prison (Gunnison, Bernat, & Goodstein, 2016). For those fortunate female offenders who are able to regain custody of their children, they soon find that having their children back in their care places additional burdens on them—

particularly in the acquisition of housing. For many women seeking subsidized housing, they quickly learn that a barrier to entry into these homes is their children as most of the subsidized housing programs do not allow children (Leverentz, 2010). Thus, some female parolees who are mothers face a difficult choice to either live within subsidized housing by themselves or forgo this housing option to reside with their children.

For many female parolees, the stress of reunification with their children and regaining custody is compounded by their efforts to remain sober. Parsons and Warner-Robbins (2002) add that sustaining recovery from substance abuse problems is a chief concern of females reentering the community, resulting in the reunification with their child(ren) becoming a secondary goal. Additionally, many female parolees are faced with overcoming personal problems such as prior sexual abuse, previous domestic violence victimization, a HIV-positive diagnosis, coping with depression, earning money, maintaining sobriety, finding and acquiring reliable transportation, and trying to regain their parental rights (Arditti & Few, 2006; Gunnison et al., 2015; Michalsen, 2011; Sharp, 2014). Thus, a multitude of demands and tasks are placed on females upon reentry.

In sum, female parolees attempting to reenter society successfully are not faced with one challenge but a whole host of challenges which may or may not be visible. They struggle to acquire housing, and those with children may find that their housing options are even further limited. Additionally, they struggle with reunification with their children and regaining custody of them. They battle these struggles while also overcoming their own personal problems and traumas (e.g., depression, prior sexual abuse, domestic violence), health issues (e.g., sobriety, HIV diagnosis), and daily life struggles (e.g., transportation, money to buy food and personal hygiene products).

Conclusion

In conclusion, this chapter provided an overview of the number and types of offenders that are under various community corrections sentences. Demographic data does not exist on offenders serving all forms of community corrections sentences. Despite the significant gaps in data, those serving community corrections sentences are predominately male, Caucasian, and are in their mid-20s to late 30s. Community corrections sentences can add a difficult layer of complexity for sex offenders, mentally ill offenders, offenders with drug and/or alcohol addictions, domestic violence offenders, and female offenders. The difficulties that these offenders experience while serving community sentences was discussed. Overwhelmingly, not all offenders serving community corrections sentences are the same, thus, correctional administrators should carefully consider the needs and unique difficulties that various groups of offenders may experience while serving these sentence—particularly if administrators want to achieve successful reintegration and ultimately reduced recidivism rates.

Key Terms

Adam Walsh Child Protection and Safety Act

Adoption and Safe Families Act

Community Mental Health Centers Act

Jacob Wetterling Crimes Against Children and Sexually Violent Offender Act

Megan's Law

Parole

Probation

Sex Offender Registration and Notification Act

Discussion Questions

1. Research the number of offenders serving community corrections sentences in your state. Be sure to note the age, gender, race/ethnicity, and trends for those serving these sentences.

2. Research sex offenders residing in your county. What did you find? Should sex offenders be required to register their status? If so, for how long? If not, why not? What could be done to mitigate their difficulties in obtaining housing?

3. What policies should be implemented throughout the criminal justice system to help mentally ill offenders? What policies should be in place to divert them from the criminal justice system?

4. What steps or measures are needed to assist specialized offender groups serving community correction sentences?

References

Almazar, Y. (2008, December 16). 27 Years later, case is closed in slaying of abducted child. *New York Times*. Retrieved from http://www.nytimes.com/2008/12/17/us/17adam.html.

Anglin, M. D., & Perrochet, B. (1998). Drug use and crime: A historical review of research conducted by the UCLA Drug Abuse Research Center. *Substance Use & Misuse, 33*, 1871–1914.

Arditti, J. A., & Few, A. L. (2006). Mothers' reentry into family life following incarceration. *Criminal Justice Policy Review, 17*, 103–123. doi: 10.1177/0887403405282450.

Barnes, J. C., Dukes, T., Tewksbury, R., & De Troye, T. M. (2009). Analyzing the impact of a statewide residence restriction law on South Carolina sex offenders. *Criminal Justice Policy Review, 20*, 21–43. doi: 10.1177/0887403408320842.

Belknap, J. (2007). *The invisible woman: Gender, crime, and justice*. Belmont, CA: Thomson, Wadsworth.

Bonczar, T. P. (1977). *Characteristics of adults on probation, 1995*. Washington, DC: Bureau of Justice Statistics, U.S. Department of Justice.

Brazzell, D., & La Vigne, N. D. (2009). *Prisoner reentry in Houston: Community perspectives*. Washington, DC: Urban Institute Justice Policy Center.

Camp, C. G., & Camp, G. M. (2000). The corrections yearbook 2000—Adult corrections. Middletown, CT: Criminal Justice Institute.

Carson, E. A. (2015). Prisoners in 2014. Washington, DC: Bureau of Justice Statistics, U.S. Department of Justice.

Castro, H. (2008, January 1). Police still searching for Capitol Hill killer. *Seattle Post-Intelligencer*. Retrieved from http://www.seattlepi.com/local/article/Police-still-searching-for-Capitol-Hill-killer-1260422.php.

Cavanaugh, M. M., & Gelles, R. J. (2005). The utility of male domestic violence offender typologies: New directions for research, policy, and practice. *Journal of Interpersonal Violence, 20*(2), 155–166. doi: 10.1177/0886260504268763.

Chajewski, M., & Mercado, C. C. (2009). An evaluation of sex offender residency restriction functioning in town, county, and city-wide jurisdiction. *Criminal Justice Policy Review, 20*, 44–61. doi: 10.1177/0887403408320845.

Clark, L. M. (2007). Landlord attitudes toward renting to released offenders. *Federal Probation, 71*(1), 20–30.

Cochrane, D. L., & Kennedy, M. A. (2010). Attitudes towards Megan's Law and juvenile sex offenders. *Justice Police Journal, 7*(1), 1–35. Retrieved from http://www.cjcj.org/uploads/cjcj/documents/attitudes_towards.pdf.

Crayton, A., Ressler, L., Mukamal, D. A., Jannetta, J., & Warwick, K. (2010). *Partnering with jails to improve reentry: A guidebook for community-based organizations*. Washington, DC: Urban Institute.

Davis, L., & Pacchiana, S. (2004). Health profile of the state prison population and returning offenders: Public health challenges. *Journal of Correctional Health Care, 10*, 303–331. doi: 10.1177/107834580301000305.

Federal Bureau of Investigation (FBI). (2014). *Uniform Crime Reports, 2014*. Washington, DC.

Filler, D. M. (2001). Making the case for Megan's Law: A study in legislative rhetoric. *Indiana Law Journal, 76*(2), 315–365.

Fontaine, J., Roman, C. G., & Burt, M. R. (2010). *System change accomplishments of the Corporation for Supportive Housing's Returning Home Initiative*. Washington, DC: Urban Institute.

Forliti, A. (2010, September 28). Minn. officials: No break in 1989 abduction case. *Boston.com*. Retrieved from http://www.boston.com/news/nation/articles/2010/09/28/minn_officials_no_break_in_1989_abduction_case/.

Glaze, L. E., & Parks, E. (2012). *Correctional populations in the United States, 2011*. Washington, DC: Bureau of Justice Statistics, U.S. Department of Justice.

Goldhill, R. (2013). What was she thinking? Women who sexually offend against children — implications for probation practice. *Probation Journal, 60*(4), 415–424. doi: 10.1177/0264550513502248.

Golgowski, N. (2015, February 25). Wisconsin man arrested for setting sex offender's future home on fire: Sheriff. *New York Daily News*. Retrieved from http://www.ny dailynews.com/news/national/wis-man-busted-torching-sex-offender-home-sheriff-article-1.2129307.

Gover, A. R., Richards, T. N., & Tomsich, E. A. (2015). *Colorado's innovative response to domestic violence offender treatment: Current achievements and recommendations for the future: A Buechner crime briefing.* Denver, CO: University of Colorado, Denver.

Grubesic, T. H., Murray, A. T., & Mack, E. A. (2011). Sex offenders, residence restrictions, housing, and urban morphology: A review and synthesis. *Cityscape: A Journal of Policy Development and Research, 13*(3), 7–31.

Gunnison, E., Bernat, F., & Goodstein, L. (2016). *Women and crime: Balancing the scales.* UK: Wiley-Blackwell.

Gunnison, E., & Helfgott, J. B. (2013). *Offender reentry: Beyond crime and punishment.* Boulder, CO: Lynne Rienner.

Hammet, T. M., Roberts, C., & Kennedy, S. (2001). Health-related issues in prisoner re-entry. *Crime and Delinquency, 47*(3), 446–461. doi: 10.1177/001112870104 7003006.

Harding, A., & Harding, J. (2006). Inclusion and exclusion in the re-housing of former prisoners. *Probation Journal, 53*(2), 137–153. doi: 10.1177/026455050 6063566.

Heinrich, S. (2000). *Reducing recidivism through work: Barriers and opportunities for employment of ex-offenders.* Chicago: Great Cities Institute.

Helfgott, J. B. (1997). Ex-offender needs versus criminal opportunity in Seattle, Washington. *Federal Probation, 61,* 12–24.

Hirschel, D., Buzawa, E., Pattavina, A., & Faggiani, D. (2007). Domestic violence and mandatory arrest laws: To what extent do they influence police arrest decisions? *Journal of Criminal Law and Criminology, 98*(1), 255–298.

Huebner, B. M., & Bynum, T. S. (2006). An analysis of parole decisions making using a sample of sex offenders: A focal concerns perspective. *Criminology, 44*(4), 961–991. doi: 10.1111/j.1745-9125.2006.00069.x.

Hughes, T., & Wilson, D. J. (2002). Reentry trends in the United States: Inmates returning to the community after serving time in prison. Washington, DC: Bureau of Justice Statistics.

Hynes, K. (2013). The cost of fear: An analysis of sex offender registration, community notification, and civil commitment laws in the United States and the United Kingdom. *Penn State Journal of Law & International Affairs, 2*(2), 351–379.

Inciardi, J. A. (1992). *The war on drugs II: The continuing epic of heroin, cocaine, crack, crime, AIDS, and the public policy.* Mountain View, CA: Mayfield.

Inciardi, J. A., Martin, S. S., Butzin, C. A., Hooper, R. M., & Harrison, L. D. (1997). An effective model of prison-based treatment for drug-involved offenders. *Journal of Drug Issues, 27*(2), 261–278. doi: 10.1177/002204269702700206.

Jannetta, J., Dodd, H., & Elderbroom, B. (2011). *The elected official's toolkit for jail reentry.* Washington, DC: Urban Institute.

Kaeble, D., Glaze, L., Tsoutis, A., & Minton, T. (2016). *Correctional Populations in the United States, 2014.* Washington, DC: U.S. Department of Justice.

Kaeble, D., Maruschak, L. M., & Bonczar, T. P. (2015). *Probation and parole in the United States, 2014.* Washington, DC: U.S. Department of Justice.

Kondo, L. L. (2000). Therapeutic jurisprudence. Issues, analysis and applications: Advocacy of the establishment of mental health specialty courts in the provision of therapeutic justice for mentally ill offenders. *Seattle University Law Review, 24,* 373–464.

LeBel, T. P. (2012). "If one doesn't get you another one will": Formerly incarcerated persons' perceptions of discrimination. *Prison Journal, 92*(1): 63–87. doi: 10.1177/0032885511429243.

Levenson, J. S., & Hern, A. L. (2007). Sex offender residence restrictions: Unintended consequences and community reentry. *Justice Research and Policy, 9*(1), 59–73. doi: 10.3818/JRP.9.1.2007.59.

Levenson, J. S., & Tewksbury, R. (2009). Collateral damage: Family members of registered sex offenders. *American Journal of Criminal Justice, 34,* 54–68. doi: 10.1007/s12103-008-9055-x.

Leverentz, A. M. (2010). People, places, and things: How female ex-prisoners negotiate their neighborhood context. *Journal of Contemporary Ethnography, 39*(6), 646–681. doi: 10.1177/0891241610377787.

Lewis, B. F., & Ross, R. (1994). Retention in therapeutic communities: Challenges for the nineties. In F. M. Tims, G. De Leon, & N. Jainchill (Eds.), *Therapeutic community: Advances in research and application* (pp. 99–116). Washington, DC: U.S. Government Printing Office.

Lurigio, A. J., & Swartz, J. A. (2000). *Changing contours of the criminal justice system to meet the needs of persons with serious mental illness.* Washington, DC: National Institute of Justice.

MacCoun, R. J., & Reuter, P. (2001). *Drug war heresies: Learning from other vices, times, and places.* New York: Cambridge University Press.

Mapson, A. (2013). From prison to parenting. *Journal of Human Behavior in the Social Environment, 23*(2), 171–177. doi: 10.1080/10911359.2013.747402

Marino, K. M. (2009). Probation management of sex offenders: An analysis of co-facilitators' perceptions of offender progress in treatment. *Criminal Justice Review*, *34*(3), 382–403. doi: 10.1177/0734016808328671.

Marshall, C. (2005, September 7). Man charged in killings of sex offenders. *New York Times*. Retrieved from http://www.nytimes.com/2005/09/07/national/07murder. html?pagewanted=print&_r=0.

Martin, J., & O'Hagan, M. (2005, August 30). Killings of 2 Bellingham sex offenders may have been by vigilante, police say. *Seattle Times*. Retrieved from http://www. seattletimes.com/seattle-news/killings-of-2-bellingham-sex-offenders-may-have-been-by-vigilante-police-say/.

Martin, J., & Singer, N. (2008, January 29). Suspect charged with first-degree murder in Capitol Hill stabbing. *Seattle Times*. Retrieved from http://www.seattletimes. com/seattle-news/suspect-charged-with-first-degree-murder-in-capitol-hill-stabbing/.

Michalsen, V. (2011). Mothering as a life course transition: Do women go straight for their children? *Journal of Offender Rehabilitation*, *50*(6), 349–366. doi: 10.1080/ 10509674.2011.589887.

Miller, H. V., & Miller, J. M. (2010). Community in-reach through jail reentry: Findings from a quasi-experimental design. *Justice Quarterly*, *27*(6), 893–910. doi: 10.1080/07418825.2010.482537.

National Alliance on Mental Illness. (2008). *A guide to mental illness and the criminal justice system*. Arlington, VA: National Alliance on Mental Illness, Department of Policy and Legal Affairs.

National Association of State Mental Health Program Directors Research Institute. (2000). *Closing and reorganizing state psychiatric hospitals: 2000*. Alexandria, VA.

Office of Justice Programs. (2015). *Legislative history*. Retrieved from http://ojp.gov/ smart/legislation.htm.

Olson, D. E., Alderden, M., & Lurigio, A. J. (2003). Men are from Mars, women are from Venus, but what role does gender play in probation recidivism? *Justice Research and Policy*, *5*(2), 33–54. doi: 10.3818/JRP.5.2.2003.33.

Osher, F., Steadman, H. J., & Barr, H. (2003). A best practice approach to community reentry from jails for inmates with co-occurring disorders: The Apic model. *Crime and Delinquency*, *49*(1): 79–96. doi: 10.1177/0011128702239237.

Parsons, M. L., & Warner-Robbins, C. (2002). Factors that support women's successful transition to the community following jail/prison. *Health Care for Women International*, *23*(1), 6–18. doi: 10.1080/073993302753428393.

Perez, A., Leifman, S., & Estrada, A. (2003). Reversing the criminalization of mental illness. *Crime and Delinquency*, *49*(1): 62–78. doi: 10.1177/0011128702239236.

Petersilia, J. (2003). *When prisoners come home: Parole and prisoner reentry*. New York: Oxford University Press.

Presser, L., & Gunnison, E. (1999). Strange bedfellows: Is sex offender notification a form of community justice? *Crime and Delinquency, 45*(3), 299–315. doi: 10. 1177/0011128799045003001.

Richards, T., Jennings, W. G., Tomsich, E. A., & Gover, A. R. (2014). A ten year analysis of re-arrests among a cohort of domestic violence offenders. *Violence and Victims, 29*(6), 1–20.

Richie, B. E. (2001). Challenges incarcerated women face as they return to their communities: Findings from life history interviews. *Crime and Delinquency, 47*(3), 368–389. doi: 10.1177/0011128701047003005.

Roman, C. G., & Travis, J. (2006). Where will I sleep tomorrow? Housing, homelessness, and the returning prisoner. *Housing Policy Debate, 17*(3): 389–418.

Sanburn, J. (2014, September 16). Life inside a community of sex offenders. *Time.* Retrieved from http://time.com/3705637/life-inside-a-community-of-sex-offenders/.

Scott-Hayward, C. S. (2009). *The fiscal crisis in corrections: Rethinking policies and practices.* New York: Vera Institute of Justice.

Sharp, S. F. (2014). *Mean lives, mean laws: Oklahoma's women prisoners.* Newark, NJ: Rutgers University Press.

Simpson, A. I. F., McMaster, J. J., & Cohen, S. N. (2013). Challenges for Canada in meeting the needs of persons with serious mental illness in prison. *Journal of the American Academy of Psychiatry & Law, 41*(4), 501–509.

Simpson, D. D., Joe, G. W., & Brown, B. S. (1997). Treatment retention and follow-up outcomes in the Drug Abuse Treatment Outcome Study (DATOS). *Psychology of Addictive Behaviors, 11*(4), 294–307. doi: 10.1037/0893-164X.11.4.294.

Slate, R. N., Roskes, E., Feldman, R., & Baerga, M. (2003). Doing justice for mental illness and society: Federal probation and pretrial service officers as mental health specialists. *Federal Probation, 65*(3), 13–19.

Solomon, A. L., Osborne, J. W. L., LoBuglio, S. F., Mellow, J., & Mukamal, D. A. (2008). *Life after lockup: Improving reentry from jail to the community.* Washington, DC: Urban Institute.

Stromberg, M. (2007). Locked up, then locked out. *Planning, 73*(1), 20–25.

Sullivan, J. (2009, May 29). Man gets 35-year sentence in New Year's Eve slaying on Capitol Hill. *Seattle Times.* Retrieved from http://www.seattletimes.com/seattle-news/man-gets-35-year-sentence-in-new-years-eve-slaying-on-capitol-hill/.

Tennen, E. (2014). Risky policies: How effective are restrictions on sex offenders in reducing reoffending? *Boston Bar Journal, 58*(4). Retrieved from http://boston barjournal.com/2014/10/07/risky-policies-how-effective-are-restrictions-on-sex-offenders-in-reducing-reoffending/.

Tewksbury, R., & Copes, H. (2013). Incarcerated sex offenders' expectations for successful reentry. *Prison Journal, 93*(1), 101–122. doi: 10.1177/ 0032885512467318

Thompson, A. C. (2004). Navigating the hidden obstacles to ex-offender reentry. *Boston College Law Review, 45*(2), 255–306.

Travis, J., Solomon, A., & Waul, M. (2001). *From prison to home: The dimensions and consequences of prisoner reentry.* Washington, DC: Urban Institute.

Ventura, L. A., Cassel, C. A., Jacoby, J. E., & Huang, B. (1998). Case management and recidivism of mentally ill persons released from jail. *Psychiatric Services, 49*(10), 1330–1337. doi: 10.1176/ps.49.10.1330

Visher, C., & Courtney, S. M. E. (2007). *One year out: Experiences of prisoners returning to Cleveland.* Washington, DC: Urban Institute.

Walker, S., Spohn, C., & DeLone, M. (2007). *The color of justice: Race, ethnicity, and crime in America.* Belmont, CA: Wadsworth.

Wodahl, E. J. (2006). The challenges of prisoner reentry from a rural perspective. *Western Criminological Review, 7*(2), 32–47.

Wootan, C. R. (2016). Danny Heinrich admits he abducted and killed Jacob Wetterling, ending a 27-year-old mystery. *The Washington Post.* Retrieved from https://www. washingtonpost.com/news/true-crime/wp/2016/09/06/danny-heinrich-admits-he-abducted-and-killed-jacob-wetterling-ending-a-27-year-old-mystery/.

Wyatt v. Stickney. 344 F. Supp. 373 (1972).

Zandbergen, P. A., & Hart, T. C. (2006). Reducing housing options for convicted sex offenders: Investigating the impact of residency restriction laws using GIS. *Justice Research and Policy, 18*(2), 1–24.

Zhang, S. X., Roberts, R. E. L., & Callanan, V. J. (2006). Preventing parolees from returning to prison through community-based reintegration. *Crime and Delinquency, 52*(4), 551–571. doi: 10.1177/0011128705282594.

Chapter 4

Probation:
Historical Overview &
Current Status

Student Learning Outcomes

After reading this chapter, you should be able to:

• Describe the history of probation.

• Explain the current status of probation in the United States.

• Summarize the effectiveness of probation.

Introduction

It is hard to escape the reality that the sentence of probation is one punishment that the criminal justice system hands out quite frequently in the United States. Citizens' understanding of what a probation sentence is and who is sentenced to probation is often shaped by the news and media. If the offender is a celebrity and is being sentenced to probation, then a greater awareness of this punishment tends to surface. While there have been many celebrities that have been sentenced to probation for a variety of offenses, there are a few celebrities whose probation sentences have captivated the attention of citizens due to intense media coverage. In fact, some of the celebrity probation sentences have garnered international attention. In February of 2009, Chris Brown and Rihanna, both music entertainment artists and a romantic couple, were driving in Brown's rented Lamborghini in the Hollywood Hills when Brown received a text message from another woman (Nudd, 2009). Rihanna was upset by the text and pressed Brown for details. Brown refused to discuss the text, and the more Rihanna questioned Brown about the text, the angrier Brown became. Unfortunately, Brown lost his composure and he ended up beating Rihanna (Nudd, 2009). The case garnered international attention as both entertainment artists were revered and many were shocked that Brown would engage in domestic violence. Later that year, Brown was sentenced to a five-year probation sentence as well as community service (Duke, 2009). However, discussions of Brown's probation sentenced resurfaced in 2013 when he violated his probation sentence when he hit someone outside a hotel in Washington, DC (Winton, 2014). Since he violated his probation terms, in 2014, he was sentenced to a one-year jail sentence and his original probation sentence was extended to 2015 (Winton, 2014).

Another celebrity whose probation sentences have been in the news quite a bit is actress Lindsay Lohan. Lohan was sentenced to probation in 2007 for two separate driving under the influence (DUI) cases. While on probation, she violated the terms of the probation sentence when she was arrested for the theft of a necklace in 2011. She also picked up another probation sentence in 2012 for a reckless driving offense (Associated Press, 2014). In 2013, she was sentenced to a 120-day jail sentence for violating the terms of her probation sentence with the theft case (Duke, 2013). She was later sentenced to probation for that offense. By 2014, her probation sentence for the theft of the necklace, which also included a requirement of a designated number of hours of community service, was ended by a judge (Associated Press, 2014). However, she is still serving her probation sentence for the 2012 reckless driving offense. The sheer extent of Lohan's sentences has confused many; after all, her arrests and violations are hard to keep straight! Additionally, her continued probation sentences have led some to question whether she was receiving such sentences because of her celebrity status.

The aforementioned cases highlight the fact that probation is one type of punishment that many in the U.S. are familiar with most likely due to the media coverage of celebrities who find themselves ensnared with such sentences in the criminal justice system. This chapter devotes attention to defining probation and providing a historical overview tracing the origin of probation in the United States to how it has taken a foothold in community corrections today. Additionally, this chapter will discuss the current status of probation in the United States and will include discussion of the characteristics of those serving probation sentences. Further, a thorough review of research regarding the effectiveness of probation is provided.

Defining Probation

While probation as a sentence is one that many have heard about in some form or fashion, a clear definition of probation is needed as well as a discussion of the nuts and bolts regarding how a probation sentence works. According to the American Probation and Parole Association (2014), "**Probation** is a court-order through which an offender is placed under the control, supervision and care of a probation field staff member in lieu of imprisonment, so long as the probationer meets certain standards of conduct." That is, rather than being sentenced to a jail or prison term, a convicted offender can serve his/her sentence in the community under the supervision of a corrections official—a probation officer. The length of a probation sentence any given offender may receive can vary. Some offenders may receive a one-year probation sentence while others, such as in Brown's case, may receive a five-year probation sentence. For instance, in 2013, an affluent teen from Texas who drove drunk and killed four people and injured two others, was sentenced to a 10-year probation sentence (Ford, 2013). What determines the length of a probation sentence an offender may receive depends on several factors including, but not limited to: prior record age of the offender offense committed, and history of a past probation sentence (see Text Box 4.1). While it is not uncommon for a convicted offender to receive a probation sentence by itself with no other forms of punishment, it is possible for a convicted offender to serve a small amount of time in jail, receive a probation sentence, and perhaps pay a fine or perform a designated number of community service hours. As you may recall, one of Lohan's probation sentences included the completion of community service hours.

Text Box 4.1: 2015 California Rules of Court, Rule 4.414

Criteria affecting the decision to grant or deny probation include facts relating to the crime and facts relating to the defendant.

(a) Facts relating to the crime

Facts relating to the crime include:

(1) The nature, seriousness, and circumstances of the crime as compared to other instances of the same crime;

(2) Whether the defendant was armed with or used a weapon;

(3) The vulnerability of the victim;

(4) Whether the defendant inflicted physical or emotional injury;

(5) The degree of monetary loss to the victim;

(6) Whether the defendant was an active or a passive participant;

(7) Whether the crime was committed because of an unusual circumstance, such as great provocation, which is unlikely to recur;

(8) Whether the manner in which the crime was carried out demonstrated criminal sophistication or professionalism on the part of the defendant; and

(9) Whether the defendant took advantage of a position of trust or confidence to commit the crime.

(b) Facts relating to the defendant

Facts relating to the defendant include:

(1) Prior record of criminal conduct, whether as an adult or a juvenile, including the recency and frequency of prior crimes; and whether the prior record indicates a pattern of regular or increasingly serious criminal conduct;

(2) Prior performance on probation or parole and present probation or parole status;

(3) Willingness to comply with the terms of probation;

(4) Ability to comply with reasonable terms of probation as indicated by the defendant's age, education, health, mental faculties, history of alcohol or other substance abuse, family background and ties, employment and military service history, and other relevant factors;

(5) The likely effect of imprisonment on the defendant and his or her dependents;

(6) The adverse collateral consequences on the defendant's life resulting from the felony conviction;

(7) Whether the defendant is remorseful; and

(8) The likelihood that if not imprisoned the defendant will be a danger to others.

Source: Judicial Council of California, http://www.courts.ca.gov/cms/rules/index.cfm?title=four&linkid=rule4_414.

Probation is considered a privilege, not a right. Thus, offenders cannot claim that they have a constitutional right to receive a probation sentence as it is an act of grace meted out by the courts (Sklar, 1964). Convicted offenders who receive a probation sentence are required to follow guidelines or conditions as probation is a **contract** between the offender and the state/federal government. That is, the offender agrees to follow conditions or rules while on probation, and, if he/she violates any of the conditions, the offender can be sent to jail and/or prison to serve the remainder of their sentence. All offenders who receive a probation sentence must follow **general conditions**. General conditions are rules that apply to all probationers regardless of their offense. Examples of general conditions include: obtaining employment, not committing a new crime, not associating with other convicted felons, following a curfew, not taking illegal substances, random drug testing, the prohibition of moving and/or traveling out of state, and meeting with the assigned probation officer for a specified time (e.g., once per week). (See Text Box 4.2).

On the other hand, **specific conditions** are rules that apply to a specific offender based on their offense and needs. In addition to following general conditions applied to all probationers, an offender may, for instance, be prohibited from consuming alcohol or frequenting any establishment where the primary service is the serving of alcohol (i.e., a bar). Another example of a specific condition applied to a probationer with an anger problem would be the requirement that the offender participate in an anger management rehabilitation program. Moreover, convicted sex offenders, for example, would be required to register as a sex offender with their local police department. In many cases, probationers report that following the conditions is more difficult than actually serving the original jail or prison sentence. After all, the probationer need only make one mistake and *voila* they are locked back up. In some studies, probationers have reported that they prefer to serve a prison term than to be hassled with following all the guidelines required for their probation or worrying about violating a condition that would send them back to jail or prison anyway (May, Wood, Mooney, & Minor, 2005; Wood & Grasmick, 1999).

Text Box 4.2: General Conditions of Probation in Oregon

1) The court may sentence the defendant to probation subject to the following general conditions unless specifically deleted by the court. The probationer shall:

(a) Pay supervision fees, fines, restitution or other fees ordered by the court.

(b) Not use or possess controlled substances except pursuant to a medical prescription.

(c) Submit to testing of breath or urine for controlled substance or alcohol use if the probationer has a history of substance abuse or if there is a reasonable suspicion that the probationer has illegally used controlled substances.

(d) Participate in a substance abuse evaluation as directed by the supervising officer and follow the recommendations of the evaluator if there are reasonable grounds to believe there is a history of substance abuse.

(e) Remain in the State of Oregon until written permission to leave is granted by the Department of Corrections or a county community corrections agency.

(f) If physically able, find and maintain gainful full-time employment, approved schooling, or a full-time combination of both. Any waiver of this requirement must be based on a finding by the court stating the reasons for the waiver.

(g) Change neither employment nor residence without prior permission from the Department of Corrections or a county community corrections agency.

(h) Permit the parole and probation officer to visit the probationer or the probationer's work site or residence and to conduct a walk-through of the common areas and of the rooms in the residence occupied by or under the control of the probationer.

(i) Consent to the search of person, vehicle or premises upon the request of a representative of the supervising officer if the supervising officer has reasonable grounds to believe that evidence of a violation will be found, and submit to fingerprinting or photographing, or both, when requested by the Department of Corrections or a county community corrections agency for supervision purposes.

(j) Obey all laws, municipal, county, state and federal.

(k) Promptly and truthfully answer all reasonable inquiries by the Department of Corrections or a county community corrections agency.

(L) Not possess weapons, firearms or dangerous animals.

(m) If recommended by the supervising officer, successfully complete a sex offender treatment program approved by the supervising officer and submit to polygraph examinations at the direction of the supervising officer if the probationer: (A) Is under supervision for a sex offense under ORS 163.305 to 163.467; (B) Was previously convicted of a sex offense under ORS 163.305 to 163.467; or (C) Was previously convicted in another jurisdiction of an offense that would constitute a sex offense under ORS 163.305 to 163.467 if committed in this state.

(n) Participate in a mental health evaluation as directed by the supervising officer and follow the recommendation of the evaluator.

(o) Report as required and abide by the direction of the supervising officer.

(p) If required to report as a sex offender under ORS 181.596, report with the Department of State Police, a chief of police, a county sheriff or the supervising agency: (A) When supervision begins; (B) Within 10 days of a change in residence; (C) Once each year within 10 days of the probationer's date of birth; (D) Within 10 days of the first day the person works at, carries on a vocation at or attends an institution of higher education; and (E) Within 10 days of a change in work, vocation or attendance status at an institution of higher education.

Source: Oregon Judicial Department. (2008, October). *General Conditions of Probation.* http:// courts.oregon.gov/Multnomah/docs/CriminalActions/GeneralConditionsOfProbation.pdf.

History of Probation

Probation in the United States can be traced back to the nineteenth century with the work of **John Augustus.** To this day, in fact, Augustus is referred to the "inventor" or "father" of probation (Panzarella, 2002). Augustus was a wealthy shoemaker in Boston who began observing court cases in 1841 and noticed that often non-violent offenders were receiving harsh sentences. In particular, Augustus was concerned that individuals appearing in the court for infractions such as public intoxication were receiving too harsh of sentences. He was affiliated with the **temperance movement,** a social movement that advocated for moderate consumption of alcohol and the reformation of alcoholics, thus, those appearing in court for alcohol related crimes particularly bothered him (Panzarella, 2002). It was one case that Augustus observed in 1841 that changed the course of corrections in the United States (Lindner, 2007). As he observed a man being found guilty for being a drunkard, his passion for assisting offenders was instantly ignited. The man, who was going to be sentenced to the House of Corrections, appealed to Augustus for help stating that if Augustus could help him, he would refrain from using alcohol ever again (Lindner, 2007). With the man's appeal and promise of reformation, Augustus asked the court that the offender be placed in his custody. The judge granted Augustus's wish, thus, Augustus, using his own monetary funds, bailed the man out of court and required that the convicted offender sign a pledge of sobriety (Lindner, 2007). After three weeks, Augustus returned to court with the offender for sentencing, and, it was at this moment, that fruits of Augustus's supervision paid off. Augustus recalls (1852, p. 5),

> ... I accompanied him into the courtroom; his whole appearance was changed and no one, not even the scrutinizing officers, could have believed that he was the same person who less than a month before, had stood trembling on the prisoner's stand. The Judge expressed himself much pleased with the account we gave of the man, and instead of the usual penalty—imprisonment in the House of Correction—he fined him one cent and costs, amounting to $3.76, which was immediately paid. The man continued industrious and sober, and without doubt has been, by this treatment, saved from a drunkard's grave.

His ability to demonstrate the reformation of the convicted man led to the creation of probation. At first, Augustus concentrated his efforts on reforming men, but later he expanded his efforts in assisting women and children—particularly those with alcohol problems (Panzarella, 2002). Besides assisting his clients with abstaining from alcohol use, his reformation efforts also included assisting them with obtaining employment, an education, or finding a suitable place for them to live. Again, Augustus utilized his own money to assist in the reformation of his clients. By the mid-1840s, Augustus began to assist madams and young prostitutes (Panzarella, 2002). All of his care, however, was not necessarily appreciated or well received by many in his community. With Augustus bailing offenders out of jail in order to reform them, jail administrators were losing operating funds, as jail administrators received fees from those they incarcerated. Therefore, jail administrators were not supportive of his efforts whatsoever (Lindner, 2007). Additionally, reformation, or rehabilitation, was not the prevailing ideal of the correctional system at the time nor was it embraced by citizens—rather the focus of the correctional system was on punishment (Lindner, 2007). Rehabilitation as a goal of corrections would not emerge until the late 1800s. Despite his lack of popularity and noble efforts that were not appreciated by most, before his death in 1859, Augustus had secured probation for several thousand adults and children. Thus, his efforts were extremely impactful.

During the same time era, by coincidence, in Birmingham, England, **Matthew Davenport Hill**, a lawyer, also developed a probation program in 1841 (Lindner, 2007). However, he did not refer to his practice of providing services for young offenders as *probation*. There were some distinct differences between Hill's probation model and Augustus's model. Hill promulgated the use of a one-day incarceration sentence for youth engaging in minor crimes followed by releasing the young offender to a guardian—not necessarily a parent but someone who would watch over or supervise the offender. In this sense, requiring the offender to serve a short incarceration term was distinctly different from Augustus's ideals. Additionally, Hill would have the guardian of the offender keep a record of the juvenile's behavior (Lindner, 2007). It is this addition, a guardian in charge of supervision, that makes Hill's model of probation distinctly different from Augustus's model. Essentially, Hill introduced the element of monitored supervision to probation and, of course, supervision is still an integral and important component of probation as it operates today. His model of probation appeared to be effective, as he tracked reconviction rates of those who were supervised. Over a 12-year period, 80 offenders out of 417 offenders who were part of the program were reconvicted (Lindner, 2007). Given Hill's efforts, many consider him to be a co-founder of probation, thus, he also has a prominent role in the history of probation.

Following Augustus' death, the practice of probation was continued by uncompensated volunteers in the United States. It was not until Massachusetts passed the first probation statute in 1878 that the work of probation shift from an unpaid and unprofessional practice to a paid and professional correctional practice (Panzarella, 2002). The passage of the probation statute created an official state probation system as well as paid probation officers. After the establishment of probation in Massachusetts, the next state to implement probation was Missouri about twenty years later, in 1897 (Champion, 2001). It was not long after probation implementation in Missouri before other states followed suit. By 1957, all states had adult and juvenile probation statutes (Petersilia, 1998).

Efforts to establish probation at the federal level began as early as 1909; however, its proponents found that it was met with quite a bit of resistance (Evjen, 1975). Some of the early resistance to the implementation of federal probation came from prohibitionists who were concerned that individuals who violated the Prohibition Amendment would be placed on probation—many didn't believe that probation was a proper punishment for such an offense (Evjen, 1975). One of the more prominent advocates for the establishment of probation at the federal level was **Charles L. Chute**, who was active with the New York State Probation Commission and later served as the general secretary for the National Probation Association (Evjen, 1975). Chute not only strongly advocated for the implementation of federal probation, but he also invested quite a bit of time writing to judges across the nation asking for their opinions about federal probation. He soon discovered that many judges were opposed to probation—regarding it to be too lenient of a punishment, thereby, they resisted the establishment of a federal probation system. For other judges, the term "probation" caused some confusion for them as they often referred to probation as "parole" when providing Chute with their opinions about probation (Evjen, 1975). Further, some judges favored the use of probation for juveniles, but not adults (Evjen, 1975). Moreover, many judges believed "salaried probation officers were unnecessary and that United States marshals and volunteers could perform satisfactorily the functions of a probation officer" (Evjen, 1975, p. 4). In 1923, Judge J. Foster Symes from the District of Colorado wrote to Chute regarding his opinion about a federal probation law, which sums up the feeling of many judges across the nation stating,

> I have your letter of December 10th, asking my endorsement for a Federal probation act. Frankly, permit me to say that I do not favor any such law, except possibly in the case of juvenile offenders. My observation of probation laws is that it has been abused and has tended to weaken the enforcement of our criminal laws. What we need in this country is not a movement such as you advocate, to create new officials with resulting expense, but a movement to make the enforcement of our criminal laws more certain and swift. I believe that one reason why the Federal laws are respected more than the state laws is the feeling among the criminal classes that there is a greater certainty of punishment (Evjen, 1974, p. 5).

Other judges were a bit harsh in their response to Chute's inquiry about their position on federal probation. Also in 1923, Judge John F. McGee of the District of Minnesota, wrote to Chute stating,

> I most sincerely hope that you will fail in your efforts, as I think they could not be more misdirected. The United States district courts have already been converted into police courts, and the efforts of your Association are directed towards converting them into juvenile courts also.... In this country, due to the efforts of people like yourselves, the murderer has a cell bedecked with flowers and is surrounded by a lot of silly people. The criminal should understand when he violates the law that he is going to a penal institution and is going to stay there. Just such efforts as your organization is making are largely responsible for the crime wave that is passing over this country today and threatening to engulf our institutions.... What we need in the administration of criminal laws in this country is celerity and severity (Evjen, 1975, p. 5).

Despite such resistance for several decades, the federal government formally established probation in 1925 when President Coolidge, a former governor of Massachusetts, signed the **National Probation Act** (Champion, 2001; Evjen, 1975). The act initially authorized the judge to appoint one or more unpaid probation officers and one paid probation officer to serve and supervise probationers, utilizing many of the founding probation principles of August and Hill. With federal probation approved, many offenders were now sentenced to probation and these early officers found themselves with high caseloads (Evjen, 1975). For instance, by 1932, there were 63 probation officers supervising approximately 25,000 probationers, which resulted in an average caseload of 400 probationers per officer (Evjen, 1975). Thus, it appeared that federal probation quickly became readily used by many judges, and it by then had a significant foothold in the federal correctional system.

Text Box 4.3: Probation Around the World

While probation practices were implemented in England in the 1840s, it was not more widely used until around 1876 (Harris, 1995). In fact, it was not until the passage of the *Probation of Offenders Act* in 1907 that probation was formally adopted throughout the United Kingdom (Harris, 1995). Although probation had been well established in England, in Scotland, probation was not adopted until the 1950s (McIvor & McNeill, 2007). Thus, despite the implementation of probation in the United States and England, across the world, probation was not quickly adopted in other countries. For example, although Australia had adopted probation legislation in 1887, probation was not first formally implemented until 1946 in the commonwealth of Tasmania (O'Toole, 2006; Tulett, 1990). Similarly to Australia, in Canada, legislation for probation was adopted in the 1880s, however, probation was not fully adopted and implemented across the nation until the 1950s (Harris, 1995). In European countries, probation was formally implemented at various rates: Austria in 1980; Belgium in 1964; France in the 1950s; Germany in the 1950s; and Switzerland in the 1930s (Harris, 1995). For other countries, probation has been implemented, but it has not developed into a formalized service for offenders. This has been the case for probation in India. Although the *1923 Code of Criminal Procedure* permitted probation for juvenile offenders in India and additional probation legislation was passed in the 1930s and 1950s, probation is not widely used (Harris, 1995). There are several reasons why probation is not utilized as much in India. A few reasons include: (1) probation is deemed not as important by many; (2) lack of funding for probation services; (3) no training for probation officers; and (4) lack of knowledge by probation officers to assist offenders (Harris, 1995).

Organization of Probation

With the use of probation spreading quickly in both the state and federal system, the growth of state and probation agencies has burgeoned as well. According to Nieto (2003), the administration of state probation is carried out by more than 2,000 separate state and private agencies with the majority of probation administration handled at the state level. Nieto (2003) describes probation as being organized into five administrative models: (1) juvenile, (2) municipal/county, (3) state, (4) state combined, and (5) federal. In the first mode or organization, juvenile probation, services for this group are administered at the local level, a combination of local and state agencies, or solely by state agencies (Nieto, 2003). All juvenile probation services are administered separately from adult probation services (Nieto, 2003). The municipal/county probation administrative model only exists in California and Washington, DC (Nieto, 2003). For this model, Nieto (2003, p. 27) explains, "probation units are directed by the trial courts following state law and guidelines and are operated and funded by local governments." With a state model, a probation agency is operated solely by the state (Nieto, 2003). Additionally, in a state combined probation agency model, probation is administered at the local level but the funding for the local administration comes from state funds (Nieto, 2003). Finally, in the federal model, probation administration is operated solely by the federal court system (Nieto, 2003).

Apart from the five main models including local, state, or federal probation administration, a handful of states are utilizing private, or for-profit, agencies to administer probation sentences. Such private probation services began in 1992 in the state of Florida (Human Rights Watch, 2014). In some states, such as in Georgia, state statutes allow for the privatization of misdemeanor probation services (Human Rights Watch, 2014). However, oftentimes, due to budget constraints, many states are now more focused on having individuals convicted of felonies on probation supervision rather than having these same individuals serving time in jails or prisons. With the attention of the state on having more individuals convicted of felonies serving probation sentences, a gap in the supervision of probation for offenders convicted of misdemeanors has arisen. This gap has been readily filled by private companies, such as Judicial Correction Services and Sentinel Offender Services, which can provide misdemeanor probation supervision to jurisdictions that need it and without any financial support from state and/or local budgets or taxpayer monies. The growth of private probation has been burgeoning and such agencies can be found in another dozen states (Human Rights Watch, 2014). In 2012, for example, that state of Georgia assigned more than 250,000 offenders to private probation companies (Human Rights Watch, 2014). It is clear that the growth of the use of probation in both the state and federal system has resulted in the need to serve these clients using a variety of models.

Status of Probation

Without a doubt, probation is the largest component of the correctional system, with approximately 4.7 million adults on state and federal probation in 2014 (Kaeble, Maruschak, & Bonczar, 2015). Specifically, probationers accounted for 58% of the total corrections population—more than prison, jails, and parolees combined (Kaeble et al., 2015). As highlighted in Figure 4.1, the number of adults on probation has fluctuated somewhat since 2000. Overall, the number of adults serving probation has remained relatively stable over time. The larger increase in numbers of those serving probation sentences between the years 2006 and 2009 corresponds to the economic recession in the United States during that same time period. During the economic recession, many state criminal justice agencies (e.g., courts, corrections) found their operating budgets slashed. Scott-Hayward (2009) reports that cuts to the department of corrections budgets were a national problem plaguing 26 states in 2010 (Scott-Hayward, 2009). Because of this, many states utilized cheaper forms of punishment, such as probation sentences, as an alternative to using much more costly incarceration sentences. After all, probation is a much cheaper correctional sentence. For instance, at the federal level, probation has an average annual cost of $3,400 per offender versus an annual average cost of $25,000 per offender to incarcerate the individual (La Vigne & Samuels, 2012).

Figure 4.1: Trends in Adult Probation, 2000–2014

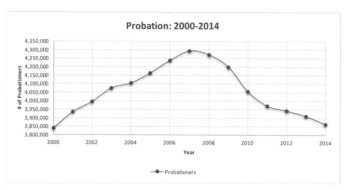

Source: Kaeble, D., Maruschak, L. M., & Bonczar, T. P. (2015). *Probation and parole in the United States, 2014*. Washington, DC: U.S. Department of Justice.

Image 8. © hafakot/Fotolia.

Characteristics of Probationers

Despite the national trends and fluctuations in the number of individuals sentenced to probation over the last decade, the characteristics of probationers have not changed much. For instance, adults sentenced to probation in 2014 were predominately male and Caucasian (see Text Box 4.4) (Kaeble et al., 2015). When comparing statistics on the percentages of adult probationers for the years 2000 and 2014, the percentage of male probationers dipped from 78% in 2000 to 75% in 2014, while the percentage of female probationers increased slightly from 22% in 2000 to 25% in 2014 (see Text Box 4.4) (Kaeble et al., 2015). Researchers have also noted that women probationers were arrested at an older age and committed less serious criminal offenses compared to women who had been incarcerated (The Sentencing Project, 2007). In regards to race and ethnicity, Kaeble et al. (2015, p. 5) report that in 2014, "more than half (54%) of probationers were non-Hispanic white, 30% were non-Hispanic black, and 13% were Hispanic or Latino—a similar distribution for race and Hispanic origin observed in 2000" (see Text Box 4.4). Additionally, in 2014, most adult probationers received the sentence for committing a felony offense, however, the offense was predominately non-violent in nature (see Text Box 4.4) (Kaeble et al., 2015). Moreover, the percentage of adults serving a probation sentence for committing a felony increased slightly from 52% in 2000 to 56% in 2014 (see Text Box 4.4) (Kaeble et al., 2015). Further, the majority (73%) of adult probationers were under active supervision with only 7% on inactive probation or no-contact supervision, and only 7% absconded (i.e., violated probation and his/her whereabouts are unknown (see Text Box 4.4) (Kaeble et al., 2015).

Text Box 4.4: Characteristics of Adult Probationers, 2000, 2013, & 2014

Characteristic	2000	2013	2014
Sex			
Male	78%	75%	75%
Female	22%	25%	25%
Race/Origin			
White	54%	54%	54%
Black/African American	31%	30%	30%
Hispanic/Latino	13%	13%	14%
American Indian/Alaska Native	1%	1%	1%
Asian/Pacific Islander	1%	1%	1%
Status of Supervision			
Active	76%	69%	73%
Inactive	9%	6%	5%
Absconder	9%	9%	7%
Residential/Other treatment program	—	1%	1%
Financial conditions remaining	—	1%	1%
Supervised out of jurisdiction	3%	2%	2%
Warrant status	—	9%	6%
Type of Offense			
Felony	52%	55%	56%
Misdemeanor	46%	43%	42%
Other infractions	2%	2%	2%
Most Serious Offense			
Violent	—	19%	19%
Property	—	29%	28%
Drug	24%	25%	25%
Public Order	24%	17%	16%
Other[1]	52%	10%	10%

— Less than .05%

[1] Includes violent and property in 2000 as data were not collected separately.

Source: Kaeble, D., Maruschak, L. M., & Bonczar, T. P. (2015). *Probation and parole in the United States, 2014*. Washington, DC: U.S. Department of Justice.

Statistics on juveniles sentenced to probation are not updated as frequently as figures for adults sentenced to probation. In 2009, there were approximately 500,000 juveniles sentenced to probation (Livsey, 2012). Juveniles may serve probation sentences as a court-ordered punishment following conviction or they may be given an option to serve a probation sentence *prior* to a conviction. With the latter option, juveniles agree to serve a probation sentence and abide by conditions. If they successfully complete their probation sentence, their case will be dismissed (Livsey, 2012). The characteristics of juveniles who are serving probation sentences closely mirror the characteristics of their adult counterparts. For example, in 2011, more male and Caucasian juveniles were serving probation sentences (Office of Juvenile Justice and Delinquency

Prevention, 2011). Additionally, the majority of juveniles were aged 16 at the time they were referred to their probation sentences, and the majority of juveniles on probation were convicted of a property offense (Office of Juvenile Justice and Delinquency Prevention, 2011). More detail and discussion on the experiences of juveniles serving community corrections sentences will be explored in Chapter 7.

Financial Costs of Probation

Due to reductions in operating budgets, virtually all states collect some form of probation supervision fee. These fees collected from the probationer help to subsidize the cost of probation and save taxpayers money. The cost of the supervision fee varies widely by state. It can cost a probationer as little as $20/month in Rhode Island or a $300 probation enrollment fee in Iowa (Iowa Courts, 2014; Rhode Island Department of Corrections, 2008). Human Rights Watch (2014) estimates that, in 2012, private probation companies collected more than 1.1 million dollars in supervision fee payments. While such fees are great in theory, they often overwhelm the offender.

Convicted offenders have many legal financial obligations (LFOs), which include fees administered by the courts such as filing fees, fees for a jury trial, jail fees, warrant fees, fees for a public defender, DNA collection fee, and restitution orders (Evans, 2014; Harris, Evans, & Beckett, 2010). In Washington State Superior Courts, judges have the option of imposing 17 fees and fines for felony defendants during sentencing (Harris et al., 2010). To make matters worse, unpaid LFOs are subject to interest and collection fees (Harris et al., 2010). Harris and colleagues (2010) report that the interest rate on unpaid LFOs in Washington State is 12.7%. Such LFOS are a significant concern to probationers as their debt accumulates when they are required to pay for their supervision. Further, probationers may also accrue other forms of court debt if they perhaps are engaged in a fight for custody of their child/children as well as other personal debt, such as securing housing or purchasing household goods. Since convicted offenders have difficulties obtaining employment or finding employment that has a suitable wage, probationers really struggle with paying their LFOs (Evans, 2014; Gunnison & Helfgott, 2013). As one component of a research investigation to explore the impact of LFOs had on offenders, Harris et al. (2010) interviewed 50 residents of Washington State who had a felony conviction. One subject reported on the gravity of the debt burden,

> My biggest question is like uh, you know, am I ever going to pay this amount off? At the rate I'm going now, I'll never pay it off. That amount now is about $44,000. Because of the interest, and in spite of me paying the payments pretty religiously (Harris et al., 2010, p. 1779).

Some of this debt is collected by debt collection agencies, but in many states, probation officers are tasked with collecting LFOs (Evans, 2014). Failure in meeting financial obligations often results in probation revocation, or suspension of the probation sentence (Evans, 2014). Another subject in Harris et al.'s (2010, p. 1783) study reports:

> If you miss a payment, then you get a probation violation. And that means like you go back to jail, you know, or they give you some time: it depends

on who your probation officer is…. And so like, if, say I don't pay this much, they'll send something in the mail saying that if I don't make the payment then they'll issue a probation warrant out for my arrest.

The concern over fees imposed on offenders has arisen with much concern directed towards the economically disadvantaged who are crippled by such costs and other disenfranchised members of our community — that is, convicted offenders.

Effectiveness of Probation

With so many individuals on probation, the natural question arises about whether it is effective, or whether the punishment "works" (Petersilia, 1998). The evidence on whether probation is effective is rather mixed. One difficulty that researchers have in attempting to ascertain probation effectiveness is how best to go about measuring "effectiveness." That is, researchers grapple with whether successful completion of a probation sentence, the absence of a probation violation, or the absence of a re-arrest, conviction, or even re-incarceration should be the driving measures of probation effectiveness. Another difficulty researchers have had in determining the effectiveness of probation revolves around what type of offender is being examined — a probationer convicted of a misdemeanor or a felony (Allen, Eskridge, Latessa, & Vito, 1985). Clearly, if the probationer is convicted of a misdemeanor offense, he/she has a greater likelihood of being successful on probation given that these offenders are fairly low risk to begin with compared to their felony counterparts. Additionally, researchers have raised concerns about the length of follow-up in determining probation effectiveness. For example, if re-arrest rates of probationers are examined three months after completion of a probation sentence versus three years after completion of a probation sentence, the outcome of probation success may be different. After all, it is expected that those probationers who completed their sentences would be less likely to **recidivate**, or re-offend, in the short-term. However, as time passes, the likelihood of these same probationers re-offending would be much higher. Thus, the time period that researchers utilize is critical to their determination of probation effectiveness. All the aforementioned problems have raised doubts as to whether the little research that has been conducted on probation can be trusted as the "truth" about the actual effectiveness of probation.

Upon review of the existing early literature on probation effectiveness, it has been found that the types of offenders on probation, the follow-up period, and definitions of recidivism have yielded failure rates for probation anywhere from 16% to 55% (Allen et al., 1985). Recidivism rates, however defined, at 30% or less are ideal and the 30% mark is considered standard by many researchers in determining whether anything that is being evaluated is indeed effective (Allen et al., 1985). One of the most infamous examinations of probation effectiveness was conducted by the RAND Corporation in 1985. In this research investigation, 1,672 male felony probationers from several counties in California, who had faced convictions for offenses such as auto theft, robbery, assault, and drug sales/possession, were tracked following completion of their probation sentence for 40 months (Petersilia, 1985). Results from the research revealed that 65% of the sample were re-arrested, 51% were convicted of a new crime, and 34% of the sample were incarcerated in jail or prison (Petersilia, 1985). For those who had convictions for a new criminal offense, some of the crimes were offenses such as homicide, rape, and aggravated assault. Other earlier studies have yielded different results on the effectiveness of probation. For example, Vito (1986), using a sample of 317 probationers in Kentucky and tracking them for three years, found that 22% of the probationers were rearrested. Given the 30% success standard, probation was found to be effective in Vito's (1986) study. However, arguments could be made about whether the results of either could give an accurate picture of probation effectiveness given that both studies were limited to one particular state. Thus, perhaps probation was effective in certain states for certain probationers, but the results of these studies could not necessarily be generalized to all probationers across the nation.

A more comprehensive research investigation of probation effectiveness occurred in the early 1990s. Langan and Cunniff (1992) examined recidivism rates for 79,000 probationers across 17 states. The researchers found that 43% of the sample were re-arrested for a felony within three years and 36% of the sample were incarcerated in a jail or prison. Given the robust nature of the study in terms of sample size and probationer representation from a multitude of states, probation was not deemed to be effective. In 1993, Morgan examined the literature on probation outcomes through 1991 and concluded that, overall, probation was effective with failure rates (i.e., reconviction, probation revocation, or absconding) ranging from 14% to 60%. Morgan (1993, p. 27) noted the following factors to be most associated with failure: "employment status; prior criminal record, low income; age; sex; and marital status. Instability, as measured by employment status, marital status, and length of stay at residence, was also related to probation failure or success. Probationers who were married with children, adequately employed, and had lived in an area for more than 2 years, were often successful under supervision. When discussing probation failures, most of the studies indicated that reconviction offenses tended to be minor misdemeanors rather than felonies." While Morgan (1993) did find probation to be effective, she did caution the interpretation of her findings due to various methodological differences. She noted the lack of uniformity in the definition of failure across the studies, the lack of a control group for a comparison, and the wide range of follow-up periods, which ranged from anywhere from 6 months in some studies to 11 years in other studies. Thus, the results of Morgan's analysis again left many researchers scratching their heads about whether probation is effective.

Following Morgan's 1993 investigation, researchers thereafter began to further examine factors associated with successful probation outcomes and probation agencies began to alter their supervision practices in hopes of improving probation outcomes while ensuring public safety with cost-effective methods given the financial crisis plaguing the correctional system. Since Morgan's investigation, research on probation effectiveness fell rather flat. That is, very few research investigations have been conducted since then to examine probation outcomes. One reason for the faltering of probation research is the sheer complexity of it, given some of the aforementioned issues. Also, probation agencies often lacked the knowledge or expertise necessary to best conduct their own investigations or lacked funding to hire a researcher to root out the answers on their behalf. One of the more "recent" probation outcome investigations was conducted by Gray, Fields, and Maxwell in 2001. The researchers examined 1,500 probationers in the state of Michigan in 1996 over a 30-month follow-up period. Gray et al. (2001) found that most probationers in their sample had committed a probation violation on some sort of technicality (e.g., failing to report, or a failed drug test) rather than for committing a new crime and tended to commit the violation early in the probation period (i.e., within the first three months). Of those probationers who did commit a new crime, they tended to commit it later in their probation period. Further, the researchers found that "minority, less educated offenders with prior drug use were more likely to have technical violations" (Gray et al., 2001, p. 554). On the other hand, "unemployed probationers, those with previous misdemeanor convictions, those who committed assaultive crimes, and those with more technical violations were more likely to commit a new crime while on probation" (Gray et al., 2001, p. 554). Finally, the researchers reported that the "type" of offender who was most likely to commit a technical violation and a new crime was the offender whose had committed an assault offense. Most recently, in an examination of 257 women probationers in a midwestern state using a three-year follow-up period, Stalans and Lurigio (2015) found that women with intimate partners that were criminal had both a higher likelihood of missing a required probation appointment as well as being arrested for substance abuse or a misdemeanor crime. While the findings of this study cannot give an overall complete picture of the effectiveness of probation for all women, the results do highlight that for these women probationers, having a pro-social intimate partner may help insulate them from future criminal involvement.

While research on probation effectiveness has waned over the past two decades, research on probation, or investigations into how best to improve successful outcomes, did not disappear. Due to growing research in the 1990s stressing the importance of addressing the needs and risk factors for offenders to reduce their recidivism rates (see Gendreau, 1996), many probation agencies have revised their practices to achieve better outcomes. Besides now assessing the needs and risk factors of probationers, something that was not typically done previously, probation agencies have been more mindful of tailoring the supervision to the individual offender, whereby more resources may be allocated to higher risk probationers (Solomon et al., 2007). Additionally, such research has prompted probation agencies to implement different supervision strategies. Morash (2010), who conducted a research investigation of women on probation and parole, noted that several women were critical of the supervision style of their probation officer. One subject reported,

> [My PO] had a different idea of what supervision was supposed to be about, and focused on intimidation and punishment, but I wanted to learn new skills. The PO seemed to take pleasure in making supervision a punishment, scaring the participants (Morash, 2010, p. 73).

If women are feeling that supervision style is harsh or unsupportive, this may contribute to unsuccessful probation outcomes. Often, many probationers, female or male, look to their probation officer as a pillar of support—to help them meet their needs. In many cases, the officer is the only pro-social person in their lives to guide them towards success.

One difference in supervision strategy that has been implemented is the use of swift, certain, and severe strategies to respond to violations of probation conditions (American Probation and Parole Association, 2014). Drawing on the criminological principles of **deterrence theory**, the idea is that if probationers expect to be punished if they violate a condition and expect that their punishment for the violation will be swift (i.e., will be issued immediately) and severe, then they are more likely to be deterred from violating the condition in the first place (Wilson, 1975). Such a supervisory practice promotes accountability and responsibility, fostering positive outcomes in probation clients (American Probation and Parole Association, 2013). Another strategy that has been implemented by many probation agencies is the use of incentives to increase compliance with probation conditions (American Probation and Parole Association, 2013). All too often sanctions are viewed as the stimulus needed to shape behavior, however, incentives play an important role in altering behavior as well.

Researchers have found that a combination of utilizing a swift, certain, and severe approach and incentives work the best in stimulating probationer success (Wodahl, Garland, Culhane, & McCarty, 2011). One such program that has utilized a combined approach with probationers and has been met with great success is the Hawaii Opportunity Probation with Enforcement (HOPE) program. The HOPE program is designed for probationers who are designated as being at high risk of committing a probation violation (Hawken & Kleiman, 2009). In the HOPE program, the probationer is brought before a judge and warned that if he/she violates a condition of probation, the probationer will immediately be remitted into jail—typically for a few days (Hawken & Kleiman, 2009). Besides the negative aspects, HOPE also provides incentives to probationers who produce negative drug tests and complete treatment (Hawken & Kleiman, 2009). An example of a HOPE program incentive was a reduction in the frequency of drug testing. Hawken and Kleiman (2009) compared the outcomes of participants in the HOPE program to probationers not in the program. After a one-year follow-up period, the researchers found that HOPE probationers were 55% less likely to be re-arrested, had a lower rate of failed drug tests, and were less likely to have their probation sentences revoked than their control group counterparts. The researchers also noted that although probationer officers were not initially enamored with the idea of providing incentives, as HOPE probationers succeeded, these same officers were very much impressed with how the incentives shaped their clients' behaviors.

This idea of accountability and incentives has extended beyond just the probationer. Both the public and the state legislatures have called for probation departments to be held accountable for probation outcomes. No longer can probation agencies dispense probation as usual—they are now being asked to show that their methods are effective at reducing recidivism and technical violation rates for probationers. Increasingly more probation agencies in the United States and across the globe such as in England are moving towards **evidence-based practices**, whereby departments are analyzing their practices and treatments to empirically determine if they are indeed effective (Fabelo, Nagy, & Prins, 2011; Knott, 2004). Moving to empirical assessment and demonstrating effectiveness can be lucrative for many probation agencies as incentives are in place to reward them for their efforts. In the past seven years, states such as Arizona, California, Colorado, Illinois, and South Carolina have each passed legislation that provide financial incentives for probation agencies that can reduce recidivism and technical violation rates (Pew Center on the States, 2011). Some of these states, such as in Arizona, receive partial refunds for the costs of delivering probation, which can be invested in the development of more treatment services for probationers, while in other states, such as in Colorado, departments can receive grant money to examine what programming may be effective or ineffective for probationers (Colorado Division of Probation Services, 2010). Currently, there is no federal law offering incentives for successful federal probationer outcomes. However, the Office of Probation and Pretrial Services has been working hard to have evidence-based practices implemented into probation services (Hurting & Lenart, 2011). Thus, change in probation supervision and delivery of services is well underway in hopes of improving probation outcomes.

Conclusion

In sum, this chapter provided discussion on the history of probation development in the United States. Additionally, this chapter described the organization of modern probation, trends in the use of probation as a sentence, the characteristics of those serving probation sentences, and how fiscal constraints have impacted probation agencies. Probation supervision is no longer free and now probationers are paying for the privilege of a probation sentence, which has now burdened probationers in ways that are often unforeseen. As for the effectiveness of probation, the jury is still out on that. Due to a litany of methodological issues, research on probation effectiveness has been rather mixed. From the research that has been gathered over the past several decades, probation can be effective—if the probationers' needs are being met. Further, probation success may differ based on gender, race, or ethnicity. More research is needed to determine the exact factors that promote probation success in order to ensure that these risk and needs factors are being addressed during probation supervision and treatment services. Finally, a monumental shift is underway in probation in regards to how probation operates. Traditionally, probationers were only punished for violating conditions of probation or committing a new crime. However, today, more and more probationers are receiving incentives for changing their behaviors and complying with conditions of supervision. Moreover, state probation agencies are now recognizing that providing probation agencies with incentives can produce better outcomes for probationers and a cost savings.

Key Terms

Charles L. Chute

Contract

Deterrence theory

Evidence-based practices

General conditions

John Augustus

Matthew Davenport Hill

National Probation Act

Probation

Recidivate

Specific conditions

Temperance Movement

Discussion Questions

1. What are the trends in probation in your state over the past decade? Pay careful attention to examining the characteristics of those on probation as well as the types of offenses they were convicted of.

2. What do you think about probationers having to pay for part of their probation supervision?

3. How do you feel about probationers receiving incentives for complying with rules that they are required to follow as conditions of their supervision?

4. What factors do you think promote successful probation outcomes? Why? How do you think probation outcomes can be improved?

References

Allen, H. E., Eskridge, C. W., Latessa, E. J., & Vito, G. F. (1985). *Probation and parole in America.* Encino, CA: Collier Macmillian.

American Probation and Parole Association. (2014). *Probation and parole FAQs.* Retrieved from https://www.appa-net.org/eweb/DynamicPage.aspx?WebCode= VB_FAQ.

Associated Press. (2014). Lindsay Lohan's probation ends. *USA Today.* Retrieved from http://www.usatoday.com/story/life/people/2014/11/06/lohans-probation-ended-in-necklace-theft-case/18622111/.

Augustus, J. (1852). *A report of the labors of John Augustus.* Boston: Wright & Hasty, Printers.

Champion, D. J. (2001). *Corrections in the United States: A contemporary perspective* (3rd ed.). Upper Saddle River, NJ: Prentice Hall.

Colorado Division of Probation Services. (2010). *Colorado probation and evidence-based practices: A systemic view of the past, present & future of EBP in Colorado probation, progress report.* Retrieved from http://www.courts.state.co.us/userfiles/file/Administration/Probation/APPA_Presentation_Material/EBP_Report.pdf.

Duke, A. (2009). Brown sentenced for Rihanna assault; Other incidents surface. *CNN.* Retrieved from http://www.cnn.com/2009/CRIME/08/25/chris.brown.sentencing/.

Duke, A. (2013). Lindsay Lohan goes to jail on probation violation. *CNN.* Retrieved from http://www.cnn.com/2011/CRIME/04/22/california.lindsay.lohan.case/.

Evans, D. N. (2014). *The debt penalty: Exposing the financial barriers to offender reintegration.* Research & Evaluation Center: John Jay College of Criminal Justice. Retrieved from http://justicefellowship.org/sites/default/files/The%20Debt%20Penalty_John%20Jay_August%202014.pdf.

Evjen, V. H. (1975). The federal probation system: The struggle to achieve it and its first 25 years. *Federal Probation,* (June), 3–15.

Fabelo, T., Nagy, G., & Prins, S. (2011). *A ten-step guide to transforming probation departments to reduce recidivism.* Bureau of Justice Assistance, U.S. Dept. of Justice. Retrieved from http://csgjusticecenter.org/documents/0000/1150/A_Ten-Step_Guide_to_Transforming_Probation_Departments_to_Reduce_Recidivism.pdf.

Ford, D. (2013). Texas teen Ethan Couch gets 10 years' probation for driving drunk, killing 4. *CNN.* Retrieved from http://www.cnn.com/2013/12/11/us/texas-teen-dwi-wreck/.

Gendreau, P. (1996). The principles of effective intervention with offenders. In F. X. Harland, (Ed.), *Choosing correctional options that work: Defining the demand and evaluating the supply* (pp. 117–130). Thousand Oaks, CA: Sage.

Glaze, L. E., & Kaeble, D. (2014). *Correctional populations in the United States, 2013.* Washington, DC: U.S. Department of Justice. Retrieved from http://www.bjs.gov/content/pub/pdf/cpus13.pdf.

Gray, M. K., Fields, M., & Maxwell, S. R. (2001). Examining probation violations: Who, what, and when. *Crime and Delinquency, 47*(4), 537–557. doi: 10.1177/0011128701047004003.

Gunnison, E., & Helfgott, J. B. (2013). *Offender reentry: Beyond crime and punishment.* Boulder, CO: Lynne Rienner.

Harris, A., Evans, H., & Beckett, K. (2010). Drawing blood from stones: Legal debt and social inequality in the contemporary U.S. *American Journal of Sociology, 115*(6), 1755–99.

Harris, R. (1995). Probation round the world: Origins and Development. In K. Hamai, R. Ville, R. Harris, M. Hough, & U. Zvekic (Eds.), *Probation around the world: A comparative study* (pp. 25–67). New York: Routledge.

Hawken, A., & Kleimen, M. (2009). Managing drug involved probationers with swift and certain sanctions: Evaluating Hawaii's HOPE. Retrieved from https://www.ncjrs.gov/pdffiles1/nij/grants/229023.pdf.

Human Rights Watch. (2014). *Profiting from probation: America's "offender-funded" probation industry.* Retrieved from http://www.hrw.org/sites/default/files/reports/us0214_ForUpload_0.pdf.

Hurting, J. E., & Lenart, L. M. (2011). The development of the evidence-based practice blue print and where are we now. *Federal Probation, 75*(2), 35–37.

Iowa Courts. (2014). *Fourth judicial district Department of Correctional Services informal probation program.* Retrieved from http://fourthdcs.com/uploads/3/1/2/4/3124488/informal_probation_information_for_court.pdf.

Judicial Council of California. (2015). *California rules of court.* Retrieved from http://www.courts.ca.gov/cms/rules/index.cfm?title=four&linkid=rule4_414.

Kaeble, D., Maruschak, L. M., & Bonczar, T. P. (2015). *Probation and parole in the United States, 2014.* Washington, DC: U.S. Department of Justice.

Knott, C. Evidence-based practice in the National Probation Service. In R. Burnett & C. Roberts (Eds.), *What works in probation and youth justice: Developing evidence-based practice* (pp. 14–28). United Kingdom: Willan Publishing.

Langan, P., & Cunniff, M. A. (1992). *Recidivism of felons on probation, 1986–1989.* Washington, DC: Bureau of Justice Statistics.

La Vigne, N., & Samuels, J. (2012). *The growth and increasing cost of the federal prison system: Drivers and potential solutions.* Urban Institute. Retrieved from http://www.urban.org/uploadedpdf/412693-the-growth-and-increasing-cost-of-the-federal-prison-system.pdf.

Lindner, C. (2007). Thacher, Augustus, and Hill: The path to statutory probation in the United States and England. *Federal Probation, 71*(3), 36–41.

Livsey, S. (2012). *Juvenile delinquency probation caseload, 2009.* Washington, DC: U.S. Department of Justice. Retrieved from http://www.ojjdp.gov/pubs/239082.pdf.

May, D. C., Wood, P. B., Mooney, J. L., & Minor, K. I. (2005). Predicting offender generated exchange rates: Implications for a theory of sentence severity. *Crime & Delinquency, 51*, 373–399, doi: 10.1177/0011128704271459.

McIvor, G., & McNeill, F. (2007). Probation in Scotland: Past, present, and future. In L. Gelsthorpe & R. Morgan (Eds.), *Handbook of probation* (pp. 131–154). United Kingdom: Willan Publishing.

Morash, M. (2010). *Women on probation and parole: A feminist critique of community programs and services.* Boston: Northeastern University Press.

Morgan, K. (1993). Factors influencing probation outcome: A review of the literature. *Federal Probation, 57* (2), 23–29.

Nieto, M. (2003). *Adult probation and parole in California.* Retrieved from https://www.library.ca.gov/crb/03/09/03-009.pdf.

Nudd, T. (2009). Rihanna gives painful details of Chris Brown assault. *CNN.* Retrieved from http://www.cnn.com/2009/SHOWBIZ/Music/11/06/rihanna.chris.brown/index.html?eref=ib_us.

Office of Juvenile Justice and Delinquency Prevention. (2011). *Juveniles on probation: Characteristics of adjudicated cases ordered to probation, 1985–2011, OJJDP statistical briefing book 2011.* Washington, DC. Retrieved from http://www.ojjdp.gov/ojstatbb/probation/qa07103.asp?qaDate=2011.

Oregon Courts. *General conditions of probation.* Retrieved from http://courts.oregon.gov/Multnomah/docs/CriminalActions/GeneralConditionsOfProbation.pdf.

O'Toole, S. (2006). *The history of Australian corrections.* Australia: University of New South Wales Press.

Panzarella, R. (2002). Theory and practice of probation on bail in the report of John Augustus. *Federal Probation, 66*(3), 38–42.

Petersilia, J. (1985). *Summarizing RAND's study of adult felony probation.* Santa Monica, CA: RAND Corporation. Retrieved from http://www.rand.org/content/dam/rand/pubs/papers/2008/P7058-1.pdf.

Petersila, J. (1998). *Probation in the United States: Part 1.* American Probation and Parole Association. Retrieved from http://www.appa-net.org/eweb/Resources/PPPSW_2013/docs/sp98pers30.pdf.

Pew Center on the States. (2011). *State of recidivism: The revolving door of America's prisons.* Washington, DC. Retrieved from https://www.michigan.gov/documents/corrections/Pew_Report_State_of_Recidivism_350337_7.pdf.

Rhode Island Department of Corrections. (2008). *Adult probation and parole.* Retrieved from http://sos.ri.gov/documents/archives/regdocs/released/pdf/DOC/5452.pdf.

Scott-Hayward, C. S. (2009). *The fiscal crisis in corrections: Rethinking policies and practices.* New York: Vera Institute of Justice.

The Sentencing Project. (2007). *Women in the criminal justice system: Briefing sheets.* Washington, DC.

Sklar, R. B. (1964). Law and practice in probation and parole revocation hearings. *Journal of Criminal Law, Criminology and Police Science, 55*(2), 175–198. doi: 10.2307/1140747.

Solomon, A., Osborne, J., Winterfield, L., Elderbroom, B., Burke, P., Stroker, R., Rhine, E., & Burrell, W. (2007). *Putting public safety first: 13 parole supervision strategies to enhance reentry outcomes.* Washington, DC: The Urban Institute. Retrieved from http://www.urban.org/UploadedPDF/411791_public_safety_first.pdf.

Stalans, L. J., & Lurigio, A. J. (2015). Parenting and intimate relationship effects on women offenders' recidivism and noncompliance with probation. *Women and Criminal Justice*, 1–17. doi: 10.1080/08974454.2014.909764.

Tulett, J. (1990). *The changing role of probation in South Australia.* Australian Institute of Criminology.

Vito, G. F. (1986). Felony probation and recidivism: Replication and response. *Federal Probation, 50*, 17–25.

Wilson, J. Q. (1975). *Thinking about crime.* New York: Vintage Books.

Winton, R. (2014). Chris Brown admits violating probation, gets 1 year in L.A. county jail. *L.A. Times.* Retrieved from http://www.latimes.com/local/lanow/la-me-ln-chris-brown-20140509-story.html.

Wodahl, E. J., Garland, B., Culhane, S. E., & McCarty, W. P. (2011). Utilizing behavioral interventions to improve supervision outcomes. *Criminal Justice and Behavior, 38*(4), 386–405. doi: 10.1177/0093854810397866.

Wood, P. B., & Grasmick, H. G. (1999). Toward the development of punishment equivalencies: Male and female inmates rate the severity of alternative sanctions compared to prison. *Justice Quarterly, 16*, 19–50, doi: 10.1080/07418829900094041.

Chapter 5

Intermediate Sanctions: Other Alternatives

Student Learning Outcomes

After reading this chapter, you should be able to:

• Define and explain the types of intermediate sanctions.
• Describe the historical development of intermediate sanctions.
• Summarize the effectiveness of intermediate sanctions.

Introduction

Perhaps you were an avid viewer of *The Montel Williams Show* as it aired from 1991 until 2008. If you did happen to watch the show or catch it on occasion, you may have watched an episode where Montel was trying to reform unruly juveniles, who often were delinquent and sometimes criminal. Montel would interview the combative teenagers and their family members, then proceed to send them to a juvenile boot camp to reform their behavior. The hope, of course, was that the juvenile would change his/her behavior. While juvenile boot camps may be sensationalized on television, in reality, they are an integral part of community corrections. Besides being profiled on television on occasion, you don't often hear about boot camps in the news—unless the boot camp made the headlines for some specific reason, such as the death of a juvenile at the camp. In 2006, 14-year-old Martin Lee Anderson died in a Florida juvenile boot camp (Sexton, 2006). Initial accounts of his death stated that Anderson collapsed on the exercise area, and his death was later ruled by the medical examiner as being due to his sickle cell disease (Klatell, 2006). This ruling was made despite the fact that there was video evidence showing seven guards beating and coercing Anderson, apparently because Anderson did not want to participate in the exercise regimen, before his collapse (Sexton, 2006). Also shown in the video was a nurse standing by and not intervening in the officer treatment of Anderson (Klatell, 2006). The video, of course, ignited community outrage and resulted in a second inquiry into Anderson's death. After a second autopsy investigation, Anderson's death was changed to death by suffocation (Klatell, 2006). Subsequently, the seven officers and the nurse were charged with Anderson's death, but they were later acquitted (Goodnough, 2007; Klatell, 2006). Following this case, the state of Florida permanently closed all juvenile boot camps in the state (Goodnough, 2007). The death of

Anderson at a juvenile correctional boot camp was a rare occurrence, and it is certainly not the norm.

The general public probably does not think about forms of punishment that occur in corrections besides jail or prison sentences. However, when an athlete or celebrity gets ensnared in the criminal justice system, other forms of correctional punishment, such as house arrest, often come to light. Former NFL Falcons star, Michael Vick, was thrust into the media spotlight when his involvement in funding and hosting illegal dogfighting events at one of his properties surfaced as well as his participation in the killing of underperforming dogs in 2007 (Macur, 2007). Vick agreed to a plea bargain, and he was sentenced to a 23-month prison sentence (Macur, 2007). He was released a few months early to serve the rest of his sentence under house arrest and was required to wear an electronic monitoring device (Macur, 2007; Maske, 2009). His case, due to his status, raised awareness about other forms of punishment (i.e., house arrest, electronic monitoring) in the correctional system.

This chapter will provide a definition and overview of intermediate sanctions. In particular, attention will be paid to the historical development of intermediate sanctions and the many types of intermediate sanctions (e.g., day reporting centers, work release, halfway houses incarceration, boot camps) will be discussed. Additionally, the chapter will provide a review of research regarding the effectiveness of the various types of intermediate sanctions, including how these sanctions compare in terms of effectiveness to traditional probation sentences.

History of the Development of Intermediate Sanctions

Between the 1970s and the 1990s, both state and federal governments began to shift their funding from rehabilitation and funnel it instead to crime prevention (e.g., policing of hot spots, enhanced surveillance) and other forms of deterrent punishments, known as **intermediate sanctions**, which are sentences that are alternatives to probation such as house arrest (Seiter & Kadela, 2003). With prisons becoming overcrowded during this time, correctional administrators needed cost-effective alternatives to traditional incarceration that ensured public safety and were considered to be tough by both politicians and the public (Latessa & Smith, 2011). Because intermediate sanctions attempted to fill these lofty goals, the implementation and use of these sanctions exploded during this time period. Intermediate sanctions have been defined as "a punishment option that is considered on a continuum to fall between traditional probation and traditional incarceration" (U.S. Department of Justice, 1990, p. 3). Latessa and Smith (2011) state that intermediate sanctions allowed the punishment to be individually tailored to the offender, and the offender is still held accountable for his or her behavior. A wide range of punishments fall under the intermediate sanctions umbrella, including day fines, intensive supervision probation, day-reporting centers, house arrest, electronic monitoring, and boot camps (Latessa

& Smith, 2011). These punishments were designed to enhance the surveillance and control of offenders in society and to perhaps increase the severity of punishments, such as probation, which were often seen as a slap on the wrist by many in the public. The following sections describe the historical development of many types of these intermediate sanctions as well as how they operate.

Day Fines

Historically, fines, or payment of a fee, have often been utilized in the criminal justice system as a form of punishment. However, one of the chief problems with relying only on a fine as punishment is the obvious fact of how such a punishment is advantageous to those with great financial wealth and disadvantageous to those from low socioeconomic backgrounds. Given the disparity that arises with traditional fines, **day fines** have emerged. Rather than requiring a flat fee, day fines are assigned based on the individual's normal work pay for one day of work. That is, if the individual typically made $100 per day for his/her work, then this would be the fine that would be accessed. On the other hand, if the individual made $1,000 in the course of one working day, then a fine of $1,000 would be assigned. Thus, day fines attempt to improve on traditional fines by making the use of a fine more equitable (Zedlewski, 2010). Additionally, day fines can be viewed as advantageous as the punishment may be viewed as punitive, they reduce costs to the criminal justice system (e.g., incarceration, court appearances), and they divert the individual from other forms of punishment, such as incarceration, that often disrupt family networks and cause the individual to lose ties to employment (Zedlewski, 2010).

The use of day fines is not a U.S. invention, but rather their use has its roots in Europe. In 1921, Finland was the first country to implement day fines (Zedlewski, 2010). Other countries soon followed suit, including Sweden, Germany, the United Kingdom, and the Dominican Republic (Zedlewski, 2010). It was not until the 1980s that day fines had begun to be used in various jurisdictions in the United States for not just misdemeanor offenses but also felony offenses. The first jurisdiction to implement a day fine, and only for misdemeanor offenses, was Staten Island, New York, in 1988 (Zedlewski, 2010). Following implementation in New York, other states soon followed, including Arizona, Iowa, Connecticut, Oregon, Alaska, and Oklahoma (Zedlewski, 2010). While day fines may be assigned as the only form of punishment, typically they are utilized in conjunction with other forms of intermediate sanctions. One of the chief problems with the use of day fines is the court's access to the offender's income information (Zedlewski, 2010). For instance, the court cannot require the Internal Revenue Service (IRS) to provide tax information about an offender — such information can only be released by the IRS with consent (Zedlewski, 2010). Therefore, the court has to rely on the offender self-disclosing his/her income, whereby the offender may underreport income in hopes of obtaining a lower day fine. Of course, such self-disclosure is based on legal income. Overall, while day fines are one type of intermediate sanction, the sanction has not been adopted or used universally in the nation, perhaps due to the difficulties in the acquisition of income information or because policymakers and the public view day fines as not too tough, or severe, or a punishment.

Text Box 5.1: Alternative Community Sanctions in Europe

In Europe, other forms of intermediate, or community, sanctions are utilized that have yet to be adopted in the United States. For instance, in the Netherlands, a task penalty is utilized (Subramanian & Shames, 2013). The task penalty requires the offender to complete a task that can be either a work order or training order for no greater than 480 hours (Subramanian & Shames, 2013). Similarly to the U.S. sanction of community service, a work order requires that the offender work in the community, either with a government agency or a private organization, to assist them with their needs in some way (e.g., improving the community, assisting in cultural work). However, the training order aspect of this punishment is a definite distinction from the U.S. model of service as training orders require that the offender "learn specific behavioral skills and are often imposed on offenders who need to improve their communication skills or social abilities" (Subramanian & Shames, 2013, p. 8).

House Arrest/Home Confinement

House arrest, or home confinement, is a soft form of incarceration. Rather than incarcerating offenders in a jail or prison, they serve their period of confinement in their own homes. Those under house arrest sentences are required to be at their residences during specified hours, and they can only be outside their homes for designated activities such as attending educational classes, therapeutic sessions, or working. Offenders sentenced to this sanction are monitored for compliance by a probation officer—even if the offender is not sentenced to probation. That is, a house arrest sentence can be made in lieu of or, in addition to, a probation sentence. Therefore, regardless of whether the offender also has a formal probation sentence, his/her behavior is monitored by a probation officer. The clear advantage of the house arrest sentence is the lower cost, as it is a much cheaper alternative than the use of a prison or jail sentence. After all, it is the responsibility of the offender to pay for his/her residence and purchase his/her own food. Apart from the cost savings, house arrest sentences allow the offender to maintain ties to family and to continue working if he/she was employed. The use of house arrest can be traced back to the 1600s in Rome (Lilly & Ball, 1987). Other countries also used forms of house arrest, including Russia, South African, Poland, South Korea, and India (Lilly & Ball, 1987). In the United States, house arrest, sometimes referred to as home detention, was implemented in St. Louis in 1971 for juveniles (Lilly & Ball, 1987). The use of house arrest proliferated across the nation through the 1970s. It was not until 1983 that the first house arrest program was implemented for adults in Florida (Lilly & Ball, 1987). Within just a few years, over 30 states had developed house arrest programs (Lilly & Ball, 1987). By 1986, the federal government adopted the use of home arrest for federal probation and parole offenders (Lilly & Ball, 1987). Despite the wide implementation of this sanction, many worried about community safety and whether the offender was adequately being supervised and truly at home when he/she was required to do so.

Image 9. © iStockphoto.com/StockSolutions.

Electronic Monitoring

Electronic monitoring (EM) is a technological device that is adhered to the offender that tracks his/her movements to ensure that he/she is in compliance with release terms. More often than not, EM is used in conjunction with a house arrest sanction. That is, EM is the technology that ensures that the offender is in his/her residence when required to be so. The development and use of EM has not only an interesting history, but the technology behind EM devices has advanced quite a bit. With the implementation of house arrest for both juvenile and adult offenders by the early 1980s, in 1983, a judge in New Mexico was concerned about offender compliance. In fact, the judge was so concerned with compliance that he was inspired to take action and develop some sort of electronic device that could ensure compliance. His inspiration for such a device from a Spiderman comic strip that he viewed wherein Spiderman was tracked by a transmitter affixed to his wrist (Lilly & Ball, 1987). Yes, a Spiderman comic strip was the inspiration for the modern-day EM devices! Lilly and Ball (1987, p. 362) explain,

> The judge approached an engineer, who designed a device consisting of an electronic bracelet approximately the size of a pack of cigarettes that emitted an electronic signal that was picked up by a receiver placed in a home telephone. This bracelet could be strapped to the ankle of an offender in such a way that if he or she moved more than approximately 150 feet from the home telephone, the transmission signal would be broken, alerting authorities that the offender had left the premises.

These early EM devices, utilizing radio wave frequencies, were considered passive systems, or random calling devices, as it required the offender to wear the device and have a receiver device installed at their residence next to their phone (Renzema & Mayo-Wilson, 2005). Since probation officers supervised EM clients, they would call the offender at his/her residence when he/she was required to be there. When the probation officer called, the offender had a certain amount of time to insert the EM device into the receiver in order for the device to register them as being in their residence when they were required to be. Alternatives to the EM device soon developed, such as those working on an active system. For those EM devices working on the active system, or continuous signal devices, the device would send a radio transmission to the probation office if the offender went out of designated zones at specific times (e.g., not being home during curfew hours) (Renzema & Mayo-Wilson, 2005). Regardless of whether the EM device utilized the passive or active system, they both had similar problems. First, responses to violations were not immediate. That is, the device would indicate a violation, but the probation officer probably didn't notice it until the next day when they reviewed the data from the device from the previous day. At that point, the probation officer would not begin immediately searching for the offender to determine his whereabouts—thus, there was not an instantaneous response to the violation. Second, as with any technology, there were some reliability issues (Renzema & Mayo-Wilson, 2005). The devices, on occasion, would register a false positive (i.e., indicating a violation where there, in fact, was none) or a false negative (i.e., indicating there was no violation when, in fact, the offender was in violation). Finally, these early EM devices did not do a great job in tracking the identity of the offender. Thus, the device could not necessarily identify that the person who was wearing the device was, in fact, the offender. This was due to the fact that these devices were not initially fitted specifically for each offender, thus, more than one device could register as the offender since the devices were not unique or had specific transmissions for any given offender.

Despite some of the problems with EM devices, they continued to be utilized as they offered a cost savings solution to corrections department. With technological advancements in the 1990s, EM devices soon became more sophisticated and were able to overcome some of their earlier shortcomings. Renzema & Mayo-Wilson (2005, p. 217) explain, "In late 1997, two vendors began marketing systems that mated CS [continuous signal], wireless phone, and Global Positioning System (GPS) technologies. Although GPS tracking is limited by cellular network coverage and blockage of satellite coverage by structures, agencies were attracted by the ability to track offenders in real-time." Therefore, agencies began shifting from the old active and passive systems based on radio technology and began using new GPS active and passive systems. More recently, GPS hybrid systems have been adopted. The International Association of Chiefs of Police (2008, p. 5) describes these three systems as follows:

> **Active GPS monitoring**: Active systems allow the PTD [portable tracking device] to transmit offender location information to a monitoring center in near-real time. Therefore, active GPS systems require a cellular telephone to communicate location information and determine whether a transmitter is out of range or whether someone has tampered with it.

> **Passive GPS monitoring**: Location and time data are stored in the PTD, and this information is downloaded when the PTD is charged each day. The

Table 5.1: Trends in GPS Units Adopted in the U.S., 1999–2009

Year	1999	2000	2001	2002	2003	2004	2005	2006	2007	2008	2009
GPS Units	230	395	647	1,276	2,394	5,000	10,250	20,046	37,299	62,121	91,329

Source: DeMichele, M., & Payne, B. (2009). *Offender supervision with electronic technology.* Washington, DC: U.S. Department of Justice. Retrieved from http://www.appa-net.org/eweb/docs/appa/pubs/OSET_2.pdf.

charger is connected to a landline telephone to transfer information to the monitoring center.

Hybrid systems: Hybrids, the newest type of GPS system, combine both passive and active monitoring capabilities, and differ from active units because they are programmed to report data at much longer time intervals, such as every few hours or two or three times each day. If the transmitter is out of range or someone has tampered with it, hybrid systems react just like active systems, by reporting data in near-real time using cellular telephone communications.

Regardless of which system agencies adopt, the devices can be programmed with inclusion or exclusion zones (Gowen, 2001; International Association of Chiefs of Police, 2008). When an inclusion zone is programmed into the device, this permits that offender to be at certain locations at specific times (e.g., work). The exclusion zone, on the other hand, restricts the offender from entering or being near specific locations such as a bar or a school. Due to the costs, most agencies employ the passive GPS system (Pattavina, 2009). The growth of GPS units for EM has increased greatly since the late 1990s (see Table 5.1). EM devices are utilized for a wide range of offenders including low- and high-risk offenders. In fact, many states require that those convicted of sex offenses or gang related offenses be placed on EM along with other sanctions, with over 40 states requiring mandatory EM monitoring of certain ex-offenders for life (International Association of Chiefs of Police, 2008; Savage, 2015). Currently, the Supreme Court is reviewing the constitutionality of lifetime EM monitoring for ex-offenders (Savage, 2015).

Many states have now adopted specific EM devices designed for alcohol offenders called Secure Continuous Remote Alcohol Monitor (SCRAM) devices (Sullivan, 2011). You may have heard about this device in the news when Lindsay Lohan volunteered to wear it in an effort to prove to the courts that she was in compliance with the required probation condition that she remain sober (Friedman, 2007). The device operates as other EM devices do, with the added feature of alcohol monitoring, and it is designed to be tamperproof as it is firmly secured on one's ankle and has a security screw and clasp (Friedman, 2007). SCRAM detects alcohol consumption through "a process called 'transdermal alcohol testing,' which essentially takes samples from the hard-to-see layer of sweat that is on everyone's skin" (Friedman, 2007). About every 30 minutes, SCRAM takes alcohol readings and then the data is transmitted wirelessly to a private monitoring company (Sullivan, 2011). This company reports the data on the offender as well as if the offender has attempted to tamper with the device to the probation agency and/or courthouse (Sullivan, 2011). Some believe that such devices are an improvement over traditional forms of monitoring for alcohol offenders such as breathalyzer test or ignition interlock systems, which can be tampered with or compromised.

With the pervasive adoption of GPS EM devices promising better surveillance of offenders at a lower cost, there are a few drawbacks. One drawback of EM devices is the workload placed on probation officers and unforeseen costs that probation agencies will incur that are associated with operating and monitoring these devices. The International Association of Chiefs of Police (2008, p. 9) cautions that agencies must be prepared for several tasks including "monitoring GPS equipment; responding to alerts; reviewing GPS data; fitting offenders with GPS units; teaching offenders how the equipment works; connecting a charger in offenders' homes; and maintaining equipment, procurement, inventory, and product replacement." Given the cost and time investment of probation officers, probation agencies will need to assess whether they can handle and sustain the use of such devices in the long run. Another drawback to EM devices is that they provide the community with a false sense of security. Even though an offender is being monitored, they are still freely moving in society and can commit a new crime. Additionally, these devices are thought to be foolproof or tamperproof. However, it is possible for offenders to find ways or methods to compromise the device, thus, circumventing the design of enhanced surveillance of the offender (International Association of Chiefs of Police, 2008).

Day Reporting Centers

Day reporting centers (DRC) are facilities that offenders report to during business hours for treatment services and for monitoring. DRCs were first implemented in Great Britain in the 1960s (Craddock, 2004). With the explosion in the adoption of alternative or intermediate sanctions in the U.S., the first official DRC in the United States opened in 1986 in Springfield, Massachusetts (Curtin, 1996). Given their potential cost savings, the implementation of DRCs proliferated from 13 DRCs operational in the early 1990s to 114 in the mid-1990s (Martin, Lurigio & Olson, 2003; Parent et al., 1995). Typically, offenders serving DRC sentences include: persons over the age of 18; persons charged with a crime who are incarcerated or facing incarceration; pre-trial detainees, sentenced offenders, and post sentence violators; misdemeanants and felons; and non-violent offenders (Latessa & Smith, 2011). It should be noted that there is jurisdiction variability in programming delivered to clients as well as the target population of clients that are served in DRCs (Parent, 1990; Roy, 2002; Roy & Barton, 2006; Spencer, 2012). That is, one jurisdiction may predominately serve probation violators while another jurisdiction may focus their services on pre-trial defendants (Marciniak, 1999; Parent et al., 1995). Additionally, there is jurisdictional variability as to how DRCs are referred to in the community. For instance, in some jurisdictions, DRCs are referred to as DRCs; community resource centers; day treatment centers; day incarceration centers; and even restorative justice centers (Craddock, 2004). In Seattle, Washington, for example, the King County Department of Adult and Juvenile Detention Community Corrections Division operates a day reporting center called the Community Center for Alternative Programs (CCAP), which was established in 2002. Regardless of the name of the facility or program, the offenders are supervised by a probation officer or a counselor, reside in their own residences, and are required to report to the center on a daily basis (Roy & Barton, 2006). In 2014, approximately 4,400 offenders under jail supervision were participating in DRC programs (Minton & Zeng, 2015).

At the DRC, the offender will also be required to participate in programming such as mental health counseling, education programs, social skills training, and substance abuse treatment (Martin et al., 2003). A common thread among the clients, regardless of their status in the criminal justice system, is their substance abuse histories (Parent et al., 1995). Thus, participants in DRC programs are monitored and treated for drug and/or alcohol use (Lurigio, Olson, & Sifferd, 1999; Marciniak, 1999; Parent et al., 1995). In the Seattle CCAP program, a wide range of programming options exists for clients, including domestic violence education; family relations; choices-life skills; social responsibility; financial management; health education; re-licensing program; fight the power of tobacco; anger management; drug treatment (out-patient); drug treatment (intensive out-patient); alcohol treatment; work-life skills; and GED education (Gunnison & Helfgott, 2016). Since pre-trial detainees can be included as participants in DRC programs, the time served in these programs for offenders can range from less than one week for such offenders to as much as one year for those offenders who have been formally sentenced to a DRC as punishment (Humphrey, 1992; Marciniak, 1999). In Seattle, for instance, clients of the CCAP participate for various amounts of time from as little as five days to as long as nine months.

Work Release

Work release programs can be described as a community-based treatment correctional program where an offender, after serving most of his/her prison sentence, resides in a work release facility to assist him/her in reintegrating back into society (Elder & Cohen, 1978). While selection criteria for eligible offenders may vary slightly between jurisdictions, ex-offenders released from prison to a work release center are nonviolent offenders and those who are usually classified as lower risk offenders but not always. For instance, in 2013, in the state of Washington, of the 658 offenders who were currently serving work release sentences, only 9% were classified as low risk, while 12% were classified as moderate risk, 29% were classified as high non-violent risk, and 49% were classified as a high violent risk (Washington State Department of Corrections, 2013). Besides their risk classification, prisoners' institutional adjustment, prior record, and substance abuse histories are examined before they are possibility released to a work release center.

The first work release program established in the United States was in Wisconsin in 1913, and other states began to follow suit and implement such programs throughout the 1950s and thereafter (Long, 1965). However, the proliferation of work release programs across the nation did not occur until after Congress passed the **Prisoner Rehabilitation Act of 1965**, which established work release as an option for federal offenders (Long, 1965; Zalba, 1967). Due to the passage of this legislation, and given that these programs offered a potential cost savings over traditional incarceration for offenders, correctional agencies across the nation began implementing these programs in greater numbers (Johnson, 1967). Each state will stipulate when an offender may be eligible for possible release to work release, which could be six months to eight months before their release from prison. The state of Washington, for example, stipulates that offenders are only eligible within six months of release (Washington State Department of Corrections, 2013). It should also be noted that offenders can also be directly sentenced to a work release program in lieu of serving a jail sentence first. At the work release program, offenders participate in programming, search for employment, and begin to re-establish family connections. The offender is required to abide by the work release program rules (e.g., curfew and drug/alcohol testing) while participating in the program. Work release programs provide the structure and support that many ex-offenders need to reintegrate successfully into society while, at the same time, offer supervision and surveillance of the offenders to ensure that they are meeting program expectations as well as remaining crime free (see Text Box 5.2).

Text Box 5.2: Expectations of Work Release Offenders, Washington State

- All offenders must abide by the rules and regulations of the program. Deviations can result in disciplinary action, to include termination from the program.

- Offenders work on job development, search, placement, and retainment of employment. On-site job visits and verifications are completed to assure the offender is employed at the designated site. Offenders are also monitored on their trips back and forth to work to ensure their movements allow enough time to get to work without any pre-arranged stops.

- Offenders are only allowed out of the facility if they work, are conducting business or are on a supervised outing to visit family members. These outings are always in the presence of a sponsor who has undergone a criminal background check and been adjudged responsible for the offender's actions.

- Offenders must continue therapy, parenting classes, anger management training, and substance abuse treatment that may also include participation in Alcoholics Anonymous or Narcotics Anonymous, as identified in their reentry plan.

- Offenders must submit to frequent tests for substance abuse.

Source: Washington State Department of Corrections. (2015). *Work release data fact sheet: A structured transition back into the community*, page 2. Retrieved from http://www.doc.wa.gov/docs/publications/fact-sheets/006-F1.pdf.

Halfway Houses

Halfway houses, also referred to as residential reentry centers, are utilized to assist ex-offenders in their transition from prison to the community and may also be used as an alternative to an incarceration term. Prisoners who are near the end of their prison sentence (e.g., state level: 12–18 months; federal level: 6 months) and have had good institutional adjustment and participated in treatment are eligible to be released to a halfway house to serve the remainder of their sentence. Alternatively, halfway houses may be utilized as a sanction for higher risk offenders. For instance, an offender may be sentenced to probation as well as to a halfway house if he/she is deemed to be in need of assistance or therapy or perhaps at a higher risk of reoffending.

Halfway houses were first utilized in the United States in the 1800s and were found in states such as New York, Pennsylvania, and Massachusetts (McCartt & Mangogna, 1973). These early halfway houses were designed to provide short-term shelter to ex-offenders and to assist them in making a successful transition from prison to their communities, and most lacked a treatment component. Despite their early implementation, halfway houses were not considered a part of the correctional system and many were very critical of their implementation, including citizens and even leaders of the American Prison Association (McCartt & Mangogna, 1973). It was not until the 1950s that halfway houses underwent a revival in the corrections system (McCartt & Mangogna, 1973). At this time, many were now viewing halfway houses as a useful tool in helping offenders transition from prison to their communities and they began to be implemented across the nation. By 1964, the halfway house movement was in full swing, at both the state and federal level, and the International Association of Halfway Houses was established (McCartt & Mangogna, 1973). The legitimization of halfway houses as a tool to help ex-offenders resulted in the establishment of both public and private halfway houses, which served ex-offenders in general or specialized in assisting ex-offenders with specific needs such as the treatment of alcoholism (McCartt & Mangogna, 1973). Additionally, by the late 1960s, the federal government began utilizing halfway house for federal offenders. With the budget crisis plaguing the correctional system, the use of halfway houses for offenders has become increasingly more popular.

The burgeoning use of halfway houses for offenders has caused concerns for some referring to halfway houses as "an industry plagued with problems" (Gilna, Clarke, & Patel, 2015, p. 1). For instance, some halfway houses are driven more for profit than to help offenders, escapes are common, and residents and even sometimes staff are often involved in criminal behavior (Gilna et al., 2015). In the state of New Jersey, escape attempts from halfway houses were so common in 2011, that they averaged about 40 per month (Gilna et al., 2015). In comparison, there were no prison escapes in New Jersey in 2011 (Dolnick, 2012). One senior corrections investigator who spent four years tracking escaped offenders from halfway houses describes the situation as follows: "The system is a mess. No matter how many escaped, no matter how many were caught, no matter how many committed heinous acts while they were on the run, they still kept releasing more guys into the halfway houses, and it kept happening over and over again" (Dolnick, 2012). When reforms were put into place by the New Jersey governor in 2012, escape attempts had dropped to just 18 during the first six months of 2012, however, clearly they were not entirely curtailed (Gilna et al., 2015). Such escape problems were not isolated to the state of New Jersey, as they occurred at other state and federal facilities (Gilna et al., 2015). Additionally, allegations of misconduct by staff members from former residents have included rape, sexual re-lations with residents, diverting funds for treatment to the purchase of drugs, per-mitting residents to have unsupervised urine tests, warning residents about upcoming drug tests, and even altering drug test reports (Gilna et al., 2015). While such problems do not define halfway houses and their utility, they do highlight that reforms may be needed to ensure that they are operating as they should be and that client needs are being met.

Boot Camps

Image 10. © iStockphoto.com/Lorado.

Boot camps are a form of correctional sanction that is aimed at non-violent, young, and first-time offenders. Rooted in militaristic ideals, these camps mirror military basic training camps whereby participants engage in marching drills, strenuous ex-ercises, and endure being yelled at by correctional staff (Benda, 2005). This form of incarceration is sometimes referred to as **shock incarceration**, as offenders are sen-tenced to a short period of confinement and the "shock" of the experience is supposed to deter them from committing future crime. In 1971, this sanction was first imple-mented for adult offenders in Idaho with other states such as Georgia and Oklahoma opening their own adult boot camp programs in 1983 and 1984 respectively (Benda, 2005). The following year, in Louisiana, the first boot camp for juveniles in the nation was opened. Since boot camps offered a "get-tough" form of punishment and were deemed to be a punishment that was harsher than probation and yet would be a de-terrent to offenders as well, these programs soon began to be fervently implemented in the United States in the 1980s and throughout the 1990s (Benda, 2005; Cullen et al., 2005). Because boot camp sentences are short-term, ranging from 90–180 days, they are appealing to correctional administrators since many offenders can be punished at once at a lower cost than a traditional jail or prison sentence. The popularity of boot camps reached their pinnacle in the mid-1990s with over 75 boot camps operating in the United States (Benda, 2005). Despite their popularity, many correctional administrators became disillusioned with boot camps and many began to shut their doors. By 2000, there were only 51 boot camps in operation (Benda, 2005). There are no national statistics kept on boot camps, thus, it is not known how many may be in operation currently. It should be noted that the early boot camp programs offered no rehabilitation components. However, today, there are some boot campus that are operating which provide some form of treatment to offenders, but even for these programs, rehabilitation is not the chief goal.

Intensive Supervision Probation

Intensive Supervision Probation (ISP) is a probation sanction that is designed to be more intense than a traditional probation sentence. The philosophy of intense punishment fits well with the get-tough-on-crime movement. The ISP sanction was first adopted in the United States in the 1980s, and by 1990 all states offered this form of sanction (Petersilia & Turner, 1993). At the federal level, ISP sanctions were also slowly adopted (Petersilia & Turner, 1993). This sanction requires more frequent contact between offenders and probation officers, more random drugs tests, and more monitoring of offenders to ensure that they are adhering to conditions of their release (e.g., curfew). Wiliszowski et al. (2010, p. 376) explain that

Examples of ISP components are:

- screening and assessment of offenders' substance abuse problems;
- treatment;
- education;
- intensive supervision;
- self-help (e.g., commit to lifestyle changes including sobriety, required attendance by offenders at Alcoholics Anonymous [AA] meetings, required attendance at victim impact panels [VIPs], finding employment);
- submission to random alcohol and other drug testing;
- driver's licensing sanctions;
- vehicle actions (e.g., ignition interlocks, special license plates, sale of vehicles);
- submission to home confinement and controlled movement (through electronic monitoring and/or compliance checks); and
- community service.

Since this sanction is more intense than traditional probation, it is most typically meted out to higher risk offenders—or offenders not necessarily suitable for regular probation. While treatment may be a component of an ISP sanction, it is not the chief focus. In fact, in a review of ISP programs, Gendreau et al. (2000) uncovered that only 18% of the ISP programs offered treatment.

Effectiveness of Intermediate Sanctions

With the growing implementation of intermediate sanctions in the 1970s and 80s, researchers soon turned their attention to whether these sanctions were effective in reducing recidivism, reducing prison overcrowding, ensuring community safety, and if they were cost effective (Harris, Peterson, & Repoza, 2001). Unfortunately, as researchers began to examine the effectiveness of various intermediate sanctions, the outlook was rather grim. For the most part, researchers were finding that intermediate sanctions, as a whole, were no more effective than traditional probation—the only exception were day fines, which had a high completion rate (see MacKenzie, 1997). In fact, the new sanctions resulted in **net widening**, whereby now more offenders, many of whom may not have received these sanctions had they not existed, were getting ensnared in the criminal justice system (Johnson & Dipietro, 2012). The following sections highlight the empirical status of various intermediate sanctions.

Day Reporting Centers

Clients of DRCs experience a myriad of needs and challenges and report that programming at DRCs can assist them in getting their needs met (Gunnison & Helfgott, 2016). Several researchers have explored the effectiveness of DRCs (Anderson, 2002; Boyle et al., 2011; Boyle et al., 2013; Champion et al., 2012; Craddock, 2000; 2004; 2009; Kim et al., 2007; Martin et al., 2003; McBride & VanderWaal, 1997; McDevitt & Miliano, 1992; Ostermann, 2009; Roy & Barton, 2006) and have found DRC programs to be successful. Craddock and Graham (2001, p. 95), for example, examined two DRC programs in a midwestern state and concluded that, "DRCs may provide a viable correctional treatment option for moderately high-risk offenders supervised in the community." Anderson (2002), in an examination of a DRC program in Illinois for parolees, found that parolees who participated in the DRC program had lower recidivism rates than parolees who did not participate in DRC or other programming. In an examination of 1,391 DRC clients in Cook County, Illinois, Martin et al. (2003) found the DRC program to be successful, as participants in the program demonstrated reductions in illegal drug use, re-arrest rates, and court-appearance rates following completion of the program. More recently, Ostermann (2009) compared recidivism results from four male and female ex-offender groups in New Jersey (n=714): (1) individuals who maxed out their prison sentences; (2) individuals released to the community without supervision; (3) individuals who were paroled to a DRC program; and (4) individuals who were paroled to a Halfway Back program. Results from his investigation revealed that DRC clients were significantly less likely to be re-arrested than all the other comparison groups except for the Halfway Back clients, who had the overall lowest re-arrest rates.

It appears that DRC programs that can offer intensive supervision in tandem with intensive service delivery may offer the most promise for DRC clients (Steiner & Butler, 2013). Champion and colleagues (2012) also found that day reporting centers saved incarceration costs and reduced recidivism in a Western Pennsylvanian county with an estimated cost of $52.00 per day and a rate of offender treatment completion of 76.9%.

However, several researchers have not uncovered such success in all evaluations of DRC programs (Boyle et al., 2011; Boyle et al., 2013; Brunet, 2002; Marciniak, 1999; Craddock & Graham, 2001; Roy & Grimes, 2002). Boyle et al. (2011), who compared DRC parolees to parolees assigned to intensive supervision parole in New Jersey found that DRC clients did not have lower recidivism rates compared to their counterparts. In a subsequent study, Boyle and colleagues (2013) found that medium- and high-risk parolees in New Jersey who were assigned to a DRC program did not have lower re-cidivism rates (i.e., arrests, convictions) than similar offenders who were on traditional parole. Other researchers, however, caution the quick dismissal of DRC programs for higher risk offenders based on Boyle et al.'s (2013) findings given the parameters of their investigation and weaknesses associated with it (see Ostermann, 2013).

Work Release

The effectiveness of the work release programs in reducing recidivism has also been questioned. Several early researchers found that work release offenders exhibited lower levels of recidivism after completion of the program (Beha, 1977; Dunlavey, 1969; Jeffrey & Wolpert, 1974; Rudoff & Esselstyn, 1973; Waldo & Chiricos, 1977; Zalba, 1967). However, the results of many of these early studies have been called into question (Katz & Decker, 1982; Turner & Petersilia, 1996; Waldo & Chiricos, 1977). In a review of more than 41 evaluations conducted on work release programs, Katz and Decker (1982) cautioned that most early studies finding recidivism reductions for work release programs were plagued with methodological weaknesses in the study designs. For in-stance, many of the earlier studies of work release programs lacked an experimental design whereby offenders are randomly assigned into control and experimental groups (Katz & Decker, 1982). Of the few earlier studies that did have experimental designs, Waldo & Chiricos (1977), who examined work release offenders in Florida, found no reductions in recidivism rates for work release offenders, whereas Jeffrey and Wolpert (1974), who examined work release offenders in California, did find reductions in re-cidivism rates. Despite the mixed results, other researchers continued to examine work release offenders in the context of identifying the type of offender who is likely to suc-ceed on work release. For example, Elder and Cohen (1978) examined 90 nonviolent male offenders and concluded that those offenders who had no prior history of drug use and who had not been first arrested at an early age were more likely to be successful in a work release program. Butzin and colleagues (2006) also found that prior criminal history and earlier age at first arrest were significant predictors of recidivism.

Subsequent studies on work release programs have continued to yield mixed results (Gordon, & Chiricos, 1986; LeClair, 1988; LeClair & Guarino-Ghezzi, 1991; Turner & Petersilia, 1996). LeClair and Guarino-Ghezzi (1991), in an evaluation of male of-fenders on work release in Massachusetts, found that male offenders who participated in work release programs have lower recidivism rates after one year than males who were directly released from prison into the community. However, Gordon and Chiricos (1986), who examined work release in Florida, found no differences in recidivism rates after a two-year follow-up period between those offenders who had served work release sentences and those offenders who had not. Similarly, Turner and Petersilia (1996, p. 161), who examined male offenders on work release in Washington State, found that "the work release program did not reduce offender recidivism rates." More recently, research has emerged suggesting that work release programs can be effective in reducing recidivism and that these programs may also be effective in improving employment opportunities for these offenders (Cheliotis, 2008, 2009; Drake, 2007; Marion, 2002). Drake (2007), in an evaluation of work release programs in Washington State, reported that the programs lowered total recidivism by 2.8%. However, Drake (2007, p. 1) also noted that work release programs have "a marginal effect on felony recidivism by 1.8%," and have "no effect on violent felony recidivism." Upon reviewing the literature on temporary release, Cheliotis (2009, p. 427) concludes that: "Work release programs also showed considerable promise in lowering reconviction rates and were found to be effective in enhancing post-release employment prospects." In 2012, Gunnison examined 170 males and females sentenced to work release in Washington State and found that 40% of offenders had at least one post-release violation—although no differences emerged in recidivism rates between the genders. While Gunnison (2012) did not find differences in recidivism rates between the genders, the researcher found differences and similarities in offender needs by gender. For example, offender needs factors such as level of conflict with partner, mental health problem ever, suicidal considerations ever, threatening/aggressive/violent behavior ever, and alcohol use/problem distinguished females from males. Specifically, males were found to be more likely to have ever had mental health problems, a result that is consistent with previous research finding that male offenders suffer from mental health issues (Kenemore & Roldan, 2006; Petersilia, 2003). Thus, work release offenders, similar to other ex-offenders serving sentences in the community, are in need of mental health support (Lurigio, 1996; White et al., 2006). The finding that females were more likely to have experienced an alcohol problem in the past six months is consistent with previous research finding that alcohol use contributed both to onset and persistence in offending (Belknap, 2007; Mullings et al., 2004).

Halfway Houses

Since there is wide diversity in the offenders (i.e., low, moderate, and high risk) that are placed in halfway houses and since halfway houses are used at different points in the correctional system (i.e., as a standalone sentence, pre-release, and post-release), it has been difficult for researchers to conclude with certainty whether halfway houses are indeed effective. When comparing offenders sentenced to halfway houses as a condition of their probation or in lieu of jail or incarceration to those offenders sentenced to probation, researchers have found no significant differences in their recidivism rates (Hartmann, Friday, & Minor, 1994). Additionally, for those researchers who have compared offenders released to halfway houses from prison to offenders released on parole, it appears that halfway houses are not effective at the pre-release and post-release points. For instance, in an earlier examination of the previous evaluations examining the effectiveness of prisoners released to halfway houses compared to prisoners released on parole, Seiter et al. (1977) found no significant differences between the groups and concluded that halfway houses did little to assist ex-offenders during reentry. Lowenkamp and Latessa (2002) examined the effectiveness of halfway houses in Ohio and found recidivism rates were higher for low-risk offenders but the rates were actually lower for higher risk offenders. In a later follow-up evaluation of 40 halfway houses in Ohio, Latessa, Lovins, and Smith (2010) again found the same results—halfway house participants that were a higher risk had lower recidivism rates. More recently, in an examination of halfway houses in New Jersey, Hamilton and Campbell (2014) found that halfway house participants did not have lower recidivism rates (rearrest, reconviction, or reincarceration) than parolees not released to halfway houses. Despite the findings, the researchers conclude that halfway house participants did return to prison less frequently than parolees. Overall, the assessment of halfway houses is that they are not universally effective and not more effective than other traditional forms of punishments, such as probation and parole. Part of the problem is due to the diversity of offenders entering such programs as well as the diversity of halfway houses in operation, with some more dedicated to addressing offender needs than others.

Boot Camps

Research conducted to date on boot camps has not been favorable for this intermediate sanction. Overwhelmingly, researchers have not found boot camps to be more effective than other forms of punishment (Bottcher & Ezzell, 2005; Duwe & Kerschner, 2008; Meade & Steiner, 2010; Parent, 2003; Steiner & Giacomazzi, 2007). In fact, boot camp participants may have higher rates of recidivism than similar offenders who did not partake in the program and served sentences in jail or prison (see Aos et al., 1999). In the rare case when a boot camp was deemed to be successful, it was due to additional programmatic features, such as the incorporation of an educational and/or treatment component (Duwe & Kerchner, 2008). Recent research has revealed that the aftercare of boot camp participants can result in lower recidivism rates for this group if the aftercare continues for at least 90 days (Kurlychek et al., 2011). At a minimum, boot camps offer a cost savings for correctional agencies compared to traditional costs of incarceration (Meade & Steiner, 2010). Given the unfavorable findings, many states have closed their boot camp programs.

ISP

With the creation of the ISP sanction, more offenders were being sentenced to ISP rather than to probation. Early investigations into the effectiveness of ISP sentences in reducing recidivism were not favorable (Bryne & Kelley, 1989; Petersilia & Turner, 1992). In fact, several researchers found that recidivism rates for ISPs were not different from those offenders sentenced to traditional probation, and, in some cases, even higher (Gendreau et al., 2000; Petersilia & Turner, 1992; Smith & Akers, 1993). In an evaluation of approximately 2,000 adult offenders in 14 ISP programs, both probation and parole, Petersilia and Turner (1993, p. 5) found "that in 11 of the 14 sites, arrest rates during the one-year follow up were in fact higher for ISP participants than for the control group (although not significantly so). At the end of the one-year period, about 37 percent of the ISP participants and 33 percent of control offenders had been arrested." Additionally, Gendreau et al. (2000) conducted a meta-analytic review of 47 ISP programs across the nation and found that ISP programs had higher recidivism rates, about 6% higher, than traditional probation programs. Some have argued that it is to be expected that ISP participants to have higher recidivism rates than traditional probationers as there was a reason why these participants were sentenced to ISP programs—that is, they are higher risk. Further, others have stated that since ISP programs offer enhanced surveillance of clients, then it should not be surprising that they fail more given that they are being monitored much more than traditional probationers. Other researchers have concluded that only those ISP programs that have a treatment component are more likely to achieve lower recidivism rates (Fulton et al., 1997). More recently, Lowenkamp et al. (2010) examined the effectiveness of 58 ISP programs by analyzing whether the program philosophy and treatment integrity were at all associated with reductions in recidivism. The researchers discovered that ISP programs that incorporated the principles of effective intervention (i.e., targeting risk and needs factors) and had a human service philosophy, rather than a deterrence orientation, were more likely to achieve reductions in recidivism rates.

Conclusion

In sum, this chapter provided a definition and overview of intermediate sanctions. In particular, attention was paid to the historical development of intermediate sanctions and the many types of intermediate sanctions (e.g., day reporting centers, work release, halfway houses, boot camps) were discussed. The creation of these types of sanction has created net widening, whereby offenders, who may not have ever been sentenced to probation, may find themselves sanctioned to such sentences since they are now available. Additionally, the chapter provided a review of research regarding the effectiveness of the various types of intermediate sanctions, including how these sanctions compare in terms of effectiveness to traditional probation sentences. Overwhelmingly, the effectiveness of intermediate sanctions in reducing recidivism is limited and the best hope for these sanctions to be successful is the incorporation of a treatment component.

Key Terms

Active GPS monitoring

Boot camps

Day fines

Day reporting centers

Electronic monitoring

Halfway houses

House arrest

Hybrid systems

Intensive Supervision Probation (ISP)

Intermediate sanctions

Net widening

Passive GPS monitoring

Prisoner Rehabilitation Act of 1965

Shock incarceration

Work release

Discussion Questions

1. Research the types of intermediate sanctions that exist in your state. When was the first intermediate sanction established? Has your state abolished any types of intermediate sanctions? If so, when?

2. Given the empirical status of intermediate sanctions, should these punishments be abolished? Why or why not?

3. How can current intermediate sanctions be improved upon? What suggestions do you have to increase their effectiveness?

4. Can you think of other intermediate sanctions, not yet developed, that may be useful? What ideas do you have? For which type of offenders? How would the sanction operate?

References

Anderson, J. L. (2002). Overview of the Illinois DOC high-risk parolee re-entry program and 3-year recidivism outcomes of program participation. *Cognitive Behavioral Treatment Review, 11,* 4–6.

Aos, S., Phipps, P., Barnoski, R., & Lieb, R. (1999). *The comparative costs and benefits of programs to reduce crime: A review of national research findings with implications for Washington State.* Washington State Institute for Public Policy. http://www.wsipp.wa.gov/ReportFile/1319.

Beha, J. A. (1977). Innovation at a county house of correction and its effect upon patterns of recidivism. *Journal of Research in Crime and Delinquency, 14*(1), 88–106.

Belknap, J. (2007). *The invisible women: Gender, crime, and justice.* Belmont, CA: Wadsworth.

Benda, B. B. (2005). Introduction: Boot camps revisited: Issues, problems, prospects. *Journal of Offender Rehabilitation, 40*(3/4), 1–25. doi: 10.1300/J076v40n03_01.

Bottcher, J., & Ezell, M. E. (2005). Examining the effectiveness of boot camps: A randomized experiment with a long-term follow up. *Journal of Research in Crime and Delinquency, 42*(3), 309–332. doi: 10.1177/0022427804271918.

Boyle, D. J., Ragusa, L., Lanterman, J., & Marcus, A. (2011). *Outcomes of a randomized trial of an intensive community corrections program—day reporting centers—for parolees.* U.S. Department of Justice.

Boyle, D. J., Ragusa-Salerno, L., Lanterman, J. L., & Marcus, A. (2013). An evaluation of day reporting centers for parolees. *Criminology & Public Policy, 12*(1), 119–143. doi: 10.1111/1745-9133.12010.

Brunet, J. (2002). Day reporting centers in North Carolina: Implementation lessons for policymakers. *The Justice System Journal, 23*(2), 135–156.

Butzin, C. A., O'Connell, D. J., Martin, S. S., & Inciardi, J. A. (2006). Effect of drug treatment during work release on new arrest and incarcerations. *Journal of Criminal Justice, 34*(5), 557–565. doi: 10.1016/j.jcrimjus.2006.09.010

Byrne, J. M., & Kelly, L. M. (1989). *Restructuring probation as an intermediate sanction: An evaluation of the implementation and impact of the Massachusetts intensive probation supervision program.* Washington, DC: National Institute of Justice.

Champion, D. R., Harvey, P. J., & Schanz, Y. Y. (2012). Day reporting center and recidivism: Comparing offender groups in a Western Pennsylvania County. *Journal of Offender Rehabilitation, 50*(7), 433–446. doi: 10.1080/10509674.2011.583718.

Cheliotis, L. K. (2008). Reconsidering the effectiveness of temporary release: A systematic review. *Aggression & Violent Behavior, 13*(3), 153–168.

Cheliotis, L. K. (2009). Before the next storm: Some evidence-based reminders about temporary release. *International Journal of Offender Therapy and Comparative Criminology, 53*(4), 420–432. doi: 10.1177/0306624X08316710.

Craddock, A. (2000). *Exploratory analysis of client outcomes, costs, and benefits of day reporting centers—Final report.* Washington, DC: U.S. Department of Justice. https://www.ncjrs.gov/pdffiles1/nij/grants/182365.pdf.

Craddock, A. (2004). Estimating criminal justice system costs and cost-savings benefits of day reporting centers. *Journal of Offender Rehabilitation, 39*(4), 69–98.

Craddock, A. (2009). Day reporting center completion: Comparison of individual and multilevel models. *Crime & Delinquency, 55*(1), 105–133. doi: 10.1177/001 1128707305743.

Craddock, A., & Graham, L. A. (2001). Recidivism as a function of day reporting center participation. *Journal of Offender Rehabilitation, 34*(1), 81–97. doi: 10.1300/J076v34n01_06.

Cullen, F. T., Blevins, K. R., Trager, J. S., & Gendreau, P. (2005). The rise and fall of boot camps: A case study in common-sense corrections. *Journal of Offender Rehabilitation, 40*(3/4), 53–70. doi: 10.1300/J076v40n03_03.

Curtin, E. L. (1996). Day reporting centers. In A. C. Association, *Correctional issues: Community corrections.* Lanham, MD: American Correctional Association.

DeMichele, M., & Payne, B. (2009). *Offender supervision with electronic technology.* Washington, DC: U.S. Department of Justice. Retrieved from http://www.appa-net.org/eweb/docs/appa/pubs/OSET_2.pdf.

Dolnick, S. (2012, June 16). As escapees stream out, a penal business thrives. *New York Times.* Retrieved from http://www.nytimes.com/2012/06/17/nyregion/in-new-jersey-halfway-houses-escapees-stream-out-as-a-penal-business-thrives.html.

Drake, E. K. (2007). *Does participation in Washington's work release facilities reduce recidivism?* Olympia, WA: Washington State Institute for Public Policy.

Dunlavey, D. (1969). Work release in Minnesota. *American Journal of Corrections, 31*(4), 28–29.

Duwe, G., & Kerschner, D. (2008). Removing a nail from the boot camp coffin. *Crime and Delinquency, 54*(4), 614–643. doi: 10.1177/0011128707301628.

Elder, J. P., & Cohen, S. H. (1978). Prediction of work release success with youthful, nonviolent, male offenders. *Criminal Justice and Behavior, 5*(2), 181–192. doi: 10.1177/009385487800500209.

Friedman, E. (2007, July 17). A different kind of bling: Bracelet tracks alcohol consumption. *ABC News.* Retrieved from http://abcnews.go.com/US/story?id=3383679&page=1.

Fulton, B., Latessa, E. J., Stichman, A., & Travis, L. F. (1997). The state of ISP: Research and policy implications. *Federal Probation, 61*, 65–75.

Gendreau, P., Goggin, C., Cullen, F. T., & Andrews, D. A. (2000). The effects of community sanctions and incarceration on recidivism. *Forum on Corrections Research, 12*, 10–13.

Gilna, D., Clarke, M., & Patel, P. (2015). When halfway houses pose full-time problems. *Prison Legal News, 26*(1), 1–18.

Goodnough, A. (2007, October 13). 8 acquitted in death of boy, 14, in Florida. *New York Times.* Retrieved from http://www.nytimes.com/2007/10/13/us/13bootcamp.html.

Gordon, W., & Chiricos, T. G. (1986). Work release and recidivism: An empirical evaluation of social policy. *Evaluation Quarterly, 1*(1), 87–108.

Gowen, D. (2001). Remote location monitoring — A supervision strategy to enhance risk control. *Federal Probation, 65*(2), 38–41.

Gunnison, E. (2012). An examination of female and male work release offenders: Risk factors, needs, and recidivism. *Journal of Community Corrections, 21*(4), 9–16.

Gunnison, E., & Helfgott, J. B. (2016). A day in the life of a day reporting center: A profile of needs & challenges of clients entering and exiting. *The Journal of Community Corrections, 25*(4), 5–14.

Hamilton, Z. K., & Campbell, C. M. (2014). Uncommonly observed: The impact of New Jersey's halfway house system. *Criminal Justice & Behaviour, 41*(11), 1354–1375. doi: 10.1177/0093854814546132.

Harris, P. M., Peterson, R. D., & Rapoza, S. (2001). Between probation and revocation: A study of intermediate sanctions decision-making. *Journal of Criminal Justice, 29*(4), 307–318. doi: 10.1016/S0047-2352(01)00090-3.

Hartmann, D. J., Friday, P. C., & Minor, K. I. (1994). Residential probation: A seven-year follow up study of halfway house discharges. *Journal of Criminal Justice, 22*(6), 503–515. doi: 10.1016/0047-2352(94)90092-2.

Humphrey, E. S. (1992). *Day reporting program profile.* Albany: State of New York Correctional Services.

International Association of Chiefs of Police. (2008). *Tracking sex offenders with electronic monitoring technology: Implications and practical uses for law enforcement.* Alexandria: VA. https://www.bja.gov/publications/IACPSexOffenderElec Monitoring.pdf.

Jeffrey, R., & Wolpert, S. (1974). Work furlough as an alternative to incarceration: An assessment of its effects on recidivism and social cost. *Journal of Criminal Law and Criminology, 65*(3), 405–415. doi: 10.2307/1142610.

Johnson, B. D., & Dipietro, S. M. (2012). The power of diversion: Intermediate sanctions and sentencing disparity under presumptive guidelines. *Criminology, 50*(3), 811–849. doi: 10.1111/j.1745-9125.2012.00279.x.

Johnson, E. H. (1967). Work release: A study of correctional reform. *Crime and Delinquency, 13*, 521–530. doi: 10.1177/001112876701300406.

Katz, J. F., & Decker, S. H. (1982). An analysis of work release: The institutionalization of unsubstantiated reforms. *Criminal Justice and Behavior, 9*(2), 229–250. doi: 10.1177/0093854882009002009.

Kenemore, T. K., & Roldan, I. (2006). Staying straight: Lessons from ex-offenders. *Clinical Social Work Journal, 34*(1), 5–21. doi: 10.1007/s10615-005-0003-7.

Kim, D.-Y., Spohn, C., & Foxall, M. (2007). An evaluation of the DRC in the context of Douglas County, Nebraska: A developmental perspective. *The Prison Journal, 87*(4), 434–456. doi: 10.1177/0032885507307144.

Klatell, J. (2006, November 28). 8 charged in teen's boot camp death. *CBS News.* Retrieved from http://www.cbsnews.com/news/8-charged-in-teens-boot-camp-death/.

Kurlycheck, M. C., Wheeler, A. P., Tinik, L., & Kempinen, C. A. (2011). How long after? A natural experiment assessing the impact of the length of aftercare service delivery on recidivism. *Crime & Delinquency, 57*(5), 778–800. doi: 10.1177/001 1128710382262.

Latessa, E., Lovins, L. B., & Smith, P. (2010). Follow-up evaluation of Ohio's community based correctional facility and halfway house programs—Outcome study. Cincinnati, OH: Center for Criminal Justice Research.

Latessa, E. J., & Smith, P. (2011). *Corrections in the community,* (4th ed.). Cincinnati, OH: Anderson.

LeClair, D. P. (1988). *The effect of community reintegration on rates of recidivism: A statistical overview of the data for the years 1971 through 1985.* Boston, MA: Massachusetts Department of Corrections, Research Division.

LeClair, D. P., & Guarino-Ghezzi, S. (1991). *Evaluating the prison furlough program in Massachusetts.* Boston, MA: Massachusetts Department of Corrections, Research Division.

Lilly, R. A., & Ball, R. (1987). Brief history of house arrest and electronic Monitoring. *Northern Kentucky Law Review, 13*(3), 343–373.

Long, E. V. (1965). The prisoner rehabilitation act of 1965. *Federal Probation, 4,* 3–7.

Lowenkamp, C. T., Flores, A. W., Holsinger, A. M., Makarios, M. D., & Latessa, E. J. (2010). Intensive supervision programs: Does program philosophy and the principles of effective intervention matter? *Journal of Criminal Justice, 38,* 368–375. doi: 10.1016/j.jcrimjus.2010.04.004

Lowenkamp, C. T., & Latessa, E. J. (2002). *Evaluation of Ohio's community based correctional facilities and halfway house programs* (Evaluation No. 56350044). Cincinnati, OH: Center for Criminal Justice Research.

Lurigio, A. J. (1996). Responding to the mentally ill on probation and parole: Recommendations and action plans. In A. J. Lurigio (Ed.). *Community corrections in America: New directions and sounder investments for persons with mental illness and codisorders* (pp. 166–171). Seattle, WA: National Coalition for Mental and Substance Abuse Health Care in the Justice System.

Lurigio, A. J., Olson, D. E., & Sifferd, K. (1999). A study of the Cook County day reporting center: The third in a series of evaluations. *Journal of Offender Monitoring, 12,* 5–12.

MacKenzie, D. L. (1997). Criminal justice and crime prevention. In L. W. Sherman, D. Gottfredson, D. MacKenzie, J. Eck, P. Reuter, & S. Bushway (Eds.), *Preventing crime: What works, what doesn't, what's promising.* Washington, DC: NIJ.

Macur, J. (2007, December 11). Vick receives 23 months and a lecture. *New York Times.* Retrieved from http://www.nytimes.com/2007/12/11/sports/football/11vick.html?pagewanted=all.

Marciniak, L. M. (1999). The use of day reporting as an intermediate sanction: A study of offender targeting and program termination. *The Prison Journal, 79*(2), 205–225.

Martin, C., Lurigio, A. J., & Olson, D. E. (2003). An examination of rearrests and reincarcerations among discharged day reporting center clients. *Federal Probation, 67,* 24–30.

Maske, M. (2009, February 26). Vick approved for home confinement. *Washington Post.* Retrieved from http://views.washingtonpost.com/theleague/nflnewsfeed/2009/02/vick-reportedly-approved-for-home-confinement.html.

McBride, D., & VanderWaal, C. (1997). Day reporting centers as an alternative for drug using offenders. *Journal of Drug Issues, 27*(2), 379–397. doi: 10.1177/002204269702700212.

McCartt, J. M., & Mangogna, T. J. (1973). *Guidelines and standards for halfway houses and community treatment centers.* Washington, DC: NCJRS. https://www.ncjrs.gov/pdffiles1/Digitization/9989NCJRS.pdf.

McDevitt, J., & Miliano, R. (1992). Day reporting centers: An innovative concept in intermediate sanctions. In J. M. Byrne, A. J. Lurigio, & J. Petersilia (Eds.), *Smart sentencing: The emergence of intermediate sanctions* (pp. 152–165). Newbury Park, CA: Sage Publications.

Meade, B., & Steiner, B. (2010). The total effects of boot camps that house juveniles: A systematic review of the evidence. *Journal of Criminal Justice, 38*(5), 841–853. doi: 10.1016/j.jcrimjus.2010.06.007.

Minton, T. D., & Zeng, Z. (2015). *Jail inmates at midyear 2014 — Statistical tables.* Washington, DC: United States Department of Justice, Bureau of Justice Statistics.

Mullings, J. L., Hartley, D. J., & Marquart, J. W. (2004). Exploring the relationship between alcohol use, childhood maltreatment, and treatment needs among female prisoners. *Substance Use & Misuse, 29*(2), 277–305. doi: 10.1081/JA-120028491.

Ostermann, M. (2009). An analysis of New Jersey's day reporting center and halfway back programs: Embracing the rehabilitative ideal through evidence based practices. *Journal of Offender Rehabilitation, 48*(2), 139–153. doi: 10.1080/10509670802640958.

Ostermann, M. (2013). Using day reporting centers to divert parolees from revocation. *Criminology & Public Policy, 12*(1), 163–171. doi: 10.1111/1745-9133.12013.

Parent, D. (1990). *Day reporting centers for criminal offenders: A descriptive analysis of existing programs.* Washington, DC: U.S. Department of Justice.

Parent, D. E. (2003). *Correctional boot camps: Lessons learned from a decade of research.* Washington, DC: NIJ. https://www.ncjrs.gov/pdffiles1/nij/197018.pdf.

Parent, D., Byrne, J. M., Tsarfaty, V., Valade, L., & Esselman, J. (1995). Day reporting centers, Vols. 1 and 2. Washington, DC: Department of Justice, National Institute of Justice.

Pattavina, A. (2009). The use of electronic monitoring as persuasive technology: reconsidering the empirical evidence on the effectiveness of electronic monitoring. *Victims & Offenders, 4*, 385–390.doi: 10.1080/15564880903260611.

Petersilia, J. (2003). *When prisoners come home: Parole and prisoner reentry.* New York: Oxford University Press.

Petersilia, J., & Turner, S. (1992). An evaluation of intensive probation in California. *The Journal of Criminal Law and Criminology, 82*, 610–658. doi: 10.2307/1143747.

Petersilia, J., & Turner, S. (1993). *Evaluating intensive supervision probation/parole: Results of a nationwide experiment.* Washington, DC: NCJRS. https://www.ncjrs. gov/pdffiles1/Digitization/141637NCJRS.pdf.

Renzema, M., & Mayo-Wilson, E. (2005). Can electronic monitoring reduce crime for moderate to high-risk offenders? *Journal of Experimental Criminology, 1*, 215–237.

Roy, S. (2002). Adult offenders in a day reporting center: A preliminary study. *Federal Probation, 66*, 44–50.

Roy, S., & Barton, S. (2006). Convicted drunk drivers in electronic monitoring home detention and day reporting centers: An exploratory study. *Federal Probation*, 49–55.

Roy, S., & Grimes, J. N. (2002). Adult offenders in a day reporting center: A preliminary study. *Federal Probation, 66*(1), 44–50.

Rudoff, A., & Esselstyn, T. C. (1973). Evaluating work furlough: A follow-up. *Federal Probation, 37*(2), 48–53.

Savage, D. (2015, March 30). Supreme court questions lifetime monitoring of sex offenders. *L.A. Times.* Retrieved from http://www.latimes.com/nation/la-na-supreme-court-sex-offenders-20150330-story.html.

Seiter, R. P., Carlson, E. W., Bowman, H. H., Grandfield, J. J., & Beran, N. J. (1977). *Halfway houses.* Washington, DC: U.S. Department of Justice. https://www.ncjrs. gov/pdffiles1/Digitization/148740NCJRS.pdf.

Seiter, R., & Kadela, K. (2003). Prisoner reentry: What works, what does not, and what is promising. *Crime and Delinquency, 49*(3): 360–388. doi: 10.1177/001112 8703049003002.

Sexton, C. J. (2006, May 6). Autopsy ties boy's death to boot camp. *New York Times.* Retrieved from http://www.nytimes.com/2006/05/06/us/06bootcamp.html?_r=0.

Smith, L. G., & Akers, R. L. (1993). A comparison of recidivism of Florida's community control and prison: A five-year survival analysis. *Journal of Research in Crime and Delinquency, 30*, 267–292. doi: 10.1177/0022427893030003002

Spencer, S. (2012). Day reporting centers: A service delivery model. *Journal of Community Corrections, 21*(2), 11–26.

Steiner, B., & Butler, H. D. (2013). Why didn't they work? Thoughts on the application of New Jersey day reporting centers. *Criminology & Public Policy, 12*(1), 153–162. doi: 10.1111/1745-9133.12014.

Steiner, B., & Giacomazzi, A. L. (2007). Juvenile waiver, boot camp, and recidivism in a Northwestern State. *Prison Journal, 87*(2), 227–240. doi: 10.1177/003288550 7303750.

Subramanian, R., & Shames, A. (2013). *Sentencing and prison practices in Germany and the Netherlands: Implications for the United States.* Vera Institute of Justice.

Retrieved from http://www.vera.org/sites/default/files/resources/downloads/european-american-prison-report-v3.pdf.

Sullivan, J. (2011, May 10). Seattle courts to trade jail for ankle bracelets. *Seattle Times.* Retrieved from http://www.seattletimes.com/seattle-news/seattle-courts-to-trade-jail-for-ankle-bracelets/.

Turner, S., & Petersilia, J. (1996). Work release in Washington: Effects on recidivism and corrections costs. *The Prison Journal, 76*(2), 138–164. doi: 10.1177/003285 5596076002003.

U.S. Department of Justice. (1990). *Survey of intermediate sanctions.* Washington, DC: U.S. Government Printing Office.

Waldo, G. P., & Chiricos, T. G. (1977). Work release and recidivism: An empirical evaluation of a social policy. *Evaluation Quarterly, 1*(1), 87–108.

Washington State Department of Corrections. (2013). *Work release data sheet.* Retrieved from http://doc.wa.gov/facilities/workrelease/docs/WRDataFactSheet.pdf.

White, M. D., Goldkamp, J. S., & Campbell, S. P. (2006). Co-occurring mental illness and substance abuse in the criminal justice system: Some implications for local jurisdictions. *The Prison Journal, 86*(3), 1–26. doi: 10.1177/0032885506290852.

Wiliszowski, C. H., Fell, J. C., McKnight, A. S., Tippetts, A. S., & Ciccel, J. D. (2010). An evaluation of three intensive supervision programs for serious DWI offenders. *Annuals in Advances of Automotive Medicine, 54*, 375–387.

Zalba, S. R. (1967). Work-release-a two-pronged effort. *Crime and Delinquency, 13*, 506–512. doi: 10.1177/0032885506290852.

Zedleeski, E. W. (2010). *Alternatives to custodial supervision: The day fine.* Washington, DC: NIJ. https://www.ncjrs.gov/pdffiles1/nij/grants/230401.pdf.

Chapter 6

Parole: Historical Overview & Current Status

Student Learning Outcomes

After reading this chapter, you should be able to:

- Describe the history of parole.
- Explain the current status of parole in the United States.
- Summarize the effectiveness of parole.

Introduction

Unlike probation, parole tends to get less media press—unless the offender commits a heinous crime on parole. One infamous parolee that captivated the attention of the nation and the international community in the early 1990s and whose case spawned sentencing legislation was a parolee named Richard Allen Davis. Davis was an offender with a significant rap sheet who first entered into the criminal justice system at the age of 12. Throughout Davis's life, he committed a variety of crimes, ranging from burglaries to kidnapping to attempted sexual assaults. For these criminal acts, he had received numerous forms of punishment such as probation and incarceration sentences, and he had been granted parole in the past as well. However, it was his abduction, sexual assault, and killing of 12-year-old Polly Klaas in Petaluma, California, in 1993 that caused national outrage (Associated Press, 1996). The crime was egregious by any measure, but the fact that Davis, a hardened criminal, had committed the crime while on parole for a previous kidnapping infuriated the nation. Davis had only been on parole for three months when he wandered into Petaluma, stalked Klaas, and later entered her home through an open window (Associated Press, 1996). Then, he abducted Klaas from her bedroom where she was having a sleepover with friends and later sexually assaulted and murdered her (Associated Press, 1996). The fact that a parolee committed such a horrific act on an innocent girl rattled citizens, who then demanded that community members should be protected from predators such as Davis. In 1993, a **"three strikes law"** was passed in Washington State, whereby offenders who were convicted of a third felony would receive life without the possibility of parole. With the outrage over the Klaas murder, many states, including California in 1994, quickly adopted sentencing enhancements for serious of-

Image 11. © hafakot/Fotolia.

fenders utilizing the terminology of the "three strikes law" (Clark, Austin, & Henry, 1997). These three strikes laws still exist in many states today. Ultimately, Davis was convicted for the Klaas murder in 1996 and sentenced to death (Associated Press, 1996). He is still on death row.

More often than not, it is the cases where a parolee has committed a crime while on parole that draws citizens' attention to the use of parole in the criminal justice system. However, there are a few exceptions where parolees are not vilified in the media. One exception might be Animal Planet's show entitled, *Pit Bulls and Parolees*. This show depicts two groups (i.e., pit bulls and ex-offenders) in society that are viewed rather unfavorably by the general public, and the struggles each face to reenter society. In this show, parolees are reforming their lives through working with pit bulls. Specifically, the parolees rehabilitate and train pit bulls in order to facilitate adoption of these dogs to the general public. The pairing of these two groups not only serves as entertainment, but it also demonstrates that parole can be successful for some offenders and should perhaps not be abolished as it has in some states (e.g., Washington).

The aforementioned case and television show highlight the fact that parole is a concept that many in the U.S. are familiar with in some capacity. This chapter devotes attention defining parole and providing a historical overview of parole, including a discussion of the origin of parole in the United States and its role in the criminal justice system. Additionally, this chapter will discuss the current status of parole in the United States and will include discussion of the characteristics of those serving parole sentences. Further, a thorough review of research regarding the effectiveness of parole is provided.

Defining Parole

Oftentimes, individuals mix up the terms probation and parole and regard parole as the same sentence as probation, but this could not be farther from the truth. Thus, a clear definition of parole is needed as well as a discussion of the nuts and bolts regarding how the parole sentence works. According to the American Probation and Parole Association (2014), "**Parole** refers to the term of supervision that occurs once offenders are conditionally released to the community after serving a prison term. Parolees are subject to being returned to jail or prison for rule violations or other offenses." That is, individuals first serve a prison term, and then are granted release early from their term to serve the remainder of their sentence in the community under the supervision of a corrections official—a parole officer.

The determination of whether an offender may be released from prison early is made by the **parole board**. A parole board is a panel of individuals such as retired judges, former law enforcement officers, and/or victim advocates who determine whether an inmate who is eligible for parole, should be released on parole. Each state has its own eligibility criteria which list the conditions that must be satisfied for offenders to be considered for parole. For example, in the state of Connecticut, offenders who have been convicted of felony murder or aggravated sexual assault in the first degree are not eligible to be considered for parole (Connecticut Board or Pardons and Parolees, 2013). Additionally, offenders considered to be high risk or to have criminal charges pending in Connecticut are also not eligible (Connecticut Board or Pardons and Parolees, 2013). Many states also require that offenders serve a significant portion of their sentence before they are eligible for parole. One reason that offenders must serve a significant portion of their sentences stems from **truth-in-sentencing laws** that were passed in the 1980s. Truth-in-sentencing laws usually require that violent offenders serve a greater percentage of their sentences, typically 85% or more, in order to be considered for parole (Travis, 2001). The federal government also encouraged states to adopt truth-in-sentencing laws and provided states with financial incentives for the implementation of these laws with the passage of the Violent Offender Incarceration and Truth-in-Sentencing Grants Program as part of the Violent Crime Control and Law Enforcement Act of 1994 (Seiter & Kadela, 2003; Shepherd, 2002; Turner, Greenwood, Fain, & Chiesa, 2006; Weinstein & Wimmer, 2010). Thus, many states, such as Connecticut, do require offenders to serve at least 85% of their original sentence.

When deciding whether to grant parole, the parole board will consider many factors, such as prior record, the offense the offender committed, behavior while incarcerated, and whether the offender will likely adjust into the community successfully upon release (see Text Box 6.1).

Text Box 6.1: Criteria Utilized in Parole Decisions by Board in Maryland

By law, the Commission must consider the following criteria when making any decisions about parole:

- The circumstances surrounding the crime;
- The offender's physical, mental, and moral qualifications;

- The offender's progress during confinement;
- Whether there is a reasonable probability the offender will not violate the law if paroled;
- Whether the offender's parole would be compatible with the welfare of society;
- Any original or updated victim impact statement, and/or any information presented by the victim at a meeting with a Commissioner and/or at the time of an open parole hearing; and
- Any sentencing judge's recommendation.

In assessing these criteria, the Commission may also consider other relevant information, such as:

- Prior criminal and juvenile record:
- Prior substance abuse;
- Attitude and emotional maturity;
- Home and employment plans.

Source: Maryland Department of Public Safety and Correctional Services. Frequently asked questions: Maryland Parole Board: Parole and Parole Hearings. http://www.dpscs.state.md.us/about/FAQmpc.shtml#parol.

The board can have other functions, such as assessing whether parole should be revoked for a parolee, which will be explored more in Chapter 10. The size of parole a board varies by state, ranging from three members to nineteen (Michigan Department of Corrections, 2014; New York State Division of Parole, 2014). Similar to probation, parole is an act of grace extended by the board, thereby offenders cannot claim that they have a constitutional right to receive parole (Savage, 2011). Some researchers have been critical of parole boards, questioning whether they can accurately determine whether the offender is truly capable of reintegrating back into society successfully (Walker, 2013). After all, these critics wonder if members of the parole board are adequately trained in assessing risk in offenders—especially if these members are only considering a few risk factors in their decision such as prior record and offense history. The concern over whether parole boards are indeed effective in making release decisions has led to some states adopting computerized software programs, such as Compas, that can calculate the offender's odds of recidivating to aid parole boards in their decision-making process (Walker, 2013).

Additionally, like probationers, parolees must follow guidelines while on parole as they are under "conditional release." The released offender agrees to follow conditions or rules while on parole, and, if he/she violates any of the conditions, the offender can be returned to prison to serve the remainder of their sentence. All offenders who receive a parole sentence must follow **general conditions**. General conditions are rules that apply to all parolees. Examples of general conditions include: not possessing a firearm, not committing a new crime, not associating with other convicted felons, following a curfew, not taking illegal substances, random drug testing, the prohibition of moving and/or traveling out of state, and meeting with the assigned parole officer for a specified time (e.g., once per week). (See Text Box 6.2). Additionally, parolees must abide by **specific conditions**—are rules that apply to the specific offender based on his/her offense and needs. In addition to following general conditions applied to all parolees, an offender may, for instance, be prohibited from consuming alcohol or frequenting any establishment where the primary service is the serving of alcohol (i.e., a bar) or where children are likely to congregate if the individual is a child sexual offender.

Text Box 6.2: General Conditions of Federal Parole

The General Conditions of Release for Parole are established by the United States Parole Commission:

1. You shall go directly to the district named in the certificate (unless released to the custody of other authorities). Within three days after your release, you shall report to the supervision office named on the certificate. If in any emergency you are unable to get in touch with the supervision office, you shall communicate with the United States Parole Commission, Chevy Chase, MD 20815-7286.

2. If you are released to the custody of other authorities, and after release from the physical custody of such authorities, you are unable to report to the supervision office within three days, you shall instead report to the nearest U.S. Probation Officer.

3. You shall not leave the geographic limits fixed by the certificate of release without written permission from your Supervision Officer.

4. You shall make a complete and truthful written report (on a form provided for that purpose) to your Supervision Officer between the first and third day of each month, and on the final day of parole. You shall also report to your Supervision Officer at other times as your Supervision Officer directs, providing complete and truthful information.

5. You shall not violate any law. You shall not associate with persons engaged in criminal activity. You shall get in touch within two (2) days with your Supervision Officer if you are arrested or questioned by a law-enforcement officer.

6. You shall not associate with persons who have a criminal record without the permission of your Supervision Officer.

   You shall not enter into any agreement to act as an informer or special agent for any law-enforcement agency without permission from your Supervision Officer.

7. You shall work regularly unless excused by your Supervision Officer and support your legal dependents, if any, to the best of your ability. You shall report within two (2) days to your Supervision Officer any changes in employment. You shall notify your Supervision Officer within two (2) days any change in your place of residence.

8. You shall not drink alcoholic beverages to excess. You shall not purchase, possess, sell, manufacture, use or distribute any controlled substance or drug paraphernalia unless such usage is pursuant to a lawful order of a practitioner and you promptly notify your Supervision Officer of same.

9. You shall not frequent places where such drugs are illegally sold, dispensed, used or given away.

10. You shall not own, possess, use, sell, or have under your control any firearm, ammunition, or other dangerous weapons.

11. You shall permit visits by your Supervision Officer to your residence and to your place of business or occupation. You shall permit confiscation by your Supervision Officer of any materials which the officer believes may constitute contraband in your possession and which he observes in plain view of your residence, place of business or occupation, vehicle(s), or on your person. The Commission may also, when a reasonable basis for so doing is presented, modify the conditions of parole to require you to permit the Supervision Officer to conduct searches and seizures of concealed contraband on your person, and in any building, vehicle, or other area under your control, at such times as the Supervision Officer shall decide.

12. You shall make a diligent effort to satisfy any fine, restitution order, court costs or assessment and/or court ordered child support or alimony payment that has been, or may be, imposed, and shall provide such financial information as may be requested, by your Supervision Officer, relevant to the payment of the obligation. If unable to pay the obligation in one sum, you will cooperate with your Supervision Officer in establishing an installment payment schedule.

13. You shall be screened for the presence of controlled substances by appropriate tests as may be required by your Supervision Officer.

14. You shall cooperate fully with those responsible for your supervision.

15. You shall carry out the instructions of your Supervision Officer and report that failure to do so may be sufficient to cause your return to the institution.

16. You shall submit to the sanctions imposed by your Supervision Officer (within the limits established by the approved Schedule of Accountability Through Graduated Sanctions), if the Supervision Officer finds that you have tested positive for illegal drugs or that you have committed any non-criminal violation of the release conditions.

    Graduated sanctions may include community service, curfew with electronic monitoring and/or a period of time in a community treatment center. Your failure to cooperate with a graduated sanction imposed by your Supervision Officer will subject you to the issuance of summons or warrant by the Commission, and a revocation hearing at which time you will be afforded the opportunity to contest the violation charge(s) upon which the sanction was based. If the Commission finds that you have violated parole as alleged, you will also be found to have violated this condition. In addition, the Commission may override the imposition of a graduated sanction at any time and issue a warrant or summons if it finds that you are a risk to the public safety or that you are not complying with this condition in good faith.

17. If you have been convicted of any sexual offense under District of Columbia or federal law (including the Uniform Code of Military Justice), you must report for registration with your state (including the District of Columbia) sex offender registration agency as directed by your Supervision Officer. You are required to report for registration in any state (including the District of Columbia) in which you live, work, attend school or have local convictions for sexual offenses, and in compliance with 42 U.S.C. §14072(i) (which makes it a federal crime for any offender covered by 18 U.S.C. §4042 not to register in accordance with state law). If there is any question as to whether or where you are required to register, you must seek and follow the guidance of your Supervision Officer.

Source: Court Services and Offender Supervision Agency. Parole: General conditions of release. Retrieved from http://www.csosa.gov/supervision/types/parole/release-conditions.aspx.

History of Parole

The origins of parole in the United States can be traced to penal system practices in England and across Europe (Witmer, 1927a). Beginning in the 1600s, England transported poor women, men, and children as well as convicted and pardoned criminals to both North America and Australia. Initially, the pardoned and convicted criminals sent to the developing countries had no conditions placed on them, however, this practice changed as many evaded being transported or returned to England. Eventually, English officials instituted specific conditions for convicted and pardoned offenders. If, for example, a pardoned offender returned to England, the pardon would be nullified, which would result in the offender facing punishment in England—typically death (Witmer, 1927a). When pardoned offenders reached North America, their services were sold to the highest bidder, and they became indentured servants. Additionally, convicted offenders to be transported to North America were expected to report to a contractor, who was paid by officials to transport him/her to the colonies (Witmer, 1927a). Many convicted offenders lingered around in England and did not report for transportation, even though the punishment was hanging, due to the harsh conditions of the journey, which was fraught with disease (Witmer, 1927a). For convicted offenders sent to North America, some were allowed to go free, yet others were also required to become indentured for a specified period of time (Pisciotta, 1982). England ceased transporting offenders to North America following the end of the American Revolutionary War in 1783 (Witmer, 1927a).

Apart from the conditional release of offenders in North America, the use of conditional liberation for prisoners of war in France also provided the foundation for parole. In 1791, during the French Revolution, French officials allowed prisoners of war to be released if they promised to give their "word of honor," or **parole d'honneur**, that they would not rejoin the war efforts (Cohen, 2014). As early as 1811, England had established a **ticket-of-leave system** whereby those offenders who were transported from England to other countries could return after their sentences were completed (Witmer, 1927a). However, upon return, offenders were not supported in their reintegration back into their community, which created problems and some public outrage (Witmer, 1927a). One of the first early conditional release systems began in 1835 in a prison in Spain. This early precursor to parole allowed offenders to receive up to a one-third reduction in their sentence if they demonstrated good behavior while incarcerated and also demonstrated a commitment to reform their behavior (Lindsey, 1925). A similar system was implemented in Germany in the 1840s (Lindsey, 1925). Despite these early efforts, it is the work by **Alexander Maconochie** that led to the development of parole. Maconochie is considered the founder of parole and is often referred to as the "father of parole" (Witmer, 1927a). In 1840, Maconochie, a former British naval officer, became superintendent of the penal colony on Norfolk Island— an island approximately 1,000 miles off the coast of Australia that held over 2,000 hardened convicted offenders (Witmer, 1927a). He established the **marks system**, whereby the convicts were granted credits for good behavior and these credits were taken away when they behaved poorly. For example, the offenders could use their credits to buy goods, such as food, or receive reductions in their sentence (i.e., one-day reductions of sentence for every 10 marks earned) (Witmer, 1927a). His focus was on reforming the individual, instilling self-discipline, and requiring offenders to earn release. Maconochie advocated for sentences that were not fixed but indeterminate in length in order for offenders to work for their release. Thus, his philosophy of punishment provided the foundation for **indeterminate sentences** that operate today in the U.S. criminal justice system. While Maconochie achieved great success on Norfolk Island, he was still not able to quell all the riots that occurred at the prison or to satisfy critics of his work who disapproved of his efforts and viewed him as too soft on offenders. By 1844, he was relieved of his duties at the prison, and by 1867, prisoners were no longer transported from England to Australia (Morris, 2002). Although he was relieved of his duties, Maconochie wrote and spoke extensively about his ideals, and his philosophy of punishment influenced others (Morris, 2002).

One individual who was very much influenced by Maconochie was **Sir Walter Crofton**, the director of the Irish prison system in the 1850s (Witmer, 1927a). He established the **Irish system**, whereby offenders were first placed in solitary confinement, followed by placement in a prison to work alongside others, and then they transferred to another prison facility where they could earn early release. It is in this third stage that Crofton adopted Maconochie's mark system, and with a few modifications, implemented his own version of a ticket-of-leave system (Witmer, 1927a). Unlike the system in England, his system allowed offenders to leave the institution and work in the community before their sentence officially had ended, however, they had to earn their release. Additionally, this ticket, or license, required that offenders follow certain conditions, such as not committing a new crime or checking in with Crofton or another assigned supervisor (e.g., a police officer) at various times, or they would be returned to the institution (Witmer, 1927a). Essentially, Crofton and others assigned to supervise offenders served the function of a parole officer. Offenders in his system fared much better than offenders who partook in England's original ticket-of-leave system due to the level of support and supervision they received (Witmer, 1927a).

The United States had been already dabbling a bit with parole concepts even before Crofton's efforts. For instance, in 1817, New York passed a **good time law** where offenders received a slight deduction in their sentence for good behavior, and thus, these offenders could earn a bit of early release (Roth, 2010). Despite the implementation of good time credits in New York and many other states in the following decades, it was really the work by Crofton which was widely publicized and greatly influenced the development of parole in the United States. **Zebulon Brockway**, an American penologist, was inspired by Crofton's work and pushed for the implementation of a parole system in the United States (Hinkle & Whitmarsh, 2014). In 1876, Brockway got his chance to implement such a system when he was appointed to the new Elmira Reformatory in New York—a prison designed for male offenders age 16–30 (Hinkle & Whitmarsh, 2014). With the establishment of an indeterminate sentencing law in New York the same year, Brockway immediately began his efforts at reformation. He adopted a system of marching and discipline, vocational training, and required offenders to earn release (Hinkle & Whitmarsh, 2014). For offenders with good behavior, they would be granted early release, but they were still required to be supervised by a guardian in the community for at least six months. Thus, early release for offenders was conditional. Parole had now been officially established in the United States. It also did not take long to spread to other states as well. Less than 15 years later in 1900, almost 20 states had adopted a parole system, and by 1944, all states had adopted parole (Lindsey, 1925; O'Toole, 2006). It was also not long before the federal government established parole in 1910 in a few federal penitentiaries and by 1930 formally established a federal parole board, known as the United Stated Parole Board and later renamed the U.S. Parole Commission in 1976 (Hoffman, 2003). Part of the popularity of parole was due to a few factors including: (1) the focus on reformation, which was a key ideal during the early 1900s; (2) the approval of it by prison administrators who found that prisoners behaved better due to parole serving as sort of a "light at the end of the tunnel" for offenders; and (3) the potential cost savings to the institution by creating a release valve where overcrowded and underfunded facilities could save money by releasing offenders early. Despite the spread of parole and its popularity, it did experience quite a bit of backlash beginning in the 1970s.

One reason for the backlash against parole was due to an abandonment by many of the rehabilitative ideal—a core foundation of the principle of parole. The abrupt departure from rehabilitation can also be partly attributed to research conducted by Martinson (1974). In 1974, Martinson, who reviewed 231 studies of prison rehabilitation programs, declared that nothing works in regards to rehabilitation and that offender treatment was essentially ineffective. This research shook the foundation of correctional administrators and the public. If rehabilitation was as ineffective as Martinson claimed, then perhaps it should not be the focus in corrections anymore. The abandonment of rehabilitation became the platform for the conservatives, who were already disillusioned with the use of rehabilitation. Many conservatives viewed the use of rehabilitation to be indicative of being soft on crime, which was at odds with their "get-tough-on-crime" philosophy. This view would come to be shared by many. The pendulum had swung in the criminal justice system from a rehabilitative model to more of a crime control model.

With rehabilitation no longer the concern of administrators, sentencing practices also had shifted from an indeterminate model to a determinate model. With the departure from indeterminate sentencing, concerns about disparity in the parole system, concerns about public safety with parolees comingling with the general U.S. population, and the view that parole was too soft, many states began to abolish parole. Maine was the first state to do so in 1976 with six other states following suit by 1979 (Krajick, 1983). The federal system soon followed. The Comprehensive Crime Control Act of 1984 established the use of determinate sentencing via its Sentencing Reform Act provision and the federal system began to phase out of the use of parole for federal offenders (Hoffman, 2003). Approximately 15 states have abolished parole for all offenders (Seiter & Kadela, 2003). Washington State is one such example, having abolished parole in 1984. The Board of Prison Terms and Paroles, as it was then known, was disbanded and replaced with the Indeterminate Sentence Review Board (ISRB) in 1986. The ISRB Board makes parole decisions for felony offenders who committed crimes before July 1, 1984, and were sentenced to prison terms (Indeterminate Sentencing Review Board, 2008). Additionally, the ISRB Board makes decisions regarding release for sex offenders who committed offenses after August 31, 2001 (Indeterminate Sentencing Review Board, 2008). If, based on evidence, it is believed that a sex offender will likely commit another sex offense upon release, the ISRB Board may add up to 60 additional months to the original sentence for the sex offender. A few other states have not necessarily abolished parole but scaled back its use. For instance, the passage of the Sentencing Reform Act of 1998 in the state of New York, also referred to as Jenna's Law, abolished the use of parole for all offenders who commit violent offenses (New York State Division of Parole, 2014). See Text Box 6.3 for information about parole in other countries.

Text Box 6.3: Parole Around the World

While parole was implemented in England in the 1700s and in the United States in the 1800s, across the globe, parole was implemented in many countries much later. For example, in South Africa, parole was not established until 1910 (Department of Correctional Services, 1992). Parole was established in India in 1919, and its use is very limited (Roth, 2005). Although parole can be traced back to practices in Australia, the country did not formally adopt parole until the 1950s (O'Toole, 2006). In other countries, such as in China, the use of parole is rarely implemented. For instance, parole will not be granted to a prisoner in China unless he/she has exhibited exceptional good behavior (Dui Hua, 2010). It has been estimated that only 3–5% of prisoners are released on parole in China each year (Dui Hua, 2010). The only other means of parole release in China besides good behavior is medical parole, or early release on parole due to a medical condition (Dui Hua, 2010). Thus, unlike probation, parole has not been implemented or used as widely as its counterpart.

Organization of Parole

Those states which still grant parole employ a state parole board to provide recommendations for which offenders that are eligible may be granted parole. Within these states, parole officers are hired to supervise parolees as part of the Department of Corrections or an independent parole agency. The most recent survey of state parole revealed that there were 52 agencies with approximately 2,200 parole agency offices (Bonczar, 2008). Although the federal government eliminated parole for federal crimes with the passage of the Sentencing Reform Act of 1984, parole is still an option for federal offenders who committed crimes before November 1, 1987 (U.S. Department of Justice, 2014). Therefore, there are offenders who committed federal crimes on parole today. The United States Parole Commission is the official authority that grants release decisions, establishes parole conditions, and determines when parole supervision will be terminated (U.S. Department of Justice, 2014). The officers who supervise federal parolees work in the federal district courts across the nation in divisions referred to as the U.S. Courts Probation and Pretrial Services. While these officers primarily supervise probationers, they are assigned some federal parolees to supervise as well (Federal Judicial Center, 2014). Thus, it is possible for a federal probation officer to have a dual role as a parole officer!

Status of Parole

In comparison to probation and incarceration, parole is the smallest component of the correctional system with approximately 856,000 adults on state and federal parole in 2014 (Kaeble, Maruschak, & Bonczar, 2015). Specifically, parolees accounted for a mere 18% of the total corrections population (Kaeble et al., 2015). As highlighted in Figure 6.1, the number of adults on parole has steadily increased since 2000. The larger increase in numbers of those serving parole sentences beginning in the year 2006 corresponds to the economic recession in the United States during that same time period. During the economic recession, many budgets of state criminal justice agencies (e.g.,

Figure 6.1: Trends in Adult Parole, 2000–2014

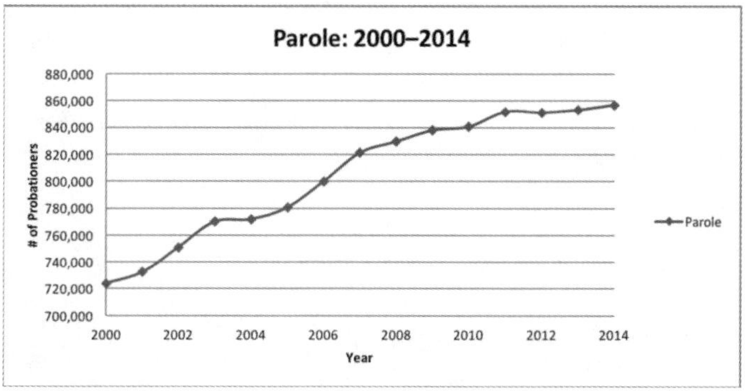

Source: Kaeble, D., Maruschak, L. M., & Bonczar, T. P. (2015). *Probation and parole in the United States, 2014.* Washington, DC: U.S. Department of Justice.

courts, corrections) found their operating budgets slashed. Scott-Hayward (2009) reported that cuts to the department of corrections budgets was a national problem plaguing 26 states in 2010. Because of this, many states began rethinking their parole release policies and began releasing offenders from prisons and placing more on parole due to cost. The use of parole is much more cost effective per year than incarcerating offenders in prison for the same year (La Vigne & Samuels, 2012). The Pew Center on the States (2009) reports that in 2008, the average cost of incarcerating an offender per year in prison is 29K, however, the average annual cost of parole ranges from $1,250 to $2,750.

Characteristics of Parolees

While the number of individuals granted parole over the last decade has increased, the characteristics of probationers have not changed much. For instance, adults sentenced to parole in 2014 were predominately male and Caucasian (see Text Box 6.4) (Kaeble et al., 2015). When comparing statistics on the percentages of adult parolees for the years 2000 and 2014, the percentage of both male and female parolees remained the same with 88% in 2000 and in 2014 for males and 12% in 2000 and 2014 for females (see Text Box 6.4) (Kaeble et al., 2015). In regards to the race and ethnicity of parolees, Kaeble et al. (2015, p. 7) report that in 2014, "16% of the parole population was Hispanic or Latino, compared to 17% in 2013 and 21% in 2000, and 43% percent of parolees were white, up from 38% in 2000" (see Text Box 6.4). Additionally, in 2014, 31% of adult parolees under supervision had committed a violent offense (see Text Box 6.4) (Kaeble et al., 2015). Further, the majority (84%) of adult parolees were under active supervision with only 5% on inactive parole, and only 6% absconded (i.e., violated probation and his/her whereabouts are unknown (see Text Box 6.4) (Kaeble et al., 2015).

The actual statistics of juveniles placed on parole are non-existent. This is due to the fact that parole is not an integral part of the juvenile justice system. It is estimated that 100,000 youth are released from the juvenile justice system each year and not on parole per se (Nellis & Wayman, 2009). In fact, juvenile parole boards are rare with

---

Text Box 6.4: Characteristics of Adult Parolees, 2000, 2013, & 2014

Characteristic	2000	2013	2014
Sex			
Male	88%	89%	88%
Female	12%	12%	12%
Race/Origin			
White	38%	43%	43%
Black/African American	40%	38%	39%
Hispanic/Latino	21%	17%	16%
American Indian/Alaska Native	1%	1%	1%
Asian/Pacific Islander	—	1%	1%
Status of Supervision			
Active	83%	84%	84%
Inactive	4%	5%	5%
Absconder	7%	6%	6%
Financial conditions remaining	—	—	0
Supervised out of state	5%	4%	4%
Most Serious Offense			
Violent	—	29%	31%
Property	—	22%	22%
Drug	—	32%	31%
Weapon	—	4%	4%
Other	—	13%	12%

— Less than .05%

Source: Kaeble, D., Maruschak, L. M., & Bonczar, T. P. (2015). *Probation and parole in the United States, 2014.* Washington, DC: U.S. Department of Justice.

---

only five states even having such a board (Frendle, 2004). Rather, when juvenile offenders complete their incarceration sentences, they are released on "aftercare" as opposed to "parole." Upon release, aftercare programs are designed to assist juveniles upon release by syncing them up to mentors and/or case managers, and to help them in reunification with family and seeking employment (Nellis & Wayman, 2009). More detail and discussion on the experiences of juveniles on aftercare, or parole in some states, will be explored in Chapter 7.

Financial Costs of Parole

With budget cuts abounding in corrections, virtually all states collect some form of parole supervision fee (Scott-Hayward, 2009). The fees collected from the parolee help to subsidize the cost of parole and save taxpayers money (Peterson, 2012). The cost of the supervision fee varies widely by state. It can cost a parolee as little as $21/month in Montana, up to $45/month in Tennessee, and supervision fees are on a sliding scale for parolees in South Carolina (Montana Department of Corrections, 2014; South Carolina Board of Probation, Parole, and Pardon Services, 2014; Tennessee Board of Parole, 2014). As Peterson (2012, p. 40) explains, "Policies on supervision fees across the country are geared almost exclusively toward raising revenue and generally give local departments a high degree of discretion to institute and collect fees as they see fit. The patchwork of policies has proved an obstacle to national data on how much is being collected, and local departments vary greatly in claims of success." In some states, such as New Jersey, parolees, particularly sex offenders, receive parole sentences for life (New Jersey State Parole Board, 2014). Thus, the collection of supervision fees is of grave concern as these parolees are saddled with fees for the remainder of their lives.

Similar to probationers, parolees also have many legal financial obligations (LFOs), which include fees administered by the courts such as filing fees, fees for a jury trial, jail fees, warrant fees, fees for a public defender, DNA collection fee, and restitution orders (Evans, 2014; Harris, Evans, & Beckett, 2010). In addition, parolees may be saddled with other debt such as tax deficiencies, child support payments, and out-standing bills (e.g., credit card or utility bills) (Griswold & Pearson, 2005; Richards & Jones, 2004). Thus, debt for the parolee mounts while they are incarcerated and, upon release, additional LFOs are added, resulting in almost unsurmountable obstacles in their bid at successful reentry (Pogrebin, West-Smith, Walker, & Unnithan, 2014).

Parolees have difficulties obtaining employment or finding employment that has a suitable wage and, thus, really struggle with paying their LFOs (Evans, 2014; Gun-nison & Helfgott, 2013; Pogrebin et al., 2014). Pogrebin et al. (2014) interviewed 70 men and women parolees in Colorado to explore the role of employment and LFOs in regards to reentry.

One subject reported on the difficulties of LFOs, "I have restitution, which is $152 every month. And then I have three UA's a month, so that's $45 a month and a $10 parole supervision fee, so that's about $207 a month" (Pogrebin et al., 2014, p. 402). If parolees are unable to pay for their required treatment program, their urine analysis (UA), or other supervision fees, their failure to pay can result in a technical violation (Evans, 2014). For example, Pogrebin et al. (2014, p. 404) report, "Respondents ex-plained that if one shows up for a UA and is unable to pay, the company giving the test for drug use counts the parolee as a no-show. Two or more missed UA's are grounds for a technical parole violation." Some subjects in their study absconded due to their inability to pay. If parolees are required to pay fees, but they are unable to due to the lack of sufficient finances or the inability to obtain legal employment, it appears that the stage has been set for failure rather than successful reentry (Pogrebin et al., 2014).

The concern over fees imposed on offenders has arisen with much concern directed towards the economically disadvantaged, who are crippled by such costs, and other disenfranchised members of our community—that is, convicted offenders. Addition-ally, further refining the lens of disenfranchisement, Pogrebin and colleagues (2014) express concern regarding how such LFOs may further inhibit successful reentry for parolees of color. Employment, for example, is difficult for any ex-offender to obtain given the stigma associated with their conviction status; African American men and women may encounter greater difficulties in reaching success in this arena (Gunnison

& Helfgott, 2013). Previous research has found that minorities in the general law-abiding U.S. society, who do not possess a criminal record, have experienced employment discrimination (Holzer et al., 2003; Toth, Crews, & Burton, 2008). Research has revealed that African Americans face employment discrimination in getting hired and promoted (Queralt, 1996). Further, several researchers have uncovered employment discrimination for African American job applicants when compared to Caucasian job applicants (Beauchamp & Bowie, 1993; Turner, Fix, & Struyk, 1991; Weatherspoon, 1996). With this reality, minority ex-offenders have experienced employment difficulties (Pager, 2007). Thus, for parolees of color, gaining legal employment to pay for LFOs may be more difficult compared to their Caucasian counterparts.

Effectiveness of Parole

Although parolees represent a smaller proportion of the corrections population in comparison to those under incarceration or probation, researchers have fervently been trying to assess the effectiveness of parole since the 1920s. Despite such research efforts, the evidence on whether parole is effective is rather mixed — mostly due to different methodologies utilized to tap effectiveness. One difficulty that researchers have in attempting to ascertain parole effectiveness is how best to go about measuring "effectiveness." That is, researchers grapple with whether successful completion of a parole sentence, the absence of a technical violation, or the absence of a re-arrest, conviction, or even re-incarceration should be the driving measures of parole effectiveness. Typically, the absence of re-arrest is used as the indicator of parole effectiveness. However, by just focusing on whether parolees were arrested or not as a measure of effectiveness, valuable information is lost. For example, with arrest only as a measure of success, researchers can miss whether the arrest was for a minor or severe criminal offense and whether the arrest led to a conviction.

Another difficulty researchers have in determining parole effectiveness is the length of follow-up after parolees have completed their sentences. If parolees are examined too quickly following their parole term, there is a much higher chance that they will have not been successful since they are undergoing many stressful events including transitioning to being on their own, obtaining employment, and navigating without the guidance of their parole officer. Thus, to best determine the effectiveness of parole, a follow-up period of two years or greater is ideal since the majority of parolees are most likely to "fail during the first two years" (Flanagan, 1982). Further complicating the selection of the "best" follow-up period is the consideration of the crime that the parolee had committed. Sex offenders, due to their higher recidivism rates, would require a longer follow-up period to ensure that they were indeed successful following their parole term. All the aforementioned problems have raised doubts as to whether the research that has been conducted on parole can be trusted as the absolute bottom line about whether parole is indeed effective.

Upon review of the existing early literature on parole effectiveness, there has been a wide range of outcomes. In the 1920s, several researchers began to investigate the effectiveness of parole. Warner (1923) examined male parolees in Massachusetts to identify the factors related to parole effectiveness. Lacking statistical rigor in his analysis, he "eyeballed" his findings and concluded that prior record was the only factor that could predict parole success (Hart, 1923). Another early research investigation into parole effectiveness for males occurred in Wisconsin and was conducted by Witmer (1927b). She found several factors related to parole failure: (1) age, (2) marital status, (3) alcohol use, and (4) previous institutional commitment. Specifically, Witmer (1927b) found that male parolees who were under age 30, unmarried, used alcohol, and had one or more previous institutional commitment were more likely to fail on parole. Witmer (1927b) found that parole failure was relatively low and recommended that community members not be afraid of parolees in their cities and towns. Unfortunately, Witmer (1927b) did not employ solid statistical analyses in her study, resulting in research conclusions that were questioned by many. Following both Warner (1923) and Witmer's (1927b) research investigations, researchers were inspired to create a **parole actuarial tool**, a predictive tool comprised of various risk factors that would assist parole boards in identifying which offenders would be successful on parole. Discussions of such tools dominated the literature around parole in the late 1920s and 1930s (Vold, 1927). Many researchers during this time were applying statistical and methodological rigor in the correctional literature — a step that researchers had not taken either due to lack of knowledge or the understanding of fundamental research design.

The discussion of parole prediction tools was continued by a variety of researchers through the 1970s with various parole risk assessment tools being adopted and implemented across the nation in states and by the federal government (Harcourt, 2006). With the focus of attention on predicting parole success, researchers had lost sight of actually investigating whether parole was indeed effective (for an exception, see: Zuckerman, Barron, & Whittier, 1953). A revival into the examination of parole effectiveness occurred in the late 1970s and early 1980s. Some of this early research on parole effectiveness yielded either support, modest support, or no support for its effectiveness (Gottfredson, Mitchell-Herzfeld, & Flanagan, 1982; Jackson, 1983; Lerner, 1977; Sachs & Logan, 1979). In an investigation into whether the New York misdemeanant parole program was successful, Lerner (1977) examined 195 inmates who were either released to parole supervision or were released from prison due to completing their incarceration term in full. Lerner (1977) concluded that, after a two-year follow-up period, those offenders on parole supervision had significantly lower levels of recidivism that those offenders not on parole. While Lerner (1977, p. 222) did not explore why supervision was successful for offenders in his sample, he speculates that "this effect is probably due to the deterrent or law-enforcement aspects of parole supervision and not to the popular notions of rehabilitation." Following Lerner's (1977) examination of parole, several other researchers also examined parole effectiveness, but their results were not as positive. For example, Gottfredson and colleagues (1982), who examined the effects of parole supervision using a five-year follow-up period in a northeastern state, found that adult offenders on parole had lower recidivism rates than those offenders not on parole. However, the researchers note that the reductions in recidivism were very small. Early findings on youth who were paroled also demonstrated a lack of parole effectiveness. Jackson (1983), in an investigation of youth both on parole and not on parole in California, found no significant differences in recidivism rates between the groups.

Researchers have reported that recidivism rates for parolees are high (Durose, Cooper, & Snyder, 2014; Solomon, 2006). More recently, subsequent studies have also found mixed support for parole effectiveness through the examination of parole supervision (Schlager & Robbins, 2008; Solomon, Kachnowski, & Bhati, 2005). Findings from one of the more rigorous research investigations of parole have painted a rather grim picture about its effectiveness. In an examination of approximately 38,000 released prisoners across 14 states, Solomon et al. (2005, p. 1) found that "parole supervision has little effect on rearrest rates of released prisoners." The researchers provided a few insights into why parole supervision is not working and point to the role of parole officers as a possible reason for why parole is not more successful for offenders. First, Solomon et al. (2005) point out the fact that parole officers have very high caseloads, resulting in less quality time spent with their clients. That is, parole officers are managing quite a few offenders at one time, thus, to expect parole officers to change the life of parolee is an exceptionally difficult task. Second, the researchers explain that in many states when parolees violate their parole terms, responses to their violations may be inconsistent or punishment may not occur from their parole officer. If parolees are not being punished for violations, then their behavior is not being altered, therefore, they are more at risk for maintaining current behavior patterns such as committing crime. Finally, the researchers discuss how parole is now more surveillance oriented than treatment oriented. Parole officers are now equipped with high-tech monitoring equipment to assist in watching the offender. Thus, parole officers are more focused on surveillance than on rehabilitating their client. With so much of the focus in the literature in using recidivism as a measure of success as well as looking at the parole officer as perhaps the reason for *why* parolees are not successful following the completion of a parole sentence, a wealth of research on factors that may contribute to parole success factors is often been overlooked.

Evidence has emerged that incarcerated offenders who participated in treatment that addressed their criminogenic needs tend to demonstrate lower recidivism rates upon return to the community than offenders who do not participate in such treatment (Smith & Gendreau, 2007). If offenders' needs are not addressed before they return to the community, it can be expected that parolees would have increased recidivism rates. Apart from treatment while incarcerated, there are several factors that can increase the likelihood of parole reentry success. One of the most important keys to their success is ensuring that male and female parolee's basic needs continue to be met upon release— the initial stage of the reentry process (Gunnison & Helfgott, 2013). If parolees are able to securing housing, employment, and food, then this lays the foundation for success. Getting these needs met can be difficult given the multiple barriers that ex-offenders face in regards to job restrictions, exclusions from public assistance, and a reduction in the number of housing options available to them due to their criminal record (Petersilia, 2005). Johnson (2014), through interviews with 60 female parolees, found that struggles in obtaining employment were one of the more difficult challenges for female parolees. One female parolee describes her troubles with gaining employment as follows,

> I was so desperate for a job and knowing that my parole officer was pressuring me to get a job, I lied on one application. I told them that I had never been arrested. I did have an interview and was hired. I worked there for four months until the criminal background check was done. The employer was willing to hire me, but the headquarters of the company rejected my application because of my criminal record. How am I suppose to make it out here when I can't get a job? (Johnson, 2014, p. 375).

Other research has yielded that female parolees need gender-responsive supervision, suggesting that parole officers may need to alter their supervision style depending on the gender of their client (Morash, 2010). Despite the wealth of literature on what may be needed to assist ex-offenders in successful reintegration, other researchers have cast doubt on whether it really is having basic needs met such as housing and employment that provide the foundation for parole success. In an examination of male and female parolees in Pennsylvania, Bucklen and Zajac (2009, p. 239) found that parolees who were successful were less likely to possess "antisocial attitudes, poor problem-solving and coping skills, and unrealistic expectations about life after release from prison." Clearly, more methodologically rigorous research is needed to assess the effectiveness of parole beyond recidivism measures as well more research pinpointing the exact factors that are related to parole success for all parolees.

Conclusion

In sum, this chapter provided discussion on the history of parole development in the United States. Additionally, this chapter described the organization of modern parole, trends in the use of parole as a sentence, the characteristics of those serving parole sentences, and how fiscal constraints have impacted parolees. Parolees are being charged for their supervision, further burdening their attempts at successful reentry. Due to a wide range of methodological issues, research on parole effectiveness has been rather mixed. From the research that has been gathered over the past several decades, parole can be effective—if offenders' needs are being met and their parole officers are supportive. More research is needed to determine the exact factors that promote parole success in order to ensure that these risk and needs factors are being addressed both before release from prison and during reentry.

Key Terms

Alexander Maconochie

General conditions

Good time law

Indeterminate sentences

Irish system

Marks system

Parole

Parole actuarial tool

Parole board

Parole d'honneur

Sir Walter Crofton

Specific conditions

"Three strikes law"

Ticket-of-leave system

Truth-in-sentencing laws

Zebulon Brockway

Discussion Questions

1. Does your state have parole? If so, what are the trends in parole in your state over the past decade? If not, when did your state abolish parole?

2. What do you think about parolees having to pay for part of their probation supervision?

3. Does your state utilize a parole actuarial tool? If so, what is currently used? If your state does not have parole, research the closest state that has parole and identify its actuarial tool.

4. What factors do you think promote successful parole outcomes? Why? How do you think parole outcomes can be improved?

References

American Probation and Parole Association. (2014). *Probation and parole FAQs.* Retrieved from https://www.appa-net.org/eweb/DynamicPage.aspx?WebCode=VB_FAQ#10.

Associated Press. (1996, September 27). Before being sentenced to die, killer disrupts a courtroom. *New York Times.* Retrieved from http://www.nytimes.com/1996/09/27/us/before-being-sentenced-to-die-killer-disrupts-a-courtroom.html.

Beauchamp, T. L. & Bowie, N. E. (1993). *Ethical theory and business* (4th ed.). Englewood Cliffs, NJ: Prentice-Hall, Inc.

Bonnczar, T. P. (2008). *Characteristics of state parole agencies, 2006*. Washington, DC: U.S. Department of Justice. Retrieved from http://www.bjs.gov/content/pub/pdf/cspsa06.pdf.

Bucklen, K. B., & Zajac, G. (2009). But some of them don't come back (to prison!) resource deprivation and thinking errors as determinants of parole success and failure. *The Prison Journal, 89*(3), 239–264, doi: 10.1177/0032885509339504.

Clark, J., Austin, J., & Henry, D. A. (1997). "Three strikes and you're out": A review of state legislation. Washington, DC: U.S. Department of Justice. Retrieved from http://sjra1.com/index_files/cjreports/1997%20NATL%20INST%20OF%20JUST-3-STRIKES%20REPORT-1997-165369.pdf.

Cohen, L. (2014). Freedom's road: Youth, parole, and the promise of *Miller v. Alabama* and *Graham v. Florida. Cardozo Law Review, 35*, 1031–1089.

Connecticut Board or Pardons and Parolees. (2013). *Parole eligibility information.* Retrieved from http://www.ct.gov/bopp/cwp/view.asp?a=4330&q=508186.

Court Services and Offender Supervision Agency for the District of Columbia. (2014). *Parole: General conditions of release.* Retrieved from http://www.csosa.gov/supervision/types/parole/release-conditions.aspx.

Department of Correctional Services. (1992). *Annual report, 1991/92.* Pretoria: Commissioner of Correctional Services.

Department of Public Safety and Public Services. (2014). *Probation and parole hearings.* Retrieved from http://www.dpscs.state.md.us/aboutdpscs/FAQmpc.shtml.

Dui Hua (2010). *Systemic sickness: Diagnosing the ills of medical parole in China.* Retrieved from http://duihua.org/wp/?p=2608.

Durose, M., Cooper, A. D., & Snyder, H. N. (2014). *Recidivism of prisoners released in 30 states: Patterns from 2005 to 2010.* Washington, DC: U.S. Department of Justice. Retrieved from http://www.bjs.gov/content/pub/pdf/rprts05p0510.pdf.

Evans, D. N. (2014). *The debt penalty: Exposing the financial barriers to offender reintegration.* Research & Evaluation Center: John Jay College of Criminal Justice. Retrieved from http://justicefellowship.org/sites/default/files/The%20Debt%20Penalty_John%20Jay_August%202014.pdf.

Federal Judicial Center. (2014). *Who does what? Probation officer: Q & As.* Retrieved from http://www.fjc.gov/federal/courts.nsf/autoframe!openform&nav=menu1&page=/federal/courts.nsf/page/360.

Flanagan, T. J. (1982). Risk and the timing of recidivism in three cohorts of prison releasees. *Criminal Justice Review, 7*, 34–45.

Frendle, J. W. (2004). An overview of juvenile parole boards in the United States. New Mexico: New Mexico Sentencing Division.

Gottfredson, M. R., Mitchell-Herzfeld, S. D., & Flanagan, T. J. (1982). Another look at the effectiveness of parole supervision. *Journal of Research in Crime & Delinquency, 19*, 277–288. doi: 10.1177/002242788201900209.

Gunnison, E., & Helfgott, J. B. (2013). *Offender reentry: Beyond crime and punishment.* Boulder, CO: Lynne Rienner.

Griswold, E. A., & Pearson, J. (2005). Turning offenders into responsible parents and child support payers. *Family Court Review, 43,* 358–371. doi: 10.1111/j.1744-1617. 2005.00039.x.

Harcourt, B. E. (2006). *Against prediction: Profiling, policing, and punishing in an actuarial age.* Chicago, IL: University of Chicago Press.

Harris, A., Evans, H., & Beckett, K. (2010). Drawing blood from stones: Legal debt and social inequality in the contemporary U.S. *American Journal of Sociology, 115*(6), 1755 99. doi: 10.1086/651940.

Hart, H. (1923). Predicting parole success. *American Institute of Criminal Law & Criminology, 14,* 405–413.

Hinkle, W., & Whitmarsh, B. (2014). *Elmira reformatory.* Charleston, South Carolina: Arcadia Publishing.

Hoffman, P. B. (2003). *History of the federal parole system.* Washington, DC: U.S. Department of Justice. Retrieved from http://www.justice.gov/sites/default/files/uspc/legacy/2009/10/07/history.pdf.

Holzer, H. J., Raphael, S., & Stoll, M. A. (2003). *Employer demand for ex-offenders: Recent evidence from Los Angeles.* Washington, DC: Urban Institute.

Indeterminate Sentencing Review Board. (2008). *Access Washington.* Retrieved from http://www.srb.wa.gov/index.shtml.

Jackson, P. G. (1983). Some effects of parole supervision on recidivism. *British Journal of Criminology, 23*(1), 17–34.

Johnson, I. M. (2014). Economic impediments to women's success on parole: "We need someone on our side." *The Prison Journal, 94*(3), 365–387. doi: 10.1177/ 0032885514537760.

Kaeble, D., Maruschak, L. M., & Bonczar, T. P. (2015). *Probation and parole in the United States, 2014.* Washington, DC: U.S. Department of Justice.

Krajick, K. (1983). Abolishing parole: An idea whose time has passed. *Corrections Magazine, 9*(3), 33–40.

La Vigne, N., & Samuels, J. (2012). *The growth and increasing cost of the federal prison system: Drivers and potential solutions.* Urban Institute. Retrieved from http://www. urban.org/uploadedpdf/412693-the-growth-and-increasing-cost-of-the-federal-prison-system.pdf.

Lerner, M. J. (1977). The effectiveness of a definite sentence parole program. *Criminology, 15*(2), 211–224. doi: 10.1111/j.1745-9125.1977.tb00062.x.

Lindsey, E. (1925). Historical sketch of the indeterminate sentence and parole system. *Journal of the American Institute of Criminal Law & Criminology, 16,* 9–69.

Martinson, R. (1974). What works? Questions and answers about prison reform. *The Public Interest,* 22–54.

Michigan Department of Corrections. (2014). *The parole consideration process.* Retrieved from http://www.michigan.gov/corrections/0,4551,7-119-1384-22909—,00.html.

Montana Department of Corrections. (2014). *Probation and parole.* Retrieved from http://www.cor.mt.gov/Facts/pandp.mcpx.

Morash, M. (2010). *Women on probation and parole: A feminist critique of community programs and services.* Boston, MA: Northeastern University Press.

Morris, N. (2002). *Maconochie's gentleman: The story of Norfolk Island and the roots of modern prison reform.* New York: Oxford University Press.

Nellis, A., & Wayman, R. H. (2009). *Back on track: Supporting youth reentry from out-of-home placement to the community.* Washington, DC: Youth Reentry Task Force of the Juvenile Justice and Delinquency Prevention Coalition.

New Jersey State Parole Board. (2014). *Supervision.* Retrieved from http://www.state.nj.us/parole/supervision.html.

New York State Division of Parole. (2014). *Frequently asked questions.* Retrieved from https://www.parole.ny.gov/faq.html.

O'Toole, S. (2006). *The history of Australian corrections.* Australia: University of New South Wales Press.

Pager, D. (2007). *Marked: Race, crime, and finding work in an era of mass incarceration.* Chicago, IL: University of Chicago Press.

Petersilia, J. (2005). Meeting the challenges of prisoner reentry. In American Correctional Association (Ed.), *What works and why: Effective approaches to reentry* (pp. 175–192). East Peoria, IL: Versa Press.

Peterson, P. (2012). Supervision fees: State policies and practice. *Federal Probation, 76*(1), 40–45.

Pew Center on the States. (2009). *One in 31: The long reach of American corrections.* Washington, DC. Retrieved from http://www.pewtrusts.org/en/research-and-analysis/reports/0001/01/01/one-in-31.

Pisciotta, A. (1982). Saving the children: The promise and practice of parens patria, 1838–1898. *Crime & Delinquency, 28*(3), 410–425. doi: 10.1177/001112878202800303.

Pogrebin, M., West-Smith, M., Walker, A., & Unnithan, N. P. (2014). Employment isn't enough: Financial obstacles experienced by ex-prisoners during the reentry process. *Criminal Justice Review, 39*(4), 394–410. doi: 10.1177/0734016814540303.

Queralt, M. (1996). *The social environment and human behavior: A diversity perspective.* Needham Heights, MA: Allyn & Bacon.

Richards, S., & Jones, R. (2004). Beating the perpetual incarceration machine: Overcoming structural impediments to re-entry. In S. Maruna & R. Immarigeon (Eds.), *After crime and punishment: Pathways to offender reintegration* (pp. 201–232). Collompton, England: Willan Publishing.

Roth, M. P. (2005). *Prisons and prison systems: A global encyclopedia*. Westport, CT: Greenwood.

Roth, M. P. (2010). *Crime and punishment: A history of the criminal justice system.* Belmont, CA: Wadsworth.

Sachs, H., & Logan, C. (1979). *Does parole make a difference?* West Hartford: University of Connecticut Law School.

Savage, D. G. (2011). *Supreme Court says state prisoners have no constitutional right to parole.* Retrieved from http://articles.latimes.com/2011/jan/25/nation/la-na-supreme-court-20110125.

Schlager, M., & Robbins, K. (2008). Does parole work? — Revisited. Reframing the discussion of the impact of postprison supervision on offender outcome. *The Prison Journal, 88*(2), 234–251. doi: 10.1177/0032885508319164.

Scott-Hayward, C. S. (2009). *The fiscal crisis in corrections: Rethinking policies and practices.* New York: Vera Institute of Justice.

Seiter, R., & Kadela, K. (2003). Prisoner reentry: What works, what does not, and what is promising. *Crime and Delinquency, 49*(3), 360–388.

Shepherd, J. (2002). Police, prosecutors, criminals, and determinate sentencing: The truth about truth-in-sentencing laws. *Journal of Law and Economics, 45*, 509–534.

Smith, P., & Gendreau, P. (2007). The relationship between program participation, institutional misconduct and recidivism among federally sentenced adult male offenders. *Forum on Corrections Research, 19*, 6–10.

Solomon, A. L. (2006). *Does parole supervision work? Research findings and policy opportunities.* Urban Institute. Retrieved from http://www.urban.org/uploadedpdf/1000908_parole_supervision.pdf.

Solomon, A. L., Kachnowski, V., & Bhati, A. (2005). *Does parole work? Analyzing the impact of postprison supervision on rearrest outcomes.* Washington, DC: The Urban Institute. Retrieved from http://www.northstarnews.com/userimages/references/Does_Parole_Work.2005_Urban%20Institute.pdf.

South Carolina Board of Probation, Parole, and Pardon Services. (2014). *Offender supervision strategies.* Retrieved from http://www.dppps.sc.gov/what_we_do_sanctions.html.

Tennessee Board of Parole. (2014). *Frequently asked questions about parole.* Retrieved from http://www.tn.gov/bop/bopp_faq.htm.

Toth, R. C., Crews, G. A., & Burton, C. E. (2008). *In the margins: Special populations and American justice.* Prentice Hall.

Travis, J. (2001). But they all come back: Rethinking prisoner reentry. *Corrections Management Quarterly, 5*(3), 23–33.

Turner, M. A., Fix, M., & Struyk, R. J. (1991). Hiring discrimination against Black men. The *Urban Institute Policy and Research Report, Summer*, 4–5.

Turner, S., Greenwood, P. W., Fain, T., & Chiesa, J. R. (2006). An evaluation of the federal government's violent offender incarceration and truth-in-sentencing incentive grants. *Prison Journal, 86*(3), 364–385. doi: 10.1177/0032885506291026.

U.S. Department of Justice. (2014). *Organization, mission and functions manual: United States parole commission.* Retrieved from http://www.justice.gov/jmd/ organization-mission-and-functions-manual-united-states-parole-commission.

Vold, G. B. (1927). Prediction methods applied to problems of classification within institutions. *American Institute of Criminal Law, & Criminology, 14,* 405–413.

Walker, J. (2013). State parole boards use software to decide which inmates to release. *Wall Street Journal.* Retrieved from http://www.wsj.com/articles/SB100014240 52702304626104579121251595240852.

Warner, S. B. (1923). Factors determining parole from the Massachusetts reformatory. *Journal of Criminal Law and Criminology, 14*(2), 172–207.

Weatherspoon, F. D. (1996). Remedying employment discrimination against African-American males: Stereotypical biases engender a case of race plus sex discrimination. *Washburn Law Journal, 36*(1), 23–87.

Weinstein, J. B., & Wimmer, C. (2010). Sentencing in the United States. In H. A. Dlugacz (Ed.), *Reentry planning for offenders with mental disorders* (pp 1-1–1-49). Kingston, NJ: Civic Research Institute.

Witmer, H. L. (1927a). The history, theory and results of parole. *Journal of the American Institute of Criminal Law, & Criminology, 18,* 24–64.

Witmer, H. L. (1927b). Some factors in success or failure on parole. *Journal of the American Institute of Criminal Law, & Criminology, 18,* 384–403.

Zuckerman, S. B., Barron, A. J., & Whittier, H. B. (1953). A follow-up study of Minnesota State Reformatory inmates: A preliminary report. *Journal of Criminal Law, Criminology, & Police Science, 43,* 622–636.

Chapter 7

Juveniles in the Community Corrections Mix

Student Learning Outcomes

After reading this chapter, you should be able to:

- Describe the history of and current use of probation and parole for juveniles.
- Explain the conditions placed on juvenile probationers and parolees and the types of risk assessments that are used with juvenile populations.
- Summarize the outcomes of juvenile probation and parole, the risk factors for juvenile recidivism, and what is needed to assist juvenile community corrections offenders.

Introduction

Curtis Jackson. The name Curtis Jackson may not be familiar to you when you first read it, but the rapper named 50 Cent should ring a bell—Curtis Jackson is his birth name. Sure, you may be familiar with some of his most popular tracks, such as "In Da Club," or that you have heard that he was number four on Forbes' top five wealthiest hip hop artists in 2015, at a cool $155 million (Greenburg, 2015). You also be familiar with the fact that 50 Cent has been arrested on several occasions in the past. In fact, his first arrest occurred when he was in tenth grade for possession of drugs (Green, 2015). It was during this time of 50 Cent's life that he was dealing cocaine and marijuana, and he was quite the businessman, earning upwards of $5,000 per day (Green, 2015). Since 50 Cent was a juvenile and this was his first arrest, he was sentenced to a juvenile community corrections boot camp (Green, 2015). After serving his sentence, 50 Cent did not make an immediate switch to law-abiding behavior. Rather, he dropped out of school, continued to sell drugs, and was later arrested again (Green, 2015). Perhaps, this was due to the environment he lived in, his lack of education, or because his criminogenic needs he had were not met in the boot camp program. Whatever may be the exact contributing factors, his reformation from drug dealer to entertainment mogul and superstar would come later in his life—once he left the drug business. While your familiarity with 50 Cent did not begin due to his sentence as a juvenile given his lack of fame at that time, he is an example of a former offender who entered the criminal justice system as a juvenile and beat the odds, turning his life around and escaping the entrapment of the criminal justice system—a feat that so many of his African American peers have been unable to accomplish.

Although you may not have been familiar with 50 Cent's past juvenile history, there are likely other juvenile cases, not involving celebrities, that you may be aware of. It is not uncommon to hear news reports of teens driving at excessive speeds or under the influence of drugs and/or alcohol. In 2013, sixteen-year-old Ethan Couch was driving while intoxicated, which resulted in the deaths of four people in Texas (Mitchell, 2013). Unfortunately, while this type of case is not rare, it did garner national attention due to Couch's "affluenza" defense. It was claimed that Couch was a "victim" of affluenza, whereby his parents indulged his every want and need, never setting any limits for him or punishing him for his bad behavior, thus, he was somehow not responsible for his actions due to his insulation by his parents (Ford, 2014; Mitchell, 2013). Many in society were outraged by his defense and viewed it as another example of how those with wealth are able to escape responsibility for their actions. Couch was later sentenced to a ten-year probation sentence and required to go to a residential treatment facility (Ford, 2014; Mitchell, 2013). His parents agreed to pay for his rehabilitation at a facility near Newport Beach, California, that costs $450,000 per year (Mitchell, 2013). If he violated any of his conditions of probation, which included refraining from substance use and driving, he could return to prison to serve the remainder of his sentence (Ford, 2014). It did not take long for Couch to violate a condition of his probation—specifically the use of alcohol. He was subsequently incarcerated for a two-year term for the violation (Hanna, 2016).

Oftentimes, in discussions of community corrections, the place of juveniles is overlooked or missed. This chapter will devote attention to the history of the use of probation and parole for juveniles, the current numbers of juveniles serving these sentences, conditions that juveniles serving these sentences must follow, assessment tools that are used with these populations, and juvenile probation and parole outcomes. Additionally, discussion regarding risk factors for juvenile recidivism as well as what is needed in juvenile community corrections will be provided.

Juvenile Probation

Brief History

As highlighted in Chapter 4, probation in the United States can be traced back to the 1840s with the work of John Augustus in Boston. At first, Augustus was focused on reforming adult men and women, however, he later assisted young prostitutes as well (Panzarella, 2002). Large-scale implementation of juvenile probation would come many years later, after the development of the first juvenile court in Chicago in 1899 (Chute, 1923). The implementation of this first juvenile court in a sense legitimatized the wide-scale adoption and use of probation, as when future juvenile courts were established in subsequent states, juvenile probation sentences were con-

Image 12. © hafakot/Fotolia.

sidered an essential component of their mission (Chute, 1923). However, it should be noted that the adoption of probation did not occur as rapidly as it did for adult offenders (Kehoe, 1994). This may stem from the broader social views on juveniles at the time as during the 1800s and early 1990s, children were often viewed as "little adults," thereby not needing special care or even protection. For many of the courts that were early adopters of probation, there was a tendency to utilize probation "unofficially." Unofficial probation was utilized for juveniles before they were convicted as a method of both helping them and diverting them from the court system (Chute, 1923). Rather than proceed forward with processing the juvenile through the court for their offenses, some juvenile courts would require that juveniles first serve an unofficial probation sentence under the supervision of a probation officer. If the juveniles completed the unofficial probation successfully, their case was disposed of and no further formal actions were taken. Today, unofficial probation, now referred to as *informal probation*, is still utilized for juveniles in state and federal probation systems (Livsey, 2012).

Beginning in the 1970s, in the context of the "get-tough-on-crime" movement, intensive supervision probation (ISP) was implemented for use with the juvenile offender population (Wiebush, 1993). Many in society viewed traditional probation as a slap on the wrist and wanted more stringent punishments—ISPs offered that. **Intensive supervision probation** refers to increased monitoring and supervision of offenders on probation (Wiebush, 1993). ISP sentences are reserved for juveniles who have committed serious offenses, such as violent or sex crimes, or those that are chronic offenders. Under ISP sentences, juvenile offenders adhere to stricter conditions, maintain more contact with their probation officer, are held accountable for their actions, and participate in required treatment programs (Wiebush, 1993). Also during the 1970s, the first school-based probation program opened in a high school in California (Griffin, 1999a). **School-based probation** refers to probation whereby the probation officer manages the juvenile probationers from inside school walls rather than at a traditional program agency. Such an arrangement allows for probation officers to directly monitor their clients, speak with the teachers of their clients, and have access to grades and other reports pertaining to their clients (Griffin, 1999a). Despite the possible advantages of implementing school-based probation sentences, such as increased contact with clients, direct observation of clients, increased school success for probationers, and reduced misconduct at school for the juveniles, most states did not follow California's lead right away. Rather, other states, such as Pennsylvania and Arizona, later implemented their own programs in the 1990s (Griffin, 1999a; Griffin & Torbet, 2002). Pennsylvania, for instance, has invested heavily in the use and implementation of school-based probation with over $20 million dollars spent (Torbet, Ricci, Brooks, & Zawacki, 2001). The use of school-based probation has continued to expand with four schools in Los Angeles adding such programming in 2009 (Hennessy-Fiske, 2009).

Statistics

With over 1.5 million juvenile delinquency cases processed each year, juvenile probation sentences represent about 60% of the sanctions that a convicted juvenile may receive (Livsey, 2012). The majority of juveniles receiving probation sentences are Caucasian at 68%, male at 73%, and between the ages of 14–16 at 65% (Livsey, 2012). For all juvenile age groups, the use of formal probation sentences has increased since 1985—particularly for those convicted of drug offenses (Hockenberry & Puzzanchera, 2015). Overall, the use of probation for juveniles convicted of **status offenses**, crimes that only apply to juveniles due to their age, is down (see Text Box 7.1) (Hockenberry & Puzzanchera, 2015). For instance, in 2000, the use of probation for juveniles convicted of status offenses reached a high of approximately 65,000 offenders, however, by 2013, less than 30,000 offenders were receiving such a sentence—the most recent statistics available (Hockenberry & Puzzanchera, 2015). For those juveniles receiving probation sentences for status offenses, the most common offenses were truancy at 43% and liquor law violations at 22% (Hockenberry & Puzzanchera, 2015).

For juveniles receiving probation sentences, formal or informal, outside of status offenses, the most common offenses committed were property crimes (see Text Box 7.2) (Livsey, 2012). Since 1985, the use of formal and informal probation sentences for juveniles has increased for person, drug, and public order offenses (Livsey, 2012). By 2013, the use of formal probation was still highest for those juveniles convicted of property crimes at 34%, followed by person at 27%, public order at 26%, and drug offenses at 13% (Hockenberry & Puzzanchera, 2015). See Text Box 7.3 for juvenile probation examples in another country.

Text Box 7.1: 1995–2013 Juvenile Probation Status Offenses Sentences

Adjudicated cases resulting in probation

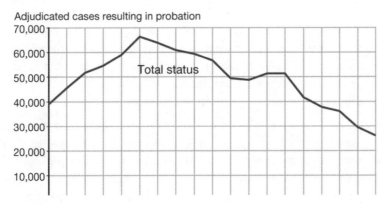

Source: Hockenberry, S., & Puzzanchera, C. (2015). *Juvenile court statistics, 2013.* Retrieved from http://www.ojjdp.gov/ojstatbb/njcda/pdf/jcs2013.pdf.

Text Box 7.2: 1995–2009 Juvenile Probation Sentences: Formal & Informal

Most serious offense	Formal probation		Informal probation	
	1985	2009	1985	2009
Total	100%	100%	100%	100%
Person	16	26	13	19
Property	60	36	66	44
Drugs	8	13	8	14
Public order	16	25	12	12

Source: Livsey, S. (2012). *Juvenile delinquency probation caseload, 2009.* Washington, DC: U.S. Department of Justice.

Text Box 7.3: Juvenile Probation in Denmark

Throughout the world, many countries utilize probation for juvenile offenders. However, some countries, such as Denmark, do not. Denmark is rather unique in that the country does not have a juvenile justice system (Kyvsgaard, 2004). In Denmark, the age of criminal responsibility is 15 years old, and those who commit offenses under that age are handled by social welfare agencies (Kyvsgaard, 2004). Additionally, the country does not have status offenses for juveniles that the U.S. does (Kyvsgaard, 2004). Thus, if an individual aged 15 years old or older commits an offense, he/she proceeds to a regular adult criminal court for adjudication. For those under the age of 18, this procedure means that these juveniles are held to the same legal standard as their adult peers (Kyvsgaard, 2004). Despite this similarity, efforts are made to divert juvenile offenders from prison and probation (Kyvsgaard, 2004). More often than not, juveniles are diverted from formal sanctions, such as incarceration and probation, and are referred to social service agencies for monitoring and assistance. Therefore, juveniles in Denmark do not serve probation sentences—such sentences are reserved for adults only.

Conditions

Similar to adult probationers, juvenile probationers also must abide by conditions (see Text Box 7.4). Even some juveniles released from custody and not having served official probation sentences often have to abide by conditions per their release order, such as attending school or being required to appropriately maintain, "clean up," or even delete their social media sites. Juveniles released from custody in Texas, not on probation, will find the following condition of release on their release order:

> My Space, Facebook and/or similar website must be age and content appropriate. All references to drugs, alcohol, guns or other weapons, gambling, sex and/or derogatory comments about women, race, color or creed shall be deleted. No profanity or nudity in any videos, music and pics shall be on the site. "Friends" who are on probation or parole shall be deleted from the site. The child shall provide the parent/guardian with their email address and password (Galveston County Texas, 2015).

Offenders released from custody but having to abide by such conditions are serving **conditionary probation** sentences. More traditionally, the conditions that are imposed on juveniles are consistent with conditions placed on adult probationers, such as abiding by a curfew, abstaining from drug and alcohol use, and participating in treatment. However, there are a few conditions of probation that are unique to this group. For instance, all juveniles receiving probation as a sentence are required to attend school. Additionally, the parents of juvenile probationers can be held criminally responsible in the courts if their child does not abide by the conditions of probation. In a sense, when the child is placed on probation, the parent is also placed on probation by proxy (Cook & Gordon, 2012). This aspect adds a different level of complexity to probation supervision for juveniles as the parent(s) is now also required to monitor his/her child's behavior, perhaps for the first time, and the pressures of monitoring his/her child may result in the fostering of anger towards the child due to the added pressure and burden (Cook & Gordon, 2012). Further, some parents may feel that his/her child may be a lost cause in the system and may begin to pull back and not be a reliable support for his/her child, resulting in poor probation outcomes (Cook, 2013). Moreover, probation officers view strong parental support and working with the officer as imperative to successful juvenile probation outcomes (Maschi, Schwalbe, & Ristow, 2013).

Text Box 7.4: Exhibit A: Idaho Juvenile Probation Order

Exhibit A
TERMS AND CONDITIONS OF PROBATION ORDER
UNDER IDAHO CODE 20-520

Any juvenile offender placed on probation and his/her parents/guardians shall abide by the following terms and conditions. The probation officer will explain the requirements of Exhibit A and will require the juvenile and his/her parents/guardians to sign and date Exhibit A. All juvenile offenders are required to obey the following rules of probation unless waived in writing:

1. The parents/guardians shall assure compliance with, and the juvenile shall:

A. Maintain contact with your probation officer and obtain the officer's written consent to move, leave Bannock County, or leave the state of Idaho. If your address changes, these rules apply to the new residence as well.

B. Avoid any contact with individuals not approved of by your probation officer and your parent(s)/guardian(s).

C. Follow all of the rules at home and school.

D. Abide by the following curfew: Sunday–Thursday: 10:00 PM; Friday and Saturday: 11:30 PM (unless told differently).

E. Attend school every day unless you have a physician's excuse. Truancies are reported to your probation officer and may constitute a new juvenile offense. Your probation officer will have access to your report cards and attendance records.

F. Obey the law and not use or possess any illegal narcotics, paraphernalia, or prescription medication.

G. Not use or possess alcohol, any form of tobacco, pornography, sexually explicit or violent materials, including music, or any weapons, including BB guns, pocket knives, slingshots, and razor blades. You may not be at any place outside your home where any of these items are being used.

H. Have a parent or legal guardian with you at all times when you are in retail stores, and never enter any stores that have trespassed you. If you do enter such stores, you may be charged with trespassing. You may not enter any store property where an offense occurred.

I. Obtain your probation officer's consent to apply for a driver's license or take drivers training. If you already have a license, it may be suspended by your probation officer or the Court, if you do not follow the rules of probation.

J. Not go to any school or school event where you are not registered without permission of your probation officer. If you are found on such school grounds, you may be charged with trespassing.

K. Pay Juvenile Justice $25.00 for each month you are on probation. Payments are due on the last day of the month.

L. Not spend any nights away from home unless accompanied by parent or guardian.

2. **Restitution:** If the court orders any restitution paid to the juvenile offender's victim and the juvenile and/or the parents/guardians object to the amount ordered, they may request a Restitution Hearing. The juvenile and/or the parents/guardians must provide the court written notice of their objection within twenty (20) days of the restitution order. A failure to do so makes the restitution order final. Parents/guardians are legally responsible for paying any restitution that the juvenile fails to pay. Restitution shall be paid to: Bannock County Courthouse, Bonds & Fines, 624 E. Center, Room 220, Pocatello, Idaho, 83201. If the court terminates probation or the juvenile or the parents/guardians fail to obey the restitution order, the court may convert the restitution order to a civil judgment for the unpaid balance against the juvenile and the parents/guardians who are designated in the restitution order.

3. **Home Detention:** The probation officer may require the juvenile offender to remain at home at all times unless he/she is at school and/or work. The probation officer may use an electronic monitor while the juvenile is on home detention. A daily fee for the monitor is charged.

4. **Community Service:** A juvenile offender must perform twenty (20) hours of community service for each offense. The probation officer has discretion to suspend hours as he/she deems appropriate. If in school, the juvenile shall perform twenty (20) hours per month. If not in school, the juvenile shall perform forty (40) hours per month. The juvenile and the parents/guardians shall pay $.60 per hour for workmen's compensation coverage. The

fee shall be paid to: Bannock County Courthouse, Bonds & Fines, 624 E. Center, Room 220, Pocatello, Idaho, 83201. If the fee is not paid, Bannock County may obtain a civil judgment against the juvenile and the parents/guardians.

5. **Classes:** A juvenile offender and the parents/guardians shall attend, participate in, and complete all ordered classes and programs at the scheduled date and time.

6. **Law Violations:** A juvenile offender and the parents/guardians shall not encourage, participate in, or commit any act that constitutes a violation of the laws of the United States, Idaho, or its cities. A juvenile and/or the parents/guardians who violate the law may be charged criminally for the violation. The probation officer may also file a probation violation and seek contempt sanctions against the juvenile and/or the juvenile's parents.

7. **Warrantless Home Checks and Searches:** The juvenile and parents or guardians are ordered by the Court to maintain a crime-free home and property. The home and property must be free from illegal items including: drugs, prohibited intoxicating substances, weapons, pornography, stolen property, drug paraphernalia and gang paraphernalia. All of the home, outbuildings, property, vehicles, school lockers, and bags may be searched without a warrant. A juvenile offender and the parents/guardians shall submit to periodic unannounced and warrantless home checks and searches by probation officers at any time and without probable cause. During such home checks, a law enforcement officer may assist the probation officer for the probation officer's safety. No unapproved juveniles or adults may spend the night in the home. Probation officers, along with a law enforcement officer, may, at their discretion, search the juvenile's and the parents/guardians home, secured rooms, safes, grounds, outbuildings, vehicles, and/or school locker without obtaining a search warrant. The juvenile and the parents/guardians specifically *waive* their constitutional right to be free from such searches.

8. **Detention Costs:** A juvenile offender and the parents/guardians shall pay $100.00 for each day the juvenile is in detention. Probation officers have discretion to decrease or waive this fee if the juvenile and the parents/guardians are complying with probation.

9. **Probation Officer's Discretion:** When necessary a probation officer may order the juvenile offender and/or the parents/guardians to complete any of the following:

   A. Individual, group, or family counseling;

   B. Alcohol/drug evaluations and counseling;

   C. Random drug/alcohol testing within 24 hours of the probation officer's request;

   D. Victim Offender Mediation;

   E. Parent Orientation/Parent Project/Strengthening Families;

   F. Additional community service (juvenile only).

Additional Requirements for Juvenile Offenders Who Violate Probation

1. Serve detention time, home detention, or be placed on the electronic monitor and pay a fee for each day the juvenile is on the monitor.

2. Perform twenty (20) additional hours of community service for each violation.

3. Attend any additional classes that the probation officer may deem appropriate.

4. Remain on probation for additional time or be monitored at a higher probation level.

5. Receive a Juvenile Violation Report for criminal contempt or for any additional juvenile and/or misdemeanor charges.

Additional Requirements for Parents/Guardians Who Violate This or Any Court Order

If the parents/guardians of the juvenile allow, encourage, participate in, or do not report to the probation officer all violations of this Order, the parents/guardians may be required to attend an Order to Show Cause hearing before the Judge. At the Order to Show Cause hearing, the State has the burden to prove beyond a reasonable doubt that the parents/

guardians have violated the terms of Probation. Possible sanctions for a contempt conviction include: a $1,000.00 fine; up to five (5) days in jail for each violation; and/or additional classes or to be charged with the crime of contempt. See Idaho Code §§ 20-520; 18-1801.

Source: Bannock County Juvenile Probation Department. (2015). Retrieved from http://www.bannockcounty.us/juvenile/probation/.

Assessments

The development and use of risk assessment tools for juveniles first began in the 1970s (Baird et al., 2013), and their implementation has grown over the past few decades with 34 states currently using some form of risk assessment tool for juvenile probationers (Wachter, 2015). Despite rather wide adoption of a single risk assessment tool across the nation, there is quite a bit of variation in the adopted tools. For instance, several states have adopted juvenile probation risk assessment tools known as: the Positive Achievement Change Tool (PACT), the Youth Assessment and Screening Instrument (YASI), the Youth Offender-Level of Service Inventory (YO-LSI), and the Youth Level of Service/Case Management Inventory (YLS/CMI) (Baird et al., 2013; Wachter, 2015). Both the YO-LSI and YLS/CMI have been touted to predict both general and violence recidivism (Oliver, Stockdale, & Wormith, 2009). The PACT risk-needs assessment tool was developed and rolled out in the state of Florida in 2005. PACT is a 126-item assessment tool that reports both a criminal history score and a social history risk score (see Text Box 7.5). As described by Early, Hand, & Blakenship (2012, pp. 3–4),

> The criminal history score is based solely on measures of prior criminal offending, juvenile justice supervision and placement, escapes and warrants for failure to appear before the court. Scores range from a low of zero to a high of 31 points. The social history score examines individual and situational factors including the youth's sex, current school involvement, peers, dependency placements, familial criminal justice system involvement, parental supervision, alcohol and drug use, abuse and neglect, and mental health

Text Box 7.5: PACT Scoring Matrix

Criminal History Score	Social History Score		
	0–5	6–9	10–18
0–5	Low	Low	Moderate
6–8	Low	Moderate	Moderate-high
9–11	Moderate	Moderate-high	High
11–31	Moderate-high	High	High

Source: Early, K. P., Hand, G. A., & Blakenship, J. L. (2012). *Validity and reliability of the Florida PACT Risk and Needs Assessment Instrument: A three-phase evaluation*. Tallahassee, FL: Justice Research Center.

problems. A social history score of zero is indicative of low risk in terms of environmental factors that may influence the likelihood for future criminal offending. The maximum social history score a youth can receive is eighteen. The total criminal history score and social history score are factored together.

In some states, several juvenile risk assessment tools for probation are utilized (Wachter, 2015). For a few states, such as Hawaii, several different risk assessment tools are utilized, whereby a particular risk assessment tool is utilized on the island of Oahu with the a second distinct risk assessment tool utilized for juveniles in the remaining islands (Wachter, 2015). However, other states, such as Ohio, Indiana, Arizona, and Iowa have designed and implemented their own distinct and singular juvenile probation risk assessment tools (Wachter, 2015).

With such a wide range of juvenile probation risk assessment tools, the natural question may emerge as to whether such tools are indeed effective at predicting risk. Both the YO-LSI and YLS-CMI have been found to have good predictive ability for general, non-violent, and violent recidivism across gender, race, and ethnicity (Oliver et al., 2009). Assessments of PACT, for instance, have yielded good predictive ability for recidivism (see Early et al., 2012). Baird et al. (2013) examined approximately 10 juvenile risk assessment tools that were utilized in eight states in an effort to examine their validity and reliability. The researchers found mixed results with only one of the instruments having strong predictive validity and the remaining tools having moderate to low predictive validity. Other researchers have found that assessments tools may be more or less predictive for juvenile offenders depending on their race and ethnicity (Rembert, Henderson, & Pirtle, 2014). Such findings are not conclusive in regards to the value that risk assessments have for probation, but point to the fact that more research is needed on these instruments and perhaps further refinement of risk assessment tools for juveniles on probation is in order.

Juvenile Probation Outcomes

Research investigations on juvenile probation outcomes have found that juveniles classified as a higher risk are more likely to re-offend (Onifade et al., 2011; Ryans, Abrams, & Huang, 2014; Wagoner, Schubert, & Mulvey, 2015). Other researchers have explored whether there is a difference in outcomes for juveniles sentenced to formal versus informal probation. For instance, in a comparative examination of juveniles sentenced to formal and informal probation, Onifade and colleagues (2011) found that juveniles with similar risk levels and offense types did not differ in their recidivism rates. This finding suggests that regardless of the type of probation sentence a juvenile is serving (i.e., formal vs. informal), there are no distinct differences in outcomes. Ryans et al. (2014) examined recidivism rates for first-time violent juvenile probationers in Los Angeles. Given the seriousness of the crimes committed by the juveniles it may not come as a surprise to learn that the researchers found that almost half of the juveniles were re-arrested. The researchers further examined the nature of how the probation sentence was carried out (e.g., in-home, group-home placement, or a probation camp) to determine if that had an impact on juvenile outcomes. Upon inspection of the disposition of the case, the researchers found that recidivism rates were higher for juveniles serving their sentences in group-home placements and probation camps. These results suggests that the environment in which the probation sentence is carried out in can play a critical role in success.

In regards to probation condition compliance, research has found that juveniles are very likely to fail to comply with at least one of the conditions of their sentence. More specifically, researchers have found that those juveniles who have failed to comply with probation conditions previously are at risk for non-compliance, and minority juvenile offenders are also at higher risk for non-compliance (NeMoyer et al., 2014). Further, it appears that juvenile probationers are most likely to fail to comply with substance abuse conditions (e.g., non-use and treatment) (NeMoyer et al., 2014). It is clear that more research is needed on non-compliance of conditions to uncover why certain races may be more likely to be non-compliant and what can be implemented to assist all juvenile offenders to be compliant with imposed conditions. Since juveniles are being diverted from incarceration terms through the use of probation sentences, juvenile probation offenders finding themselves incarcerated due to non-compliance results in the opposite impact that the sentence was intended to achieve—that is, diversion from incarceration.

Early research on ISP for juveniles yielded mixed results, with some evaluations findings that they were a cost effective alternative to incarceration and participants had lower recidivism rates than traditional probationers, yet other studies did not find such positive outcomes (Wiebush, 1993). Wiebush (1993) explains that the discrepancies in findings were due to the use of small sample sizes and other methodological weaknesses. Today, research on the effectiveness of ISP programs for juveniles is still mixed. For example, several researchers have reported no differences in recidivism rates for juveniles placed on ISP versus traditional probation (Drake, Aos, & Miller, 2009; MacKenzie, 2006). However, in a more recent investigation of an ISP program for male juveniles in California that included structured after-school probation activities, Hanningan and colleagues (2010) found ISP programs to be favorable, in particular, for higher risk juveniles. That is, higher risk juveniles had less official and self-reported offending behaviors. Lower risk juveniles, however, did not fare well in the program. This finding is not surprising as several researchers have asserted that it is better to target high-risk, as opposed to low-risk, offenders for correctional interventions in order to achieve favorable outcomes (Lowenkamp & Latessa, 2005). Perhaps ISPs for juveniles would have more effective outcomes if there were a built-in system of interventions to assist offenders in getting their needs met while on probation, in addition to addressing their risk level.

Results from research investigations of school-based probation programs offer some positive support. In 1997, Metzger evaluated school-based probation in Pennsylvania and found several benefits, including better supervision of probationers, enhanced school attendance of probationers, increased communication between school officials and probation officers, and lower recidivism rates for participants. Other studies have yielded positive support for school-based probation programs, noting that the programs increase student attendance and participants exhibit lower school drop-out rates (Clouser, 1995; Griffin, 1999b; Lasater et al., 2008; Torbet et al., 2001). Torbet et al. (2001) conducted interviews with juvenile probationers, school administrators, and probation officers in Pennsylvania and found that school administrators and probationers stated that the program was effective in reducing recidivism. However, the researchers reported that probation officers were less likely to report the program as effective. Since the findings by Torbet et al. (2001) were based on opinions of those interviewed rather than an evaluation of recidivism outcomes, their findings do not provide an accurate assessment of whether the probation was indeed effective. Subsequent comprehensive evaluations of school-based probation programs have been sparse, and those researchers who have conducted rigorous evaluations of these programs have generally not found them to be effective (Frederique, 2010). More research is needed in this area.

Researchers have also explored the role of probation officers and their relationship to successful probation outcomes. Several research investigations have found that juvenile probation officers are more likely to adopt a rehabilitative perspective for juvenile probationers — more so than for adult probationers (Schwalbe, 2012). With the adoption of a rehabilitative ideology, there has been greater scrutiny of the role that probation officers have in fostering successful juvenile probation outcomes. On one hand, some research has explored the level of supervision that a probation officer has with the juvenile and its relation to recidivism. The idea behind such investigations is that intense or lacking supervision by the probation officer may result in unfavorable recidivism outcomes. Despite this perspective, research has yielded that the level of supervision provided by the juvenile probation officer did not have an impact on juvenile probation recidivism (Wagoner et al., 2015). On the other hand, it may not be the level of supervision provided by the probation officer that can impact juvenile probation outcomes but rather the strength of the relationship between the juvenile offender and his/her officer or other outside factors beyond the control of the probation officer. Schwalbe (2012) conducted interviews with 31 juvenile probation officers in an effort to understand probation practices. Probation officers reported that ensuring that their juvenile clients were participating and fully cooperating with the court-ordered treatment plans was critical to successful probation outcomes. They further reported that their own ability to build a strong rapport and partnership with their clients assisted them in successful outcomes. Additionally, the officers also stated that besides the support that they offer their clients it was also critical that the juvenile receive parental support as well, noting that "uncooperative parents undermine youth participation in probation" in that they are also not helping their child to be accountable for their actions while on probation (Schwalbe, 2012, p. 195). Finally, juvenile probations officers viewed being able to tap into their clients' goals and priorities and find ways to motivate them to be compliant with conditions was critical to ensuring juvenile success on probation.

Juvenile Parole

Brief History

As highlighted in Chapter 6, the use of parole, or some form of conditional release for offenders, including children, dates back to the 1600s (Witmer, 1927). In the United States, the origins of juvenile parole can be traced to Brockway's reforms in New York in the 1870s whereby offenders had to earn their conditional release (Hinkle & Whitmarsh, 2014). The conditional release process, or parole, was established in other states and by 1944, all states and the federal government offered parole to juveniles or adults (Hoffman, 2003; Lindsey, 1925; O'Toole, 2006). Part of the proliferation of the use of parole for juveniles is due to the child-saving movement (Platt, 1969). The **child-saving movement** refers to educated middle-class reformers, mostly women, who fought for reforms for delinquent youth in the late 1800s and early 1900s (Platt, 1969). Since the reformers were concerned with the welfare of children, they pushed for the implementation of policies that would be beneficial for delinquent youth. Juvenile parole was viewed as one policy that could assist delinquent youth in that the youth could obtain assistance, or aftercare, when released. This aspect of aftercare is very much part of the juvenile parole today.

Similar to what occurred in juvenile probation, during the 1970s and 1980s, also in the context of the "get-tough-on-crime" movement, intensive supervision parole was implemented for use with the juvenile offender population (Petersilia & Turner, 1993). At the time, many in society were concerned that juveniles on parole were not subject to enough supervision and concerns about dangerous juveniles being released fueled fears about public safety. **Intensive supervision parole** refers to the increased, or enhanced, monitoring and supervision of offenders on parole (Petersilia & Turner, 1993). These sentences are typically used for juveniles who have committed serious offenses, such as violent or sex crimes. Under intensive supervision parole sentences, juvenile offenders adhere to stricter conditions, maintain more contact with their parole officer, undergo more random drug testing, and participate in required treatment programs (Petersilia & Turner, 1993).

Image 13. © Lisa F. Young/Fotolia.

More recently, much of the discussion surrounding parole for juveniles has centered on the fact that juveniles were often sentenced to life *without* the possibility of parole (National Conference on State Legislatures, 2015). Many viewed this sentence for juveniles as too stringent and the Supreme Court agreed. In 2012, the Supreme Court ruled in the *Miller* v. *Alabama* decision that a life sentence without the possibility of parole for juveniles was unconstitutional and violated the Eighth Amendment, which prohibits against "excessive sanctions" (National Conference on State Legislatures, 2015). With this decision, parole now became an option again for juveniles sentenced to confinement. However, the approximately 1,500 offenders who were sentenced to this punishment prior to 2012 are still incarcerated (Stroud, 2015). At the present time, the Supreme Court is considering whether the *Miller* v. *Alabama* should apply retroactively and whether these affected offenders should be re-sentenced (Stroud, 2015). Additionally, juvenile sex offenders who were originally sentenced to life without parole are now finding themselves indefinitely civilly confined to institutions, which is raising concerns about violations of the Eight Amendment (Shute, 2015).

Statistics

Although there are over 1.5 million juvenile delinquency cases processed each year, it is unknown how many juvenile offenders, who received incarceration as a sentence, ultimately were released on parole. The Office of Juvenile Justice and Delinquency Prevention (2015) notes that statistical information on this is limited, however, they are working towards building such information in the future. Given that juvenile probation sentences represent about 60% of the sanctions that a convicted juvenile may receive, it is fair to assume that the other 40% if sanctions may be a combination of incarceration and other community corrections sentences, such as boot camp sentences (Livsey, 2012). Thus, the juvenile parole population is likely to be a much smaller slice of the 40% — but how much smaller is unknown. The data on juveniles that are actually incarcerated is also extremely limited. Upon further inspection of juvenile incarceration data, the most recent data collection was performed in 1995. At that time, there were approximately 108,000 juvenile offenders held in public, private, or shelter facilities (Office of Juvenile Justice and Delinquency Prevention, 1996). Again, with outdated data that also mixes counts of juveniles held in shelter facilities, it is extremely difficult to pinpoint what possible percentage of juveniles that may be serving parole sentences. Clearly, more data collection is critically needed in this area.

Conditions

Similar to adult parolees, juvenile parolees also must abide by conditions (see Text Box 7.6). Examples of conditions, for instance, that juveniles on parole in Texas are required to follow include not absconding, abiding by a curfew, not owning or possessing a weapon, attending school, participating in treatment, refraining from drug/alcohol use, refraining from tampering with any monitoring device, cleaning up or deleting social media sites they belong to, and not committing a new crime (Texas Juvenile Justice Department, 2015). For paroled juvenile sex offenders, for example, additional conditions may be placed on them such as not having any unsupervised contact with minors and prohibiting them from babysitting or other activities that may place them into contact with minors (Texas Juvenile Justice Department, 2015).

With growing concerns about successful reentry, some jurisdictions are utilizing new models to assist juveniles in reintegrating back into society besides just releasing offenders on parole with the general conditions to follow. In 2011, Illinois created aftercare specialist positions whose job it is to first work with juveniles while they are incarcerated to develop a parole, or aftercare, plan and then continue to do so upon their release. With this model, the Illinois Department of Juvenile Justice (2015) claims that "youth will no longer be subject to the ineffective DOC-run, adult-focused parole system which only serves as a surveillance and revocation mechanism." During the first 90 days on parole, the juvenile offender meets with his/her aftercare specialists weekly, and, after 90 days, the juvenile meets the aftercare specialist monthly. Throughout the parole process, the aftercare specialist is meeting with school personnel, family, counselors, and service provides on a monthly basis in an effort to identify any challenges faced by the juvenile and provide a continuum of care (Illinois Department of Juvenile Justice, 2015). Additionally, many states are either eliminating the use of parole for most juvenile offenses or shortening the length of time juvenile offenders may be on parole to as little as six months in order to foster successful reentry. For example, in the state of Washington, only juveniles classified as high risk or who are sex offenders or auto thieves can actually receive parole. A juvenile offender in Washington State will receive a 20-week parole sentence for auto theft crimes whereas higher risk juvenile offenders will serve a six-month intensive parole sentence (Washington Association of Juvenile Court Administrators, 2013). However, juvenile sex offenders could receive a parole sentence of anywhere from 2–3 years in the state (Washington Association of Juvenile Court Administrators, 2013).

Text Box 7.6: Washington State Juvenile Parole Release Guidelines

Following the release of any juvenile, the secretary may require the juvenile to comply with a program of parole to be administered by the department in his or her community which shall last no longer than eighteen months, except that in the case of a juvenile sentenced for rape in the first or second degree, rape of a child in the first or second degree, child molestation in the first degree, or indecent liberties with forcible compulsion, the period of parole shall be twenty-four months and, in the discretion of the secretary, may be up to thirty-six months when the secretary finds that an additional period of parole is necessary and appropriate in the interests of public safety or to meet the ongoing needs of the juvenile. A parole program is mandatory for offenders released under subsection (2) of this section and for offenders who receive a juvenile residential commitment sentence for theft of a motor vehicle, possession of a stolen motor vehicle, or taking a motor vehicle without permission 1. A juvenile adjudicated for unlawful possession of a firearm, possession of a stolen firearm, theft of a firearm, or drive-by shooting may participate in aggression replacement training, functional family therapy, or functional family parole aftercare if the juvenile meets eligibility requirements for these services. The decision to place an offender in an evidence-based parole program shall be based on an assessment by the department of the offender's risk for reoffending upon release and an assessment of the ongoing treatment needs of the juvenile. The department shall prioritize available parole resources to provide supervision and services to offenders at moderate to high risk for reoffending.

The secretary shall, for the period of parole, facilitate the juvenile's reintegration into his or her community and to further this goal shall require the juvenile to refrain from possessing a firearm or using a deadly weapon and refrain from committing new offenses and may require the juvenile to: (i) Undergo available medical, psychiatric, drug and alcohol, sex offender, mental health, and other offense-related treatment services; (ii) report as directed to a parole officer and/or designee; (iii) pursue a course of study, vocational training, or employment; (iv) notify the parole officer of the current address where he or she resides; (v) be present at a particular address during specified hours; (vi) remain within prescribed geographical boundaries; (vii) submit to electronic monitoring; (viii) refrain from using illegal drugs and alcohol, and submit to random urinalysis when requested by the assigned parole officer; (ix) refrain from contact with specific individuals or a specified class of individuals; (x) meet other conditions determined by the parole officer to further enhance the juvenile's reintegration into the community; (xi) pay any court-ordered fines or restitution; and (xii) perform community restitution. Community restitution for the purpose of this section means compulsory service, without compensation, performed for the benefit of the community by the offender. Community restitution may be performed through public or private organizations or through work crews.

The secretary may further require up to twenty-five percent of the highest risk juvenile offenders who are placed on parole to participate in an intensive supervision program. Offenders participating in an intensive supervision program shall be required to comply with all terms and conditions listed in (b) of this subsection and shall also be required to comply with the following additional terms and conditions: (i) Obey all laws and refrain from any conduct that threatens public safety; (ii) report at least once a week to an assigned community case manager; and (iii) meet all other requirements imposed by the community case manager related to participating in the intensive supervision program. As a part of the intensive supervision program, the secretary may require day reporting.

After termination of the parole period, the juvenile shall be discharged from the department's supervision.

The department may also modify parole for violation thereof. If, after affording a juvenile all of the due process rights to which he or she would be entitled if the juvenile were an adult, the secretary finds that a juvenile has violated a condition of his or her parole, the secretary shall order one of the following which is reasonably likely to effectuate the purpose of the parole and to protect the public: (i) Continued supervision under the same conditions previously imposed; (ii) intensified supervision with increased reporting requirements; (iii) additional conditions of supervision authorized by this chapter; (iv) except as provided in (a)(v) and (vi) of this subsection, imposition of a period of confinement not to exceed thirty days in a facility operated by or pursuant to a contract with the state of Washington or any city or county for a portion of each day or for a certain number of days each week with the balance of the days or weeks spent under supervision; (v) the secretary may order any of the conditions or may return the offender to confinement for the remainder of the sentence range if the offense for which the offender was sentenced is rape in the first or second degree, rape of a child in the first or second degree, child molestation in the first degree, indecent liberties with forcible compulsion, or a sex offense that is also a serious violent offense as defined by RCW 9.94A.030; and (vi) the secretary may order any of the conditions or may return the offender to confinement for the remainder of the sentence range if the youth has completed the basic training camp program as described in RCW 13.40.320.

The secretary may modify parole and order any of the conditions or may return the offender to confinement for up to twenty-four weeks if the offender was sentenced for a sex offense as defined under *RCW 9A.44.130 and is known to have violated the terms of parole. Confinement beyond thirty days is intended to only be used for a small and limited number of sex offenders. It shall only be used when other graduated sanctions or interventions have not been effective or the behavior is so egregious it warrants the use of the higher level intervention and the violation: (i) Is a known pattern of behavior consistent with a previous sex offense that puts the youth at high risk for reoffending sexually; (ii) consists of sexual behavior that is determined to be predatory as defined in RCW 71.09.020; or (iii) requires a review under chapter 71.09 RCW, due to a recent overt act. The total number of days of confinement for violations of parole conditions during the parole period shall not exceed the number of days provided by the maximum sentence imposed by the disposition for the underlying offense pursuant to RCW 13.40.0357. The department shall not aggregate multiple parole violations that occur prior to the parole revocation hearing and impose consecutive twenty-four week periods of confinement for each parole violation. The department is authorized to engage in rule making pursuant to chapter 34.05 RCW, to implement this subsection, including narrowly defining the behaviors that could lead to this higher level intervention.

If the department finds that any juvenile in a program of parole has possessed a firearm or used a deadly weapon during the program of parole, the department shall modify the parole under (a) of this subsection and confine the juvenile for at least thirty days. Confinement shall be in a facility operated by or pursuant to a contract with the state or any county.

A parole officer of the department of social and health services shall have the power to arrest a juvenile under his or her supervision on the same grounds as a law enforcement officer would be authorized to arrest the person.

Source: Washington State Legislature. (2015). *RCW 13.40.210. Setting of release date—Administrative release authorized, when—Parole program, revocation or modification of, scope—Intensive supervision program—Parole officer's right of arrest.* Retrieved from http://app.leg. wa.gov/rcw/default.aspx?cite=13.40.210.

Assessments

As mentioned previously, risk assessment tools were first developed for juveniles in the 1970s (Baird et al., 2013). In an effort to make juvenile parole release decisions with more precision as opposed to being based on professional judgements, juvenile parole boards do examine risk assessment tool information to guide their decisions. Currently, a universal juvenile risk assessment tool is not utilized, thus, states utilize their own risk assessment tools. In many cases, states utilize the same risk instrument for juveniles placed either on probation or parole, therefore, separate juvenile parole risk assessment tools may not exist in a particular state. For instance, several states have adopted juvenile risk and risk/needs assessment tools utilized for those on probation or parole known as: the Arizona Risk/Needs Assessment, the Risk and Resiliency Checkup (RRC), the Youth Offender Level of Service Inventory (YO-LSI), Youth Level of Service/Case Management Inventory System (YLS/CMI), the Positive Achievement Change Tool (PACT), and the Youth Assessment and Screening Instrument (YASI) (Administrative Office of the Courts, 2011; Baird et al., 2013). Additional instruments may be utilized by states to predict violent recidivism, including the Psychopathy Checklist-Youth Version (PCL-YV) and the Structured Assessment of Violence Risk in Youth (SAVRY) (Oliver et al., 2009). The RRC is a 60-item risk/needs assessment tool which contains questions tapping delinquency, education, family, peers, substance use, and individual factors (Vincent, Terry, & Maney, 2009). In each of the scales, questions assess both protective and risk factors for the juvenile. A lower score on the RRC indicates that the juvenile is at a higher risk for offending (Vincent et al., 2009).

Although many evaluations have been conducted with several of the aforementioned tools, such as the PCL-YV and SAVRY, demonstrating their predictive ability for violent recidivism, there have been a limited number of evaluations of assessment tools specifically for juvenile parolees (Oliver et al., 2009). The little research that has been conducted with this sample only has yielded rather mixed support for some of these instruments. For instance, in an examination of three different risk assessment tools, Ashford & LeCroy (1990), found that only one tool adequately predicted recidivism for juvenile parolees. Additionally, Turner, Fain, & Sehgal (2005), examined an RRC instrument used in L.A. County to investigative its ability to predict recidivism for juvenile probationers. Overall, the researchers found that the instrument was predictive of recidivism for juvenile probationers, both male and female, and for various races/ethnicities — except for Hispanic youth (Turner et al., 2005). Unfortunately, their examination did not include exploring how the RRC instrument predicted recidivism for juvenile *parolees*. Despite the difference in the study population, Turner et al.'s (2005) results suggests that juvenile risk assessments may need some modifications for different races and ethnicities — perhaps for both juvenile probationers and parolees. The lack of empirical investigations may also be an artifact of the reduced use of juvenile parole across the nation. With a limited number of comprehensive evaluations of risk assessments for parolees, more research is needed on these instruments and perhaps further refinement of risk assessment tools for juveniles on parole is required — especially since many tools are designed for use on probationers and parolees, which clearly are two distinct populations.

Juvenile Parole Outcomes

There have been several research investigations into recidivism rates for juveniles on parole with most evaluations being individual state analyses. Unfortunately, the results have not yielded strong support of reductions in recidivism for juveniles placed on parole. The sparse number of investigations into juvenile parole is also hampered by the fact that some states do not utilize parole very much for juvenile offenders or even track recidivism rates for juveniles released from prison or following parole (National Reentry Resource Center, 2014). Perhaps the lack of strong support is not all that surprising given the fact that there is a reason why a juvenile is released onto parole rather than just discharged from an institution. That is, there is concern regarding his/her risk for re-offending, which is why the juvenile is released with supervision. Barnoski and Aos (2001), examined juvenile recidivism rates for about 1,500 juveniles on parole and juveniles released without parole in 1999 in Washington State. The researchers found comparable recidivism rates after a 12-month follow-up period where both groups had been convicted of new felonies at a rate of about 30%. In a subsequent evaluation of juvenile parolees and non-parolees, using a longer follow-up period of 36 months, Drake and Barnoski (2006) again found no differences in recidivism rates between the groups. Additionally, in an examination of approximately 3,700 juveniles in Virginia, the Virginia Department of Justice (2014) found that juveniles on parole were 1.5 times more likely to be rearrested than juveniles not receiving parole sentences.

With only approximately four states having a distinct and separate juvenile parole board that is not part of the adult parole board, readily available data on juvenile parole revocation rates do not exist (Frendle, 2004). Additionally, research on the rates of juvenile parole revocation, at the national level, are lacking. In order to get a sense of the rate of parole revocation, inspection of individual state investigations would first need to be examined. In Illinois, juveniles seeking parole represent about 6.5% of all cases brought forth to the parole board year each, but a research investigation uncovered that nearly 54% of all juveniles granted parole had it revoked and were re-incarcerated, mostly due to a technical violation (Schiffman, 2011). The high revocation rate for such a small population coupled with allegations that juveniles were being denied access to their constitutionals rights during the revocation hearing, such as remaining incarcerated after being acquitted for a charge or not being informed that an attorney could be present during their revocation hearing, prompted a class action lawsuit (Schiffman, 2011; Schmadeke, 2013). By 2014, the state settled the lawsuit, which resulted in the protection of juvenile rights during revocation which processes about 1,000 parole revocations for juveniles each year (Schmadeke, 2014).

Factors Related to Juvenile Recidivism

Despite the gaps in knowledge, researchers have explored the factors that are predictive of recidivism for juveniles. Cottle, Lee, and Heilbrun (2001) conducted a meta-analysis of 23 studies in order to isolate specific risk factors that predict recidivism. Upon completion of their analysis, the researchers found that offense history was the strongest predictor of juvenile recidivism (Cottle et al., 2001). Additionally, the researchers found that family problems, conduct problems, and association with delinquent peers were also strong predictors of juvenile recidivism (Cottle et al., 2001). Other researchers have discovered that the social context of where juveniles may reside (i.e., neighborhood context), their offense history, and parental behaviors are predictive of drug and/or violent re-offending (Grunwald et al., 2010). More recently, Thompson and Morris (2013) examined approximately 3,200 male and female juveniles in Arizona to identify risk factors. The researchers found that offense severity was not predictive of recidivism but emotional disabilities was predictive of recidivism for both sexes (Thompson & Morris, 2013). While some research has found race to be a significant factor for juvenile recidivism, whereby African American juveniles are more likely to recidivate, Mbuba (2005) found in his research that race was not a significant predictor of juvenile recidivism. For juvenile female offenders, prior sexual abuse has been found to be the strongest predictor of their recidivism—even more so than other risk factors (Conrad et al., 2014).

Overall, it appears that prior offense history may be the best predictor of recidivism for juveniles. However, it is important to highlight that risk factors will not necessarily be the same for all offenders as there may be gender differences and perhaps even race/ethnicity differences. Additionally, research has revealed that differences in the types of predictors for juvenile offenders may vary by the type of offenses (e.g., drug or violent offenses) they commit.

What Is Needed in Juvenile Community Corrections

One of the chief problems with effectively meeting the needs of juveniles centers around the lack of consistent collection and tracking of juvenile recidivism data at the state and federal levels. If states, for instance, are not collecting this data or information on juvenile offender needs, then information cannot be gleaned as to *when* and perhaps *why* juveniles are re-offending. That is, if lack of parental support is a contributor to juvenile recidivism, this factor cannot be isolated and addressed if data do not exist to support services to enhance parent support to foster successful juvenile reentry. The National Reentry Resource Center (2014, p. 2) recommends the following changes: "1) Measure recidivism for youth involved with the juvenile justice system, considering the multiple ways they may have subsequent contact with the justice system; 2) Analyze recidivism data to account for youth's risk levels, as well as other key youth characteristics and variables; 3) Develop and maintain the infrastructure necessary to collect, analyze, and report recidivism data; and 4) Make recidivism data available to key constituents and the general public." In regards to the first recommendation, the National Reentry Resource Center (2014) encourages recidivism to be measured in a variety of ways including, but not limited to: rearrest; readjudication/reconviction; recommitment/reincarceration; and technical violations/revocations. For the second recommendation, if states are also not collecting data on risk and needs factors or even analyzing the data they do collect, they are doing a disservice to youth in that opportunities to offer assistance are missed. Finally, the last recommendation really speaks to the fact that in order for change to be implemented, key individuals need to be educated. All too often, the general public is clueless as to what is needed to help juvenile offenders. Thus, in order for meaningful changes to be implemented in juvenile community corrections, there has to be data and shared information to support those changes that both policymakers and members of the community can rally behind.

The Illinois Juvenile Justice Commission (2011, p. 9) poignantly states, in regards to juvenile community corrections in their own state, "In human terms, we must do better for our young people and our communities. In fiscal terms, we simply cannot afford to continue business as usual." In other words, juvenile community corrections needs to be overhauled. Specifically, the commission suggests moving away from the traditional surveillance-only practice for supervising youth on parole and moving towards a focus on aftercare. This suggestion, while aimed at the Illinois system, has universal application across all states. Additionally, the Illinois Juvenile Justice Commission (2011, p. 19) noted their juvenile corrections system is broken and "fails to identify youth needs and does not match identified needs with the services provided to the youth during incarceration." Thus, meeting the needs of juveniles while incarcerated and also while under supervision is critical (Peterson-Badali, Skilling, & Haqanee, 2015). Using assessment tools across all of juvenile community corrections should assist in this endeavor. Research has demonstrated that probation officers are capable of utilizing such tools effectively and routinely utilize results to make decisions about the conditions and care of the juvenile while under supervision (Models for Change, 2011). Therefore, the continued use of these instruments will assist in isolating those factors that are predictive of recidivism for all offenders, such as offense history, and those factors that are more predictive of recidivism for one gender, such as prior sexual abuse for female juvenile offenders. Further, the Illinois Juvenile Justice Commission (2011, p. 25) states that parole board members should receive the following training:

- Adolescent brain development and decision making
- Trauma, its impact on youth development and effective trauma-informed services
- Evidence-based practices in identifying youth needs, strengths and assets
- Evidence-based, youth-oriented services, supervision and support before and after release from secure detention
- Principles of effective institutional case management, including family engagement in positive behavioral change and use of community-based services and support
- Behavioral health (mental health and substance abuse) needs of justice-involved youth and effective means of addressing those needs
- Effective interactions with youth, families and staff, including age-appropriate communication, special attention to issues impacting fundamental fairness, and motivational interviewing and other procedural justice strategies.

While the recommendations were directed at improving youth parole practices, they certainly have applicability within probation as well. Appropriate rehabilitation and interventions for juvenile probation offenders can be successful in diverting these youth from detention and avoiding the stigma and label of "ex-offender" (Braithwaite, 1989; NPR, 2015).

Conclusion

In sum, this chapter devoted attention to the history of the use of probation and parole for juveniles, the current numbers of juveniles serving these sentences, conditions that juveniles serving these sentences must follow, assessment tools that are used with these populations, and juvenile probation and parole outcomes. Additionally, discussion regarding risk factors for juvenile recidivism as well as what is needed in juvenile community corrections was also provided. The research suggests that a focus on rehabilitation and appropriate aftercare is needed to foster successful juvenile offender reentry. Without a commitment to striking changes in approaches to managing and assisting juvenile community corrections offenders, these youth will likely recidivate and slip quietly into the adult corrections system.

Key Terms

Child-saving movement

Conditionary probation

Intensive supervision parole

Intensive supervision probation

School-based probation

Status offenses

Discussion Questions

1. Research juvenile probation and parole in your state. Describe the age, race, and gender of juvenile probationers and parolees in your state. What trends do you notice in your state with these populations?

2. How do you feel about parents being held accountable for their child's non-compliance with probationer orders? Do you feel this is fair? Should this practice continue? Why or why not? If not, what might be a better alternative?

3. Research the type of risk assessments utilized in your state for juvenile probationers and parolees. Identify the instruments and how they are used. Have there been empirical investigations into their effectiveness? If so, summarize the findings of these studies.

4. Reflect on the risk factors for juvenile recidivism as well as what is needed in community corrections for juveniles. What policy(ies) would you suggest that your state implement to better assist this often overlooked population?

References

Administrative Office of the Courts. (2011). *Screenings and assessments used in the juvenile justice system.* Retrieved from http://www.courts.ca.gov/documents/AOCBrief_RiskAndNeedsAssessement_rev011012.pdf.

Ashford, J. B., & LeCroy, C. W. (1990). Juvenile recidivism: A comparison of three prediction instruments. *Adolescence, 25*(98), 441–450.

Baird, C., Healy, T., Johnson, K., Bogie, A., Dankert, E. W., & Scharenbroch, C. (2013). *A comparison of risk assessment instruments in juvenile justice.* Washington, DC: U.S. Department of Justice.

Bannock County Juvenile Probation Department. (2015). Retrieved from http://www. bannockcounty.us/juvenile/probation/.

Barnoski, R., & Aos, S. (2001). The effects of parole on recidivism: Juvenile offenders released from Washington State institutions. Retrieved from http://www.wsipp. wa.gov/ReportFile/753.

Braithwaite, J. (1989). *Crime, shame, and reintegration.* Cambridge, UK: Oxford University Press.

Chute, C. L., (1923). Juvenile probation. *Annals of the American Academy of Political and Social Science, 105,* 223–228.

Clouser, M. (1995). School-based juvenile probation. *Pennsylvania Progress, 2*(1), 1–4.

Conrad, S. M., Tolou-Shams, M., Rizzo, C., Placella, N., & Brown, L. K. (2014). Gender differences in recidivism rates for juvenile justice youth: The impact of sexual abuse. *Law & Human Behavior, 38*(4), 305–314. doi: 10.1037/lhb0 000062.

Cook, A. K. (2013). I'm tired of my child getting into trouble: Parental controls and supports of juvenile probationers. *Journal of Offender Rehabilitation, 52*(8), 529–543. doi: 10.1080/10509674.2013.840352.

Cook, A. K., & Gordon, J. A. (2012). Get him out of my house: Parental competencies of juvenile probationers. *Youth Violence & Juvenile Justice, 10*(2), 205–223. doi: 10.1177/1541204011418352.

Cottle, C. C., Lee, R. J., & Heilbrun, K. (2001). Prediction of criminal recidivism in juveniles: A meta-analysis. *Criminal Justice & Behavior, 28*(3), 367–394. doi: 10.1177/0093854801028003005.

Drake, E. K., Aos, S., & Miller, M. G. (2009). Evidence-based public policy options to reduce future prison construction, criminal justice costs, and crime rates. *Victims & Offenders, 4,* 170–196. doi: 10.1080/15564880802612615.

Drake, E., K. & Barnoski, R. (2006). *The effects of parole on recidivism: Juvenile offenders released from Washington State institutions final report.* Retrieved from http://www.wsipp.wa.gov/ReportFile/948.

Early, K. P., Hand, G. A., & Blakenship, J. L. (2012). *Validity and reliability of the Florida PACT Risk and Needs Assessment Instrument: A three-phase evaluation.* Tallahassee, FL: Justice Research Center.

Ford, D. (2014, Feb. 6). Judge orders Texas teen Ethan Couch to rehab for driving drunk, killing 4. *CNN.* Retrieved from http://www.cnn.com/2014/02/05/us/ texas-affluenza-teen/.

Frederique, N. P. (2010). *The effectives of school based intensive probation for reducing recidivism: An evaluation of Maryland's Spotlight on Schools program.* University of Maryland: Dissertation.

Frendle, J. W. (2004). *An overview of juvenile parole boards in the United States.* New Mexico Sentencing Commission. Retrieved from http://nmsc.unm.edu/reports/2004/JuvParoleBoards.pdf.

Galveston County Texas. (2015). *Order of release with conditions: Juvenile not currently on probation.* Retrieved from http://www.galvestoncountytx.gov/Forms%20Library/Conditions%20of%20Release—NOT%20on%20Probation.pdf.

Green, M. (2015). *Celebrity biographies: The amazing life of Jay Z and 50 Cent.* Google Play Books.

Greenburg, Z. O. (2015, May 5). The Forbes five: Hip-hop's wealthiest artists 2015. *Forbes.* Retrieved from http://www.forbes.com/sites/zackomalleygreenburg/2015/05/05/the-forbes-five-hip-hops-wealthiest-artists-2015/.

Griffin, P. (1999a). *Juvenile probation in the schools.* Pittsburgh, PA: National Center on Juvenile Justice.

Griffin, P. (1999b). *Developing and administering accountability-based sanctions for juveniles.* Washington, DC: Office of Juvenile Justice and Delinquency Prevention.

Griffin, P., & Torbet, P. (2002). *Desktop guide to good juvenile probation practice.* Pittsburgh, PA: National Center on Juvenile Justice.

Grunwald, H., Lockwood, B., Harris, P., & Mennis, J. (2010). Influences of neighborhood context, individual history and parenting behavior on recidivism among juvenile offenders. *Journal of Youth & Adolescence, 39*(9), 1067–1079. doi: 10.1007/s10964-010-9518-5.

Hanna, J. (2016, April 14). 'Affluenza' teen Ethan Couch gets tentative order for 2-year jail term. *CNN.* Retrieved from http://www.cnn.com/2016/04/13/us/texas-affluenza-ethan-couch/.

Hannigan, K., Kolnick, K., Tian, S. T., Maxson, C., & Poplawski, J. (2010). *Five year outcomes in a randomized trial of a community-based multi-agency intensive supervision juvenile probation program.* Washington, DC: U.S. Department of Justice.

Hennessy-Fiske, M. (2009, March 30). Valley campuses added to school-based probation program. *L.A. Times.* Retrieved from http://articles.latimes.com/2009/mar/30/local/me-probation30.

Hinkle, W. & Whitmarsh, B. (2014). *Elmira reformatory.* Charleston, South Carolina: Arcadia Publishing.

Hockenberry, S. & Puzzanchera, C. (2015). *Juvenile court statistics, 2013.* Retrieved from http://www.ojjdp.gov/ojstatbb/njcda/pdf/jcs2013.pdf.

Hoffman, P. B. (2003). *History of the federal parole system.* Washington, DC: U.S. Department of Justice. Retrieved from http://www.justice.gov/sites/default/files/uspc/legacy/2009/10/07/history.pdf.

Illinois Department of Juvenile Justice. (2015). *Youth reentry.* Springfield, IL: Illinois Department of Human Services. Retrieved from https://www.dhs.state.il.us/page.aspx?item=58039.

Illinois Juvenile Justice Commission. (2011). *Youth reentry improvement report.* Springfield, IL. Retrieved from http://www.dhs.state.il.us/OneNetLibrary/27896/documents/By_Division/DCHP/RFP/IJJC_YouthRentryImprovement.pdf.

Kehoe, C. J. (1994). Dramatic changes in store for juvenile probation agencies. *Corrections Today, 56*(7), 96.

Kyvsgaard, B. (2004). Youth justice in Denmark. In M. Tonry & A. N. Doob (Eds.), *Youth crime and youth justice: Comparative and cross-national perspectives* (pp. 349–390). Chicago, IL: University of Chicago Press.

Lasater, L., Willis, T., Sherman, T., Schaaf, D., & Petak, F. (2008). *School-based probation intervention results with high-risk youth in Montana.* Boulder, CO: Character Development Systems.

Lindsey, E. (1925). Historical sketch of the indeterminate sentence and parole system. *Journal of the American Institute of Criminal Law, & Criminology, 16,* 9–69.

Livsey, S. (2012). *Juvenile delinquency probation caseload, 2009.* Washington, DC: U.S. Department of Justice.

Lowenkamp, C. T., & Latessa, E. J. (2005). Increasing the effectiveness of correctional programming through the risk principle: Identifying offenders for residential placement. *Criminology & Public Policy, 4*(2), 263–290. doi: 10.1111/j.1745-9133.2005.00021.x.

MacKenzie, D. (2006). *What works in corrections: Reducing the criminal activities of offenders and delinquents.* New York: Cambridge University Press.

Maschi, T., Schwalbe, C., & Ristow, J. (2013). In pursuit of the ideal parent in juvenile justice: A qualitative investigation of probation officers' experiences with parents of juvenile offenders. *Journal of Offender Rehabilitation, 52*(7), 470–492. doi: 10.1080/10509674.2013.829898.

Mbuba, J. M. (2005). A refutation of racial differentials in the juvenile recidivism rate hypothesis. *African Journal of Criminology & Justice Studies, 1*(2), 52–68.

Metzger, D. S. (1997). *School-based probation in Pennsylvania.* Philadelphia, PA: University of Pennsylvania, Center for Studies of Addiction.

Mitchell, M. (2013, December 10). Teen sentenced to 10 years probation, rehab in 4 deaths. *Star-Telegram.* Retrieved from http://www.star-telegram.com/news/local/crime/article3839368.html.

Models for Change. (2011). *Can risk assessment improve juvenile justice practices?* Washington, DC: Justice Policy Institute. Retrieved from http://www.umassmed.edu/uploadedFiles/cmhsr/NYSAP/KnowledgeBrief%20Can%20Risk%20Assessment.pdf.

National Conference on State Legislatures. (2015). *Miller v. Alabama*: Mandatory life without parole sentences are unconstitutional for juveniles. Retrieved from http://

www.ncsl.org/research/civil-and-criminal-justice/miller-v-alabama-mandatory-life-without-parole.aspx.

National Reentry Resource Center. (2014). *Measuring and using juvenile recidivism data to inform policy, practice, and resource allocation.* Retrieved from https://cs-gjusticecenter.org/wp-content/uploads/2014/07/Measuring-and-Using-Juvenil-e-Recidivism-Data-to-Inform-Policy-Practice-and-Resource-Allocation.pdf.

NeMoyer, A., Goldstein, N. S., McKitten, R. L., Prelic, A., Ebbecke, J., Foster, E., & Burkard, C. (2014). Predictors of juveniles' noncompliance with probation requirements. *Law & Human Behavior, 38*(6), 580–591. doi: 10.1037/lhb0000083.

NPR. (2015, July 29). Probation with a therapeutic approach keeps kids out of juvenile hall. *NPR, Youth Radio.* Retrieved from http://www.npr.org/2015/07/29/427464695/probation-with-a-therapeutic-approach-keeps-kids-out-of-juvenile-hall.

Office of Juvenile Justice and Delinquency Prevention. (1996). *Children in custody: Census of public and private juvenile detention, correctional, and shelter facilities 1994/1995.* Washington, DC: Bureau of the Census.Data Source: Office of Juvenile Justice and Delinquency Prevention. Children in Custody Census of Public and Private Juvenile Detention, Correctional, and Shelter Facilities 1994/95 [machine-readable data files]. Washington, D.C.: Bureau of the Census, 1996. Data Source: Office of Juvenile Justice and Delinquency Prevention. Children in Custody Census of Public and Private Juvenile Detention, Correctional, and Shelter Facilities 1994/95 [machine-readable data files]. Washington, D.C.: Bureau of the Census, 1996.

Office of Juvenile Justice and Delinquency Prevention. (2015). *Juvenile reentry and aftercare.* Washington, DC: Office of Justice Programs.

Oliver, M. E., Stockdale, K. C., & Wormith, J. S. (2009). Risk assessment with young offenders: A meta-analysis of three assessment measures. *Criminal Justice & Behavior, 36*(4), 329–353. doi: 10.1177/0093854809331457.

Onifade, E., Wilkins, J., Davidson, W., Campbell, C., & Petersen, J. (2011). A comparative analysis of recidivism with propensity score matching of informal and formal juvenile probationers. *Journal of Offender Rehabilitation, 50*(8), 531–546. doi:10.1080/10509674.2011.618526.

O'Toole, S. (2006). *The history of Australian corrections.* Australia: University of New South Wales Press.

Panzarella, R. (2002). Theory and practice of probation on bail in the report of John Augustus. *Federal Probation, 66*(3), 38–42.

Petersilia, J., & Turner, S. (1993). Intensive probation and parole. *Crime and Justice, 17*, 281–335.

Peterson-Badali, M., Skilling, T., & Haqanee, Z. (2015). Examining implementation of risk assessment in case management for youth in the justice system. *Criminal Justice & Behavior, 42*(3), 304–320. doi: 10.1177/0093854814549595.

Platt, A. (1969). The rise of the child-saving movement: A study in social policy and correctional reform. *Annals of the American Academy of Political and Social Science, 381,* 21–38.

Rembert, D. A., Henderson, H., & Pirtle, D. (2014). Differential racial/ethnic predictive validity. *Youth Violence & Juvenile Justice, 12*(2), 152–166. doi: 10.1177/1541204013485606.

Ryan, J. P., Abrams, L. S., & Huang, H. (2014). First-time violent juvenile offenders: Probation, placement, and recidivism. *Social Work Research, 38*(1), 1–12. doi: 10.1093/swr/svu004.

Schiffman, L. (2011, December 14). Illinois juvenile justice commission: Broken parole system traps young offenders. *The Huffington Post.* Retrieved from http://www.huffingtonpost.com/2011/12/14/illinois-juvenile-justice-commission-report-parole_n_1145752.html.

Schmadeke, S. (2013, November 10). Lawsuits challenge Illinois' parole revocation process. *Chicago Tribune.* Retrieved from http://articles.chicagotribune.com/2013-11-10/news/ct-met-parole-hearings-prison-20131111_1_parole-violation-alexa-van-brunt-revocation.

Schmadeke, S. (2014, May 19). State agrees to settlement in lawsuit alleging a 'kangaroo court.' *Chicago Tribune.* Retrieved from http://articles.chicagotribune.com/2014-05-19/news/chi-state-agrees-to-settlement-in-lawsuit-alleging-a-kangaroo-court-20140519_1_juvenile-offenders-parole-revocation-hearings-alexa-van-brunt.

Schwalbe, C. S. (2012). Toward an integrated theory of probation. *Criminal Justice & Behavior, 39*(2), 185–201. doi: 10.1177/0093854811430185.

Shute, T. M. (2015). Cruel and unusual: The effect of *Miller v. Alabama* on the indefinite civil commitment of juvenile sex offenders. *New England Journal on Criminal & Civil Commitment, 41*(1), 225–251.

Stroud, M. (2015, March 23). The Supreme Court takes one more look at life sentences for teens. *Bloomberg Business.* Retrieved from http://www.bloomberg.com/news/articles/2015-03-23/the-supreme-court-takes-one-more-look-at-life-sentences-for-teenagers.

Texas Juvenile Justice Department. (2015). *General administrative policy manual: Rules and consequences for youth on parole.* Retrieved from https://www.tjjd.texas.gov/policies/gap/380/95/gap3809504.pdf.

Thompson, K. C., & Morris, R. J. (2013). Predicting recidivism among juvenile delinquents: Comparison of risk factors for male and female offenders. *Journal of Juvenile Justice, 3*(1), 36–47.

Torbet, P., Ricci, R., Brooks, C., & Zawacki, S. (2001). *Evaluation of Pennsylvania's school-based probation program.* Pittsburg, PA: National Center of Juvenile Justice.

Turner, S., Fain, T., & Sehgal, A. (2005). Validation of the risk and resiliency assessment tool for juveniles in the Los Angeles County probation system. Los Angeles: RAND.

Vincent, G. M., Terry, A. M., & Maney, S. M. (2009). Risk/needs tools for antisocial behavior and violence among youthful populations. In J. T. Andrade (Ed.), *Handbook of violence risk assessment and treatment: New approaches for mental health professionals* (pp. 377–424). New York, NY: Springer.

Virginia Department of Juvenile Justice. (2014). *Predictors of recidivism for juveniles released from direct care.* Retrieved from http://www.djj.virginia.gov/pdf/AboutDJJ/RecidivismPredictors.pdf.

Wachter, A. (2015). *Statewide risk assessment in juvenile probation.* Pittsburgh, PA: Juvenile Justice: Geography, Policy, Practice, & Statistics.

Wagoner, R. C., Schubert, C. A., & Mulvey, E. P. (2015). Probation intensity, self-reported offending, and psychopathy in juveniles on probation for serious offenses. *Journal of the American Academy of Psychiatry & the Law, 43*(2), 191–200.

Washington Association of Juvenile Court Administrators. (2013). *Washington State model for juvenile justice.* Retrieved from https://www.dshs.wa.gov/sites/default/files/JJRA/jr/documents/WashingtonStateModelforJuvenileJustice.pdf.

Washington State Legislature. (2015). *RCW 13.40.210. Setting of release date—Administrative release authorized, when—Parole program, revocation or modification of, scope—Intensive supervision program—Parole officer's right of arrest.* Retrieved from http://app.leg.wa.gov/rcw/default.aspx?cite=13.40.210.

Wiebush, R. G. (1993). Juvenile intensive supervision: The impact on felony offenders diverted from institutional placement. *Crime and Delinquency, 39*(1), 68–89. doi: 10.1177/0011128793039001005.

Witmer, H. L. (1927). The history, theory and results of parole. *Journal of the American Institute of Criminal Law, & Criminology, 18,* 24–64.

Chapter 8

Reentry:
Challenges and Obstacles

Student Learning Outcomes

After reading this chapter, you should be able to:

- Describe the many obstacles that offenders face within community corrections.

- Explain how the obstacles and challenges faced by community corrections offenders may be more pronounced for certain groups of offenders in society.

- Summarize what policy changes could be implemented that could assist community corrections offenders in overcoming their challenges in reentry.

Introduction

Each day millions of community corrections offenders are attempting to reintegrate successfully into society while serving probation, reporting to day reporting center sentences, or even transitioning from prison to serving parole sentences. As you may imagine there are many obstacles in their way as these offenders attempt to abide by the conditions of their sentence and assimilate back into society. Given the many challenges, successful reentry is an evasive goal for many, and those offenders who are successful upon reentry often face setbacks. For California probationer Toni Botai, her successful reentry story is a glimmer of hope that reformation is possible—even for offenders who have been involved in the system for years (Johnson, 2013). Botai's journey into the criminal justice system is a familiar one for many offenders. She first tried heroin at age 15 and soon her life revolved squarely around the drug (Johnson, 2013). Her use of the drug at such a young age resulted in an addiction that lasted four decades. The crimes that she engaged in to support her heroin habit, such as drug-dealing, resulted in her serving multiple sentences in prison over that time period. As she reports, "Before I knew it, my whole life passed me by," she said. "That drug took my youth, my adulthood, and I allowed it" (Johnson, 2013). Most in society would view Botai as a lost cause—a person that is so engrained in the criminal justice system that successful transformation is highly unlikely. Fortunately for Botai, while serving yet another sentence for one of her criminal offenses, her probationer officer was able to finally help Botai break away from her criminal past, and this time she was ready to accept his assistance (Johnson, 2013). With the help and support of her probationer officer, she was eventually able to kick her drug habit, obtain employment, and secure housing (Johnson, 2013). All too often, citizens do not hear about such success stories for the "average" community corrections offender. More often than not, the news media reports on those who have failed while serving community corrections sentences or those offenders who have inflicted some harm on communities while serving such sentences.

Another former offender who surpassed the odds regarding reentry is Dave Dahl, founder and creator of Dave's Killer Bread. Dahl, whose family was in the bread making profession in Oregon, found himself entangled in the criminal justice system after he developed a methamphetamine addiction, which propelled him to sells drugs and engage in property and personal crimes, including an armed robbery, to support his habit (Schulzke, 2012). Facing a potential incarceration term of 20 years for the various offenses he was arrested for, Dahl opted to take a plea bargain, and in doing so served just a 7-year prison sentence (Schulzke, 2012). Upon release from prison in 2004, Dahl rejoined the family business and launched his own special organic breads the following year, which he named Dave's Killer Bread (Schulzke, 2012). Sales of the organic breads soon skyrocketed into the millions, and it appeared that Dahl had successfully reentered society (Schulzke, 2012). However, in 2013, Dahl had started to unwind and began drinking to cope with mental health problems (Duin, 2014). During a mental health crisis he had, he rammed a few police cars and engaged in a brief police chase, resulting in his arrest in Oregon (Duin, 2014; Theen, 2015). Despite the setback, Dahl rebounded and was able to avoid another prison sentence for his offenses. Instead, in 2015, the judge granted him conditional release under the supervision of the Oregon State Psychiatric Review Board as Dahl suffers from bipolar disorder (Smith, 2015). Later that year, Dahl sold his bread line to another company for $275 million (Theen, 2015). Given that his needs have been recognized by the state, Dahl will likely be successful during reentry since he will be obtaining the help and support he currently needs.

This chapter will discuss the myriad of challenges and obstacles that community corrections offenders face upon reentry. These include, but are not limited to, housing, employment, transportation, social acceptance, personal relationships, legal complications, loss of constitutional rights, substance abuse, and re-offending. Additionally, some of these challenges may be more pronounced for certain groups (e.g., minority offenders, sex offenders, female offenders). Finally, this chapter will highlight policy changes that could be implemented that could assist community corrections offenders in overcoming their challenges in reentry.

Challenges & Obstacles

There are a wide range of community corrections offenders who are attempting to reenter into society. Some of these offenders serve long sentences in prison and then are released on parole—in many cases for several more years. Other community corrections offenders are serving shorter sentences. Examples of community corrections offenders serving shorter sentences include those individuals serving probation sentences as well as any other form of an intermediate sanction (e.g., day reporting center, halfway house, work release center). Research on offender reentry over the past thirty years has demonstrated that an offenders' ability to reintegrate successfully is hindered by numerous obstacles, such as difficulty in obtaining employment, acquiring housing, and being admitted to higher education, as well as any number of medical problems (Gunnison & Helfgott, 2013; Petersilia, 2003). For instance, newly released offenders from prison who are serving parole sentences encounter stigmatization and are often in need of social support, substance abuse treatment, and mental health treatment (Cullen, 1994; Gunnison & Helfgott, 2013; Petersilia, 2003). Offenders serving short-term community corrections sentences, such as probation, also suffer from these same difficulties. Given the wide range of obstacles offenders face when reintegrating back into society and the various resources that may be available to these assist these offenders, community corrections offenders face an uphill battle in the bid to successfully reenter their communities. The following sections highlight some of the pervasive problems that community corrections offenders can encounter during reentry.

Housing

Housing has been identified as one of the most difficult obstacles offenders encounter in their reentry by both ex-offenders and correctional administrators (Gunnison & Helfgott, 2013; Gunnison, Helfgott, & Wilhelm, 2015; Helfgott, 1997). Housing is such an obstacle for all offenders transitioning back into their communities that Roman and Travis (2006, p. 389) state that the question for these offenders quickly becomes "Where will I sleep tomorrow?" One reason for the difficulties that community corrections offenders experience with securing housing is due to their lack of income. Offenders often have limited credit, rental history, and finances, which restrict their housing opportunities and options (Helfgott, 1997; Phillips & Spencer, 2013). McLean and Thompson (2007) report that offenders are saddled with a large amount of debt upon release from jails and prisons. This debt includes supervision fees (e.g., jail, probation, and mandatory urine screens), court costs, victim restitution, and child support (McLean & Thompson, 2007; Shivy et al., 2007). Additionally, McLean and Thompson (2007, p. 7) explain "people released from prisons and jails typically have insufficient resources to pay their debts to their children, victims, and the criminal justice system." Thus, the limited income in addition to the debt experienced by community corrections offenders further compounds their inability to acquire housing.

Some community corrections offenders are fortunate enough to be able to return to their own home or reside with family members upon release from jail or prison. For example, in a study of parolees conducted by Nelson, Deess, and Allen (1999), the researchers found that approximately 80% of the former offenders lived with family members following their release. While some parolees may return to their home with their families, this is often not an option available to many. If a parolees' family members are also criminal, then returning to the family home would not be a suitable residence for them per parole guidelines (Phillips & Spencer, 2013). This is a similar concern for offenders serving probation sentences, as their housing has to be approved by their probation officer. Unfortunately, for some parolees there has been a breakdown in the family structure (e.g., marriage, relationships with other family members) stemming from their incarceration (Clear, 2007; Fontaine & Biess, 2012; Martinez & Christian, 2009). With prisons typically being located far away from the family of the incarcerated individual, the offender may not receive many visits from family members, leading to a natural disconnection between the offender and his/her family over time. This is especially the case for incarcerated female offenders. Additionally, it may be the case that the family supported the offender for many years, but after their latest conviction and sentence family members severed their ties with him/her, resulting in the newly released parolee having no stable home to return to.

Another significant barrier that many community corrections offenders face with housing is limited availability options. Many landlords are reluctant to rent to offenders due to their fear for community safety or losing current tenants who may become fearful of being a neighbor to the offender (Clark, 2007; Harding & Harding, 2006; Helfgott, 1997). This is especially true for registered sex-offenders (Evans & Porter, 2015). For sex offenders, housing is often a greater obstacle for them as opposed to other offenders as many states have passed legislation that further restricts their residency (i.e., not near schools, daycares, playgrounds, and parks) (Barnes, Dukes, Tewksbury, & De Trove, 2009; Grubesic, Murray, & Mack, 2011). Stromberg (2007, p. 20) refers to this group as being "locked up, then locked out," since sex offenders are excluded from many housing options due to fear for community safety. Zandbergen and Hart (2006, p. 1), in a case study of housing options for registered sex offenders in Florida, found "that housing options for registered sex offenders within urban residential areas are limited to only 5% of potentially available parcels and that bus stop restrictions impact the amount of livable area the most, followed by daycares, schools, parks, and attractions. The limited options to establish residency exist mostly in low-density rural areas." Thus, sex offenders may be pushed out to rural communities, which pose their own unique challenges for successful reentry (see Wodhal, 2006). Additionally, drug offenders are another group whose housing options may be limited more so than other community corrections offenders. Their conviction status as a drug offender results in this group being denied federally assisted housing, impacting thousands of these offenders (United States Government Accountability Office, 2005). It is not uncommon for offenders who were convicted of a drug-related crime to be ineligible for housing for at least three years (Mukamal, 2000).

Without suitable housing, former offenders must resort to being homeless or residing in an environment (i.e., a high crime community) that undermines their likelihood of being able to successfully complete rehabilitation programming and reintegrate into their community (Clear, 2007; Gunnison & Helfgott, 2013). Kirk (2012), who examined residential changes of parolees after Hurricane Katrina, found that parolees three years post-release, who returned to a different neighborhood in New Orleans than where they had resided during their conviction, were less likely to

Image 14. © iStockphoto.com/zimmytws.

recidivate than parolees who returned to their original neighborhood. This finding suggests that it is not just obtaining housing that matters for community corrections offenders but the particular community and situational and environmental context that these offenders are returning to is also critical for their success. Therefore, community corrections offenders may find that the only place they can find housing is in impoverished neighborhoods where they are less likely to find employment—another key obstacle to successful offender reentry (Gunnison & Helfgott, 2013).

Employment

With get-tough-on-crime policies, many community corrections offenders have found more doors closed, as opposed to open, for employment (Henry & Jacobs, 2007; Lucken & Ponte, 2008). In fact, the overall unemployment rate for offenders is estimated to be between 25 to 40 percent (Petersilia, 2003). Possessing a felony record disqualifies many offenders from certain occupations (Petersilia, 2001) and criminal background checks create barriers to employment for them as well (Harris & Kellar, 2005). Besides the external barriers that exist for community corrections offenders, they often have internal barriers that limit their employability. Holzer, Raphael, and Stoll (2003) explain that offenders have several characteristics that limit their ability to obtain employment or high paying jobs such as limited education, deficient cognitive skills, and limited legal work experience. Berg and Huebner (2011,

p. 388) add that "many offenders lack much-needed work skills, educational qualifications, and a stable history of employment." Deficits in education play a large role
in the ability of offenders to find jobs since almost two-thirds of offenders have
dropped out of high school (Travis, Solomon, & Waul, 2001). In one particularly
study, Hirsch and colleagues (2002) report that nearly 50% of offenders are "func-
tionally illiterate." The prohibition of the use of Pell grants by the federal government
in 1994 in state and federal prisons further stymied offenders' access to higher education and their ability to obtain a college degree (Erisman & Contardo, 2005; Heinrich, 2000; Lockwood, Nally, Ho, & Knutson, 2012; Stevens & Ward, 1997). With
the access to higher education severed, incarcerated offenders lost an opportunity to
develop skills which would enhance their likelihood of securing employment when
paroled and probationers lost the chance to pursue higher education in an effort to
raise their employability.

Attaining employment is hampered by offenders' inability to search for employment
via the internet or newspaper or even fill out a job application. It is not uncommon
to find offenders who lack the skills to construct an e-mail, utilize e-mail, or even
create a resume in a word processing program. This is particularly a problem for
parolees. Without a little technological savvy, their efforts to find legitimate legal employment are further hampered. If offenders are able to secure a coveted interview
for a job, they are often deficient in life skills such as proper interview attire and interview preparation skills that would ensure success for most job candidates (Brown,
2004a; Helfgott, 1997). Thus, many offenders rely on personal connections to find
a job (Visher, La Vigne, & Travis, 2004). However, offenders often do not have many
pro-social contacts that they can rely on for job referrals or may lack the ability to
form social networks which could assist them in their search for employment (Shivy
et al., 2007). Further, if offenders are successful in landing a job, they have a "limited
knowledge of workplace culture and need to develop certain interpersonal and conflict
resolution skills to be able to retain a job" (Heinrich, 2000, p. 5). The absence of ex-
hibiting proper social skills in a work environment stems from their lack of an ex-
tensive, or any, past legal work history.

Another common barrier that offenders face is that many employers are reluctant
to hire them, which is often associated with the stigma of their record (Gunnison &
Helfgott, 2013; Travis et al., 2001). Offenders have reported experiencing discrimination in regards to employment (LeBel, 2012). Fahey, Roberts, and Engel (2006),
in a focus group study of 28 employers in the Boston area, found that employers
were often reluctant to be the first place of employment for an offender. That is, employers were more comfortable hiring an offender as his/her second or third job upon
release from prison as it would allow the offender to prove his/her value through his/
her employment track record. Apart from discrimination experienced by community
corrections offenders due to their conviction record, many offenders also experience
discrimination due to their race, or **double discrimination** (Gunnison & Helfgott,
2013). Holzer and colleagues (2003, p. 5) explain "most ex-offenders are minorities—nearly half are African-American, and nearly a fifth are Latino or Asian. To

the extent that minorities continue to suffer labor market discrimination, this will further impede the ability of ex-offenders to gain employment or earn higher wages." Previous research has revealed that racial discrimination in hiring is indeed a problem for minorities without a conviction record, thus, minority community corrections offenders experience additional invisible barriers in their search for gainful employment (Toth, Crews, & Burton, 2008).

Additional concerns employers have when hiring offenders surround the issue of legal liability (Lucken & Ponte, 2008). While all employers can be held liable for employee misconduct, there is a heightened sense of concern for many employers on this issue when considering the hiring of offenders, with certain types of crime of more concern to employers than others such as violent crime and property crimes (e.g., theft and embezzlement) (Helfgott, 1997). Thus, many employers may be reluctant to hire offenders, not to due to the desire not to hire them, but out of fear for being on the reverse end of a lawsuit on the grounds of negligent hiring. Employers are aware of offenders' criminal history when they are hired, and this knowledge could more easily be used against the employer in a lawsuit—particularly if the offender commits a similar crime for which he/she was convicted while on the job.

Offenders often experience legal obstacles which do not permit them to be considered for employment in particular occupations, such as healthcare or education (Heinrich, 2000; Petersilia, 2003; Petersilia, 2005). Unless an offender has had previous employment experience in the healthcare field and obtains government waivers, then the offender will be excluded from any form of employment in the healthcare field (Heinrich, 2000). Other common employment restrictions for offenders include government positions (e.g., holding a political office position, civil service jobs), criminal justice occupations (e.g., law enforcement officers, prosecutors, correctional officers), teaching positions in the K–12 level, childcare work, and private security (Heinrich, 2000). Petersilia (2005) adds that offenders are often excluded from unionized jobs and face additional obstacles in meeting licensing requirements for certain job positions such as garbage collecting.

Further complicating the quest for legal employment is the formal state guidelines requiring offenders to obtain employment within a specified period of time. In Washington State, for example, residents of work release programs are required to obtain employment within 10 days per Department of Corrections' policy. As one can imagine, particularly in the past few years with the fluctuations in the economy, this can be a difficult endeavor for offenders. When national unemployment rates were looming high a few years ago, offenders found themselves at an increased disadvantage in their job hunt. After all, when unemployment rates were rather high, employers who were hiring were inundated with many applications from highly qualified individuals who lost their jobs and were also on the job market. With a plethora of applications, employers during this time period could afford be more selective in who they decide to hire. This sentiment was echoed in research conducted by Fahey et al. (2006), who found that employers viewed job candidates with a criminal record to be less desirable than job candidates who did not possess a criminal record. Sex offenders especially

Image 15. © iStockphoto.com/KatarzynaBialasiewicz.

have difficulties in obtaining employment, which is further complicated by the fact that sex offenders are required to pay for their treatment programs, which cost thousands of dollars (Gunnison & Helfgott, 2013). If these offenders cannot secure a job, they are then unable to pay for their treatment, which results in them being in violation of their probation or parole sentence conditions—meaning that they could be returned to jail or prison.

Substance Abuse

Previous research has established a link between substance use and criminal involvement (Anglin & Perrochet, 1998; Inciardi, 1992; Inciardi et al., 1997; MacCoun & Reuter, 2001). With substance abuse being a significant factor in the onset of criminal involvement for many offenders, it also poses a significant hurdle to reentry success for offenders (Phillips & Spencer, 2015; Travis et al., 2001; Wodhal, 2006). Solomon and colleagues (2008, p. 32) state that "more than two-thirds (68 percent) of all jail inmates meet the criteria for substance abuse or dependence, as defined by the *Diagnostic and Statistical Manual of Mental Disorders*, fourth edition. In comparison, only nine percent of the U.S. population abuse or are dependent on drugs or alcohol." Other researchers have reported that, in general, up to 75% of all offenders have a history of substance abuse or addiction (Travis et al., 2001).

Research has uncovered that offenders who participate in treatment while incarcerated, in community-based substance abuse programs while serving community correction sentences, and after release from prison have lower rates of substance use and recidivism (Anglin, Prendergast, Farabee, & Cartier, 2002; Jannetta, Dodd, & Elderbroom, 2011; Miller & Miller, 2010; Visher & Courtney, 2007; Wexler et al., 1999; Zhang, Roberts, & Callanan, 2006). For instance, Zhang and colleagues (2006), who examined the Preventing Parolee Crime Program in California—a program that provided a wide range of services to parolees including substance abuse assistance, found this program modestly reduced recidivism and parole absconding.

The length of time an offender has spent in treatment appears to be a significant factor in reentry success. Researchers have found that the longer offenders participate in treatment the greater their likelihood of committing future crimes is reduced (French et al., 1993; Simpson, Joe, & Brown, 1997). For those offenders fortunate enough to have received treatment during their incarceration term, Brazzell and La Vigne (2009) point out that the stress following incarceration and attempts to successfully reintegrate back into the community can be significantly thwarted. It seems that stress of reintegration, even for those who have participated in treatment, often puts this group at a high risk for relapse. Offenders with substance abuse histories (the majority of the offender population) making the transition from incarceration to the community are in the precarious position of having to manage extraordinary stressors without engaging in old habits of substance use and abuse as a way to manage everyday stressors and problems in life. Substance abuse problems often interfere with an offender's ability to obtain or maintain employment. The stress and strain of reentry pulls some offenders into familiar, yet dysfunctional, coping patterns.

It is important to note that not all offenders have access to community-based treatment programs during their probation and parole sentences or even post-completion of these sentences (Crayton et al., 2010; Thompson, 2004). Crayton and colleagues (2010, p. 21) explain that "lack of insurance, conviction-based bans on receiving public assistance, or the lack of available treatment can create substantial barriers to post-release substance abuse treatment." Without access to formal treatment, parolees, for instance, may come to rely on their parole officer for assistance (Thompson, 2004). It may be the case that the community corrections officer is the only pro-social individual in the life of the offender, and thus, the offender really must rely on his/her parole officer for support and guidance. Unfortunately, community corrections officers generally have a large client caseloads and are not trained treatment providers, which clearly inhibits their ability to navigate offenders to the pathway of recovery from addiction or abstinence of drug and/or alcohol consumption. With community-based substance abuse programs being unreachable or unattainable for many offenders, many researchers have found that these offenders will continue consuming drugs and/or alcohol during and after their sentences.

The problems associated with substance abuse spread into other challenge areas during reentry, such as employment (Shivy et al., 2007). Therefore, the challenge of overcoming substance abuse should not be viewed in isolation but rather as a factor that seeps into other areas of an individual's life, further complicating successful reentry. Drug addiction is indeed a struggle for many community corrections offenders (McKean & Raphael, 2002) and many of these individuals are also in need of mental health support (White, Goldkamp, & Campbell, 2006). The stress of successfully reintegrating into society is high and some offenders resort to drastic measures such as suicide in response to the stress and strain that they are experiencing during this tumultuous time (Biles, Harding, & Walker, 1999).

Mental Health

The **Community Mental Health Centers Act** of 1963 required the deinstitution-alization of the mentally ill from treatment institutions to community based treatment programs (Solomon et al., 2008). While the act was intended to eliminate involuntarily institutionalization of the mentally ill and the abuses they experienced due to their conditions, the impact of deinstitutionalization resulted in many mentally ill individuals being shifted out of state hospitals finding themselves instead entering into the criminal justice system (Barrenger & Canada, 2014). For instance, of offenders incarcerated in jails, Crayton et al. (2010) report that approximately 24% demonstrate symptomatic evidence of mental illness. Additionally, persons with mental illness are overrepresented in jails and prisons, with 6–8% having a serious mental illness in state prisons, 7.2% in jails, and many more that have contact with the criminal justice system but are not incarcerated (National Alliance on Mental Health, 2008). James and Glaze (2006) report that female inmates, in state and federal prisons and jails, had higher rates of mental health issues than male inmates at these same institutions. An earlier study by Acoca (1998) indicates that the percentage ranges from 25% to 60% for women incarcerated, with 45% as being the average percentage of women suffering from mental illness who are incarcerated. Given these percentages reported and the trauma experienced early in their lives, female ex-offenders are in need of mental health support (e.g., access to medications) and treatment, and these needs have been identified as a serious problem for this group (Gunnison & Helfgott, 2013; Teplin, Abram, & McClelland, 1996). Prior sexual and physical abuse female offenders have experienced often results in severe depression, posttraumatic stress disorder, and suicidal ideation and/or attempts (Belknap, 2007; Pollock, 2002).

For those offenders who suffer from mental illness and are incarcerated in jails and prison, their ability to succeed upon release while serving community corrections sentences is greatly hindered by the institutional environment. With correctional administrators unable to offer comprehensive services to those suffering from such problems due to budgetary constraints, the mental health problems for these individuals often worsen. Further complicating treatment in the prison environment is the adherence to get-tough-on-crime policies, which have resulted in tougher punishments for offenders, such as the increased use of solitary confinement, and the creation of super-max prisons which impose a strict form of solitary confinement (Haney, 2003). Haney (2003, p. 130) states that, "Empirical research on solitary and supermax-like confinement has consistently and unequivocally documented the harmful consequences of living in these kinds of environments." Confinement in these facilities and solitary confinement has resulted in a wide range of psychological problems exhibited by incarcerated individuals, such as cognitive dysfunction, paranoia, psychosis, and depression (Metzner & Fellner, 2010). Since the emphasis in super-max facilities is on punishment and surveillance, rehabilitation is non-existent. Thus, any offenders who had a pre-existing mental illness prior to incarceration in this facility would likely have their problems exacerbated by this type of confinement. Moreover, if offenders did not have a pre-existing mental illness prior to incarceration, they may develop one due to the experiences of ongoing solitary confinement (Haney, 2003). Untreated mental illness and conditions of confinement that elicit mental health conditions are a grave concern in principle and even more so of a concern as many of these offenders may be released on parole.

Further complicating successful reentry for those incarcerated with mental illness is often inadequate transition planning when they are released from jail or prison (Osher, Steadman, & Barr, 2003). These offenders need a wide range of available services that will meet their needs during reentry. Unfortunately, the lack of adequate transition planning for this group increases their likelihood of recidivating. Some researchers have found recidivism rates as high as 70% for those offenders with mental illnesses returning to their communities post-incarceration (Cate et al., 2012). Apart from those offenders leaving prison to serve parole sentences, mental health issues are indeed a challenge for all offenders attempting to reenter society while serving community corrections sentences such as probation, as approximately 16% of all offenders have a diagnosable mental disorder (Travis et al., 2001). For many offenders, mental health problems are not isolated but are experienced in tandem with other problems such as substance abuse. The mental health problems also cross over and present challenges for offenders in other areas of their reentry such as obtaining employment and housing, and re-establishing family connections (Fontaine, Roman, & Burt, 2010). Thus, mental health problems often inhibit offenders' ability to made strides towards success since these problems impact other aspects of their reentry.

Physical Health

For many community corrections offenders, coping with physical health problems adds another layer of challenge to their bid at successful reentry (Phillips & Spencer, 2013; Thompson, 2004). For those offenders being released from jails, this seems to be more of a serious problem. Jannetta et al. (2011, p. 6) explain, "The jail population experiences much higher rates of chronic and infectious diseases than the general population, and over a third of jail inmates report a current medical issue needing attention. Individuals passing through jails account for a substantial share of the total U.S. population infected with tuberculosis, hepatitis, and HIV/AIDS, presenting a significant opportunity to improve public health. However, fewer than half of all jail inmates nationally receive medical examinations when admitted, and few of those living with infectious diseases receive care after release." Besides infectious diseases, a high rate of chronic diseases such as asthma and heart problems plague the jail population, and unfortunately, these diseases are also rarely treated during the offenders' stay in the jail (Crayton et al., 2010). Since many community corrections offenders serve time in jail prior to their community corrections sentence or in conjunction with their sentence, these offenders are very much impacted by physical health concerns.

Physical health problems and their treatment are particularly challenging as most offenders lack quality health insurance, and thus, must rely on Medicaid for treatment of any health problems upon release from jail or prison. However, relying on Medicaid for support for physical health problems is problematic. Solomon et al. (2008, p. 16) state, "A period of incarceration often suspends or terminates benefits depending on length of stay and can disqualify inmates from Medicaid eligibility. Activating or reinstating benefits and restoring eligibility can take several months, interrupting access to prescription drugs and putting individuals at high risk of relapse." Thus, many offenders are not receiving adequate healthcare to treat their ailments during their community corrections sentence, and these gaps in service are problematic to offenders overall and certainly cause them additional stress and strain (Mears & Cochran, 2012).

The health problems experienced by offenders during reentry often impact other aspects of the reentry process such as housing and employment. For instance, in a study of approximately 1,000 male and female offenders, Mallik-Kane and Visher (2008) found that many in their sample with health problems had difficulties in maintaining stable housing after release. Additionally, the researchers discovered that women with physical health problems demonstrated an uptick in residential mobility about eight to ten months after release and were more likely to report living with anti-social individuals (i.e., offenders or drug/alcohol users) during this period. Further, the researchers uncovered that those offenders suffering from physical health problems had greater difficulties in securing employment, and that men in the sample with such problems were more likely to supplement their income through illegal means when compared to their female counterparts. Many offenders in the sample had physical problems that were so chronic that these problems prevented them from finding work, thereby requiring them to rely on disability assistance.

Physical health problems can also contribute to feelings of stigmatization and exclusion that can alter an offender's perception of self in ways that can become an obstacle to success. For example, in a study of 200 female prisoners in Russia, Moran (2012) found that one of the effects of imprisonment for the women in the sample was missing teeth, resulting from poor and invasive dental treatment that resulted in extractions while in prison. These women noted anxiety and shame associated with missing teeth upon release that contributed to feelings of stigma and exclusion. These offenders saw their missing teeth as a conspicuous stigma—a telltale sign like other visible markers (e.g., tattoos) that they had been in prison, and in their minds, this marked them as different and was seen by the women as a disadvantage in the reentry process.

In sum, physical health problems are inhibiting offenders in their efforts to successfully reenter society. Myers and colleagues (2005) report on an innovative case management plan in California for males and females leaving prison that was designed to reduce offenders' chances of acquiring HIV. Initial findings from their study yielded favorable results with reductions in participants' involvement in risky behavior (unprotected sex or the use of drugs/alcohol during sex) that could lead to the acquisition

Image 16. © iStockphoto.com/swedeandsour.

of HIV. Thus, support for existing, or the prevention of, health problems may help to facilitate successful reentry. Without community and health support for these individuals, it is inevitable that the additional burden they carry in regards to their health may put them at greater risk for re-offending.

Family

There is no doubt that family support is critical to successful reentry for offenders, and empirical research has demonstrated that family can play an important role in the offenders' success or failure post release (Aday & Krabill, 2011; DiZerega, 2011; Gunnison & Helfgott, 2013; Naser & Visher, 2006). Families can provide emotional and financial support, referrals to employers, child care, elder care, housing, transportation, positive reinforcement, monitoring of health conditions, and a source of a reconnection to the community (DiZerega, 2011). Previous research has indicated that family support can contribute to successful employment for offenders, reduced substance use, lower rates of depression, and lower recidivism rates (Berg & Huebner, 2011; La Vigne, Visher, & Castro, 2004; Martinez, 2007; Petersilia, 2003; Visher et al., 2004). Berg and Huebner (2011), in a study of 401 paroled men in a midwestern state, found that offenders who had good quality ties to family members were less likely to recidivate and more likely to be employed.

Unfortunately, many family relationships become strained due to an offender's often prolonged absence while incarcerated (Clear, 2007; Petersilia, 2003). Additionally, if there was pre-existing strain or conflict with family members prior to the incarceration of the offender, family members may not be willing to resolve this conflict upon release (Petersilia, 2003). Thus, reentry for offenders with strained family relations creates an additional layer of difficulty and stress, complicating successful reentry (Brown, 2004a; Mowen & Visher, 2015). This is particularly problematic for female offenders, as they are often incarcerated in prisons located farther away from family, which results in a breakdown of family bonds (Belknap, 2007).

In terms of the support offenders can receive from family, whether it be financial, emotional, or pro-social support, it can be limited as well. Many family members may have criminal histories or substance problems which can limit their ability to steer the offender on the pathway to reentry success (Brown, 2004a; Visher, Baer, & Naser, 2006). For some offenders returning home, it can be stressful if family members are expecting the individual to contribute financially to the household, or parents may be pressuring the individual to pursue further education or continually stressing the merits of a good work ethic (Breese, Ra'el, & Grant, 2000).

For both incarcerated males and females, ties with children are often disrupted. Many incarcerated offenders had limited contact or visits with their children during their confinement (Clear, 2007; Mumola, 2000). The passage of the **Adoption and Safe Families Act** in 1997 may make it impossible for the female offender to regain custody of her children. One provision of the act requires termination of parental rights for children who have been in foster care for at least 15 months (Petersilia, 2003). Therefore, many offenders lose custody of their children while incarcerated— especially since the female offender is more likely to have her child/ren placed in the foster care system when incarcerated, whereas men are more likely to have their children placed with a family member when incarcerated. Thus, upon release, many offenders are consumed with regaining custody of their children. For those offenders who did not lose custody of their children, there is a sense of fear in some that losing custody is a distinct possibility (Shivy et al., 2007). Pinard and Thompson (2006, p. 600) explain that "adoption laws add pressure to returning mothers by reducing the amount of time that parents have to reunite with their children before permanently losing custody." Other offenders may suddenly be burdened with the responsibility of securing childcare as well as the other responsibilities that come with raising children and this can complicate their successful reentry (Shivy et al., 2007).

The issues of childcare and its impact on successful reentry may be more of a problem for female offenders as opposed to their male counterparts (Harm & Phillips, 2001). Shivy et al. (2007, p. 472) report that, "Many female offenders have their children returned to them immediately upon release—before they successfully have secured housing or employment." Without secure and affordable childcare options, this can limit the range of jobs offenders can take, thus thwarting, or slowing down, their reentry into the workforce. For those female offenders who have addiction problems, they are often saddled with overcoming their addiction, securing employment and housing, and regularly visiting their children. Robbins, Martin, and Surratt (2009, p. 394) further explain that, "Although maternal roles may motivate substance-abusing female offenders to attain sobriety, substance abuse recovery is itself a demanding role that can compete with maternal responsibilities." Parsons and Warner-Robbins (2002) add that sustaining recovery from substance abuse problems is a chief concern of females reentering the community, resulting in the reunification with her child/ren being a secondary goal. Despite the additional strains for female offenders, children can be a source of stabilization for offenders. Some research has found that offenders who spend time with their children post-release have lower rates of recidivism (Visher, 2013).

In sum, family can be a tremendous pillar of support in the offenders' journey to successful reentry. However, family can also be a source of strain if there is conflict, if unmet expectations are placed on the offender, and if stressors are at play in regards to reunification with family members and/or children, which can further complicate the delicate transition process.

Basic Needs & Skill Deficiencies

Offenders have a wide range of basic needs that, when unmet, pose difficulties for their ability to successfully reintegrate. Besides the fundamental need of housing which was discussed earlier, offenders are often in need of basic necessities such as food (Gunnison & Helfgott, 2013; Helfgott, 1997; Shivy et al., 2007). For some offenders, the ability to obtain the basic need of sustenance is a greater challenge. Mukamal (2000) explains that the **Federal Welfare Law of 1996** permanently prohibits states to permitting ex-offenders with drug-related felony convictions to receive any form of welfare benefits, including food stamps. This permanent ban is not merely for a few years, but rather a lifetime ban (Mukamal, 2000; Petersilia, 2005). In a study conducted by Shivy et al. (2007, p. 471), the reliance on receiving food can be demoralizing, as one subject reported, "How do you like living off somebody, eating all their food?" Due to the inability to obtain employment and their conviction status, this need is often left unfulfilled. Further inhibiting the ability of offenders to obtain employment is the lack of access to transportation (Shivy et al., 2007). While many probation and parole agencies provide temporary bus passes to offenders to help them get around when they first re-enter society, it may not be enough. The provided bus passes are often temporary, but offenders are in need of longer-term solutions to their transportation limitations. This is especially critical to those serving community corrections sentences who may receive little to no support in this area (e.g., work release, day reporting).

Additionally, offenders are often in need of life skill training, including the development of problem solving skills, negotiation skills, critical reasoning skills, money management skills, and independent living skills (Brown, 2004b; McGuire & Hatcher 2001; Raynor & Vandstone 1996; Roberts, Harper, & Preszler, 1997). In a study of Canadian parole officers, the officers reported that newly released federal offenders are in need of the acquisition of problem solving and budgeting skills (Brown, 2004b). An additional study conducted by Brown (2004a), where he queried Canadian parole officers in regards to the challenges that new released federal offenders face, found that the officers identified the use of "old coping strategies" as a factor which inhibits successful reentry. According to the officers, offenders may be "overcome by pace of life," feel "fear," "loneliness," "boredom," "discouragement," "lack of patience," "lack of self-confidence," or "shame" (Brown, 2004a, p. 28). Thus, offenders, who have not received any cognitive skills programming prior to release may be at a disadvantage in their ability to successfully reintegrate. Again, if basic needs go unmet and offenders are not equipped with the necessary skills that any citizen would need to succeed in society, then successful reentry is less likely to occur.

Collateral Consequences

The conviction status of offenders creates many collateral consequences as they reenter society, many of which were mentioned earlier in this chapter such as access to housing, employment, and even obtaining food. However, there are other forms of collateral damage experienced by offenders not previously mentioned. Some have referred to a conviction status as being a form of **civil death** or additional, yet invisible, punishments (Ewald, 2002; Travis, 2005). As explained by Ewald (2002, p. 1049), "the term 'civil death' refers to the condition in which a convicted offender loses all political, civil, and legal rights." Pinard and Thompson (2006) explain that the loss of constitutional rights and other sanctions include the loss of voting rights, federal welfare benefits (either temporarily or permanently), educational grants, public housing, gun licenses, employment licenses, the chance to hold a political office, permission to serve on a jury, and the opportunity to serve in the military. In many states, offenders never regain their voting rights even after fully serving their probation, parole, or incarceration sentences (Ewald, 2002). The loss of voting rights, referred to as "felon disenfranchisement," significantly impacts male African Americans, with approximately 13% of this population affected by this prohibition—"a rate seven times the national average" (Ewald, 2002, p. 1053). The loss of rights and access to state and federal assistance programs has increased in the era of the get-tough-on-crime movement (Pinard & Thompson, 2006). A few states, however, allow for eventual restoration of voting rights (Pinard & Thompson, 2006). Several researchers have called for the abolition of the lifetime loss of rights for offenders, given that these bans are forms of additional punishment (see Bushway & Sweeten, 2007). Unfortunately, many offenders are unaware of many of the rights they have lost, are surprised to learn about them, and become frustrated when encountering the myriad of hurdles now in the pathway to successful reentry (Pinard & Thompson, 2006).

Besides "civil death," offenders experience other forms of collateral consequences due to their status as convicted felons (Clear, 2007). Tewksbury (2005), in a study of 121 registered sex offenders in Kentucky, found that many of these offenders experienced social stigmatization, loss of relationships, and verbal and physical assaults. However, for sex offenders, it is not just the offender who experiences these consequences, but the family member(s) of the offender may also experience damage due to the status of the offenders. In another study conducted by Levenson and Tewksbury (2009), the researchers examined the impact of sex offender registration laws on family members. The researchers found that family members experienced employment limitations, housing disruption, and sometimes threats, harassment, or property damage due to their association to a registered sex offender. Additionally, results from the research revealed that the children of the registered sex offender were treated differently at school or by peers and also may experience stigmatization due to their parent's status. Clear (2007) discusses how communities offenders come from and return to can also become stigmatized. He explains, "Locations with large numbers of people going to prison also become negatively stereotyped, and this affects how the area is perceived, thus transferring the stigma to the community" (Clear, 2007, p. 128). The stigmatization may culminate in residents relocating, businesses being reluctant to open in the community, or even property values dropping (Clear, 2007). Thus, it is important to recognize that not only are offenders experiencing such consequences but their family members and communities may also experience invisible punishments.

The average community corrections offender attempting to reenter society successfully is not faced with one challenge but a whole host of challenges which may or may not be visible (see Text Box 8.1). Without support to obtain food, housing, and employment, it is difficult for these offenders to succeed. Additionally, family and community support play a vital role in the success of the offender. Further, a wide range of invisible punishments are experienced by offenders after their formal punishment, which certainly undermines not only their ability to succeed but further weakens their drive to succeed.

Text Box 8.1: Offender Reentry in Hong Kong

The challenges faced by offenders in the United States during reentry are not unique to just this group. Rather offenders attempting to reintegrate into society in other countries, such as Hong Kong, experience many challenges—both shared and distinct from those of U.S. offenders. Chui and Cheng (2014) interviewed 16 young (i.e., average age 21 years) Chinese males to uncover some of the challenges the former offenders faced upon release from prison. The researchers discovered that the men received little family support and they had great difficulty in obtaining employment (Chui & Cheng, 2014). With difficulties in obtaining employment, many struggled to obtain housing and even food. One subject reported,

> The most important things are finding a place to live and work. Work is the most important thing because without work, how can I find a place to live? I really want to be able to apply for an apartment (with government subsidy) because renting is very expensive out there ... I am facing the problem of not being able to pay the rent. Even living in the residential home, I have to pay rent ... After paying the rent, I need to eat. I need to take the bus to look for work. A lot of the time it's not enough ... Sometimes I only eat one meal a day, sometimes I don't eat. I've even tried only drinking water. Sometimes the people at the residential home treat me to a meal. I have no choice, no one in my family is willing to accept me ... After a year I'll have to leave ... Maybe I will go back to living on the streets (Chui & Cheng, 2014, pp. 420–421).

Upon release, many of the former offenders felt alone and had no one to assist them in their adjustment to society. While Chui & Cheng's (2014) research focused on those being released from prison, they did note that efforts are made for probation offenders, unlike released prisoners, to receive family support in hopes that the community corrections offenders can be reformed. In a more specific examination of adult probation offenders, Chui (2004) reports that probationers experience drug addiction problems, troubled family relationships, and employment difficulties, which inhibit their ability to succeed while serving this sentence. Again, reestablishing family support was viewed as a very important challenge to overcome. This is also a challenge for U.S. community corrections offenders, but it is not as critical a challenge for reentry as it seems to be for offenders in Hong Kong. Thus, efforts to address these issues (i.e., drugs, family, employment) for both male and female probationers in Hong Kong may be helpful in increasing positive reentry outcomes for community corrections offenders.

Policy Recommendations

Community corrections offenders may be more successful in reentry with several reforms and policies put into place in the criminal justice system. First, offenders are in need of financial support and training (Martin, 2011). Rather than just simply being pushed toward obtaining employment, offenders need to be given skills to manage their money. If offenders cannot budget their earned income effectively, they will not develop the assets that are a critical factor to successful reintegration. Apart from financial training, community corrections offenders need to be released from burdening **legal financial obligations** (LFO) that are compounding their inability to successfully reintegrate (Beckett & Harris, 2011). With legal and supervision costs passed onto offenders, they are saddled with these debts along with other personal debts. These debts make it particularly difficult for offenders to seek custody of their children due to the costs incurred in doing so. Second, community corrections offenders need assistance in securing housing, employment, and even food. Getting these needs met can be difficult, given the multiple barriers that offenders face in regard to job restrictions, exclusions from public assistance, and a reduction in the number of housing options available to them due to their criminal record, the offense they committed, or because they also need housing for themselves and their child(ren) (Gunnison & Helfgott, 2013; Petersilia, 2005). Thus, more housing options are needed for community corrections offenders and community support, including community buy-in, is also needed for offenders. All too often, when housing initiatives are proposed, such as building affordable housing for offenders in neighborhoods, public support for helping offenders can wane (Garland, Wodahl, & Mayfield, 2011). Additionally, Apel (2011) cautions that giving offenders jobs or helping them find jobs is not enough, but rather a clear need exists for the enhancement of the employability of offenders. That is, many offenders are in need of job skill enhancements in order to reduce their chances of job termination and recidivism. Moreover, additional support may be needed for sex offenders and minority offenders who face much discrimination in obtaining employment. Further, "ban the box" campaigns may be helpful in curbing some employment discrimination. The "ban the box" movement allows job applicants to no longer be forced to check a box on a job application and reveal their previous conviction history (Henry & Jacobs, 2007).

Third, simply ensuring that offenders obtain housing or employment is not sufficient. Offenders also must receive the appropriate treatment for other physical health conditions as well as substance abuse and/or mental illness treatment and support (Culhane, Metraux, & Hadley, 2002; Gunnison & Helfgott, 2013; Haimowitz, 2004; Worcel et al., 2009). For offenders being released from prisons to serve parole sentences, adequate pre-release planning is needed (Petersilia, 2003). That is, a reentry plan needs to be in place before release to ensure that parolees are receiving treatment for substance abuse or mental health issues when re-released to their communities. Additionally, healthcare should be included in such planning. Since offenders are at high risk of contracting hepatitis C, HIV/AIDS, and tuberculosis, preventative healthcare efforts also should be part of these pre-planning conversations (Woods et al., 2013). Fourth, family support and reunification is needed for community corrections offenders. The fact that jail and prison sentences often disrupt stable family relationships and that offenders often do not have stable family relationships to begin with warrants the need for programming that addresses building and strengthening family relationships where healthy for offenders. Moreover, female community corrections offenders are in need of assistance in regaining custody of their children. All in all, family members, treatment providers, community corrections officers, and members of the public need to work together to help community corrections offenders overcome the many challenges they face upon reentry.

Finally, legal reforms, including those reforms that eliminate collateral consequences, are needed to assist in offender success during reentry. One such reform would be the elimination of technical violations for probationers and parolees. In relation to this, Clear (2007, p. 189) explains, "One-third of all prison admissions are parolees or probationers who have not been accused of a new crime, but instead have failed to abide by the conditions of their supervision." He further mentions that such elimination would not harm public safety. Thus, perhaps the threat of being re-incarcerated due to technical violations is not facilitating reentry success but rather is undermining the chances for community corrections offenders to be successful. What may be needed is greater support for the offender during reentry by community corrections officers (CCOs) as opposed to CCOs searching for reasons, apart from arrest, to send the offender back to jail or prison. Another legal reform suggested by Petersilia (2005) is the passage of an act that seeks to establish procedures that would allow offenders to move past their criminal record in the future through expunging their records. That is, offenders would not have to suffer the consequences of having criminal records for the rest of their lives, but rather they could eventually have their record cleared after a period of time of no further criminal involvement. As noted earlier, the presence of a criminal record hinders offenders' opportunities to obtain employment and housing. Further, a criminal record interferes with the ability of offenders to have many of the rights the rest of the population takes for granted, like access to public assistance and custody of their children. Without having their records expunged, offenders are plagued with these difficulties for the remainder of their lives. The long-term collateral consequences of having a criminal record are pervasive for offenders. Other legal reforms that would also be useful for ex-offenders are those that allow the reestablishment of various rights that they lost due to their conviction, including the right to vote, the right to serve on a jury, the right to hold a political office, and the right to serve in the military (Ewald, 2002; Pinard & Thompson, 2006). Moreover, legal reforms need to be implemented to help women regain custody of their children and provide them with the financial support to do so as well as other needed support such as childcare assistance.

Conclusion

In sum, this chapter discussed the myriad of challenges and obstacles that community corrections offenders face upon reentry. These challenges include housing,

employment, transportation, social acceptance, personal relationships, legal complications, loss of constitutional rights, substance abuse, and re-offending. Additionally, some of these challenges are more pronounced for certain groups (e.g., minority
offenders, sex offenders, female offenders). Finally, this chapter suggested possible
policy recommendations that could be implemented that could assist community
corrections offenders in overcoming their challenges in reentry. It is clear that a multi-
pronged approach is needed to help offenders. That is, challenges that offenders face
cannot be partitioned and viewed as separate issues, rather the issues faced by offenders
occur in tandem and must be addressed together as opposed to separately. Without
approaching challenges head-on and recognizing that housing, employment, substance
abuse, and mental illness are often intertwined, policies directed at one specific area
will likely result in community corrections offenders not achieving success during
reentry.

Key Terms

Adoption and Safe Families Act

Civil death

Community Mental Health Centers Act

Double discrimination

Federal Welfare Law of 1996

Legal financial obligations

Discussion Questions

1. Research the unique challenges that offenders have in your city or state. What
   unique challenges are experienced by community corrections offenders that are
   specific to your city or state?

2. Do you think probation and/or parole guidelines should be modified? What about
   the suggestion to eliminate technical violations? Do you support or oppose such
   a recommendation? Why?

3. What policies do you think are needed right now to help minority community
   corrections offenders? What policies do you think are needed right now to help
   female community corrections offenders? After some reflection, choose one policy
   for each group that you think would be beneficial to assist these offenders in your
   city or state. Explain your rationale.

4. Attend a local community or city council meeting. Bring up points regarding the
   challenges faced by community corrections offenders, both shared and unique,
   in your city, and be sure to suggest policy recommendations. Report back on
   your experience. Was the information presented well-received? Were community

members/partners receptive to your concerns? Do you have plans for a next step (e.g., such as making a more formal presentation to policymakers or interested constituents)?

References

Acoca, L. (1998). Outside/inside: The violation of American girls at home, on the streets, and in the juvenile justice system. *Crime and Delinquency, 44*(4): 561–589. doi: 10.1177/0011128798044004006.

Aday, R. H., & Krabill, J. J. (2011). *Women aging in prison: A neglected population in the correctional system.* Boulder, CO: Lynne Rienner.

Anglin, M. D., & Perrochet, B. (1998). Drug use and crime: A historical review of research conducted by the UCLA Drug Abuse Research Center. *Substance Use & Misuse, 33*(9), 1871–1914. doi: 10.3109/10826089809059325.

Anglin, M. D., Prendergast, M., Farabee, D., & Cartier, J. (2002). *Final report on the substance abuse program at the California substance abuse treatment facility (SATF-SAP) and state prison at Corcoran.* Sacramento, CA: California Department of Corrections, Office of Substance Abuse Programs.

Apel, R. (2011). Transitional jobs program: Putting employment-based reentry into context. *Criminology and Public Policy, 10*(4): 939–942. doi: 10.1111/j.1745-9133.2011.00781.x.

Barnes, J. C., Dukes, T., Tewksbury, R., & De Troye, T. M. (2009). Analyzing the impact of a statewide residence restriction law on South Carolina sex offenders. *Criminal Justice Policy Review, 20*(1), 21–43. doi: 10.1177/0887403408320842.

Barrenger, S. L., & Canada, K. E. (2014). Mental illness along the criminal justice continuum. *Journal of Forensic Social Work, 4*(2), 123–149. doi: 0.1080/193692 8X.2014.948251.

Beckett, K., & Harris, A. (2011). On cash and conviction: Monetary sanctions as misguided policy. *Criminology & Public Policy, 10*(3), 505–37. doi: 10.1111/j.1745-9133.2011.00727.x.

Belknap, J. (2007). *The invisible woman: Gender, crime, & justice.* Belmont, CA: Thomson, Wadsworth.

Berg, M. T., & Huebner, B. M. (2011). Reentry and the ties that bind: An examination of social ties, employment, and recidivism. *Justice Quarterly, 28*(2), 382–410. doi: 10.1080/07418825.2010.498383.

Biles, D., Harding, R., & Walker, J. (1999). The deaths of offenders serving community corrections orders. *Trends and Issues Australian Institute of Criminology, 107*, 1–6.

Brazzell, D., & La Vigne, N. G. (2009). *Prisoner reentry in Houston: Community perspectives.* Washington, DC: Urban Institute.

Breese, J. R., Ra'el, K., & Grant, G. K. (2000). No place like home: A qualitative investigation of social support and its effects on recidivism. *Sociological Practice: A Journal of Clinical and Applied Research, 2*(1), 1–21. doi: 10.1023/A:101010 3821490.

Brown, J. (2004a). Challenges facing Canadian federal offenders newly released to the community. *Journal of Offender Rehabilitation, 39*, 19–35. doi: 10.1300/J07 6v39n01_02.

Brown, J. (2004b). Managing the transition from jail to community: A Canadian parole officer perspective on the needs of newly released federal offenders. *Western Criminology Review, 5(2)*, 97–107.

Bushway, S., & Sweeten, G. (2007). Abolish lifetime bans for ex-felons. *Criminology and Public Policy, 6*(4), 697–706. doi: 10.1111/j.1745-9133.2007.00466.x.

Cate, M., Hoshino, M., Seale, L., Grealish, B., Fitzgerald, T., Grassel, K., Maxwell, D., Viscuso, B., Isorena, T., & Reyes, M. (2012). *California Department of Corrections and Rehabilitation: 2012 outcome evaluation report.* Sacramento, CA: Office of Research.

Chui, W. H. (2004). Adult offenders on probation in Hong Kong: An exploratory study. *The British Journal of Social Work, 34*(3), 443–454. doi: 10.1093/bjsw/bch047.

Chui, W. H., & Cheng, K. K. (2014). Challenges facing young men returning from incarceration in Hong Kong. *The Howard Journal of Criminal Justice, 53*(4), 411–427. doi: 10.1111/hojo.12088.

Clark, L. M. (2007). Landlord attitudes toward renting to released offenders. *Federal Probation, 71*(1), 20–30.

Clear, T. R. (2007). *Imprisoning communities: How mass incarceration makes disadvantaged neighborhoods worse.* New York: Oxford University Press.

Crayton, A., Ressler, L., Mukamal, D. A., Jannetta, J., & Warwick, K. (2010). *Partnering with jails to improve reentry: A guidebook for community-based organizations.* Washington, DC: Urban Institute.

Culhane, D. P., Metraux, S., & Hadley, T. (2002). Public service reductions associated with placement of homeless persons with severe mental illness in supportive housing. *Housing Policy Debate, 13*(1), 107–163. doi: 10.1080/10511482.2002. 9521437.

Cullen, F. T. (1994). Social support as an organizing concept for criminology: Presidential address to the Academy of Criminal Justice Sciences. *Justice Quarterly, 11*, 527–559. doi: 10.1080/07418829400092421.

DiZerega, M. (2011). *Why ask about family?* New York: Vera Institute of Justice.

Duin, S. (2014, August 5). The troubled summer of Dave Dahl, the good seed behind Dave's Killer Bread. *The Oregonian.* Retrieved from http://www.oregonlive.com/news/oregonian/steve_duin/index.ssf/2014/08/steve_duin_the_troubled_summer.html.

Erisman, W., & Conardo, J. B. (2005). *Learning to reduce recidivism: A 50-state analysis of postsecondary correctional educational policy.* Washington, DC: Institute for Higher Education Policy.

Evans, D., & Porter, J. (2015). Criminal history and landlord rental decisions: A New York quasi-experimental study. *Journal of Experimental Criminology, 11*(1), 21–42. doi: 10.1007/s11292-014-9217-4.

Ewald, A. C. (2002). Civil death: The ideological paradox of criminal disenfranchisement law in the United States. *Wisconsin Law Review, 5,* 1045–1135.

Fahey, J., Roberts, C., & Engel, L. (2006). *Employment of ex-offenders: Employer perspectives.* Boston, MA: Crime and Justice Institute.

Fontaine, J., & Biess, J. (2012). *Housing as a platform for formerly incarcerated persons.* Washington, DC: Urban Institute.

Fontaine, J., Roman, C. G., & Burt, M. R. (2010). *System change accomplishments of the Corporation for Supportive Housing's Returning Home Initiative.* Washington, DC: Urban Institute.

French, M. T., Zarkin, G. A., Hubbard, R. L., & Rachal, J. V. (1993). The effects of time in drug abuse treatment and employment on posttreatment drug use and criminal activity. *American Journal on Drug and Alcohol Abuse, 19,* 19–33. doi: 10.3109/00952999309002663.

Garland, B., Wodahl, E. J., & Mayfield, J. (2011). Prisoner reentry in a small metropolitan community: Obstacles and policy recommendations. *Criminal Justice Policy Review, 22*(1), 90–110. doi: 10.1177/0887403409359804.

Grubesic, T. H., Murray, A. T., & Mack, E. A. (2011). Sex offenders, residence restrictions, housing, and urban morphology: A review and synthesis. *Cityscape: A Journal of Policy Development and Research, 13*(3), 7–31.

Gunnison, E., & Helfgott, J. B. (2013). *Offender reentry: Beyond crime and punishment.* Boulder, CO: Lynne Rienner.

Gunnison, E., Helfgott, J. B., & Wilhelm, C. (2015). Correctional practitioners on reentry: A missed perspective. *Journal of Prison Education &Reentry, 2*(1), 51–73. doi: 10.15845/jper.V2i1.789.

Haimowitz, S. (2004). Slowing the revolving door: Community reentry of offenders with mental illness. *Psychiatric Services, 55*(4), 373–375. doi: 10.1176/appi.ps. 55.4.373.

Haney, C. (2003). Mental health issues in long-term solitary and "supermax" confinement. *Crime and Delinquency, 49*(1), 124–156. doi: 10.1177/0011128702239239.

Harding, A., & Harding, J. (2006). Inclusion and exclusion in the re-housing of former prisoners. *Probation Journal, 53*(2), 137–153. doi: 10.1177/0264550506063566.

Harm, N. J., & Phillips, S. D. (2001). You can't go home again: Women and criminal recidivism. *Journal of Offender Rehabilitation, 32*(3), 3–21. doi: 10.1300/J076v3 2n03_02.

Harris, P. M., & Keller, K. S. (2005). Ex-offenders need not apply: The criminal background check in hiring decisions. *Journal of Contemporary Criminal Justice, 21*(1), 6–30. doi: 10.1177/1043986204271678.

Heinrich, S. (2000). *Reducing recidivism through work: Barriers and opportunities for employment of ex-offenders.* Chicago: Great Cities Institute.

Helfgott, J. B. (1997). Ex-offender needs versus criminal opportunity in Seattle, Washington. *Federal Probation, 61*, 12–24.

Henry, J. S., & Jacobs, J. B. (2007). Ban the box to promote ex-offender employment. *Criminology and Public Policy, 6*(4), 755–762.

Hirsch, A., Dietrich, S., Landau, R., Schneider, P., Ackelsberg, I., Bernstein-Baker, J., & Hohenstein, J. (2002). *Every door closed: Barriers facing parents with criminal records.* Washington, DC: Center for Law and Social Policy and Community Legal Services.

Holzer, H. J., Raphael, S., & Stoll, M. A. (2003). *Employer demand for ex-offenders: Recent evidence from Los Angeles.* Washington, DC: Urban Institute.

Inciardi, J. A. (1992). *The war on drugs II: The continuing epic of heroin, cocaine, crack, crime, AIDS, and the public policy.* Mountain View, CA: Mayfield Publishing Co.

Inciardi, J. A., Martin, S. S., Butzin, C. A., Hooper, R. M., & Harrison, L. D. (1997). An effective model of prison-based treatment for drug-involved offenders. *Journal of Drug Issues, 27*(2), 261–278. doi: 10.1177/002204269702700206.

James, D. J., & Glaze, L. E. (2006). *Mental health problems of prison and jail inmates.* Washington, DC: U.S. Department of Justice, Bureau of Justice Statistics.

Jannetta, J., Dodd, H., & Elderbroom, B. (2011). *The elected official's toolkit for jail reentry.* Washington, DC: The Urban Institute.

Johnson, N. (2013, October 20). 'Wall of change' celebrates Marin's probation success story. *Marin Independent Journal.* Retrieved from http://www.marinij.com/general-news/20131020/wall-of-change-celebrates-marins-probation-success-story.

Kirk, D. S. (2012). Residential change as a turning point in the life course of crime: Desistance or temporary cessation. *Criminology, 50*(2), 329–358. doi: 10.1111/j.1745-9125.2011.00262.x.

La Vigne, N., Visher, C., & Castro, J. (2004). *Chicago prisoners' experiences returning home.* Washington, DC: Urban Institute.

LeBel, T. P. (2012). "If one doesn't get you another one will": Formerly incarcerated persons' perceptions of discrimination. *Prison Journal, 92*(1), 63–87. doi: 10.1177/0032885511429243.

Levenson, J. S., & Tewksbury, R. (2009). Collateral damage: Family members of registered sex offenders. *American Journal of Criminal Justice, 34*, 54–68. doi: 10.1007/s12103-008-9055-x.

Lockwood, S., Nally, J. M., Ho, T., & Knutson, K. (2012). The effect of correctional education on postrelease employment and recidivism: A 5-year follow-up study in the state of Indiana. *Crime and Delinquency, 58*(3), 380–396. doi: 10.1177/0011128712441695.

Lucken, K., & Ponte, L. (2008). A just measure of forgiveness: Reforming occupational licensing regulations for ex-offenders using BFOQ analysis. *Law and Policy, 30*(1), 46–72. doi: 10.1111/j.1467-9930.2008.00269.x.

MacCoun, R. J., & Reuter, P. (2001). *Drug war heresies: Learning from other vices, times, and places.* New York: Cambridge University Press.

Mallik-Kane, K., & Visher, C. A. (2008). *Health and prisoner reentry: How physical, mental, and substance abuse conditions shape the process of reintegration.* Washington, DC: Urban Institute.

Martin, L. L. (2011). Debt to society: Asset poverty and prisoner reentry. *Review of Black Political Economy, 38*(2), 131–143. doi: 10.1007/s12114-011-9087-1.

Martinez, D. J. (2007). Informal helping mechanisms: Conceptual issues in family support of reentry of former prisoners. *Journal of Offender Rehabilitation, 44*(1), 23–37. doi: 10.1300/J076v44n01_02.

Martinez, D. J., & Christian, J. (2009). The familial relationships of former prisoners: Examining the link between residence and informal support mechanisms. *Journal of Contemporary Ethnography, 38*(2), 201–224. doi: 10.1177/0891241608316875.

McGuire, J., & Hatcher, R. (2001). Offense-focused problem-solving: Preliminary evaluation of a cognitive skills program. *Criminal Justice and Behavior, 28*(5), 564–587. doi: 10.1177/009385480102800502.

McKean, L., & Raphael, J. (2002). *Drugs, crime, and consequences: Arrests and incarceration in North Lawndale.* Chicago: Center for Impact Research.

McLean, R., & Thompson, M. D. (2007). *Repaying debts.* New York, NY: Bureau of Justice Assistance.

Mears, D. P., & Cochran, J. C. (2012). U.S. prisoner reentry health care policy in international perspective: Service gaps and the moral and public health implications. *Prison Journal, 92*(2), 175–202. doi: 10.1177/0032885512438845.

Metzner, J. L., & Fellner, J. (2010). Solitary confinement and mental illness in U.S. prisons: A challenge for medical ethics. *Journal of American Academy of Psychiatry & Law, 38*(1), 104–108.

Miller, H. V., & Miller, J. M. (2010). Community in-reach through jail reentry: Findings from a quasi-experimental design. *Justice Quarterly, 27*(6), 893–910. doi: 10.1080/07418825.2010.482537.

Moran, D. (2012). Prisoner reintegration and the stigma of prison time inscribed on the body. *Punishment & Society, 14*(5), 564–583. doi: 10.1177/1462474512464008.

Mowen, T. J., & Visher, C. A. (2015). Drug use and crime after incarceration: The role of family support and family conflict. *Justice Quarterly, 32*(2), 337–359. doi: 10.1080/07418825.2013.771207.

Mukamal, D. A. (2000). Confronting the employment barriers of criminal records: Effective legal and practical strategies. *Georgetown Journal on Poverty Law & Policy, (January–February)*, 597–606.

Mumola, C. (2000). *Incarcerated parents and their children.* Washington, DC: U.S. Department of Justice.

Myers, J., Zack, B., Kramer, K., Gardner, M., Rucobo, G., & Costa-Taylor, S. (2005). Get connected: An HIV prevention case management program for men and women leaving California prisons. *American Journal of Public Health, 95*(10), 1682–1684.

Naser, R. L., & Visher, C. A. (2006). Family members' experiences with incarceration and reentry. *Western Criminology Review, 7*(2), 20–31.

National Alliance on Mental Illness. (2008). *A guide to mental illness and the criminal justice system.* Arlington, VA: National Alliance on Mental Illness, Department of Policy and Legal Affairs. Retrieved from http://namimarin.org/wp-content/uploads/2013/09/guide-to-mental-illness-and-the-cj-system.pdf.

Nelson, M., Deess, P., & Allen, C. (1999). *The first month out: Post incarceration experiences in New York City.* New York: Vera Institute of Justice.

Osher, F., Steadman, H. J., & Barr, H. (2003). A best practice approach to community reentry from jails for inmates with co-occurring disorders: The Apic model. *Crime and Delinquency, 49*, 79–96. doi: 10.1177/0011128702239237.

Parsons, M. L., & Warner-Robbins, C. (2002). Factors that support women's successful transition to the community following jail/prison. *Health Care for Women International, 23*(1), 6–18. doi: 10.1080/073993302753428393.

Petersilia, J. (2001). Prisoner reentry: Public safety and reintegration challenges. *Prison Journal, 81*(3), 360–375. doi: 10.1177/0032885501081003004.

Petersilia, J. (2003). *When prisoners come home: Parole and prisoner reentry.* New York: Oxford University Press.

Petersilia, J. (2005). Meeting the challenges of prisoner reentry. In American Correctional Association (Ed.), *What works and why: Effective approaches to reentry* (pp. 175–192). East Peoria, IL: Versa Press.

Phillips, L. A., & Spencer, W. M. (2013). The challenges of reentry from prison to society. *Journal of Current Issues in Crime, Law, & Law Enforcement, 6*(2), 123–133.

Pinard, M., & Thompson, A. C. (2006). Offender reentry and the collateral consequences of criminal convictions: An introduction. *NYU Review of Law and Social Change, 30*, 585–620.

Pollock, J. M. (2002). *Women, prison, and crime.* Belmont, CA: Wadsworth.

Raynor, P., & Vanstone, M. (1996). Reasoning and rehabilitation in Britain: The results of the Straight Thinking on Probation (STOP) programme. *Journal of*

Offender Therapy and Comparative Criminology, 40(4), 272–284. doi: 10.1177/0306624X96404003.

Robbins, C. A., Martin, S. S., & Surratt, H. L. (2009). Substance abuse treatment, anticipated maternal roles and reentry success of drug-involved women prisoners. *Crime and Delinquency, 55*(3), 388–411. doi: 10.1177/0011128707306688.

Roberts, R. L., Harper, R., & Preszler, B. (1997). The effects of fresh start program on Native American parolees' job placement. *Journal of Employment Counseling, 34*, 115–122. doi: 10.1002/j.2161-1920.1997.tb00988.x.

Roman, C. G., & Travis, J. (2006). Where will I sleep tomorrow? Housing, homelessness, and the returning prisoner. *Housing Policy Debate, 17*(3), 389–418. doi: 10.1080/10511482.2006.9521574.

Schulzke, E. (2012, December 1). From meth addict to businessman: Bread maker's story highlights policy aimed at changing lives. *Deseret News.* Retrieved from http://www.deseretnews.com/article/865567902/Meth-addict-to-successful-baker-New-US-incarceration-policy-aimed-at-reforming-prisoners.html?pg=all.

Shivy, V. A., Wu, J. J., Moon, A. E., Mann, S. C., Holland, J. G., & Eacho, C. (2007). Ex-offenders reentering the workforce. *Journal of Counseling Psychology, 54*(4), 466–473. doi: 10.1037/0022-0167.54.4.466.

Simpson, D. D., Joe, G. W., & Brown, B. S. (1997). Treatment retention and follow-up outcomes in the Drug Abuse Treatment Outcome Study (DATOS). *Psychology of Addictive Behaviors, 11*(4), 294–307. doi: 10.1037/0893-164X.11.4.294.

Smith, E. (2015, January 30). Dave Dahl of Dave's Killer Bread wins conditional release, avoids state hospital. *The Oregonian.* Retrieved from http://www.oregonlive.com/washingtoncounty/index.ssf/2015/01/dave_dahl_of_daves_killer_brea_8.html.

Solomon, A. L., Osborne, J., LoBuglio, S. F., Mellow, J., & Mukamal, D. A. (2008). *Life after lockup: Improving reentry from jail to the community.* Washington, DC: The Urban Institute.

Stevens, D. J., & Ward, C. S. (1997). College education and recidivism: Educating criminals is meritorious. *Journal of Correctional Education, 48*(3), 106–111.

Stromberg, M. (2007). Locked up, then locked out. *Planning, 73*(1), 20–25.

Teplin, L. A., Abram, K. M., & McClelland, G. M. (1996). Prevalence of psychiatric disorders among incarcerated women. *Archives of General Psychiatry, 53*, 505–512. doi: 10.1001/archpsyc.1996.01830060047007.

Tewksbury, R. (2005). Collateral consequences of sex offender registration. *Journal of Contemporary Criminal Justice, 21*(1), 67–81. doi: 10.1177/1043986204271704.

Theen, A. (2015, August 12). Dave's Killer Bread bought by Flowers Foods for $275M. *The Oregonian.* Retrieved from http://www.oregonlive.com/portland/index.ssf/2015/08/daves_killer_bread_bought_by_f.html.

Thompson, A. C. (2004). Navigating the hidden obstacles to ex-offender reentry. *Boston College Law Review, 45*(2), 255–306.

Toth, R. C., Crews, G. A., & Burton, C. E. (2008). *In the margins: Special populations and American justice.* Upper Saddle River, NJ: Prentice Hall.

Travis, J. (2005). *But they all come back: Facing the challenges of prisoner reentry.* Washington, DC: Urban Institute.

Travis, J., Solomon, A., & Waul, M. (2001). *From prison to home: The dimensions and consequences of prisoner reentry.* Washington, DC: Urban Institute.

United States Government Accountability Office. (2005). *Drug offenders: Various factors may limit the impacts of federal laws that provide for denial of selected benefits.* Washington, DC: U.S. Government Accountability Office.

Visher, C. (2013). Incarcerated fathers: Pathways from prison to home. *Criminal Justice Policy Review, 24,* 9–26. doi: 10.1177/0887403411418105.

Visher, C., Baer, D., & Naser, R. (2006). *Ohio prisoner's reflections on returning home.* Washington, DC: Urban Institute.

Visher, C., & Courtney, S. M. E. (2007). *One year out: Experiences of prisoners returning to Cleveland.* Washington, DC: Urban Institute.

Visher, C., La Vigne, N. G., & Travis, J. (2004). *Returning home: Understanding the challenges of prisoner reentry. Maryland pilot study: Findings from Baltimore.* Washington, DC: Urban Institute, Justice Policy Center. Retrieved from http://www. urban.org/sites/default/files/publication/42841/410974-Returning-Home-Understanding-the-Challenges-of-Prisoner-Reentry.PDF.

Wexler, H., De Leon, G., Thomas, G., Kressel, D., & Peters, J. (1999). The Amity Prison TC Evaluation: Reincarceration outcomes. *Criminal Justice and Behavior, 26*(2), 147–167. doi: 10.1177/0093854899026002001.

White, M. D., Goldkamp, J. S., & Campbell, S. P. (2006). Co-occurring mental illness and substance abuse in the criminal justice system: Some implications for local jurisdictions. *Prison Journal, 86*(3), 1–26. doi: 10.1177/0032885506290852.

Wodahl, E. J. (2006). The challenges of prisoner reentry from a rural perspective. *Western Criminological Review, 7*(2), 32–47.

Woods, L., Lanza, A. S., Dyson, W., & Gordon, D. M. (2013). The role of prevention in promoting continuity of health care in prisoner reentry initiatives. *American Journal of Public Health, 103*(5), 830–838. doi: 10.2105/AJPH.2012.300961.

Worcel, S. D., Burrus, S. W., Finigan, M. W., Sanders, M. B., & Allen, T. L. (2009). *A study of substance-free transitional housing and community corrections in Washington County, Oregon.* Portland, OR: NPC Research.

Zandbergen, P. A., & Hart, T. C. (2006). Reducing housing options for convicted sex offenders: Investigating the impact of residency restriction laws using GIS. *Justice Research and Policy, 18*(2), 1–24. doi: 10.3818/JRP.8.2.2006.1.

Zhang, S. X., Roberts, R. E. L., & Callanan, V. J. (2006). Preventing parolees from returning to prison through community-based reintegration. *Crime and Delinquency, 52*(4), 551–571. doi: 10.1177/0011128705282594.

Chapter 9

Promising Reentry Interventions

Student Learning Outcomes

After reading this chapter, you should be able to:

- Identify the many reentry interventions that ex-offenders may participate in.
- Describe the characteristics of various reentry programs and the goals that they are trying to achieve for ex-offenders.
- Summarize the effectiveness of various reentry interventions.
- Explain the principles needed for effective reentry interventions.

Introduction

For any ex-offender, getting "back on track" and reintegrating into society is no easy feat. Hector Morales, of Newark, New Jersey, is one ex-offender who exemplifies the struggles that ex-offenders have (Husock, 2012). Morales, a long-time heroin addict, spent over 18 years of his life behind bars for drug-related offenses (Husock, 2012). Upon release from serving a five-year prison sentence with no marketable job skills, no high school degree, and $9,000 in debt due to back child support, Morales was clearly in a tenuous situation when trying to reintegrate back into society (Husock, 2012). However, the Office of Reentry in Newark had a new plan in place for Morales and others just like him. Rather than providing Morales with job training and requiring him to go to counseling, the Office of Reentry instituted a different approach, whereby they push ex-offenders to develop "rapid attachment to work" (Husock, 2012). That is, the mission of the Office of Reentry is to get offenders employed first and foremost, and other aspects of reentry, such as therapy, can be supported thereafter. Their mission is definitely a different philosophy than most reentry programs where training and therapy are viewed as preliminary steps to take before the ex-offender can begin to secure employment. For ex-offenders in Newark, such as Morales, they are immediately referred to job-placement programs, which assist them in the development of their professionalism (e.g., resume writing, interviewing) (Husock, 2012). Then, these job-placement programs refer ex-offenders to various open job positions. The hope, of course, is that the ex-offenders land a job quickly, which will help to offset one major strain during reentry. Oftentimes, the strain of lack of employment can create much temptation for ex-offenders to return to criminal activity as they cannot secure housing or pay off any legal financial obligations without funds. In Morales' case, Newark's non-traditional reentry program has worked. He is currently working for the city as a trash collector and is on track to earn more than $60K per year (Husock, 2012).

In the state of Texas, big changes are underway to assist community corrections offenders in San Antonio with a program launched in 2015 called Resurgence Collaborative (Summers, 2015). This program is a comprehensive reentry program designed to provide social services from over one dozen nonprofit agencies to assist probationers transitioning into their communities (Summers, 2015). Probationers will have access to counseling, parenting classes, anger management classes, substance abuse treatment, victim services, and job training (Davis, 2015). One unique feature of this new program is that it is located near a probation office outside the city center and offers a sort of "one-stop shopping" experience for ex-offenders. That is, rather than probationers having to run from one agency to another for services, probationers can obtain all the services they need in one spot. For Vivian Childress, on probation for drug possession, the program is convenient and allows her to avoid the difficulties that she had with getting to appointments due to transportation (Davis, 2015). Rather than spending an hour to get to appointments downtown, she now spends 10 minutes to get to her needed appointments (Davis, 2015). As she puts it, "it's so convenient" (Davis, 2015).

This chapter will discuss the many interventions that are utilized within community corrections for all types of ex-offenders, including educational programs, employment programs, alcohol and/or substance abuse treatment programs, mental health programs, and specialized interventions for different groups of ex-offenders such as sex offenders and female offenders. Additionally, the effectiveness of such programming will be discussed. Finally, a discussion of the principle components needed for reentry programming will be provided.

Reentry Interventions

At both the state and federal levels, and even around the world, policymakers recognize that both offenders being released from prison and those serving community corrections sentences are in need of support during reentry (see Text Box 9.1). In 2008, the **Second Chance Act** was passed. This piece of federal legislation was designed to assist states in creating, managing, or expanding programs to assist offenders in making a successful transition from prison or jails and to reduce recidivism rates (Nayer et al., 2015). Besides proclaiming reentry as a key initiative in the criminal justice system, Congress also allotted $165 million in grant monies to fund reentry initiatives with this legislation (U.S. Department of Justice, 2016). The Second Chance Act provides "federal grants to government agencies and community and faith-based organizations to provide employment assistance, substance abuse treatment, housing, family programming, mentoring, victim support, and other services that can help reduce offending and violations of probation and parole" (Carothers, 2010, p. 5–13). In 2009, $25 million was earmarked for reentry initiatives, but the award money has grown to $68 million in 2016 (U.S. Department of Justice, 2016). Since the enactment of the act, over 137,000 ex-offenders have benefitted through various programs being funded, such as reentry courts, reentry

Image 17. © Chris Titze Imaging/Fotolia.

substance abuse treatment programs, family-based treatment programs, mentoring programs, technology career training, reentry research, mental health treatment, and education programs in prisons (Reentry Policy Council, 2011; U.S. Department of Justice, 2016). Reentry initiatives have been viewed by many policymakers as the "key" to stopping the revolving door of ex-offenders in the criminal justice system (Nayer et al., 2015). The following sections highlight some of the reentry programs that operate in the U.S. to help ex-offenders reintegrate successfully into their communities.

Employment

With employment being a clear struggle for ex-offenders upon reentry, many reentry programs are dedicated to increasing the employability of this group. If ex-offenders are able to obtain jobs, they are more likely to desist from criminal involvement. After all, if their "idle hands" are kept busy with pro-social activities, then there is less time for them to be involved in criminal activity (Duwe, 2015). In a meta-analytic review of eight employment programs, Visher, Winterfield, and Coggeshall (2005) found that the programs did not reduce future criminal involvement for ex-offenders. However, they note that their findings may be due the nature of the employment program. That is, the failure may be due to the lack of services provided to the ex-offenders as well as ongoing support that is needed but that is not being received.

Apel (2011, p. 940) states that "a comprehensive employment-based reentry program must have a dual focus on the *employment* and *employability* of ex-prisoners." While Apel (2011) made this statement in regards to ex-prisoners, it is very much applicable to those serving community corrections sentences as well. Reentry programs that aim to assist ex-offenders with employment must help them search for, locate, and apply for jobs. However, solely supporting ex-offenders in just the search for and application to positions is a recipe for disaster. Focusing on just assisting ex-offenders in getting a job is not enough. If programs just concentrate on job acquisition, it will likely result in ex-offenders recidivating (Apel, 2011). Ex-offenders need more assistance beyond getting a job, as they need help in retaining their jobs long-term. Essentially, what ex-offenders also need to acquire are job skills. For many ex-offenders, this may be the first time they have ever obtained legal employment in their life. If this is the case, these ex-offenders are likely deficient in job skills such as reporting to work on time, following orders from superiors, maintaining a positive work attitude, and proper work conflict resolution. Of course, these are needed skills for anyone employed regardless of their criminal record. Thus, job skill training is essential for all ex-offenders even if they have been employed before (Gunnison & Helfgott, 2013). The following sections highlight two employment reentry programs that are operating in the United States.

EMPLOY

In 2006, the EMPLOY program, an employment assistance program, was implemented in the state of Minnesota to assist ex-offenders with work acquisition (Duwe, 2015). Interestingly, the EMPLOY program is not funded via taxpayer money but rather through a private prison service agency known as Minnesota Correctional Industries (MINNCOR) (MINNCOR, 2016). MINNCOR (2016) touts that the EMPLOY program reduces recidivism by "empowering offenders with employee readiness, employer connections, and reinforcing positive change." The program is voluntary and is designed to help ex-offenders secure and retain employment (Duwe, 2015). Additionally, the EMPLOY program begins in the prison. Any inmate within 5 years of completing their sentence can apply to take part in the program (Duwe, 2015). Unlike many prison programs which offer services to inmates while they are incarcerated but fail to provide continued support upon release, the EMPLOY program is designed to assist ex-offenders after they step out of prison as employment assistance is offered to them for up to one year following release from prison (Duwe, 2015).

While incarcerated, if the EMPLOY program participant engages in any disciplinary infractions, they are at risk of being removed from the program (Duwe, 2015). Upon acceptance in the program, the inmates meet with a job training specialist for two sessions, eight hours in length, anywhere from 60–90 days prior to their release (Duwe, 2015). Duwe (2015, p. 564) explains, "During these meetings, the job training specialist covers material relating to skills assessments, resumes, job searching techniques, and interviewing skills. To remain in good standing with EMPLOY, participants must attend the job training sessions and complete a resume prior to their release." Besides interviewing skills, EMPLOY participants are also trained in self-identification of their skills, job retention skills, and the importance of maintaining a positive attitude and strong work ethic (MINNCOR, 2016). Approximately one week prior to release, a job development specialist assists the inmate in searching for employment based on the job skills of the inmate as well as the geographic area in which the offender will be residing (Duwe, 2015). Besides searching for open positions, the specialist also reaches out to employers to provide additional information about the work qualifications of the EMPLOY participant (Duwe, 2015). When connecting with potential employers, the specialist also provides information about the perks the employer may receive for hiring an EMPLOY participant. For instance, the specialist informs the employer that they could receive a Work Opportunity Tax Credit if they hire the EM-PLOY participant (i.e., $2,400 and no limit), and that they are protected against theft or property losses (i.e., $5,000) that they could incur from an EMPLOY participant while employed in their business via the Minnesota Federal Bonding Service (Duwe, 2015; MINNCOR, 2016). Both of these potential perks can open doors for EMPLOY participants as employers may be more willing to take a chance on hiring an ex-offender if there are incentives or protections in place for their business.

While the job search is underway, a retention specialist meets with the newly released inmate to provide additional assistance that the EMPLOY participant may need, such as copies of their resume, bus fare, and even professional attire (Duwe, 2015). After this initial meeting, the retention specialist will meet with the ex-offender as needed as well as 1 month after their release from prison and at 3, 6, and 12 months following their release (Duwe, 2015). If EMPLOY participants fail to meet with their retention specialist, then they are dropped from the program (Duwe, 2015).

Initial evaluations of the EMPLOY program appear promising. Duwe (2015), who examined recidivism and employment outcomes for approximately 460 male and female offenders who either did or did not participate in the EMPLOY program in Minnesota found that participants in EMPLOY program fared better. Specifically, EMPLOY participants have lower levels of rearrest, reconviction, and revocation of a community correction sentence (e.g., parole, work release, or boot camp). In regards to employment outcomes, EMPLOY participants were 72% more likely to gain employment than non-EMPLOY participants. Additionally, EMPLOY participants earned a slightly higher hourly wage and worked more hours than non-EMPLOY participants.

Safer Foundation: Employment Programs

The Safer Foundation is a nonprofit agency located in Chicago, Illinois, that has been assisting ex-offenders in gaining employment since 1972 (Shelden et al., 2016; Williams & Hicks, 2007). In order to increase the employability for ex-offenders, the Safer Foundation has initiated a three-pronged employment program that is designed to help ex-offenders regardless of their employment histories. First, the Safer Foundation helps ex-offenders find employment when they reenter society. Upon intake into the employment services program, ex-offenders will be assessed to determine what barriers they have which could inhibit their employment opportunities (e.g., physical, educational, or skills deficits) as well as what their employment strengths are (e.g., skills, past jobs) (Safer Foundation, 2016). After the assessment, ex-offenders will participate in a job readiness program that prepares them with the essential skills for obtaining a job (e.g., resume writing, interviewing tips, and workplace etiquette). As the ex-offenders participate in the job training program, their case managers are developing job leads and connecting with potential employers (Safer Foundation, 2016).

A second manner in which the Safer Foundation assists ex-offenders with employment is through the agency's operation of two adult transition center programs. These programs allow incarcerated offenders with anywhere from 30 days to 2 years left of their sentence to be released into the community-based facilities. At these facilities, clients receive employment services and job readiness assessments (Safer Foundation, 2016). They also receive employment support from their case managers. Finally, a third manner in which the Safer Foundation assists ex-offenders is through its transitional employment program. In this program, ex-offenders are placed in transitional jobs that are part-time (i.e., 90 days) but are paid. With these short-term jobs, ex-offenders are able to hone their employment skills and establish an employment record (Safer Foundation, 2016). As ex-offenders develop their skills, case managers assist them in obtaining permanent employment and offer additional forms of support, such as career development assistance, transportation support, and obtaining proper work attire (Safer Foundation, 2016).

The Safer Foundation programs have indeed assisted ex-offenders. It has been reported that over 40,000 ex-offenders who have participated in the Safer Foundation programs have found employment (Petersilia, 2000). In 2014, the Safer Foundation reported that recidivism rates for those who received their services was about 24% versus a 63% recidivism rate for ex-offenders who did not participate in the Safer Foundation programs during the same evaluation period. Additionally, it was found that of those clients who retained employment for 360 days, only 15% of the clients recidivated after a three-year follow-up period (Safer Foundation, 2014). Besides the lower recidivism rates, the Safer Foundation maintains that it has saved the state of Illinois $300 million dollars by putting ex-offenders back on the path to becoming law abiding citizens as opposed to returning them back to prisons.

Text Box 9.1: Community Corrections across the Globe

While community corrections have been a part of the correctional system in the United States for well over 100 years, in other countries, community corrections is a relatively new aspect of the justice system. In China, for example, community correction sentences were legalized in 1979, yet very few offenders received such sentences as prison was the preferred sentence for offenders (MacKenzie, 2011). However, the burgeoning prison population in the early 2000s, coupled with the astounding costs of sustaining an incarceration population of about 1.5 million, resulted in a shift in ideology over the use of community corrections in the country in 2003 (Li, 2014). Given the shift in thinking and the potential cost savings, the use of community corrections was implemented rather quickly across the nation, such that, by 2011, the majority of local jurisdictions in China had instituted different forms of community correction sentences (Li, 2014). With the expanded use of community corrections sentences, the government has also offered support. For instance, the government assists probationers and parolees with monetary aid, housing, and rehabilitation for drug addiction (Zhao, 2013). In Shanghai, volunteer social workers and community members work together to assist community corrections offenders with their personal problems, employment difficulties, and education deficits to facilitate successful reentry (Li, 2010).

Education

Many ex-offenders have deficient education levels (Harlow, 2003). Upon inspection of the education levels of those just incarcerated in state facilities, the majority have less

Image 18. © iStockphoto.com/michaelquirk.

than a high school education level (Harlow, 2003). For those incarcerated offenders returning to their communities serving parole sentences, it is important that their education levels be raised if they are to be successful during reentry (Gunnison & Helfgott, 2013). The problem with educational deficiencies is not limited to ex-offenders who were sentenced to prison terms. Those ex-offenders serving community corrections sentences are also deficient in their education levels. With increased education levels, ex-offenders are not only enhancing their reasoning and critical analytic skills, but they are also opening doors to gaining more employment options. Perhaps most importantly, those who can raise their educational levels may be less likely to recidivate (James, 2015).

Educational deficiencies for many ex-offenders often begin in their juvenile years. When ex-offenders begin their journey into the criminal justice system as juveniles, as is often the case, this entry disrupts their educational attainment. For juveniles who are sentenced to a correctional facility, a boot camp, or a probation group home, they are much more likely to drop out of school than their peers who do not have contact with the juvenile justice system (Abrams & Franke, 2013). Among those juveniles who do drop out of school, they are also much more likely to be poor and a minority (Abrams & Franke, 2013). Abrams and Franke (2013) report that less than 20% of juveniles who were incarcerated were likely to obtain their high school diploma or G.E.D. While it is difficult to pinpoint the exact factors for why dropout rates are high and secondary school completion is so low, researchers have indicated that there are several reasons that this may be the case, such as learning disabilities, school suspensions or expulsions, antisocial peers, and low attachment to school (Abrams & Franke, 2013). With such a small percentage of juveniles who were ensnared in the criminal justice system completing their high school degree, or equivalent, even fewer pursue postsecondary education at community colleges, four-year universities, or trade schools (Abrams & Franke, 2013).

Even ex-offenders who did not have previous entanglements with the juvenile justice system and have completed a high school degree or equivalent, are less likely to pursue post-secondary education. For the small percentage that do pursue higher education, they are more likely to be non-minority and have higher incomes. The exact number of ex-offenders who pursue higher education is not known (Abrams & Franke, 2013). However, it is clear that admission policies that restrict those with criminal records from being accepted into colleges as well as the lack of access to financial aid likely contribute significantly to the lack of those pursuing higher education. The following section highlights the educational services and programs provided to state and federal offenders.

LEARN

Each state correctional facility or community corrections center offers a basic education component for those in need. For instance, states will offer literacy training and assist those ex-offenders who have not obtained their high school diploma to obtain their G.E.D. Those ex-offenders who are deficient in the English language will also obtain support to become proficient in the language. There are a multitude of community-based educational programs that are operating in the nation to assist ex-offenders (U.S. Department of Education, 2011). One such educational program that is assisting both non-offenders and ex-offenders is the Literacy, Education, and Resource Network (LEARN) program that operates in the state of Arizona (U.S. Department of Education, 2011). This program was first launched in 1987 in Tucson, and today there are 32 LEARN centers in operation within the state (U.S. Department of Education, 2011). LEARN programs provide teacher-assisted learning programs that utilize various computer programs in an effort to increase education levels in hopes of reducing the chance of individuals becoming involved in crime due to educational deficits and, for those who have become ensnared in the criminal justice system, to reduce the chances of re-offending (U.S. Department of Education, 2011). As described by the Arizona Superior Court (2016), "the goal of the LEARN program is to provide probationers with the skills and attitudes necessary to complete a successful term of probation, become functional members of society, and pursue future educational opportunities." Educational programs offered by LEARN include Adult Basic Education and Training and Adult Secondary Education. Additionally, LEARN centers also offer G.E.D. preparation classes and testing services (U.S. Department of Education, 2011).

UNICOR

At the federal level, the Federal Prison Industries, known as UNICOR, provide educational services to incarcerated federal offenders. Federal inmates without a diploma or G.E.D. are required to participate in a literacy program until they earn their G.E.D. Additionally, those that are not proficient in the English language are required to participate in an English-as-a-Second Language program until they are competent at an eighth-grade level (UNICOR, 2016). Upon release from a federal prison, ex-offenders may be placed in a residential reentry center that will either provide educational services or be linked with a community partner that provides such services (Federal Bureau of Prisons, 2016). For those federal offenders directly sentenced to a community corrections section, educational support services are also provided.

Both the LEARN and UNICOR programs have been found to be successful in providing education, reducing recidivism, and improving outcomes for state and federal offenders (Horwitz, 2015; Siegel, 2007). For instance, an evaluation of probationers in Arizona who participated in LEARN, and whose recidivism rates were tracked for five years, revealed that the LEARN participants had lower felony arrest and conviction rates than probationers who did not participate in the program (Siegel, 2007). One LEARN probationer participant describes how pivotal the program was to his/her life:

> Before I came to the LEARN Lab, I was a lost soul with broken dreams. Being on probation is tough, but my education is so important to me. It's hard finding a job with a felony. They judge me before they get to know me. It took me four years to get my GED but my teachers never failed me. I kept coming back. I took my math test four times—I kept missing it by one or two points.... my heart sank the third time around.... I cried but my teachers pushed me and guess what? I received my GED (Siegel, 2007, p. 12).

However, the link between secondary education and recidivism is a bit murky with some researchers finding lower recidivism rates for those who earn high school diplomas or G.E.D.s, while other researchers have not found such a link (James, 2015; Rosen, 2013). Thus, while the LEARN program may be effective, other educational programs may not be. As for UNICOR, its success at assisting offenders may be limited in the future. Unfortunately, funding for UNICOR has been drastically cut, resulting in "more than 10,000 inmates on a waiting list for prison jobs and educational training" (Horwitz, 2015).

Many educational programs do not provide post-secondary education for ex-offenders or provide support for them to pursue it, perhaps due to time or budget constraints or the focus on trying to ensure all ex-offenders attain at least a secondary education. In an examination of young men who participated in a probation camp that provided reentry services (e.g., education and substance abuse treatment), three years after program completion, Abrams and Franke (2013) found that only certain probationers pursued post-secondary education. For instance, ex-offenders who were likely to pursue post-secondary education were those that had or earned a high school diploma or G.E.D., those that were not fathers, and those who had received more months of services. These findings suggest that other forms of support may need to be given to other ex-offenders to pursue post-secondary education that do not fall into those categories. Other researchers have found that the post-secondary education attainment is related to reductions in recidivism (James, 2015; Winterfield et al., 2009).

Substance Abuse

Many male and female ex-offenders struggle with substance abuse, therefore, substance abuse treatment is imperative for them to successfully reintegrate back into society (Gunnison & Helfgott, 2013). Oftentimes, policymakers are focused on ensuring that treatment is provided to those who are incarcerated. However, community corrections offenders, those outside the prison walls, are also in great need of treatment. Taxman, Perdoni, and Caudy (2013) report that a large number of community corrections offenders serving probation and parole sentences suffer from substance abuse issues, at a rate of every 7 of 10 offenders, but only about 5% of these offenders receive the appropriate treatment services that they need. While there are many substance abuse treatment programs that are designed to help community corrections offenders, there are still gaps that remain. That is, community corrections offenders need continued support beyond the initial treatment program—they need aftercare as well. The following sections describe substance abuse treatment reentry programs that are designed to assist community corrections offenders.

Step'n Out Collaborative Behavioral Management Intervention

In 2003, correctional administrators and addiction treatment specialists convened to discuss best practices for assisting parolees with their substance abuse problems (Friedmann et al., 2008). At the conclusion of their meeting, they developed a plan whereby parole officers, in conjunction with treatment providers, could work with their clients in a more collaborative fashion to address their clients' addiction issues and foster better outcomes (Friedmann et al., 2008). The culmination of the exchange of ideas resulted in the implementation of the Step'n Out Collaborative Behavioral Management (CBM) intervention program in six jurisdictions across five states.

The CBM program, which lasts 12 weeks, brings together parole officers, treatment counselors, and clients. There are four main components to the CBM intervention. The program, as summarized by Friedmann et al. (2008, p. 294), is as follows:

> First, it explicitly articulates both staff's and offenders' roles, their expectations of one another, and the consequences if offenders meet or fail to meet those expectations. Second, it negotiates a behavioral contract that specifies concrete target behaviors in which the offender is expected to engage on a weekly basis; these target behaviors include requirements of supervision and formal addiction treatment, and involvement in behaviors that compete with drug use (e.g., getting a job; enhancing non-drug social network). Third, it regularly monitors adherence to the behavioral contract, and employs both reinforcers and sanctions to shape behavior. The motto is "Catching People Doing Things Right" which is to say, the intervention creates the conditions to notice and reward offenders for achieving incremental pro-social steps as part of normal supervision. Fourth, CBM establishes a systematic, standardized, and progressive approach to reinforcement and sanctioning to ensure consistency and fairness.

One of the benefits of the program is that it allows the opportunity for parole officers to work more closely with treatment providers and foster more consistent communication between them about their clients. In addition, clients have a better expectation of what steps they are to follow and clearly understand what the sanctions may be if they fail to follow the guidance provided to them. Finally, this program allows parole officers to move beyond their surveillance role where they focused on administering sanctions, and it allows them the opportunity to reward offenders who are making positive strides in their recovery.

Initial evaluations of the Step'n Out CBM program show some promise, but more research is needed (Friedmann, Rhodes, & Taxman, 2009). For instance, Friedmann et al. (2009) found that the program increased contacts between parole officers and parolees, and that parolees also sought more individualized counseling and treatment. However, the researchers found that the increased contacts with parole officers and services did not result in increased technical violations for parolees. Additionally, Friedmann et al. (2012) examined the effectiveness of the CBM program for parolees across six different jurisdictions, and found that CBM participants had lower levels of drug use after a 9-month follow-up period. Specifically, the program had the greatest impact on those who used non-hard drugs, such as marijuana, as opposed to other substances. However, the researchers did not find significant differences in recidivism rates among non-CBM participants (Friedmann et al., 2012).

Motivational Enhancement Therapy

Developed in the early 1990s, motivational enhancement therapy (MET) is a type of intervention designed to assist individuals with substance abuse addiction through motivational interviewing techniques (Miller, Zweben, DiClemente, & Rychtarik, 1992). MET is distinct from other interventions assisting substance abusers in that is seeks to "resolve their ambivalence about engaging in treatment and stopping their drug use. This approach aims to evoke rapid and internally motivated change, rather than guide the patient stepwise through the recovery process" (National Institute on Drug Abuse, 2012, p. 54). Additionally, unlike other forms of intervention that may employ multiple therapy sessions in order to invoke change, MET only requires four individualized treatment sessions after an initial assessment is taken (Miller et al., 1992). Clients are instructed to report to the first session sober, as drug screening tests will be administered, and to also bring a support person to the session, such as a partner or close friend (Miller et al., 1992). At the first session, the therapist will provide an overview of the MET program and discuss the outcome of various assessments with the client, the history of their use of substance, and seek to elicit self-motivating statements about their use, such as, the client admitting that he/she has a problem and needs help (Miller et al., 2012; National Institute on Drug Abuse, 2012). In a sense, the therapist is allowing the client to recognize that he/she has a problem because after such recognition is made, then the client is much more open to change. With this openness to change behaviors, a plan for substance use cessation is put into place. About 1–2 weeks following the first session meeting, the second session takes place during which the therapist ensures that the client is still committed to change and continues to encourage the client to change.

Following the second session, the final two sessions take place at the week 6 and 12 marks respectively (Miller et al., 2012). Miller et al. (2012) describe the follow-up meetings as "booster sessions" whereby the client is assessed on his/her commitment to change, determining if the client is changing, and making sure they are committed to their plans of action for change. At the final session meeting, the therapist reminds clients of the reasons why they indicated they wanted to change, summarizes their commitments to change, elicits self-motivational statements from them, and encourages the client to attend follow-up sessions or seek out solutions besides the substance use when issues in their lives arise (Miller et al., 2012).

There have been several evaluations of the MET program and results are somewhat mixed as it appears to be effective for those addicted to alcohol and marijuana but less so for those addicted to other drugs, such as cocaine or heroin (Ball et al., 2007; National Institute on Drug Abuse, 2012). Some researchers have not found MET to be an effective intervention regardless of the substance used (Kinlock et al., 2005). In other evaluations of community-based reentry interventions for substance abusers that utilized a cognitive-based therapy as well as social learning based motivational interviewing techniques, researchers have not found such programs to be effective in regards to relapse and recidivism between program participants and non-program participants (Grommon, Davidson, & Bynum, 2013). Thus, MET therapies may be most effective when combined with other treatment modalities for those addicted to all types of substances.

Mental Health

Many community corrections offenders suffer from mental health issues — often in tandem with other co-occurring problems, such as substance abuse (Gunnison & Helfgott, 2013). Travis, Solomon, and Waul (2001) reported that approximately 16% of all ex-offenders have a diagnosable mental disorder. In many instances, the criminal justice system is ill-equipped to help those with mental illnesses on many levels (Petrila, Ridgely, & Borum, 2003). Despite not being properly equipped, many jurisdictions have recognized the importance of helping formerly incarcerated offenders as well as community corrections offenders with their mental health needs, which has resulted in the implementation of many reentry programs designed to help these ex-offenders. The following section describes one mental health treatment reentry program that is designed to assist mentally ill ex-offenders.

Oklahoma Collaborative Mental Health Re-Entry Program

The Oklahoma Collaborative Mental Health Re-entry program was implemented in 2007 to help those who were incarcerated and suffer from mental health problems successfully transition back into their communities. The voluntary program first begins in the prison, approximately 12 months before release, whereby inmates work through some of their problems as well as discuss care for their illness after release (Ginn, 2016). Ninety days prior to release, the program participant works with the Re-Entry Intensive Care Coordination Team (Ginn, 2015). During this time, the team assists ex-offenders in many ways, including helping them establish the necessary medical benefits that they will need so that they have access to their medications and other mental health supports (e.g., counseling). According to Ginn (2016), the ex-offender will work with a certified mental health case manager and peer recovery support specialist over the next year.

Findings from evaluations of the program are favorable. For example, the recidivism rate, after a three-year follow-up, is 25% versus 42% for non-program participants (Ollove, 2012). One successful female program participant, a former prostitute and drug runner who has been diagnosed with bipolar disorder, lauds the program, stating that without it, she "would have ended up back in prison and addicted" (Ollove, 2012). In addition to the success of the program, it is also saving the state thousands of dollars per year (Ollove, 2012). By assisting offenders and diverting their return back to prison, the state can invest in lower-cost community care as opposed to incarceration care, which can cost about twenty-five thousand per year per incarcerated offender.

Faith-Based Reentry Programs

Upon examining the history of corrections in the United States, religious ties clearly intertwine throughout. For instance, the first penitentiary in the United States, which opened in the late 1790s, was founded by a Quaker (Allen, Latessa, & Ponder, 2016). These early penitentiaries operated under the **Pennsylvania Model**, whereby inmates were housed in single cells and received religious instruction in their cells (Allen et al., 2016). With the foundation of corrections in the United States originally linked to religion, it should, perhaps, come as no surprise that there are many faith-based organizations providing reentry services and programs to ex-offenders (Roman et al., 2007). However, Mears and colleagues (2006) note that some faith-based programs assisting ex-offenders are operated by specific religious institutions and have a religious component

Image 19. © iStockphoto.com/Halfpoint.

to the programming while other faith-based programs do not have a religious component to them whatsoever. In the latter programs, clients are still exposed to faith ideals subtly through their interactions with staff and volunteers who may verbalize their commitment to religious ideals (Mears et al., 2006). The following section describes one faith-based reentry program that is designed to assist community corrections offenders.

InnerChange Freedom Initiative

In 1997, the InnerChange Freedom Initiative (IFI) reentry program was implemented in Texas (Duwe & Johnson, 2013). Today, there are a total of eight IFI programs operating across 5 states for both men and women (Duwe & Johnson, 2013). The IFI program is privately funded and relies on volunteers from churches and religious organizations to carry out the many services that the program offers (Duwe & Johnson, 2013). This program is voluntary and first begins in the prison institution approximately 18 months before an inmate's release. After admission into the program, inmates are placed into the same housing unit of the prison. During Phase 1 of the IFI program, participants receive religious instruction each morning, and in the afternoons and evenings, they receive other programming such as cognitive skills training, reentry planning, and addiction assistance (Duwe & Johnson, 2013). After successful completion of Phase 1, clients enter Phase 2, where they work in the facility, attend faith-based programming, continue to work on reentry planning, and are assigned to a mentor from the community (Duwe & Johnson, 2013). Upon release, participants enter Phase 3 of the program, which lasts 12 months, whereby they continue to work with their mentor, attend support groups, and engage in counseling as needed (Duwe & Johnson, 2013). The program also assists ex-offenders with any needs that they may have such as housing or employment.

There have been several evaluations of the IFI program which have demonstrated that the IFI program is effective at reducing recidivism (Duwe & King, 2012; Johnson & Larson, 2003). In an examination of IFI graduates and non-graduates in Texas after a two-year follow-up period, Johnson and Larson (2003) report that IFI participants had lower recidivism rates and also often undergo a spiritual transformation. One IFI participant stated, "For the first time I have respect for others. I even try to encourage others, and pray for them. The books we use here and the Bible have really helped. Praying has helped. When I stumble, now I repent. When I get out of here, the church is going to be a big part of my life" (Johnson & Larson, 2003, p. 28). In another study, Duwe and Johnson (2013) found that InnerChange programs are cost-effective and, in the state of Minnesota, an estimated $3 million dollars of tax money was saved due to reduced levels of recidivism for IFI program participants. Although the InnerChange program appears promising, other researchers have pointed to the fact that other faith-based programs may not be effective or that perhaps positive outcomes that have been found are actually due to other factors (Mears et al., 2007). For instance, the InnerChange program offers many services and support, including mentors. It may be the case that the other support services (e.g., housing and employment) or mentoring aspects of the program are driving the success of the program rather than the faith-based components (see Duwe & King, 2012). Due to the need for funding, volunteers, and community support, Mears et al. (2007, p. 362) assert that "faith-based reentry programs face the daunting challenge of maintaining the integrity of their efforts and sustaining them over time."

Other Reentry Programs

The proceeding sections only highlighted a few select reentry programs that have been implemented in the United States. There are thousands of other types of reentry programs in operation across the nation that are spearheaded by state and federal agencies, non-profit agencies, and private groups. While some reentry programs are more oriented towards addressing the specific needs of ex-offenders, other programs target specific types of ex-offenders, such as those convicted of certain offenses (e.g., sex offenses) or female offenders. For example, high-risk sex offenders may participate in a reentry program called the Circles of Support and Accountability (COSA) which first began in Canada in 1994 but today operates in several states across the nation (Daly, 2008). In this program, community volunteers, often from faith-based organizations, assist offenders by: (1) assisting the offender with getting his needs met and providing a network of individuals that can offer emotional support; (2) helping the offender develop pro-social solutions to solve problems; (3) challenging the offender's behaviors or attitudes; and (4) celebrating the successes of the offender (COSA Ottawa, 2016). Initial evaluations of the COSA programs appear to demonstrate that it can reduce recidivism for program participants, but more rigorous evaluations are needed to establish if the program is indeed effective—particularly in regards to sexual recidivism (Daly, 2008; Duwe, 2013).

Additionally, female ex-offenders encounter many difficulties in their reintegration into their communities, from coping with previous traumas to reunification with their children (Gunnison & Helfgott, 2013). In New York, the Hour Children's Hour Working Women Reentry Program assists female ex-offenders with employment assistance, skills training, mentoring, and assistance with finding care for their children when they are sick (Hour Children, 2016). The organization also assists women with mental health support and family reunification. According to organizational reports, women who participate in their programs have lower recidivism rates. More research is needed on this program as well as the many others that offer support for women struggling to reintegrate successfully.

Reentry Program Considerations

This chapter has scratched the surface in regards to the thousands of reentry programs in operation across the nation. The passage of the Second Chance Act in 2008 fostered the proliferation of the implementation of many reentry programs—many which were not rooted in theory and were often difficult to empirically evaluate (Jonson & Cullen, 2015). After all, Jonson and Cullen (2015, p. 522) state that "intervening successfully with offenders is a daunting challenge." Despite the difficulties, overall reentry programs that have been implemented have been found to be successful (Jonson & Cullen, 2015). However, some important considerations should be made to improve existing and future reentry programs. When reflecting on employment, Latessa (2012) stresses that effective employment reentry programs should target criminogenic needs and risk factors. He states that ex-offenders' attitudes about work should be a target of programming and that the programming should take a cognitive behavioral approach whereby rewards for positive behaviors and consequences for inappropriate behaviors are given to ex-offenders. It is through such an approach, Latessa (2012) maintains, that employment reentry programs are likely to be successful in terms of recidivism—much more so than those programs that merely provide job assistance to ex-offenders. Jonson and Cullen (2015) agree, stating that more effective reentry programs target risk and needs.

According to Hirschfield (2014), there are several important programming initiatives that should be in place in order to assist ex-offenders in enhancing their education levels. First, Hirschfield (2014) asserts that proper assessments of the individual's education and skill levels need to be determined. This assessment should occur regardless of whether the ex-offender is confined first to jail or prison or directly sentenced to a community corrections sanction. With proper assessment, realistic educational and career goals can be put into place. For instance, it may be recommended that ex-offenders participate in vocational training in addition to obtaining their G.E.D. certificate in order to enhance their career prospects. Second, Hirschfield (2014) states that the process of reenrollment in schools, particularly for juveniles, needs to be streamlined. All too often, there are delays in record transfers between schools resulting in increased time lags for juvenile ex-offenders to pursue education goals. Finally, Hirschfield (2014) notes that there needs to be better pre-release planning, for those incarcerated prior to serving community corrections sentences, put in place to assist ex-offenders in pursuing education upon release. With such planning, less time will be lost on secondary and post-secondary school applications and records transferring, which will result in continuity in education from the institution to the community.

For those ex-offenders suffering from substance abuse problems, there is a need for reentry programs to follow effective treatment principles—including the targeting of risk and needs factors (see Text Box 9.2) (Prendergast, 2009). Additionally, community corrections are in need of continued care after completion of the treatment program (Gunnison & Helfgott, 2013). In the case of parolees, effective interventions are those that are rooted in a cognitive-behavioral approach and offer support for relapse prevention (Prendergast, 2009). High-risk parolees with substance abuse issues would also benefit from immersion in a **treatment communities**—residential facilities that offer drug and/or alcohol abuse assistance via trained staff (Prendergast, 2009). For female community corrections offenders, their treatment should be further specialized to meet their distinct needs from male offenders. For instance, female community corrections offenders should have programming that also addresses their prior sexual abuse traumas and child reunification issues (Gunnison & Helfgott, 2013; Prendergast, 2009).

Text Box 9.2: National Institute on Drug Abuse:
Principles of Drug Abuse Treatment

1. Drug addiction is a brain disease that affects behavior.

2. Recovery from drug addiction requires effective treatment, followed by management of the problem over time.

3. Treatment must last long enough to produce stable behavioral change.

4. Assessment is the first step in treatment.

5. Tailoring services to fit the needs of the individual is an important part of effective drug abuse treatment for criminal justice populations.

6. Drug use during treatment should be carefully monitored.

7. Treatment should target factors that are associated with criminal behavior.

8. Criminal justice supervision should incorporate treatment planning for drug-abusing offenders, and treatment providers should be aware of correctional supervision requirements.

9. Continuity of care is essential for drug abusers re-entering the community.

10. A balance of rewards and sanctions encourages prosocial behavior and treatment participation.

11. Offenders with co-occurring drug abuse and mental health problems often require an integrated treatment approach.

12. Medications are an important part of treatment for many drug-abusing offenders.

13. Treatment planning for drug-abusing offenders who are living in or reentering the community should include strategies to prevent and treat serious, chronic medical conditions, such as HIV/AIDS, hepatitis B and C, and tuberculosis.

Source: Directly adapted from: National Institute on Drug Abuse. (2014). *Principles of drug abuse treatment for criminal justice populations: A research-based guide.* Rockville, MD: National Institute of Health.

Those community corrections offenders suffering from mental health problems should have access to quality in/outpatient treatment options, which are not only affordable but also accessible to them geographically (World Health Organization, 1996). Also, there should be ease in access to their medications (World Health Organization, 1996). According to the World Health Organization (2016), other important principles of treatment programs for mentally ill individuals should include the utilization of proper assessment tools for both diagnosis and ongoing treatment and that the treatment should be carried out by licensed and trained professionals. Additionally, case managers should work with clients as much as possible to assist them rather than refer their clients to others for services (Rapp & Goscha, 2004). Further, case managers should have a relatively low caseload size in order to effectively treat their clients, and case managers should work with community partners to offer support to their clients in their communities (Rapp & Goscha, 2004).

In sum, regardless of the orientation of the reentry program (i.e., substance abuse offenders, sex offenders), if reentry programs are to impact the clients (i.e., male and female community corrections offenders who have committed a wide range of offenses) that they are intended to, the programs must target criminogenic risk and needs factors (Latessa & Lowenkamp, 2006). Thus, assessment of these needs and risk factors at critical stages in the criminal justice system is needed for ex-offenders, and they certainly should be considered during program design. Moreover, continued care needs to be provided to clients following successful completion of the reentry program.

Conclusion

Over the past decade, the focus in corrections has been largely on reentry. With the increased focus on reentry, jurisdictions are either expanding their current reentry programs or implementing new ones if they had not offered such programming before. These efforts have resulted in the operation of thousands of reentry programs across the nation. As discussed in the chapter, some reentry programs are focused on meeting certain needs for ex-offenders, such as employment, education, substance abuse, and mental health, using a variety of different therapeutic techniques. Many of the reentry programs discussed in this chapter have been found to be successful. However, many more reentry programs are in need of empirical evaluations to guarantee that they are indeed effective for ex-offenders and to ensure that they are incorporating the use of assessments in their program design. Aside from the further collection of empirical evidence that is needed on existing reentry programs, it is important to recognize that regardless of what reentry program that is being implemented, all treatments are based on the principles of effective interventions.

Key Terms

Pennsylvania Model

Second Chance Act

Treatment communities

Discussion Questions

1. Research reentry efforts in your state. Are there local efforts to assist offenders in their reentry process? How about statewide?

2. Research three reentry programs in your state. Be able to discuss their inception, how they operate, and what risk/needs factors the program is targeting. Additionally, discuss whether the programs have any empirical evidence.

3. Since many reentry programs are operating without any empirical testing, find a reentry program that is operating across the nation that has not been evaluated. Research the components of the program and then develop a suggested methodological design.

4. What recommendations do you have to improve reentry programs in your state?
   What is lacking in current programs? What future reentry programs do you see
   a need for in your state? Why?

References

Abrams, L. S., & Franke, T. M. (2013). Postsecondary educational engagement among formerly-incarcerated transition-age young men. *Journal of Offender Rehabilitation, 52*(4), 233–253. doi: 10.1080/10509674.2013.782774.

Allen, H. E., Latessa, E. J., & Ponder, B. S. (2016). *Corrections in America: An introduction.* Upper Saddle River, NJ: Prentice-Hall.

Apel, R. (2011). Transitional jobs program putting employment-based reentry programs into context. *Criminology & Public Policy, 10*(4), 939–942. doi: 10.1111/j.1745-9133.2011.00781.x.

Arizona Superior Court. (2016). *Adult probation: Educational services, LEARN.* Retrieved from http://www.sc.pima.gov/?tabid=138.

Ball, S. A., Martino, S., Nich, C., Frankforter, T. L., Van Horn, D., Crits-Christoph, P., Woody, G. E., Obert, J. L., Farentinos, C., & Carroll, K. M. (2007). Site matters: Multisite randomized trial of motivational enhancement therapy in community drug abuse clinics. *Journal of Consulting & Clinical Psychology, 75*(4), 556–567. doi: 10.1037/0022-006X.75.4.556.

Carothers, C. (2010). Important role of advocacy. In H. A. Dlugacz (Ed.), *Reentry planning for offenders with mental disorders* (pp. 5-1–5-14). Kingston, NJ: Civic Research Institute.

COSA Ottawa. (2016). *What is circles of support and accountability?* Retrieved from http://cosa-ottawa.ca/.

Daly, R. (2008). *Treatment and reentry practices for sex offenders: An overview of states.* New York: Vera Institute of Justice.

Davis, V. T. (2015, May 5). Grant funds one-stop initiative to help ex-offenders reintegrate into society. *San Antonio Express-News.* Retrieved from http://www.expressnews.com/news/local/article/Grant-funds-one-stop-initiative-to-help-6244677.php.

Duwe, G. (2013). What *works* with sex offenders? Results from an evaluation of Minnesota Circles of Support and Accountability. *Corrections Today, 75,* 32–34.

Duwe, G. (2015). The benefits of keeping idle hands busy: An outcome evaluation of a prisoner reentry employment program. *Crime & Delinquency, 61*(4), 559–586. doi: 10.1177/0011128711421653.

Duwe, G., & Johnson, B. R. (2013). Estimating the benefits of a faith-based correctional program grant. *International Journal of Criminology and Sociology, 2,* 227–239.

Duwe, G., & King, M. (2012). Can faith-based correctional programs work? An outcome evaluation of the InnerChange Freedom Initiative in Minnesota. *International Journal of Offender Therapy & Comparative Criminology, 57*(7), 813–841. doi: 10.1177/0306624X12439397.

Federal Bureau of Prisons. (2016). *Reentry programs.* Retrieved from https://www.bop.gov/inmates/custody_and_care/reentry.jsp.

Friedmann, P. D., Green, T. C., Taxman, F. S., Harrington, M., Rhodes, A. G., Katz, E., O'Connell, D., Martin, S. S., Frisman, L. K., Litt, M., Burdon, W., Clarke, J. G., & Fletcher, B. W. (2012). Collaborative behavioral management among parolees: Drug use, crime and re-arrest in the Step'n Out randomized trial. *Addiction, 107*(6), 1099–1108. doi: 10.1111/j.1360-0443.2011.03769.x.

Friedmann, P. D., Katz, E. C., Rhodes, A. G., Taxman, F. S., O'Connell, D. J., Frisman, L. K., Burdon, W. M., Fletcher, B. W., Litt, M. D., Clarke, J., & Martin, S. S. (2008). Collaborative behavioral management for drug-involved parolees: Rationale and design of the Step'n Out study. *Journal of Offender Rehabilitation, 47*(3), 290–318. doi: 10.1080/10509670802134184.

Friedmann, P. D., Rhodes, A. G., & Taxman, F. S. (2009). Collaborative behavioral management: Integration and intensification of parole and outpatient addiction treatment services in the Step'n Out study. *Journal of Experimental Criminology, 5*(3), 277–243. doi: 10.1007/s11292-009-9079-3.

Ginn, J. (2016). Oklahoma helps mentally ill prisoners get on their feet. *Capitol Ideas.* Retrieved from http://www.csg.org/pubs/capitolideas/enews/issue100_3.aspx.

Grommon, E., Davidson, W. S., & Bynum, T. S. (2013). A randomized trial of a multimodal community-based prisoner reentry program emphasizing substance abuse treatment. *Journal of Offender Rehabilitation, 52*(4), 287–309. doi: 10.1080/10509674.2013.782775.

Gunnison, E., & Helfgott, J. B. (2013). *Offender reentry: Beyond crime and punishment.* Boulder, CO: Lynne Rienner.

Harlow, C. W. (2003). *Education and correctional populations.* Washington, DC: Bureau of Justice Statistics.

Hirschfield, P. J. (2014). Effective and promising practices in transitional planning and school reentry. *Journal of Correctional Education, 65*(2), 84–96.

Horwitz, S. (2015, October 29). U.S. official says prison system's best reentry program cut 'dramatically.' *The Washington Post.* Retrieved from https://www.washingtonpost.com/world/national-security/deputy-attorney-general-prison-systems-best-re-entry-program-has-dramatically-shrunk/2015/10/29/8d96713a-7e66-11e5-beba-927fd8634498_story.html.

Hour Children. (2016). *Hour working women reentry program.* Retrieved from http://hourchildren.org/?page_id=127.

Husock, H. (2012, August 3). From prison to a paycheck. *The Wall Street Journal.* Retrieved from http://www.wsj.com/articles/SB10000872396390443866404577565170182319412.

James, N. (2015). *Offender reentry: Correctional statistics, reintegration into the community, and recidivism.* Washington, DC: Correctional Research Service.

Johnson, B. R., & Larson, D. B. (2003). *InnerChange freedom initiative: A preliminary evaluation of a faith-based program.* Center for Research on Religion and Urban Civil Society: The University of Pennsylvania.

Jonson, C. L., & Cullen, F. T. (2015). Prisoner reentry programs. *Crime & Justice, 44*(1), 517–575.

Kinlock, T. W., Sears, E. A., O'Grady, K. E., Callaman, J. M., & Brown, B. S. (2005). The effect of motivational enhancement therapy on drug abuse treatment retention among drug court clients. *Journal of Community Corrections, 15*(1), 11–27.

Latessa, E. (2012). Why work is important, and how to improve the effectiveness of correctional reentry programs that target employment. *Criminology & Public Policy, 11*(1), 87–91. doi: 10.1111/j.1745-9133.2012.00790.x.

Latessa, E. J., & Lowenkamp, C. T. (2006). What works in reducing recidivism. *University of St. Thomas Law Journal, 13*(3), 521–535.

Li, E. (2010). Prisonization or socialization? Social factors associated with Chinese administrative offenses. *UCLA Pacific Basin Law Journal, 27*(2), 213–260.

Li, S. D. (2014). Toward a cost-effective correctional system: New developments in community-based corrections in China. *Victims & Offenders, 9*(1), 120–125. doi: 10.1080/15564886.2013.860936.

MacKenzie, D. L. (2011). Probation: An untapped resource in U.S. corrections. In L. Gideon & H.-E. Sung (Eds.), *Rethinking corrections: Rehabilitation, reentry, and reintegration* (pp. 97–128). Thousand Oaks, CA: Sage.

Mears, D. P., Roman, C. G., Wolff, A., & Buck, J. (2006). Faith-based efforts to improve prisoner reentry: Assessing the logic and evidence. *Journal of Criminal Justice, 34*(4), 351–367. doi: 10.1016/j.jcrimjus.2006.05.002.

Miller, W. R., Zweben A., DiClemente, C. C., & Rychtarik, R. G. (1992). *Motivational enhancement therapy manual: A clinical research guide for therapists treating individuals with alcohol abuse and dependence.* Rockville, MD: National Institute on Alcohol Abuse and Alcoholism.

MINNCOR. (2016). *About us: History of MINNCOR.* Retrieved from http://www.minncor.com/about-us/history.aspx.

National Institute on Drug Abuse. (2012). *Principles of drug addiction treatment: A research-based guide.* Washington, DC: U.S. Department of Health and Human Services.

National Institute on Drug Abuse. (2014). *Principles of drug abuse treatment for criminal justice populations: A research-based guide.* Rockville, MD: National Institute of Health.

Nayer, G., Gallo, R., Amos, C., & Colas, J. (2015). Prison reentry programs: The key to stop the revolving door. *Journal of Criminal Justice & Law Review, 4*(1/2), 1–12.

Ollove, M. (2012, October 23). Oklahoma looks for ways to keep mentally ill ex-offenders out of prison. *Kaiser Health News.* Retrieved from http://khn.org/news/stateline-oklahoma-mentally-ill-prisons/.

Petersilia, J. (2000). When prisoners return to the community: Political, economic, and social consequences. Washington, DC: U.S. Department of Justice.

Petrila, J., Ridgely, M. S., & Borum, R. (2003). Debating outpatient commitment: Controversy, trends, and empirical data. *Crime and Delinquency, 49,* 157–172. doi: 10.1177/0011128702239240.

Prendergast, M. L. (2009). Interventions to promote successful re-entry among drug-abusing parolees. *Addiction Science & Clinical Practice, 5*(1), 4–13.

Rapp, C. A., & Goscha, R. J. (2004). Principles of effective case management of mental health services. *Psychiatric Rehabilitation Journal, 27*(4), 319–333.

Reentry Policy Council. (2011). *Second Chance Act.* Lexington, KY: Justice Center, Council of State Governments. http://reentrypolicy.org.

Roman, C. G., Wolff, A., Correa, V., & Buck, J. (2007). Assessing intermediate outcomes of a faith-based residential prisoner reentry program. *Research on Social Work Practice, 17*(2), 199–215. doi: 10.1177/1049731506295860.

Rosen, H. (2013). *What works in reentry clearinghouse update — new content on the effectiveness of employment and education programs.* Washington, DC: The Justice Center.

Safer Foundation. (2014). *Safer Foundation highlights.* Retrieved from http://www.saferfoundation.org/files/documents/FINAL-SAFER-HIGHLIGHTS-7-29-14.pdf.

Safer Foundation. (2016). *Employment services.* Retrieved from http://www.safer foundation.org/services-programs/employment-services.

Shelden, R. G., Brown, W. B., Miller, K. S., & Fritzler, R. B. (2016). *Crime and criminal justice in American society* (2nd ed.). Long Grove, IL: Waveland.

Siegel, G. (2007). *The history of project LEARN.* Arizona Supreme Court. Retrieved from https://www.azcourts.gov/Portals/29/JJSD%20Publication%20Reports/corred_learn_history.pdf.

Summers, V. (2015, May 6). New probation program on East Side. *News4.* Retrieved from http://news4sanantonio.com/news/local/new-probationer-program-on-east-side.

Taxman, F. S., Perdoni, M. L., & Caudy, M. (2013). The plight of providing appropriate substance abuse treatment services to offenders: Modeling the gaps in service delivery. *Victims and Offenders, 8,* 70–93.

Travis, J., Solomon, A., & Waul, M. (2001). *From prison to home: The dimensions and consequences of prisoner reentry.* Washington, DC: The Urban Institute.

UNICOR. (2016). *Educational and vocational training.* Retrieved from http://www.unicor.gov/Education_and_Vocational_Training.aspx.

U.S. Department of Education. (2011). *Community-based correctional education.* Alexandria, VA. Retrieved from https://www2.ed.gov/about/offices/list/ovae/pi/AdultEd/cbce-report-2011.pdf.

U.S. Department of Justice. (2016). *Second Chance Act: Fact sheet.* Washington, DC. Retrieved from https://csgjusticecenter.org/wp-content/uploads/2014/08/SCA_Fact_Sheet.pdf.

Visher, C. A., Winterfield, L., & Coggeshall, M. B. (2005). Ex-offender employment programs and recidivism: A meta-analysis. *Journal of Experimental Criminology, 1,* 295–315. doi: 10.1007/s11292-005-8127-x.

Williams, B. D., & Hicks, J. (2007). Implementing coordinated and effective service systems to address offender needs—employment. *Journal of Community Corrections, 16*(4), 13–23.

Winterfield, L., Coggeshall, M., Burke-Storer, M., Correa, V., & Tidd, S. (2009). *The effects of postsecondary correctional education: Final report.* Washington, DC: The Urban Institute.

World Health Organization. (1996). *Mental health care law: Ten basic principles.* Retrieved from http://www.who.int/mental_health/media/en/75.pdf.

Zhao, R. (2013). Official responses to crime in Macao. In L. Cao, S. Liqun, Y. Ivan, & B. Hebenton (Eds.), *The Routledge handbook of Chinese criminology* (pp. 103–115). New York, NY: Routledge.

Chapter 10

Revocation of Probation or Parole

Student Learning Outcomes

After reading this chapter, you should be able to:

• Explain why probation or parole sentences can be revoked.

• Describe the probation and parole revocation process.

• Summarize the rates of revocation.

Introduction

When offenders are sentenced to probation or released from prison on parole, the expectation is that they will not engage in future crimes or violate any conditions of their release. Sadly, this is not a reality that many offenders can achieve. Occasionally, the general public will hear about a probation or parole sentence getting revoked or a battle in the courts between the defendant and the court or parole board regarding the revocation in the news. One particular case of probation revocation made headlines around the world in 2007 as it involved the socialite celebrity Paris Hilton. Hilton was serving a probation sentence for an alcohol-related reckless driving offense when she was later caught for driving with a suspended license, which was a violation of her probation conditions (Cohen, 2007). For that violation, she was sentenced to a 45-day jail sentence (Cohen, 2007). However, Hilton still continued to capture head-lines during her jail sentence when, after reporting to jail for a few days, she was re-leased early due to a medical condition. The public was rather outraged and viewed her early release as special treatment due to her celebrity status. Thirty-six hours after she was released early from jail, Hilton was returned back to jail to serve the remainder of her 45-day sentence, which was later reduced to 23 days for good behavior (Wax-man, 2007). Interestingly, her celebrity status may have contributed to her receiving more time for such a violation rather than less. Leonard and Smith (2007) reported that Hilton's several day jail sentence for violating a condition of probation was com-parable to the amount of time served by 60% of offenders like herself. In fact, Leonard and Smith (2007) reported that she "will end up serving more time than 80% of other people in similar situations." More recently, Chris Brown has been back in the news regarding his probation violation and subsequent probation revocation. Brown, who was sentenced to probation for the assault of Rihanna in 2009, violated his probation in January of 2015 when he left Los Angeles County to perform at a San Jose nightclub (Winton & Rocha, 2015). While he was at the nightclub a shooting took place, how-

Image 20. © iStockphoto.com/Hailshadow.

ever, Brown was not involved in it. Since Brown was not permitted to leave Los Angeles County, his probation was immediately revoked. Subsequently, in March of 2015, a judge officially ended his probation term despite his earlier violation and noted that Brown had completed the terms of his probation (Adejobi, 2015).

Other cases of probation or parole revocation, where the offender may not be a celebrity, garner strong interest due to the original crime that they committed as well as whether they challenge their revocation in the courts. One such case where a parole revocation made headlines occurred in Las Vegas with the case of James Meegan, who sold and also killed his infant daughter in 1990 and was later convicted for the offenses (Whaley, 2015). Meegan served 15 years for the crimes and was released on parole in 2011, however, his parole sentence was later revoked in 2013 by the Nevada State Parole Board (NSPB) after he got into an argument with his mother which resulted in him being arrested—a violation of his parole conditions (Whaley, 2015). With his parole term revoked, Meegan appealed the decision in a bid to obtain a new parole revocation hearing, claiming that the NSPB did not "meet minimal due process requirements" by failing to provide him with a written statement of evidence that was utilized in the decision (Whaley, 2015). While a lower court ruled in Meegan's favor, the NSPB ultimately ruled that the evidence provided for the revocation was sufficient and that he would not be granted a new revocation hearing (Whaley, 2015). That is, Meegan's parole revocation would stand (Whaley, 2015).

Despite the many promising interventions for offenders reintegrating back into society that were discussed in the previous chapter, unfortunately, not all offenders succeed in these treatment programs. For those offenders on probation and parole, failing (i.e., through re-arrest or violating a probation or parole condition) while on supervision often results in the revocation of their sentence. This chapter will discuss why probation or parole sentences may be revoked, the revocation process and procedures, and the rates of revocation.

Terms for Revocation

When a probationer or parolee has successfully refrained from committing a new crime or violating any conditions of their probation or parole, their sentence officially ends. With the probation or parole sentencing ended, the offender is no longer bound by any conditions nor considered to still be in the custody of the state or federal government. For instance, actor Sean Penn was sentenced to a three-year probation term as well as participation in anger management classes in 2010 after he got into a physical altercation with a photographer (Grad, 2010). He successfully stayed out of trouble during his sentence and completed the terms of his probation sentence, thus, his probation sentence was officially ended in 2013. Not all probationers or parolees are successful such as Penn. Rather, many probationers and parolees find themselves unable to complete the sentence successfully.

There are two main reasons why a probationer or parolee may have their probation or parole sentence revoked. First, if the offender commits a crime, then their sentence can be **revoked**, or terminated. In the case of Lindsay Lohan, while on probation, she was arrested for the theft of a necklace (Associated Press, 2014). Thus, her probation sentence for reckless driving was revoked. Second, if the offender violates any conditions of their sentence, their sentence may also be revoked. Recall that conditions of probation or parole typically include finding employment, remaining within the jurisdiction, abstaining from drug use, and meeting with a probation or parole officer at designated times. Chris Brown faced probation revocation in 2015 for violating one of the conditions of his sentence—not leaving the Los Angeles jurisdiction (Winton & Rocha, 2015). Offenders on probation and parole find it difficult to adhere to all the conditions of their sentence as there are many rules to follow. In fact, when given the option of serving a jail or a probation sentence, some offenders will actually choose a jail sentence. It seems that some offenders do not want to have to follow the terms of probation such as participating in treatment (Grissom, 2010). Since probation is sometimes not an attractive sentence, some have suggested reforms to probation, such as providing incentives to offenders (e.g., probation sentence reductions) for participation in treatment (Grissom, 2010). Such a strategy would not only help the offender but it also offers a cost savings to the state since probation is a cheaper sentence than jail.

Recall from Chapters 4 and 6 that probationers and parolees are required to pay for their supervision. Failing to pay for their supervision is a violation of their conditions of probation and parole, thus, offenders can face revocation for this violation as well (Clarke, 2014). However, revocation is typically not pursued in these instances unless it can be shown that the offender intentionally or willingly refused to pay their required fees. Despite the disclaimer on nonpayment of fees, offenders have had probation revoked for this violation (Clarke, 2014). For instance, in the state of Florida, fulfilling a restitution order is a mandatory condition of probation (Probation Report, 2012b). If a probationer fails to pay the restitution order, probation revocation can occur. In fact, the Supreme Court in Florida has ruled that once the state has provided sufficient evidence as to the willfulness of the nonpayment, it is then up to the probationer to refute the alleged willfulness (Probation Report, 2012b). While parole revocation is unlikely for failing to pay supervisions fees, it can still occur and the possibility of revocation for not paying fees is a huge stressor for parolees and inhibits successful reentry. In an examination of parole supervision fees in Maryland over a one-year period, which included the reviewing of payment records as well as interviews with parolees and parole agents, Diller, Greene, and Jacobs (2009, p. 17) report, "While revocation of parole is unlikely, the paper debt for failure to pay continues to accrue over the parole period. Many parolees said that the pressure of constant dunning letters that threaten revocation cause stress that undercuts prospects for successful reentry. One reentry professional explained that the DPP's computer-generated dunning letters pose a constant threat, and that the frustration created among his clients sometimes pushes some over the edge, to re-offend." Diller et al. (2009) report that parole officers aren't so supportive of these fees either. One parole agent stated, "I really want agents to get out of money collection. That would free so much time [for more important priorities]," while another reported "I don't want to be a bill collector — if the person has a drug problem it's more important to get them counseling and to stay out of trouble with police" (Diller et al., 2009, p. 21). The researchers found that only 17% of the supervisions fees for that year were actually collected in Maryland. Overwhelmingly, most parolees could not pay the fee, resulting in 75% of cases of non-payment being referred to a Central Collection Unit (CCU). Once the parolees owed $30 or more, their cases was sent to the CCU, which tacked on a 17% interest fee (Diller et al., 2009). Thus, parolees can have great difficulties in paying for their supervision, which can undermine successful reentry, and perhaps, lead them to committing crimes to garner funds to alleviate both their financial stress and the emotional stress of fearing that a warrant will be issued for nonpayment, resulting in revocation of their parole term.

If probationers or parolees commit a new crime or violate conditions of their sentences, they face revocation of their sentence. However, revocation of a sentence is not automatic. Rather, there are certain constitutional rights afforded to offenders as well as procedures that must be followed in order for their sentence to be revoked.

Revocation: Rights & Procedures

If a probation or parole sentence is to be revoked, offenders have been granted specific due process rights from two important U.S. Supreme Court rulings: (1) *Morrissey* v. *Brewer* in 1972 and (2) *Gagnon* v. *Scarpelli* in 1973 (Fisher, 1974). In the *Morrissey* v. *Brewer* case, Morrissey, who had been convicted of check fraud, was paroled from an Iowa prison in 1968 (Champion, 2001). While on parole, Morrissey committed a few new crimes, such as obtaining a false identification and buying a

car under an assumed name (Champion, 2001). For these offenses his parole was revoked. However, prior to the revocation, he had received no notification of the charges
against him, he did not receive counsel, and he did not receive any formal notification
as to the reasons why his parole was revoked (Champion, 2001). In the *Gagnon* v.
Scarpelli case, Scarpelli was sentenced to a seven-year probation sentence for a robbery
conviction (Champion, 2001). The very next day after he had received his probation
sentence, Scarpelli violated his probation when he committed a burglary (Champion,
2001). As a consequence his probation sentence was revoked, without a formal
hearing, and his original 15-year prison term was reinstated (Champion, 2001). These
cases illustrate the lack of rights that earlier probationers and parolees had in regards
to revocation. Fisher (1974, p. 50) explains that these two Supreme Court rulings
held that both probationers and parolees facing revocation are entitled to:

(a) a written notice of the claimed violations of parole [or probation]

(b) disclosure to the parolee of the evidence against him

(c) opportunity to be heard in person and to present witnesses and docu-
mentary evidence

(d) the right to confront and cross-examine adverse witnesses

(e) a 'neutral and detached' hearing body such as a traditional parole board,
the members of which need not be judicial officers or lawyers

(f) written statement by the fact finders as to the evidence relied on and the
reasons for revoking parole [or probation].

While probationers and parolees have received some due process rights surrounding
revocation proceedings, there have been additional challenges surrounding revocation—specifically if these offenders are entitled to the same due process rights that
offenders receive during a criminal trial. The following sections highlight some of
the rights that those facing revocation may or may not have.

Right to Counsel

The Sixth Amendment provides citizens with the right to counsel (Piar, 2003).
While this right is afforded to offenders who are facing conviction of various misdemeanors and all felonies, initially, probationers were not provided with this
right—particularly during revocation hearings. However, in 1967, the Supreme
Court ruled, in the case of *Mempa v. Rhay*, that a probationer is entitled to counsel
at a revocation hearing (Piar, 2003). In the *Mempa v. Rhay* case, Mempa, who was
convicted of joyriding with a stolen vehicle, had his probation revoked due to his
involvement in a burglary (Champion, 2001). At his revocation hearing, he was
not provided with any counsel and he was not permitted to cross-examine the chief
witness testifying against him—his probation officer (Champion, 2001). With the
Gagnon v. Scarpelli ruling in 1973, which afforded probationers certain rights regarding revocation, the Supreme Court did not specify that offenders have the right
to counsel necessarily, but that offenders could have counsel appointed to them or

seek private counsel (Piar, 2003). Rather, the Supreme Court stated that the decision regarding whether offenders could have counsel present at revocation hearings would be made on a case-by-case basis. The Supreme Court was concerned that if the right to counsel was mandated for all probationers during revocation hearings that the justice system would become clogged (Piar, 2003). There were no formal criteria or guidelines provided by the Supreme Court to assist authorities in making the determination about which probationers would receive counsel; however, the Supreme Court "stated that a court should consider whether the probationer appears to be capable of speaking effectively for himself in deciding whether to provide or allow counsel" (Piar, 2003, p. 136). Piar (2003, p. 136) explains the outcome of the ambiguous ruling,

> The Court's approach has had a mixed reception in both the state and the federal probation schemes. Some courts have adhered to *Gagnon*, holding that the right to counsel in revocation hearings is not absolute, and looking at the factors identified by the Court to determine whether counsel is required in each particular case. By contrast, some states have established a blanket right to counsel, either by statute or on independent state constitutional grounds. Congress likewise has provided a right to counsel in all federal probation revocation hearings.

Despite the fact that the Supreme Court did not specifically state that offenders have a constitutional right to counsel, most probationers are either granted counsel or obtain counsel during revocation hearings.

On the other hand, parolees do not necessarily obtain the right to counsel at their revocation hearings. At the parole level, citing the *Gagnon* v. *Scarpelli* ruling, parole board authorities have utilized the case as a reason for why counsel may not be granted to parolees. For the most part, parolees do not receive counsel at their revocation hearings, but this varies on a state-to-state basis. That is, many states have statutes granting the right of counsel to parolees that may either (1) grant counsel or (2) allow the parolee to request counsel. In the case of the latter, if the parole board deems counsel to be unnecessary, then the parolee is formally notified that counsel will not be appointed. At the federal level, parolees are not granted counsel, but they are able to secure counsel at their own expense (U.S. Department of Justice, 2015). Moreover, the Supreme Court has ruled that another Sixth Amendment right, the right to trial by jury, will not be granted to probationers or parolees during revocation hearings (Piar, 2003). Some scholars have voiced their concerns about the lack of probationers and parolees being judged by their peers and the idea that they are at the "mercy of judges" (Ikeda, 2006, p. 180). Ikeda (2006, p. 180) asserts that "Those facing probation revocations, like all criminal defendants facing prison time, should now have the procedural protections of twelve peers determining whether aggravating factors exist beyond a reasonable doubt when facing revocation of a stayed sentence."

Image 21. © iStockphoto.com/hfng.

Evidence

Another concern that has arisen surrounding revocation hearings has to do with the Fourth Amendment—protection from illegal search and seizure. In particular, there has been discussion that the **exclusionary rule**, or the rule that evidence obtained illegally or in violation of a defendant's rights is not admissible in court, be extended to probation revocation hearings. Piar (2003, p. 140) explains that the Supreme Court "rejected the application of the exclusionary rule to parole revocation hearings in *Pennsylvania Board of Probation and Parole v. Scott*. There the Court held that the exclusionary rule does not apply to parole revocation hearings because (1) it would 'hinder the functioning of state parole systems and alter the traditionally flexible, administrative nature' of such proceedings, and (2) the application of the rule would apply only 'minimal deterrence benefits ... because application of the rule in the criminal trial context already provides significant deterrence of unconstitutional searches.'"

Other evidentiary challenges have also arisen in the courts in regards to probation and parole revocation. One form of evidence, Facebook postings, has been challenged as evidence. With over 1 billion active Facebook users worldwide, it is quite common for offenders and non-offenders to have a Facebook account and to post updates and photos of their activities (Facebook Newsroom, 2015). In Connecticut, in 2004, Alia Altajir drove while intoxicated, which resulted in a car crash where one of her passengers died (Probation Report, 2012a). She was convicted and sentenced to a short prison term and a five-year probation sentence. While serving her probation sentence, she got into a minor car accident, which was not alcohol related. However, she was operating the vehicle without a valid driver's license and her vehicle did not have the required ignition interlock device (Probation Report, 2012a). Given that she violated conditions of her probation sentence, the state proceeded to revoke her probation.

Image 22. © iStockphoto.com/HStocks.

At her revocation hearing, the state entered in 36 photographs from Altajir's Facebook page that illustrated her consumption of alcohol while on probation—another violation of her probation conditions. As a result of this evidence, as well as other evidence, her probation sentence was revoked, resulting in her being sent to prison to serve the remainder of her sentence. She appealed the revocation.

> Altajir argued that the trial court had violated her right to due process under the Fourteenth Amendment of the U.S. Constitution by improperly admitting a number of undated photographs gathered from Facebook. The Supreme Court of Connecticut held that the photographs of Altajir showing her drinking alcohol offered the minimal indicia of reliability that are required by due process, regarding whether the behavior depicted in the photographs occurred during probation. The state had offered, uncontradicted by Altajir, a basis for determining whether each of the challenged images depicted the defendant before or during probation. Because Altajir failed to contest that the photographs did in fact depict her while on probation, the court found that the photographs contained the minimal indicia of reliability necessary to pass constitutional muster in the context of a probation revocation hearing. The sentence was upheld (Probation Report, 2012a, p. 7).

This case is another reminder to be careful as to what you decide to post on Facebook!

Self-Incrimination

The Fifth Amendment, familiar to many due to the ruling *Miranda v. Arizona* in 1966, provides the right against self-incrimination to those accused of crimes. However, the Supreme Court has ruled that this right does not extend to probation revocation hearings since the hearings are not criminal proceedings (Piar, 2003). For instance, in the state of California, an *Alford* **plea**, or no contest plea, can be used as evidence of violating the condition of the non-commission of crimes while on probation (Probation Report, 2012a). Thus, the silent guilty plea can be admissible in a probation revocation hearing in some states. Despite the Supreme Court ruling regarding self-incrimination, several states do provide protections against self-incrimination at various stages of the revocation hearing, including statements made to police or a probation officer prior to the formal hearing or even the testimony of the probationer at the hearing (Piar, 2003).

Other Rulings

Additional challenges have been made in regards to probation revocation. One such challenge occurred in Texas regarding polygraph examination results. The Texas courts ruled that polygraph results may not be used to justify probation revocation and even stated that the revocation should not be based on "junk science" but rather more solid evidence (Probation Report, 2013, p. 29). However, in the state of Pennsylvania such results may be admissible under certain conditions. As part of a condition of sex offender therapy, a probationer referred to as A.R. was required to undergo therapeutic polygraph examinations. Since A.R. was rather uncooperative and deceptive while in the program, he was dismissed from the program. Since A.R. had been dismissed from therapy, he was now in violation of his condition of probation—that he attend therapy. During his revocation hearing, evidence regarding his probation violation along with the polygraph evidence was admitted. Subsequently, probation was revoked for A.R. He appealed the revocation based on the polygraph evidence.

> The Supreme Court of Pennsylvania heard the case, and ruled that, Despite the state's general ban on the admission of polygraph results, in this case the admission was proper. The results were not offered as evidence of A.R.'s probation violation or of his motivation for the underlying crime but only to explain why he was dismissed from treatment. Because the results were not admitted to show that A.R. was lying, their admission did not implication the concerns over the bans of such evidence (Probation Report, 2014, p. 10).

In another probation revocation case in Rhode Island, the courts ruled that probation can be revoked for violating a "no contact" order. The probationer, who had been convicted of felony domestic assault, in this case violated two no-contact orders, which violated the condition of his probation to engage in "good behavior" (Probation Report, 2013). Therefore, probation was revoked and although the probationer appealed, the courts upheld the revocation. Within the state of Maryland, an interesting probation revocation case surfaced in 2010 (Probation Report, 2014). During sentencing, the probationer was upset and pretty emotional. After signing the required probation paperwork, he then proceeded to tear up his copy (Probation Report, 2014). Based on his actions, a probation revocation hearing was held and his sentence was revoked. However, the high court reversed the decision, citing that tearing up papers in courts cannot, in and of itself, justify the revocation of probation (Probation

Report, 2014). Further, a DUI offender in Pennsylvania was placed under state parole as opposed to probation as a condition of her plea deal (Probation Report, 2014). She filed a complaint alleging numerous amendment violations including that she should have been placed under probation supervision. The courts ruled that her due process rights were not violated by being placed under parole supervision as opposed to probation supervision (Probation Report, 2014).

In sum, the Supreme Court has decided to date that probationers and parolees do not have the same rights as defendants at criminal trials. While the Supreme Court has extended some due process rights to probationers and parolees during the revocation hearing, the extent of these rights are limited.

Revocation: Proceedings

Since revocation of a probation or parole sentence is a serious step, in many instances community corrections officers (CCOs) choose to engage in less formal processes in response to offender **technical violations**, or violations of the conditions (i.e., general or specific) of probation or parole. That is, CCOs can handle such violations informally before directly proceeding to revocation. For instance, CCOs in Kentucky are able to consider the severity of the current violation, the risk and needs of the offender, the prior record of the offender, and previous violations the offender had while on supervision in making a determination as to what should be the appropriate response to the violation (see Text Box 10.1) (Kentucky Department of Corrections, 2012). CCOs can choose to increase drug testing or mandate drug treatment for an offender who failed a drug test or impose additional sanctions such as electronic monitoring or community service (Kentucky Department of Corrections, 2012). Additionally, some have suggested that other informal processes in probation be utilized to address technical violations besides revocation, such as mediation (Cook, 1995). The use of mediation has not gained a strong foothold in either probation or parole when it comes to technical violations. More often, mediation tends to be utilized for juvenile probation offenders and as part of restorative justice victim and offender programming for parolees.

If informal responses to technical violations are exhausted, the violation is severe, or the offender commits a new crime, then probation or parole revocation is the next step. If revocation is sought, then either a warrant is sought for the arrest of the offender or the offender is summoned to appear in court (Nilsen, 2012). Before probation or parole may be revoked, all offenders facing probation or parole revocation are entitled to two formal proceedings: a preliminary hearing and a revocation hearing. At the **preliminary hearing,** it is decided whether there is probable cause that a violation occurred (Nilsen, 2012). Defendants are permitted to waive the preliminary hearing (Legal Information Institute, 2015). If probable cause is found, bail may be set and the case continues to a future revocation hearing (Nilsen, 2012). At the federal level, parolees not charged with a serious violation may be offered a "deal" at this point. That is, if they may choose to waive their right to a revocation hearing, acknowledge that they committed the violation, and accept the offered penalty (Hoffman & Beck, 2005). Following

Text Box 10.1: Kentucky State Probation and Parole Violation Matrix

CCOs in Kentucky utilize the following matrix when responding to probation and parole violations.

Probation and Parole Violation Matrix
Offender Risk Level

Violation	Very High	High	Moderate	Low	Admin
1st Minor	2	1	1	1	1
2nd Minor	3	2	2	2	1
3rd (or more) Minor	4	3	3	2	2
1st Major	4	3	3	2	2
2nd Major	4	3	3		
3rd (or more) Major	4	4	4		

Response Range 1	Response Range 2	Response Range 3	Response Range 4
	Any response or combination of responses in range 1 or:	Any response or combination of responses in range 1–2 or:	Any response or combination of responses in range 1–3 or:
Verbal or Written Warning	Curfew up to 60 Days	Curfew up to 120 Days	Curfew up to 180 Days
Increased Reporting	Community Service 20–30 Hours	Community Service 30–40 Hours	Community Service 40–50 Hours
Increased Frequency of Drug Testing	Electronic Monitoring	Halfway House	Jail Time up to 60 Days (requires hearing with releasing authority)
Loss of Travel or Other Privileges	Increased Treatment up to Residential	Jail Time up to 30 Days (requires hearing with releasing authority)	Request Revocation
Curfew up to 30 Days	Discretionary Detention up to 10 Days with Supervisor Approval		
Referral to the Social Service Clinician for Substance Abuse Assessment and Treatment			
Referral to Community Service Agency for Counseling or Treatment			
Community Service up to 8 Hours			

* Upon consideration of the totality of circumstances and with supervisory approval, the officer may direct the offender into appropriate interventions not included in the violation matrix or seek to impose a high level sanction, up to and including revocation.

Source: Kentucky Department of Corrections. (2012). *Graduated Sanctions and Discretionary Detention*. Retrieved from http://corrections.ky.gov/communityinfo/Policies%20and%20 Procedures/Documents/CH27/27-15-03%20-%20graduated%20sanctions%20and%20discretionary%20detention.pdf.

the preliminary hearing is the **final revocation hearing**. The final revocation hearing is a formal due process proceeding that is carried out by a judge or the probation and/ or parole authority whereby the offender has an opportunity to testify and even present witnesses regarding the alleged violation (see Text Box 10.2) (Legal Information Institute, 2015). At both hearings, hearsay evidence is admissible (Nilsen, 2012; Piar, 2003). While hearsay evidence is admissible, Nilen (2012, p. 12) explains, "if it is the sole evidence of a violation it will not be sufficient unless the court finds in writing that it is 'substantially trustworthy and demonstrably reliable.'"

As the proceeding progresses, the courts do not require that the offender be found guilty beyond a reasonable doubt as is the case at the criminal trial (Piar, 2003). Rather, the level of proof regarding the alleged violation is much lower. Most jurisdictions require that a **preponderance of evidence**, or that sufficient evidence is provided regarding the alleged violation, be met in order to render a decision about revocation (Piar, 2003). Some states have even lower thresholds when it comes to probation revocation. For instance, in Nebraska and Minnesota, the level of proof for probation revocation is not the preponderance of evidence, but rather "clear and convincing evidence" (Piar, 2003, p. 128). The reduced level of standard has resulted in lawsuits by offenders seeking to establish a higher level of proof, but the courts have not ruled in their favor, citing that raising the standard of proof would overwhelm the already overcrowded court system and reduce the flexibility that revocation proceedings offer (Piar, 2003). If the court finds that the offender violated his probation, for instance, the court may "(1) extend the term of probation, (2) modify the conditions of probation, (3) continue the client under the same probation agreement, or (4) impose the original sentence" (Nilsen, 2012, p. 9). By imposing the original sentence, the probation or parole term is thereby revoked.

Text Box 10.2: Texas Parole Revocation Process

Once the offender is detained and Parole Division decides on a hearing, the offender is interviewed by a parole officer. The offender is advised of their rights in the revocation hearing process to:

- be personally served with written notice of alleged parole violations,
- have a preliminary hearing unless the offender is accused only of administrative violations or has been convicted of a new criminal offense. The purpose of this hearing is to determine if there is probable cause to believe a condition of release was violated. In some cases, the offender may choose to waive the preliminary hearing,
- have a revocation hearing if the offender is alleged to have committed administrative violations or has been found guilty in a criminal case,
- receive full disclosure of all the evidence against the offender before the hearing,
- hire an attorney and, under certain circumstances, the conditional right to a state-appointed attorney,
- tell the hearing officer in person what happened and to present evidence, affidavits, letters, and documents to support their position, including the right to subpoena witnesses through the parole officer,
- confront and cross-examine adverse witnesses (unless the hearing officer finds good cause to deny confrontation),
- be heard on the allegations by someone designated by the Board.

If parole or mandatory supervision is revoked as a result of the hearing, the offender receives a written report by the hearing officer which describes the evidence relied upon in finding a violation. In certain cases, the offender may petition the Board to reopen the revocation hearing.

Source: Texas Board of Pardons and Parole. (2015). Parole revocation process: What happens when the Parole Division asks for a hearing? Retrieved from http://www.tdcj.state.tx.us/bpp/revocation/What_Happens_Parole_Division_Asks_for_Hearing.html.

Revocation: Rates

Assessing the exact number of revocations at both the state and federal level is extremely difficult. This is due, in part, to the data collection efforts at the state and federal level. For instance, at the federal level data has not been reported as to the specific revocation rates for probationers and parolees. Rather, what has been reported regarding probation and parole revocation is that probationers and parolees who have had their sentences revoked are less likely to be returned to jail or prison (Maruschak & Bonczar, 2013). Despite the gaps in the literature, there have been some studies that have been conducted that can provide an overall picture about probation and/or parole revocation rates. One of the most comprehensive examinations of revocation rates was recently conducted at the federal level. Johnson (2014) examined revocation rates for approximately 370,000 federal offenders who were serving either a probation sentence or a term of supervised release (TSR) sentence between 2004 and 2012. In his examination, revocation referred to either a technical violation or a new crime. Additionally, Johnson (2014) utilized a series of follow-up periods: 3 months, 6 months, 12 months, 18 months, 24 months, 36 months, 48 months, and 60 months. The researcher found that less than 4% of offenders had revocations in the first 6 months of supervision. However, at the 12-month mark, revocation rates increased to 9%, at the 24-month follow-up period, revocation rates had shot up close to 17%, and by the 60-month follow-up period, revocation rates were at 24%. Further, Johnson (2014) noted that the TSR offenders had slightly higher revocation rates than probationers. When Johnson (2014) examined the data further, he noted that up until the 36-month follow-up period, most revocations were for technical violations for both groups, but from 36 months–60 months, the majority of the revocations were due to the commission of a new crime. Upon further examination of the crimes that were committed by probationers and TSR offenders, Johnson (2014) uncovered that TSR offenders were more likely to have committed a drug offense while probationers were more likely to have committed a property offense.

There have been several state-level examinations into revocation. In a 6-month analysis of probation revocation in one Texas county, Stickels (2007) found that a majority of probation revocations were for technical violations, and the majority of these violators received a jail or prison sentence as punishment for the violation. Rodriguez and Webb (2007) reported similar findings in their analysis of probation revocation in Arizona. In their research, they found that the majority of probationers who had their probation revoked were being held accountable for technical violations. In the state of Texas, in 2011, 4% of probationers had their sentence revoked, with the majority of the revocations due to technical violations. Additionally, 15% of parolees in Texas, in 2011, had their parole sentence revoked, with the majority of those sentences revoked for the commission of a new crime (Legislative Budget Board, 2013). Those who had parole revoked were more likely to be male and approximately 40 years old (Legislative Budget Board, 2013). Overall, the Legislative Budget Board (2013) reports that parole revocations in the state of Texas have decreased since 2001.

In sum, ascertaining the exact rate of revocation is difficult since it is not data that is collected annually at either the federal or state level. At the state level, for example, data on revocation for probation or parole tends to be collected in piecemeal fashion at different times and in different years. Overall, it appears that revocation rates are not overwhelmingly high but clearly more research is needed to substantially affirm this.

Factors Influencing Revocation

While more research is needed on probation and parole revocation rates, there are a few factors that influence why revocation may occur. With the disillusionment in rehabilitation that began with Martinson (1974), the focus of the system shifted from a rehabilitative one to a control one. That is, now the focus is on controlling offender movements and watching over them more closely. This is achieved through the use of more surveillance and additional conditions added to the supervision terms for offenders. With closer supervision and monitoring (i.e., more drug tests, more curfew checks, more check-ins with an assigned community correction officer), it is not surprising that offenders would be more likely to violate a condition of their supervision and, thus, be subjected to having their sentences revoked. Additionally, the role of technology has also increased the likelihood that offenders under supervision will be "caught" for violating terms. Advancements in technology, such as global positioning, are allowing probation and parole officers to keep better tabs on the location of their clients (Sweeney, 2012). Moreover, officers are trolling social media sites such as Facebook, Twitter, and Instagram to review postings on their clients and to ensure that they are complying with their supervision terms (Sweeney, 2012).

Gender and Race

As noted earlier, the Legislative Budget Board (2013) determined that males were more likely to have their parole revoked than females. A few researchers have examined the relationship between gender and revocation. Although some researchers have found a link between gender and successful probation completion (see Morgan, 1994), other researchers have asserted that there is no difference between males and females in regards to probation success (see Gould, Pate, & Sarver, 2011). Gould et al. (2011, p. 258), who examined male and female probation success in Wisconsin, reported that "female probationers are not more likely to successfully complete their term of supervision, compared to male probationers." Additionally, the researchers found that female probationers were no more likely than male probationers to commit a new crime or have a technical violation. Although more research is needed on probation and parole revocation for women to ascertain whether their rates of revocation are lower or higher than their male counterparts', qualitative research on parole revocation for women suggests that female parolees are in great fear of revocation (Opsal, 2009). In a study of female parolees, one subject expressed her fear of revocation as follows, "'Every night you go to bed, you be like, 'Oh are they comin'?' You know what I'm sayin'? Oh yeah, they got you scared, they got you frightened. They scare you'" (Opsal, 2009, p. 321). It appears that the heightened surveillance of offenders causes much anxiety and stress for them. Clearly, more research is needed on revocation rates for both genders as the current research is rather limited to individual state-level analyses.

Until 2006, no researchers had examined the relationship between race and probation and/or parole revocation. Tapia and Harris (2006) were the first to investigate the link between race and male offender probation revocation in a south central state. The researchers found that male probationers who were young and African American were more likely to have their probation revoked than Caucasian and Hispanic American offenders. Additionally, the researchers report that Hispanic Americans were not more likely to have probation revoked than Caucasian probationers. Hartney and Vuong (2009), investigated probation and parole revocation using data from 35 states. The researchers found that, in 2003, 28% of all new admissions to prison were due to probation revocations with another 8% of admissions due to parole revocations. When the researchers examined the revocations more closely, they discovered that African Americans and Hispanic Americans had higher probation and parole revocation rates than Caucasians. To better put this into perspective, African American parolees were admitted to prisons in 2003 at a rate of 7 times more than Caucasian parolees. Moreover, "Native Americans were reincarcerated for parole revocation at almost 3 times the rate for Whites" (Hartney & Vuong, 2009, p. 18). Thus, the researchers discovered racial disparity for both probation and parole revocations. More recently, Janetta, Breaux, Ho, & Porter (2014), who examined probation revocation in four states, concluded that African American probationers had their sentences revoked at higher rates than Caucasian or Hispanic American probationers. Perhaps minorities are being targeted at a higher rate for revocation due to racial disparity, which exists not only in U.S. society, but is a pervasive problem in the criminal justice system. Since revocation is discretionary, requiring the probation officer or parole officer to initiate the proceedings and ultimately a parole board to make the final decision on revocation at the parole level, it allows for bias against minority offenders to arise (Steen, Opsal, Lovegrove, & McKinzey, 2012). More research is needed to obtain a clearer picture of the relationship between race and probation and parole revocation at the state and federal levels.

Reducing Revocation

Many probation and parole agencies across the nation are trying to strategically reduce the likelihood of revocation given the impact that revocation has on the correctional system (i.e., prisons) as well as the emergence of racial disparity in both probation and parole revocation decisions. Van Steele and Goodrich (2009, p. 1) report that in the state of Wisconsin, in collaboration with six other state correctional departments, the following plan is being instituted to reduce revocation rates:

1) Develop a coordinated system response through a Community Justice Act;

2) Refine use of risk assessment to focus efforts on high-risk offenders and customize supervision intensity and rules based on risk level;

3) Develop a departmental goal of reducing revocations by a specified percent for each supervision region and/or provide assistance to regions in decreasing revocations;

4) Consider legislative changes in sentencing guidelines to shorten the term of supervision or limit supervision to a fixed maximum time period;

5) Continue to develop a Departmental EBP-based reentry plan focusing on education, housing, and employment to support successful reentry; and

6) Impact agent decision-making and responses to offender behavior with system-level policies that encourage graduated alternatives to revocation.

Figure 10.1 represents a visual representation of the vision by the Wisconsin Department of Corrections. There is a clear effort by various correctional departments across the nation to implement changes to the revocation process. It is through such collaborations that meaningful changes can be implemented to improve the process for both offenders and the system.

Conclusion

In sum, this chapter provided discussion as to why probation or parole sentences may be revoked. Additionally, this chapter described the revocation process and procedures along with highlighting the various rights that offenders may or may not have during the revocation proceedings. Moreover, this chapter highlighted the rates of revocation as well as factors that contribute to revocation. More research is needed to determine the exact rates of revocation as well as to explore why minorities' sentences may be revoked at higher rates than Caucasians and what can be done to ameliorate this problem. Finally, it is clear that revocation procedures need to be tweaked, and it will take a comprehensive plan with interstate court and correctional agency participation in order to institute significant changes to the process.

Key Terms

Alford plea

Exclusionary rule

Final revocation hearing

Preliminary hearing

Preponderance of evidence

Figure 10.1: Best Practice Responses to Revocation

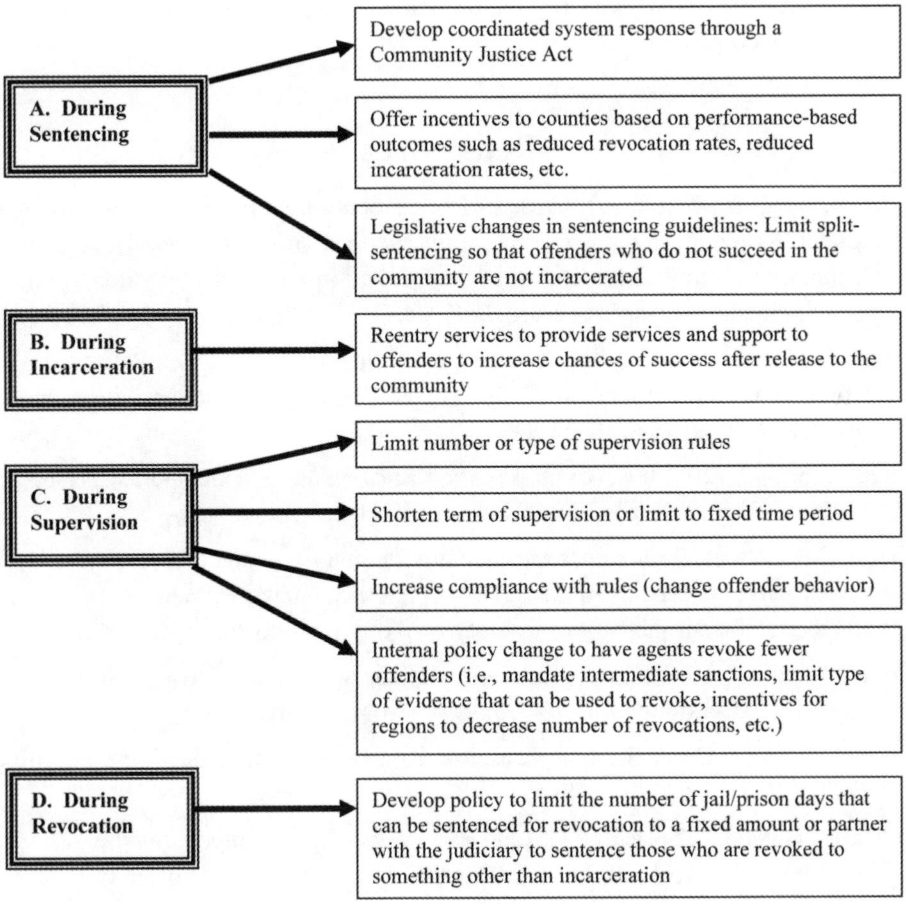

Source: Van Steele, K. R., & Goodrich, J. (2009). *2008/2009 Study of probation/parole revocation: Executive Summary.* University of Wisconsin Population Health Institute. (p. 2).

Revoked

Technical violations

Discussion Questions

1. Research the probation and parole revocation procedures in your state. Describe the specific guidelines and procedures. Be sure to identify the specific rights that offenders have.

2. Are there rights that you feel probationers and parolees should have for revocation proceedings? If so, what rights do you think should be extended to these offenders?

3. Why do you think minorities are more likely to have their probation and/or parole sentences revoked? How can disparity be reduced?

4. Do you think probation and/or parole revocation procedures need to be modified? What suggestions do you think are needed for the revocation process? Should other alternatives to revocation be implemented? If so, what ideas regarding alternatives do you have?

References

Adejobi, A. (2015, March 23). Chris Brown's probation ends six years after Rihanna assault: A timeline of his arrest record. *International Business Times.* Retrieved from http://www.ibtimes.co.uk/chris-browns-probation-ends-six-years-after-rihanna-assault-timeline-his-arrest-record-1493204.

Associated Press. (2014) Lindsay Lohan's probation ends. *USA Today.* Retrieved from http://www.usatoday.com/story/life/people/2014/11/06/lohans-probation-ended-in-necklace-theft-case/18622111/.

Champion, D. J. (2001). *Corrections in the United States: A contemporary perspective* (3rd ed.). Upper Saddle River, NJ: Prentice Hall.

Clarke, M. (2014). *Texas courts examine proof of ability to pay probation fees before revocation.* Retrieved from https://www.prisonlegalnews.org/news/2014/mar/15/texas-courts-examine-proof-of-ability-to-pay-probation-fees-before-revocation/.

Cohen, S. (2007). Paris Hilton gets 45 days in jail. *USA Today.* Retrieved from http://usatoday30.usatoday.com/life/people/2007-04-26-paris-hilton_N.htm.

Cook, S. S. (1995). Mediation as an alternative to probation revocation proceeding. *Federal Probation, 59*(4), 48–52.

Diller, R., Greene, J., & Jacobs, M. (2009). *Maryland's parole supervision fee: A barrier to reentry.* New York: Brennan Center for Justice, New York University School of Law. Retrieved from http://www.brennancenter.org/sites/default/files/legacy/publications/MD.Fees.Fines.pdf.

Facebook Newsroom. (2015). *Company info.* Retrieved from http://newsroom.fb.com/company-info/.

Fisher, H. R. (1974). Parole and probation procedures after *Morrissey* and *Gagnon. Journal of Criminal Law & Criminology, 65*(1), 46–61.

Gagnon v. Scarpelli, (1973).

Gould, L. A., Pate, M., & Sarver, M. (2011). Risk and revocation in community corrections: The role of gender. *Probation Journal, 58*(3), 250–264. doi: 10.1177/0264550511409966.

Grad, S. (2010). Sean Penn sentenced to probation for incident with photographer. *L.A. Now.* Retrieved from http://latimesblogs.latimes.com/lanow/2010/05/sean-penn-sentenced-to-probation-for-incident-with-photographer.html.

Grissom, B. (2010). Many choosing jail time over probation. *The Texas Tribune.* Retrieved from https://www.texastribune.org/2010/09/28/many-choosing-jail-time-over-probation/.

Hartney, C., & Vuong, L. (2009). *Created equal: Racial and ethnic disparities in the US criminal justice system.* National Council on Crime and Delinquency. Retrieved from http://www.nccdglobal.org/sites/default/files/publication_pdf/created-equal.pdf.

Hoffman, P., & Beck, J. (2005). Revocation by consent: The United States Parole Commission's expedited revocation procedure. *Journal of Criminal Justice, 33*(5), 451–462. doi: 10.1016/j.jcrimjus.2005.06.005.

Ikeda, S. H. (2006). Probation revocations as delayed dispositional departures: Why *Blakely v. Washington* requires jury trials at probation violation hearings. *Law & Inequality, 24*(1), 157–180.

Jannetta, J., Breaux, J., Ho, H., & Porter, J. (2014). Examining racial and ethnic disparities in probation revocation: Summary findings and implications from a multisite study. Washington, DC: Urban Institute.

Johnson, James L. (2014). Federal post-conviction supervision outcomes: Arrests and revocations. *Federal Probation, 78*(1), 1–12.

Kentucky Department of Corrections. (2012). *Graduated sanctions and discretionary detention.* Retrieved from http://corrections.ky.gov/communityinfo/Policies%20 and%20Procedures/Documents/CH27/27-15-03%20-%20graduated%20sanctions %20and%20discretionary%20detention.pdf.

Legal Information Institute. (2015). *Rule 32.1 Revoking or modifying probation or supervised release.* Cornell University of Law. Retrieved from https:// www.law.cornell.edu/rules/frcrmp/rule_32.1.

Legislative Budget Board. (2013). *Statewide criminal justice recidivism and revocation rates.* Texas State. Retrieved from http://www.lbb.state.tx.us/Public_Safety_Criminal_Justice/RecRev_Rates/Statewide%20Criminal%20Justice%20Recidivism%20 and%20Revocation%20Rates2012.pdf.

Leonard, J., & Smith, D. (2007). Hilton will do more time than most, analysis finds. *L.A. Times.* Retrieved from http://articles.latimes.com/2007/jun/14/local/ me-paris14.

Martinson, R. (1974). What works? — Questions and answers about prison reform. *The Public Interest,* 22–54.

Maruschak, L. M., & Bonczar, T. P. (2013). *Probation and parole in the United States, 2012.* Washington, DC: Bureau of Justice Statistics.

Mempa v. Rhay. 389 U.S. 128 (1967).

Miranda v. Arizona. 384 U.S. 436 (1966).

Morgan, K. (1994). Factors associated with probation outcome. *Journal of Criminal Justice, 22*(4), 341–353. doi: 10.1016/0047-2352(94)90081-7.

Morrissey v. Brewer, (1972).

Nilsen, E. (2012). Probation revocation. In E. Blumenson & A. B. Leavens (Eds.), *Massachusetts criminal practice* (4th ed.) (pp. 1–23). Boston, MA: New Law Publishing.

Opsal, T. D. (2009). Women on parole: Understanding the impact of surveillance. *Women & Criminal Justice, 19*, 306–328. doi 10.1080/08974450903224345.

Piar, D. F. (2003). A uniform code of procedure for revoking probation. *American Journal of Criminal Law, 31*(1), 117–173.

Probation Revocation. (2012a). *Probation & Parole Law Reports, 33*(1), 7–11.

Probation Revocation. (2012b). *Probation & Parole Law Reports, 33*(2), 28–30.

Probation Revocation. (2013). *Probation & Parole Law Reports, 34*(2), 27–30.

Probation Revocation. (2014). *Probation & Parole Law Reports, 35*(1), 8–10.

Rodriguez, N., & Webb, V. J. (2007). Probation violations, revocations, and imprisonment. *Criminal Justice Policy Review, 18*(1), 3–30. doi: 10.1177/088740 3406292956.

Steen, S., Opsal, T., Lovegrove, P., & McKinzey, S. (2012). Putting parolees back in prison: Discretion and the parole revocation process. *Criminal Justice Review, 38*(1), 70–93. doi: 10.1177/0734016812466571.

Stickels, J. W. (2007). A study of probation revocations for technical violations in Hays County, Texas, USA. *Probation Journal, 54*(1), 52–61. doi: 10.1177/026455 0507073328.

Sweeney, E. (2012). Probation 2.0: How technology is changing probation work. *Boston Globe.* Retrieved from http://www.bostonglobe.com/metro/regionals/south/ 2012/11/29/probation-how-technology-changing-probation-work-probation-officers-tap-social-media/Qtv52cQffcVbkAsJqcg6lK/story.html.

Tapia, M., & Harris, P. M. (2006). Race and revocation: Is there a penalty for young, minority males? *Journal of Ethnicity in Criminal Justice, 4*(3), 1–25.

Texas Board of Pardons and Parole. (2015). *Parole revocation process.* Retrieved from http://www.tdcj.state.tx.us/bpp/revocation/What_Happens_Parole_Division_ Asks_for_Hearing.html.

U.S. Department of Justice. (2015). *Frequently asked questions.* Retrieved from http:// www.justice.gov/uspc/frequently-asked-questions.

Van Steele, K. R., & Goodrich, J. (2009). *2008/2009 Study of probation/parole revocation: Executive summary.* University of Wisconsin Population Health Institute.

Waxman, S. (2007). Celebrity justice cuts both ways for Paris Hilton. *New York Times.* Retrieved from http://www.nytimes.com/2007/06/09/us/09hilton.html?_r=0.

Whaley, S. (2015). Nevada justices say no to parole hearing for man who killed his baby girl. *Las Vegas Review Journal.* Retrieved from http://www.reviewjournal.com/news/ las-vegas/nevada-justices-say-no-parole-hearing-man-who-killed-his-baby-girl.

Winton, R., & Rocha, V. (2015). Chris Brown's probation revoked in San Jose nightclub shooting. *L.A. Times.* Retrieved from http://www.latimes.com/local/lanow/ la-me-ln-chris-brown-probation-revoked—20150115-story.html.

Chapter 11

The Unsung Heroes:
Community Corrections Officers

Student Learning Outcomes

After reading this chapter, you should be able to:

- Summarize the number of community corrections officers and their duties.

- Identify the many roles that community corrections officers have and the challenges they face on the job.

- Summarize their perceptions of what offenders need for successful reentry and their thoughts on the most pressing challenges these offender face during reentry.

Introduction

Every now and again, you may hear about a particular community corrections officer in the news. In some instances, the news coverage of their work may be positive, and in other cases, it may not be. Since community corrections officers are expected to uphold the law and hold their clients to established standards and regulations, it should not come as a surprise that community members would request that the officers would also follow the law and abstain from any criminal involvement. Unfortunately, as in any profession, there are a few bad apples—that is, officers who cross the line. In 2015, in Washington State, for example, community corrections officer Michael Boone was arrested for possession of child pornography (Dickson, 2015). As a community corrections officer, Boone had worked with adult offenders in Washington State since 2003. It seems that Microsoft became aware of the fact that Boone was uploading child pornography images to his personal cloud account and reported his activities to authorities (Dickson, 2015). After his arrest, he was placed on administrative leave from his position (Dickson, 2015). Another community corrections officer, Jacquelynn Benfield, employed in Indiana, was arrested in 2015 after it was discovered that she was engaging in sexual relations with one of the clients she was supervising who was on house arrest (Gable, 2015). Gable (2015) reported that, "Benfield is facing one Level 5 felony count of sexual misconduct after she knowingly or intentionally engaged in sexual intercourse or other sexual conduct with a person who is subject to lawful detention or lawful supervision; and a Level 6 felony count of official misconduct after she knowingly or intentionally committed an offense

Image 23. © Chris Titze Imaging/Fotolia.

in the performance of the public servant's official duties." Her case is currently pending in the courts. These are two examples of cases where community corrections officers have crossed both professional and legal boundaries. However, there are many more examples of officers in the news for carrying out their jobs in a brave or professional manner.

Being a community corrections officer is by no means easy and officers experience their fair share of challenges on the job. Perhaps one of the greatest difficulties for officers is maintaining their own safety while on the job. Physical harm at the hands of their clients is a large concern for officers. For instance, in 2012, Brooklyn parole officer Samuel Salters was in his office working when his parolee, Robert Morales, walked in and shot him (Yaniv, 2013). Fortunately for Salters, Morales' gun jammed and Salters was able to recover from his injuries. Apparently, Morales did not appreciate how Salters spoke to him and that he threatened his client with parole revocation (Yaniv, 2013). Morales was subsequently convicted for his assault on Salters, and he was sentenced to a 40-years-to-life prison sentence (Yaniv, 2013). In 2011, three parole officers reported to a residence in the Bronx to arrest Jonathan Lee for failure to report for his parole (Armaghan, 2011). When the officers entered the residence, Lee tried to kill all three officers. At one point, he obtained a firearm from one of the officers and pointed it at another—fortunately, the gun did not fire as the first officer was able to slide a mechanism making the gun inoperable during their struggle (Armaghan, 2011; Halbrook, 2014). Lee was subsequently convicted and sentenced to a 40-years-to-life prison sentence (Halbrook, 2014).

Given the sheer number of offenders serving community corrections sentences, community safety is a primary concern. Community corrections officers are expected to provide safety for community members and service to their clients. Without a doubt, community corrections officers are an integral part of community corrections, with much of their work and efforts going unnoticed. That is, they don't receive the type of praise that is often afforded to police officers. Their success in keeping the community safe on a daily basis and helping their clients without the community even really noticing their efforts means these important, yet overlooked, corrections workers can be best described as the unsung heroes in the criminal justice system.

This chapter devotes special attention to the role that community corrections officers (i.e., probation or parole officers) play within community corrections. Additionally, this chapter will highlight the number of officers in the United States, the challenges they face on the job, their training, the range in their salaries, and how they carry out their duties. Further, recent research on community corrections officers' perceptions of offenders' needs and challenges during reentry will be presented.

Community Corrections Officers

A **community corrections officer** is a correctional employee who works with offenders serving a community corrections sentence (e.g., probation, parole, house arrest, day reporting center). Oftentimes, community corrections officers (CCOs) are referred to as probation and/or parole officers. However, it would be a mistake to refer to CCOs as just probation and/or parole officers. Recall from earlier chapters that the federal government and many states have abolished parole. Thus, referring to an officer working in such jurisdictions as a parole officer would be a misnomer. Therefore, the term CCO refers to the many types of correctional workers who may work as probation or parole officers but also to those officers who supervise the many other forms of community corrections sanctions that fall outside the aforementioned categories.

Numbers Employed

Without a doubt, the number of CCOs working in the United States has burgeoned over the past few decades. With the implementation of intermediate sanctions in the later part of the 1900s and the increasing use of probation and parole, there has been increasing need and demand for CCOs. To provide some historical perspective on the increased numbers working in the community corrections field during this era, in 1971, there were a total of 34,200 probation and parole officers employed in the nation, however, by 1991, the total had increased to 72,040 officers (Stinchcomb, McCampbell, & Layman, 2006). In 2005, the U.S. Bureau of Labor Statistics projected that employment for only probation officers would increase 9 to 17 percent through the year 2014. More recently, the U.S. Bureau of Labor Statistics (2015) has projected growth for probation officers at a rate of 4 percent through 2024. While it is difficult to pinpoint the exact number of all state and federal CCOs working in the field, the U.S. Bureau of Labor Statistics (2015) reports the number employed to be approximately 91,000. Within the number, the U.S. Bureau of Labor Statistics also includes correctional treatment specialists (e.g., case managers and correctional counselors) in their counts. Thus, it is impossible to disentangle these corrections workers from the overall estimation, which results in a less accurate figure as these workers may inflate the overall figure. Nevertheless, the figure points to the continued increase in hiring of CCOs.

Part of the reason for the positive hiring outlook for those seeking jobs in the community corrections sector besides the growth of use of community corrections is the fact that many CCOs from the baby boomer generation are now retiring (Stinchcomb et al., 2006). Thus, many local, state, and federal CCO agencies are finding themselves in the position of not only hiring for new positions but also hiring for replacement positions (Stinchcomb et al., 2006). Apart from the issue of growth and replacing those who retire, there is a need to hire CCOs for other organizational reasons, which are common in any workplace, such as turnover and difficulties in retaining good employees. In fact, the job outlook is so strong for those wanting work as CCOs, that these applicants ultimately have the upper hand. Agencies across the nation are looking for the best candidates to fill positions, and these agencies find themselves competing with one another to attract individuals to apply for these positions and accept these positions when offered (Stinchcomb et al., 2006).

Education and Skills Required

According to the U.S. Bureau of Labor Statistics (2015), employment as a CCO requires a bachelor's degree in criminal justice, social work, behavioral sciences, or another related field. Some agencies may require a master's degree, but typically this degree is only needed for advancement within the organization. The exact educational requirements will vary by jurisdiction. The U.S. Bureau of Labor Statistics (2015) also reports that "most employers require candidates to pass competency exams, drug testing, and a criminal background check. A valid driver's license is often required, and most agencies require applicants to be at least 21 years old." Other requirements may include that the applicant is not older than 37, must have normal or corrected vision, must have normal hearing, must be proficient in Microsoft Word, and should be in good physical condition. Candidates may also be interviewed. Additionally, the U.S. Bureau of Labor Statistics (2015) notes the following important qualities for applicants:

Communication skills. [Officers] must be able to effectively interact with many different people, such as probationers and their family members, lawyers, judges, treatment providers, and law enforcement.

Critical-thinking skills. Workers must be able to assess the needs of individual Probationers [or parolees] before determining the best resources for helping them.

Decisionmaking skills. [Officers] must consider the relative costs and benefits of potential actions and be able to choose appropriately.

Emotional stability. Workers must cope with hostile individuals or otherwise upsetting circumstances on the job.

Organizational skills. [Officers] must be able to manage multiple cases at the same time.

Given the nature of the job, other desired qualities include punctuality, ability to be meticulous in record keeping, and adherence to professionalism.

Training

For those applicants for CCO positions that successfully pass their interview, background check, and physical test (e.g., Physical Ability Test), the next step is training. Each state, as well as the federal government, requires that all CCOs must complete a corrections training program before they are permitted to work in the field (U.S. Bureau of Labor Statistics, 2015). For instance, at the state level, the length of the training can vary from four to six weeks. In the state of Nevada, training at the corrections academy lasts six weeks, while in the state of Washington, training lasts just four weeks (Vogel, 2012; Washington State Criminal Justice Training Commission, 2016). During community corrections training in Washington State, for instance, future CCOs learn about legal issues, professionalism, communication, and skills such as proper clothed searching techniques, security, and defensive tactics (Washington State Criminal Justice Training Commission, 2016). Throughout the corrections training academy, it is not uncommon for participants to take multiple written exams and quizzes, partake in skills based testing (e.g., mock scenarios), and even prepare and execute presentations (Washington State Criminal Justice Training Commission, 2016). In those state and federal jurisdictions that mandate, or grant on a voluntary basis, that a CCO carry a firearm, the training academy would include firearms training, an accuracy test, and a written exam (American Probation and Parole Association, 2006). Increasingly, more states are allowing, or requiring, CCOs to carry a firearm on the job. For instance, in 2003, a new law was passed in New York City whereby probation officers, who traditionally were not authorized to utilize a gun as part of their job, were now permitted to carry concealed Glock 9-mm pistols (von Zielbauer, 2003). By 2018, all CCOs in Tennessee will be carrying guns (Stelter, 2013). The move to equip more CCOs with weapons is due to the shifting role of CCOs from their traditional role as a social worker to more of a law enforcer role and also because the nature the work that CCOs perform can be very dangerous (von Zielbauer, 2003). Upon successful completion of the training academy, future CCOs may also be required to pass several certification tests, such as a state exam and/or a CPR or first-aid test (U.S. Bureau of Labor Statistics, 2015). Even after successful completion of the training academy and passage of any certification test(s), newly hired CCOs may still be required to work as trainees until they be officially offered a permanent position (U.S. Bureau of Labor Statistics, 2015). In some states, working as a trainee may last for one entire year (U.S. Bureau of Labor Statistics, 2015). Once officially hired in a permanent position, CCOs may be assigned to work with specific clients (U.S. Bureau of Labor Statistics, 2015). That is, CCOs may have caseloads that are only domestic violence offenders, sex offenders, or juvenile offenders. When CCOs are assigned to work with specialized clients, they do receive additional training to ensure that they can serve their clients effectively. It is also not uncommon that CCOs assigned to work with higher risk clients, such as sex offenders, would have a smaller caseload compared to their colleagues not supervising such clients.

Pay & Work Conditions

The U.S. Bureau of Labor Statistics (2015) reports that the median pay range for those working as officers is 2014 was approximately $49,000. "Although many officers and specialists work full time, the demands of the job often lead to working overtime. For example, many agencies rotate an on-call officer position. When these workers are on-call, they must respond to any issues with probationers or law enforcement 24 hours a day. Extensive travel and paperwork can also contribute to more hours of work" (U.S. Bureau of Labor Statistics, 2015). Some CCOs may belong to a union, but union membership varies by jurisdiction (U.S. Bureau of Labor Statistics, 2015). Those CCOs belonging to a union receive better pay and better working conditions (see Text Box 11.1).

Text Box 11.1: Job Ad Description for a Federal Probation Officer

Job Title: U.S. Probation Officer
Department: Judicial Branch
Agency: U.S. Courts
Job Announcement Number: 2016-01
SALARY RANGE:
$42,718.00 to $96,712.00 / Per Year
OPEN PERIOD:
Wednesday, November 18, 2015, to Thursday, November 17, 2016
SERIES & GRADE:
CL-0006-25/28
POSITION INFORMATION:
Full Time — Permanent
DUTY LOCATIONS:
1 vacancy in the following location(s):
Duluth, MN
Saint Paul, MN

WHO MAY APPLY:
Open to all U.S. citizens or permanent residents seeking U.S. citizenship
SECURITY CLEARANCE:
Public Trust — Background Investigation
SUPERVISORY STATUS:
No

JOB SUMMARY:
U.S. Probation and Pretrial Services in the District of Minnesota has its headquarters in the U.S. Courthouse located at 300 South Fourth Street, Suite 406, Minneapolis. There are field offices located in Bemidji, Duluth, Fergus Falls, and St. Paul. The Probation and Pretrial Services Office serves the Judicial District of Minnesota which includes 87 counties.
The U.S. Probation and Pretrial Services Office in the District of Minnesota is currently seeking a talented, full-time, permanent U.S. Probation Officer located in Minneapolis, Duluth, or St. Paul, Minnesota. The U.S. Probation Officer serves in a judiciary law enforcement position and assists in the administration of justice and promotes community safety. The officer gathers information, supervises offenders/defendants, interacts with col-

lateral agencies, prepares reports, conducts investigations, and presents recommendations to the court. Officer performs duties that may involve general pretrial services and/or probation cases.

TRAVEL REQUIRED
• Occasional Travel may be required
RELOCATION AUTHORIZED
• No
KEY REQUIREMENTS
• U.S. Citizenship or National
• Qualifications

DUTIES:
Under the guidance and direction of a Supervising Probation and Pretrial Services Officer, enforces court-ordered supervision components and implements supervision strategies. Maintains personal contact with defendants and offenders. Investigates employment, sources of income, lifestyle, and associates to assess risk and compliance. Addresses substance abuse, mental health, domestic violence, and similar problems and implements the necessary treatment or violation proceedings, through assessment, monitoring, and counseling.

Schedules and conducts drug use tests and DNA collection of offenders/defendants, following established procedures and protocols. Maintains paper and computerized records of test results. Testifies in court as to the basis for factual findings and (if warranted) guideline applications. Serves as a resource to the court. Maintains detailed written records of case activity.

Investigates and analyzes financial documents and activities and takes appropriate action. Interviews victim(s) and provides victim impact statement to the court. Ensures compliance with Mandatory Victims Restitution Act. Is responsible for enforcement of home confinement conditions ordered by the court.

Under the guidance and direction of a Supervising U.S. Probation Officer, analyzes and resolves disputed issues involving defendants/offenders and presents unresolved issues to the court for resolution. Assess offenders'/defendants' level of risk and develops strategies for controlling and correcting risk management.

Communicates with other organizations and personnel (such as the U.S. Parole Commission, Bureau of Prisons, law enforcement, treatment agencies, and attorneys) concerning offenders'/defendants' behavior and conditions of supervision. Identifies and investigates violations and implements appropriate alternatives and sanctions. Discusses violations with Supervising Probation and Pretrial Services Officer. Reports violations of the conditions of supervision to the appropriate authorities. Prepares written reports of violation matters, and makes recommendations for disposition.

QUALIFICATIONS REQUIRED:
The successful applicant(s) must be mature, responsible, poised, organized, and meticulous. Must possess a positive attitude, integrity, tact, good judgment, initiative, and the ability to work with a wide variety of people with diverse backgrounds. Must be able to meet all Court deadlines and dates. Proficiency with Word or similar software and excellent oral and written communication skills preferred.

Prior to appointment, the selectee considered for this position will undergo a medical examination and drug screening. Upon successful completion of the medical examination and drug screening, the selectee may then be appointed provisionally, pending a favorable suitability determination by the court. In addition, as conditions of employment, incumbent will be subject to ongoing random drug screening, updated background investigations every five years and, as deemed necessary by management for reasonable cause, may be subject to subsequent fitness-for-duty evaluations.

Officers must possess, with or without corrective lenses, good distance vision in a least one eye and the ability to read normal size print. Normal hearing ability, with or without a hearing aid, is also required. Any severe health problems, such as physical defects, disease, and deformities that constitute employment hazards to the applicant or others, may disqualify an applicant.

EDUCATION:

Qualifications include the completion of a bachelor's degree from an accredited college or university in a field of academic study, such as criminal justice, criminology, psychology, sociology, human relations, business or public administration, which provides evidence of the capacity to understand and apply the legal requirements and human relations skills involved in the work of this position is required.

A master's degree or current enrollment in a related graduate program is preferred.

First time appointees to positions covered under law enforcement officer retirement provisions must not have reached their 37th birthday at the time of appointment. Applicants 37 or over who have previous law enforcement officer experience under the Civil Service Retirement System or the Federal Employees' Retirement System and who have either a subsequent break in service or intervening service in a non-law enforcement officer position may have their previous law enforcement officer experience subtracted from their age to determine whether they meet the maximum age requirement.

Candidates selected for interviews will be required to participate in job-related testing as part of the screening process. Final candidates will undergo a background investigation with law enforcement agencies, as well as a check of financial and credit records. Prior to appointment, applicants considered for this position will undergo a full OPM background investigation, finger printing, medical examination, and drug screening. In addition, the incumbent will be subject to random drug screening and updated background investigations every five years. This position is subject to mandatory Electronic Fund Transfer (Direct Deposit) participation for payment of net pay.

The United States Probation and Pretrial Services Office require employees to adhere to a Code of Ethics and Conduct Policy. Applicants must be U.S. citizens or a permanent resident seeking U.S. citizenship. Noncitizens must execute an affidavit indicating their intent to apply for citizenship when they become eligible to do so. This position requires completion of a training academy in Charleston, South Carolina.

All final candidates are subject to FBI Fingerprints and background investigation, including criminal history. Applicants must be U.S. citizens or a permanent resident seeking U.S. citizenship. Noncitizens must execute an affidavit indicating their intent to apply for citizenship when they become eligible to do so.

Source: USA Jobs. (2016). *United States Court: Probation Officer.* Retrieved from https://www.usajobs.gov/GetJob/ViewDetails/423611100.

Job Challenges

Community corrections professionals encounter a myriad of challenges in their position on a daily basis. As Lutze (2014) notes, the work of CCOs is very much influenced by the political climate, the demands of their agencies, the needs of offenders, and the communities in which they work. One significant challenge that CCOs face on the job is their rather large **caseloads**, or the number of clients that they supervise at one time (Lutze, 2014). Since the 1960s, correctional administrators have attempted to determine what the appropriate caseload size should be for CCOs (DeMichele, 2007). In fact, during the 1960s, 50 was deemed as the perfect caseload size for CCOs

(DeMichele, 2007). Subsequent researchers, however, have stated that pinpointing an exact number of clients for every CCO is problematic due to jurisdiction variations in numbers of clients and their risk levels. After all, clients that are classified as higher risk need more attention from their CCOs. By the 1990s, the American Probation and Parole Association (APPA) (1991) recognized the differences in workload for CCOs and developed suggested caseload size standards based on the risk classification of their clients and the projected hours that the CCOs would spend with their clients. For instance, the APPA (1991) specified that CCOs with high-risk level clients should have 30 cases, those with medium-risk level clients should be assigned 60 cases, and those with low-risk level clients should supervise 120 cases.

The idea behind the caseload size recommendations, sometimes referred to as the workload model, is that those CCOs with higher risk level clients would be investing more hours of attention to these clients than those with CCOs with lower risk level clients (DeMichele, 2007). Although the APPA (1991) offered a recommendation for caseload size, the organization also noted that such a recommendation was difficult to establish as a firm standard given jurisdictional variation. Perhaps one of the chief arguments for smaller caseload sizes is that CCOs would be better able to serve their clients' needs and, thus, lower recidivism rates may be achieved overall. One study casts doubt on whether it is just caseload size that contributes to lower recidivism rates. Jalbert and colleagues (2011) examined probation officer caseloads in three states (i.e., Iowa, Oklahoma, and Colorado) to determine the impact of the caseload size on recidivism rates. In addition to caseload sizes, the researchers also examined whether probation services were being carried out in an evidence-based practices environment. **Evidence-based practices** (EBP) refer to the utilization of research principles and empirical assessments to guide treatment and supervision of offenders. The researchers found that in those jurisdictions that fully implemented EBP and whose probation officers have smaller caseloads, probationers did exhibit lower levels of recidivism. However, in those jurisdictions without fully implemented EBP practices and that also had probation officers with lower caseloads, no significant reductions in recidivism rates for probationers were observed. Thus, client outcomes are not necessarily tied to the caseload sizes of CCOs. Regarding EBP, Lutze (2014, p. 177) explains, "to effectively use evidence-based treatment, CCOs must be willing to take a holistic approach to supervision and view themselves as active agents of change who have multiple tools at their disposal, some coercive and some supportive, that in combination have the potential to make a difference."

Despite the unsuccessful attempts to implement an ideal caseload number, researchers have uncovered that indeed caseloads have increased over the past several decades. According to McGarry and colleagues (2013), in the 1970s, parole officers had an average caseload of 45 parolees, but by 2003, officers were supervising 70 parolees. Again, this is just an average number, so many parole officers had even larger caseloads. It also seems that probation officers during 2003 did not fare much better. The Vera Institute of Justice (2013) reports that in 2003, the average caseload for probation officers was 130 probationers. The concern over caseloads has prompted some states to reestablish caseload size standards. In Alaska, a bill has been put forth to cap probation officer caseloads to 60, down from the usual 100 caseload size (Reagan, 2015). While many correctional administrators may support their CCOs having a lower caseload size, it is often not realistic due to budget concerns (Reagan, 2015). Many states are facing fiscal constraints and do not have the ability to lower caseloads for their CCOs as there are no funds to hire additional CCOs to ease the caseload burden.

Another significant challenge that CCOs face in their positions is managing the stress and strain of the job. According to Gonzales, Schofield, and Hart (2005, p. ii), "the major sources of stress for community corrections officers are high caseloads, excess paperwork, and deadline pressures." Since high caseloads is a chief source of strain for CCOs, it once again raises the issue of caseload size and whether efforts should again be directed at providing CCOs with a manageable load which could result in CCOs experiencing less work-related stress and perhaps contribute to better client outcomes. In an examination of probation and parole officers, one officer reports on the strain stating, "I have 108 cases right now—I can't supervise all of them by the book—there's no time. One offender alone can eat up an enormous amount of time" (Finn & Kuck, 2003, p. 20). When examining stress and individual characteristics of CCOs, such as gender and race, it is difficult to state whether some CCOs experience more or less strain due to the paucity of research (Lutze, 2014). For female CCOs, it has been reported that they may experience more physical stress than their male colleagues, however, Lutze (2014) points out that this may be due to their willingness to report it more than their male colleagues rather than a true difference. Although, female CCOs are more likely to experience sexual harassment from their co-workers or clients than male CCOs do, which could clearly add to their stress levels (Lutze, 2014). Additionally, minority CCOs may experience discrimination on the job and may struggle with stereotypes placed on them by their colleagues and clients, which can add to their stress levels (Lutze, 2014). Furthermore, minority CCOs may struggle with the additional burden of helping "their people" succeed, while, at the same time, facing resistance from minority offenders who may perceive them as working for "the man."

Apart from the caseload size, it may be the actual clients and their offenses which can elicit much strain and stress in the CCOs and which can result in depression and burnout (Gayman & Bradley, 2013). Catanese (2010, p. 36) explains that corrections professionals who work with offenders who have committed sex crimes may be "deeply affected by the stories and the images they are exposed to during their work." For those CCOs assigned to work with sex offenders, they may experience **secondary traumatic stress**. Secondary traumatic stress (STS), also referred to as compassion fatigue or vicarious traumatization, can occur when CCOs are exposed to the suffering that their clients have inflicted on others and they then begin to develop traumatic stress symptoms as a result of their exposure (Figley, 2002; Severson & Pettus-Davis, 2013). Indicators of STS include, but are not limited to, grief, anxiety, sadness, irritability, cynicism, mood swings, and isolation (Cantanese, 2010). Additionally, indicators of STS may include physical symptoms such as headaches, hives, heartburn, migraines, ulcers, heart attacks, and strokes (Cantanese, 2010). Other indicators of STS could be the CCOs' disengagement with prior spirituality involvement or commitments, sleep disruptions, losing interest in their work, or a reduction in their desire to help their clients (Cantanese, 2010).

In a qualitative study of approximately 50 parole officers and supervisors' experiences of the symptoms of secondary trauma for those supervising sex offenders in a midwestern state, Severson and Pettus-Davis (2013) report on how supervising such a caseload can take a toll on CCOs' emotional well-being. One officer stated, "But every time you read their files, that victimizes you. I've read that officers dealing in … sex offenders, they need a break every so often because they are so victimized every time you look at them" (Severson & Pettus-Davis, 2013, p. 11). A supervisor recalls, "I had an officer who, uh, worked with us … [and] he started going out in the middle of the night and checking up on his sex offenders cuz he was worried about them; afraid that they were going to do something. Um, he ended up havin' to go on medication … and had to be transferred" (Severson & Pettus-Davis, 2013, p. 13). However, it should be noted that STS can occur for CCOs not just relegated to supervising sex offenders. CCOs whose clients commit suicide or commit violent offenses that cause significant injury or death can also cause STS (Lewis, Lewis, & Garby, 2013). In some cases, for some CCOs, encountering offenders who committed suicide may elicit primary traumas in their own lives if they have had a family member or friend commit suicide in the past (Catanese, 2010). Similarly, CCOs who have had to cope with their own violent victimization (e.g., prior sexual abuse) in the past may now be confronted with their prior victimization, which they may have previously compartmentalized, in full force as they manage offenders who have committed such offenses (Catanese, 2010).

A more manageable caseload may also ease the second source of strain that many CCOs encounter in their jobs, which is excessive paperwork (Finn & Kuck, 2003). That is, with more cases to manage, the CCOs inevitably have more paperwork to process in relation to each case. Even if the officers are not physically filling out the paperwork, they are still responsible for entering in information into various computer programs or agency computer systems or software programs (Gonzales et al., 2005). As much of the paperwork needs to be processed or entered in some form or fashion rather quickly, the stress of getting the information where it is needed on time can be very cumbersome. Apart from their usual deadlines, it is not uncommon for CCOs to experience unexpected time-sensitive deadlines that may be imposed upon them by their supervisors. In one study, a CCO explains, "A supervisor can come in and say, 'so-and-so got arrested, so you have to go to the police department and get him.' So I have to drop what I'm doing to prepare the paperwork—there's a time limit for getting the arrest report done for the hearing deadline—so all my other work backs up" (Finn & Kuck, 2003, p. 19).

Apart from the three main sources of stress that CCOs experience, Finn & Kuck (2003, p. 13) report on many other forms of strain that they experience, including:

- inadequate supervision, such as rarely receiving compliments for work well done
- lack of promotional opportunities
- low salaries that require them to hold down second jobs
- danger of physical assault or threats from offenders
- changing or conflicting State, agency, or interoffice policies and procedures
- being held—and feeling—personally accountable for offenders' misbehavior
- inconsistent demands and perceived excessive leniency on the part of courts and judges
- lack of community resources, such as treatment programs, for helping offenders.

Given the strain of the job, CCOs yearn for appropriate mentoring and supervision. Supervisors definitely need to be aware of and sensitive to the strain that CCOs are experiencing and be able to provide their employees with some recognition—either informally or formally. For some CCOs, the absence of the ability to move upwards in the organization coupled with a rather low salary is stressful for them. CNN Money (2009) describes probation/parole officer work as a stressful job that pays badly. In fact, in the CNN Money (2009) report probation/parole officer work was number *three* on their list of fifteen occupations that are stressful but pay poorly. Research conducted by Pitts (2007) revealed that CCOs reported that the number one most influential stressor for them was an inadequate salary.

Another significant stress for CCOs is concern for their own physical safety, or even the safety of their family members (Lutze, 2014). Lowry (2000), in a study of 300 probation and pre-trial officers, reported that 96% of the sample were concerned for their personal safety—particularly when making field contacts. This has been one reason why increasingly more CCOs are carrying firearms on the job (Lutze, 2014). Additionally, Finn & Kuck (2003) describe how CCOs can often encounter their clients while out in the communities with their families, and this causes much strain for CCOs who are trying to keep their professional world and personal world separate. The collision of these two worlds can be especially problematic and stressful for CCOs if their clients cross the line. Finn and Kuck (2003, p. 16) report one CC-O's concerns over family safety who stated, "When an offender found out that his children attended the same elementary school as my children, the offender made a veiled threat against my kids during an office contact." In many cases, a CCO's own family members are stressed by the work that they are doing, thus, CCOs are also experiencing vicarious levels of stress from family as well (Finn & Kuck, 2003). Apart from strain regarding the safety of their family, the strain of the job may bleed into their personal lives. The work of CCOs do not follow bankers' hours. That is, CCOs are expected to work evenings and weekends (Finn & Kuck, 2003). The long and often erratic working hours take a toll on the family life of the CCOs; for instance, important family events (e.g., birthdays, sporting events for children) may be missed. Similar to other professionals, CCOs may bring the stress they experience on the job home (Severson & Pettus-Davis, 2013). Finn and Kuck (2003, p. 25) report one CCO stating, "The job creates a lot of stress, and it's brought home. This has a negative impact on the family, so the officer returns to work with another problem."

Adding to the everyday strains on the job, CCOs are often very concerned about whether their client re-offends and if they will somehow be held accountable for the behavior of their client (Finn & Kuck, 2003). In some instances, supervisors may be very critical of a CCO whose client recidivates and question why the CCO could not prevent it. If the client commits an offense that captures the media's attention, then the CCO is under even greater scrutiny by their supervisor. CCOs may also blame themselves for why their client failed—that is, they may question themselves as to where they went wrong and be critical of their efforts and actions. Additionally, CCOs may be held legally liable for a crime committed by one of their clients (Lutze, 2014). Finn and Kuck (2003, p. 22) explain, in Washington State, this feeling has been exacerbated by the passage of the **Offender Accountability Act**, which "provides legal recourse for victims of crime committed by a reoffender by allowing personal liability lawsuits against state community corrections officers." In interviews with 49 probation officers in Washington State, Drapela and Lutze (2009) found that many in their study were concerned with being sued. As one officer stated,

> That's the worst part of the job, I think—liability. That's what brings me home with an ulcer every night because I deal with an offender and I deal with sanctions, [and I put him in treatment] ... what if that guy walks out of treatment and goes out and does bad things? You know? That was my call and we don't have any immunity like judges or a little parole board—we're open to liability on that. And I don't know who made that call, but it's not a good part of the job, it sucks, but the worst part of being on the job is liability (Drapela & Lutze, 2009, p. 377).

Further, CCOs may become frustrated when their recommendations, as prepared in presentence investigation reports, are not followed by judges or if they perceive that judges are somehow making decisions that are not in the best interest of their clients. Finally, CCOs may become strained by the absence of community resources to help their clients. The fiscal crisis experienced in corrections is not exclusive to corrections, as other agencies, such as social service agencies, have experienced significant budget cuts as well. Since many social service agencies' budgets have been cut, they are less able to offer services to community corrections offenders, such as drug and/or alcohol treatment. Thus, CCOs may experience stress and pressure to help their clients when little help is really available.

At the organizational level, the strains experienced by CCOs can have a significant impact on agencies and the organizational climate (Finn & Kuck, 2003; Lee, Phelps, & Beto, 2009). Agencies that place unreasonable demands on CCOs (e.g., caseloads, deadlines) as well as supervisors that are demanding rather than supportive will soon encounter the problem of CCO burnout. Organizational policies, such as the failure to purchase CCOs weapons for their job, neglecting to supply CCOs with good working vehicles to carry out their home visits, failing to praise employees for their hard work, disallowing CCOs to participate in meaningful discussion about future initiatives and changes, and even reimbursing CCOs a mere pittance for mileage when they must use their own vehicles while doing their job, certainly eats away at morale (Lutze, 2014; Pransky, 2015). As in any profession, employees can sometimes hit their limit, thus, CCOs are not any different than other employees working outside of criminal justice agencies. When CCOs experience burnout, they are much more inclined to leave, resulting in employee turnover and perhaps chronic employee retention problems for specific agencies (Lee et al., 2009). The problem of employee retention that agencies experience is not systemic to their veteran CCOs. Lee and colleagues (2009), who examined approximately 2,600 probation officers in regards to their employment intentions, found that those officers who were younger and who had fewer years of service were more likely to be inclined to leave their job. Other organizational factors that may impact morale and result in CCOs becoming more inclined to leave could include unequal work assignments, lack of a positive organizational culture (e.g., threatening supervisors, unsupportive colleagues), and the absence of the occasional pat-on-the-back recognition for a job well done.

Text Box 11.2: The Dutch Probation Service

The stress faced by CCOs in the United States is not unique. Probation officers in the Netherlands, for instance, also experience stress in the course of their occupation. Vogelvang and colleagues (2014) suggest that the probation profession needs resilient officers. That is, officers who can effectively assist their clients despite the myriad of challenges. In a survey of Dutch probation officers, Vogelvang et al. (2004) found that the officer resiliency can be impacted, both positively and negatively, by the organization and individual characteristics. For instance, if the organization can provide officers with proper training to cope with stress, support, and, in particular, support for coping with trauma, then the organization will benefit in numerous ways (Vogelvang et al., 2004). For instance, such training and support will allow the organization to retain high performing officers who will not be prone to burnout and will be in a better space to help their clients. Additionally, those officers with strong coping methods are also prone to be more resilient. Vogelvang et al. (2004) advocate for organizational programming, specifically any programming that can empower employees, to be effective at fostering resiliency in officers.

Coping with Challenges

CCOs may cope with the aforementioned strains in a variety of ways. They may take sick-days as a "mental health day" or because they are experiencing physical ailments as a result of their stress (Finn & Kuck, 2003). When CCOs take sick days, it negatively impacts their fellow CCOs, such that those CCOs at the office are now in charge of overseeing additional clients, thereby increasing their caseloads for the day. Other CCOs may turn to exercise as a method to control their stress (Finn & Kuck, 2003). It seems that some form of physical activity may be critical in reducing stress levels. Essentially, any form of self-care that reduces pressure and does not necessarily have a goal may be an effective stress reliever (Catanese, 2010). CCOs' fellow co-workers may also help them to reduce strain (Catanese, 2010; Finn & Kuck, 2003). With supportive colleagues, CCOs have someone to turn to that truly understands the pressure they are under, that can offer them sound advice, and that allow them to vent their frustrations. Similarly, those CCOs who have strong family and personal relationships may find these also help them cope with their strains by also offering advice and allowing the CCOs to discuss their concerns with them (Catanese, 2010). As one officer reported, "My spouse is a godsend—calm, doesn't overreact, tells me to calm down—'You can't change that idiot client'" (Finn & Kuck, 2003, p. 25).

Another approach to coping with at least the workload strain may be to prioritize clients within a CCO's caseload. That is, perhaps CCOs will need to decide to invest more time with some clients and less with others or their supervisors need to suggest this as a viable solution and support them. One supervisor reported, "We had 200 cases at one time, so we picked the 50 worst cases and took our chances with the rest. As a result, we get a feeling of making achievable goals no matter what the agency expects. We set our own expectations, not let someone else set them" (Finn & Kuck. 2003, p. 26). Perhaps CCOs should not even be expected to cope well with strains given their educational background. It may be the case that CCOs' educational background did not sufficiently prepare them for the strains in their profession. Pitts (2007), who examined approximately 2,300 probation and parole officers from fifteen states, found that officers who felt that their education did not prepare them for their work exhibited higher levels of stress than those who felt otherwise. In fact, one-third of the CCOs in this study reported this. Perhaps even more alarming, Pitts (2007) found that of these officers who felt unprepared, their stress significantly manifested into emotional outbursts, alcohol and/or drug abuse, and work errors (e.g., missed deadlines, mistakes in work products). As discussed earlier, most CCOs that are hired are required to have a bachelor's degree and the degree may be from a variety of disciplines such as criminal justice, psychology, and social work. Pitts' (2007) research suggests that additional training may be needed for all newly hired CCOs to fill any gaps in educational training that could put newly hired CCOs at increased risk for stress and assist in providing proper outlets for coping with stress. Strengthening coping via training may be key (see Text Box 11.2).

In sum, CCOs endure significant strains as they attempt to ensure community safety, their own personal safety, and also assist offenders, while at the same time holding their clients accountable for their behaviors. That is a rather tall order! It is no wonder that CCOs often feel pressure and experience significant strains. However, in spite of the workload strains, many CCOs continue to work in their profession as they are committed to helping those that they can as well as those clients who will accept their assistance.

Significant Helpers in Reentry

It is abundantly clear that CCOs are on the front lines in helping offenders successfully transition into their communities, whether their clients are transitioning from serving a lengthy prison sentence or are directly sentenced to serve community corrections sentences such as probation (Lutze, 2014). However, the clients of CCOs may not perceive their CCO as a source of help or perhaps even view CCOs as being incapable of helping them or truly understanding the needs and challenges they have during reentry.

Several researchers have explored whether criminal justice professionals are aware of ex-offenders' needs and the challenges they face upon reentry (Brown, 2004a; Brown, 2004b; Graffam et al., 2004; Gunnison & Helfgott, 2007; Helfgott, 1997; Helfgott & Gunnison, 2008). In 1997, Helfgott conducted a case study examination of the relationship between ex-offender needs and community opportunity in Seattle, Washington. One finding that Helfgott (1997) uncovered was that ex-offenders believed that their CCOs did not truly understand their needs. The offenders remarked that CCOs were unable to understand the realities of their situations and that the tightrope the officers expected them to walk, in the period immediately following release, set them up for failure. Offenders in the study did not see their CCOs as a resource in the reentry process. One offender stated, "they [CCOs] just want you to tell a good lie … they have no understanding of what it's like … take them out [of their environment] and they wouldn't be able to survive on the streets" (Helfgott, 1997, p. 16). Other researchers have surveyed officers to determine if they could indeed identify the needs and challenges faced by ex-offenders. This research has yielded the fact that CCOs are indeed capable of identifying the needs and challenges that their clients have upon reentry (Brown, 2004a; Brown, 2004b; Gunnison & Helfgott, 2007; Gunnison & Helfgott, 2011; Helfgott, 1997; Helfgott & Gunnison, 2008). However, the majority of the researchers did not explore **social distance**, the perceived social distance or barrier between CCOs and clients.

Only recently has the issue of social distance between CCOs and ex-offenders been explored. Helfgott and Gunnison (2008) surveyed CCOs and found that social distance was significantly related to officer identification of some offender needs, offender challenges, and officer attitudes towards offenders. However, social distance did not play a large role in officer ability to identify offender reentry needs, and officers do not collectively perceive officer-offender social distance as a hindrance in the reentry process. While this research was the first to explore social distance between ex-offenders and CCOs, the data were based on closed-ended survey responses and did not provide CCOs an opportunity to offer their insights and opinions about social distance.

In a qualitative exploration of 121 state and federal CCOs' opinions on social distance in Seattle, Washington, Gunnison and Helfgott (2011) found that the majority of CCOs did not view social distance as a hindrance to offenders' ability to reenter society successfully. When probed further, some CCOs believed that the offender's identification of social distance is an excuse put forth by the offender when unable to successfully reintegrate. One officer stated, "No! The offenders will find all kinds of excuses to lurk behind. It's the offenders that would want to change and the community corrections officer's (CCO) situation does not matter here" (Gunnison & Helfgott, 2011, p. 295). Similarly, another officer reported, "No, it is a ridiculous excuse. I was born and reared very practically and had good parenting. But I was exposed to other cultures and experiences as I matured. You don't need to be an addict to assist an addict. All humans have addictive personalities" (Gunnison & Helfgott, 2011, p. 295). Finally, another officer reported, "No, but offenders will attempt to use this until I explain that I was homeless for years and engaged in the same activities. I know the games as I've been there, done that" (Gunnison & Helfgott, 2011, p. 295). Gunnison and Helfgott (2013), in another qualitative study of 19 CCOs, found that several CCOs believed that the perceptions of social distance by ex-offenders about their CCOs may be due to the nature of the CCOs' role — to maintain professional boundaries between themselves and their clients. Gunnison and Helfgott (2013) explain that other CCOs do recognize that ex-offenders may perceive social distance but work to break down these barriers through establishing good communication and rapport with their clients. One female CCO in their study reported,

> No, I haven't walked in their shoes. I think that is something they feel a little bit of, of course. Especially when I was in West Seattle, I would set everything up and we would sign all our paperwork and the offender would look at me and go, 'Oh, okay thanks. Now can I meet my CCO?'... It's a matter of, with my guys, I haven't been through what you've been through, I don't have an addiction issue, you know. I didn't grow up the way you grew up. Everybody's issues are their own and we all have something. I think once you, I think I talked about this before, we do establish some rapport with people, and I think when they see that I don't judge them for the things that they did before, or choices that they've made. Then, they can understand that I don't come from where they come from, but I'm certainly not judging them because of it and that helps (Gunnison & Helfgott, 2013, p. 161).

Another CCO in their study stressed that establishing rapport is one method that CCOs can utilize to get past any perceptions of social distance by ex-offenders.

Thus, while ex-offenders often think that CCOs are unaware of their struggles or are not in a position to help them, this could not be farther from the truth. Regardless of a CCO's background, they are ready and willing to help their clients in whatever way that they can. CCOs want their clients to be successful when transitioning back into society. In many cases, CCO may be the only positive person in the ex-offender's life (Gunnison & Helfgott, 2013). Therefore, it is imperative that community corrections agencies and CCOs are aware of the potential for perceiving social distance so that proper education and training of CCOs can commence. With proper education and training, CCOs will be better equipped to break down the invisible barrier between themselves and their clients (Lutze, 2014). As these barriers are broken down, clients will be more likely to recognize their CCO as a partner in their journey to success — rather than as an adversary. To help CCOs better assist their clients during reentry, agencies need to significantly invest in CCOs and recognize the importance and value of these "boundary spanners" (Lutze, 2014).

Conclusion

In sum, this chapter provided an overview of the number of CCOs in the United States, the challenges they face on the job, their training, the range in their salaries, and how they carry out their duties. Additionally, information on how CCOs cope with the various stressors that they encounter, both internally and externally, was also presented. Finally, research on CCOs' perceptions of offenders' needs and challenges that ex-offenders face during reentry was presented. Without a doubt, CCOs toe a difficult line in their jobs as they are tasked with both assisting their clients and keeping the community safe from harm. While often a thankless or overlooked job in the criminal justice system, the job of CCOs is an important one. Hopefully, CCOs will be better recognized for their valiant efforts.

Key Terms

Caseloads

Community corrections officer

Evidence-based practices

Offender Accountability Act

Secondary traumatic stress

Social distance

Discussion Questions

1. Research the number of community corrections officers at both the state and at the federal district level in your state. How many are employed? What are their demographic characteristics? Describe the characteristics of CCOs working in your state and federal district.

2. Locate the offices in which CCOs work within your state. Are the majority employed in cities or more rural areas? What challenges do you think CCOs face when working in more rural areas?

3. Interview a community corrections officer at the local or state level about his/her background and job. What educational background do they have? What skills are most needed for CCOs to be effective in their jobs? What is the starting salary? What do CCOs report as the three most challenging aspects of their job and the three most rewarding aspects of their job?

4. Write a letter to legislators in your state. In your letter, identify the critical role CCOs have in fostering successful reintegration, the challenges the face, and concrete solutions that are needed to assist them *today* to help offenders and keep the community safe.

References

Armaghan, S. (2011, November 2). Parole officers jam Bronx court as parolee is indicted for attempted murder of 3 brethren. *New York Daily News.* Retrieved from http://www.nydailynews.com/news/parole-officers-jam-bronx-court-parolee-indicted-attempted-murder-3-brethren-article-1.971371.

American Probation and Parole Association. (1991). Caseload standards. *Perspectives, Summer.* Retrieved from http://www.appanet.org/about%20appa/caseload.htm.

American Probation and Parole Association. (2006). *Adult and juvenile probation and parole national firearm survey, second edition.* Retrieved from https://www.appanet.org/eweb/Resources/Surveys/National_Firearms/docs/NFS_2006.pdf.

Brown, J. (2004a). Challenges facing Canadian federal offenders newly released to the community. *Journal of Offender Rehabilitation, 39,* 19–35. doi: 10.1300/J076v39n01_02.

Brown, J. (2004b). Managing the transition from jail to community: A Canadian parole officer perspective on the needs of newly released federal offenders. Western Criminology Review, 5, 97–107.

Cantanese, S. A. (2010). Traumatized by association: The risk of working sex crimes. *Federal Probation, 74*(2), 36–38.

CNN Money. (2009, October 29). Stressful jobs that pay badly: Probation/parole officer. Retrieved from http://money.cnn.com/galleries/2009/pf/0910/gallery.stressful_jobs/3.html.

DeMichele, M. T. (2007). *Probation and parole's growing caseloads and working allocation: Strategies for managerial decision making.* The American Probation & Parole Association.

Dickson, A. (2015, April 8). Judge sets $5,000 bail for state community corrections officer accused of possessing child pornography. *The Olympian.* Retrieved from http://www.theolympian.com/news/local/crime/article26120044.html.

Drapela, L. A., & Lutze, F. E. (2009). Innovation in community corrections and probation officers' fears of being sued. *Journal of Contemporary Criminal Justice, 25*(4), 364–383. doi: 10.1177/1043986209344549.

Figley, C. R. (2002). *Treating compassion fatigue.* New York, NY: Routledge.

Finn, P., & Kuck, S. (2003). *Addressing probation and parole officer stress.* Washington, DC: U.S. Department of Justice.

Gable, P. (2015, October 31). Community corrections officer arrested after inappropriate relationship. *The Shelbyville News.* Retrieved from http://www.shelbynews.com/news/article_670226ae-7ff1-11e5-bb50-239686c08559.html.

Gayman, M. D., & Bradley, M. S. (2013). Organizational climate, work stress, and depressive symptoms among probation and parole officers. *Criminal Justice Studies, 26*(3), 326–346.

Gonzales, A. R., Schofield, R. B., & Hart, S. V. (2005). *Stress among probation and parole officers and what can be done about it.* Washington, DC: U.S. Department of Justice.

Graffam, J., Shinkfield, A., Lavelle, B., & McPherson, W. (2004). Variables affecting successful reintegration as perceived by offenders and professionals. *Journal of Offender Rehabilitation, 40,* 147–171. doi: 10.1300/J076v40n01_08.

Gunnison, E., & Helfgott, J. B. (2007). Community corrections officers' perceptions of ex-offender reentry needs and challenges. *Journal of Police and Criminal Psychology, 22*(1), 10–21. doi: 10.1007/s11896-007-9004-5.

Gunnison, E., & Helfgott, J. B. (2010). Factors that hinder offender reentry success: A view from community corrections officers. *International Journal of Offender Therapy and Comparative Criminology, 55*(2), 287–304. doi: 10.1177/0306624X09360661.

Gunnison, E., & Helfgott, J. B. (2013). *Offender reentry: Beyond crime and punishment.* Boulder, CO: Lynne Rienner.

Halbrook, S. (2014). Parolee who tried to kill officers gets 40 yrs-life. *The Communicator.* Retrieved from http://www.pef.org/archive/communicator/032014/parolee sentenced.htm.

Helfgott, J. B. (1997). Ex-offender needs versus criminal opportunity in Seattle, Washington. *Federal Probation, 61,* 12–24.

Helfgott, J. B., & Gunnison, E. (2008). The influence of social distance on community corrections officer perceptions of offender reentry needs. *Federal Probation, June,* 2–12.

Jalbert, S. K., Rhodes, W., Kane, M., Clawson, E., Bogue, B., Flygare, C., Kling, R., & Guevara, M. (2011). *A multi-site evaluation of reduced probation caseload size in an evidence-based practice setting.* Washington, DC: National Institute of Justice.

Lee, W.-J., Phelps, J. R., & Beto, D. R. (2009). Turnover intention among probation officers and direct care staff: A statewide study. *Federal Probation, 73*(3), 28–39.

Lewis, K. R., Lewis, L. S., & Garby, T. M. (2013). Surviving the trenches: The personal impact of the job on probation officers. *American Journal of Criminal Justice, 38*(1), 67–84. doi: 10.1007/s12103-012-9165-3.

Lowry, K. D. (2000). United States probation/pretrial officers' concerns about victimization and officer safety training. *Federal Probation, 64*(2), 51–59.

Lutze, F. E. (2014). *Professional lives of community corrections officers: The invisible side of reentry.* Los Angeles, CA: Sage.

McGarry, P., Shames, A., Yaroni, A., Tamis, K., Subramanian, R., Eisen, L.-B., Digard, L., Delaney, R., & Sullivan, S. (2013). *The potential of community corrections to improve safety and reduce incarceration.* Washington, DC: Vera Institute of Justice.

Pitts, W. (2007). Educational competency as an indicator of occupational stress for probation and parole officers. *American Journal of Criminal Justice, 32*(1/2), 57–73. doi: 10.1007/s12103-007-9010-2.

Pransky, N. (2015, March 31). Officers blow whistle on dangerous DOC 'crisis.' *10 News.* Retrieved from http://www.wtsp.com/story/news/investigations/2015/03/23/doc-penny-pinching-causing-probation-dangers/25181657/.

Reagan, K. (2015, February 26). Capping caseloads 'not realistic' for state's probation officers without funds. *KTOO Public Media.* Retrieved from http://www.ktoo.org/2015/02/26/capping-caseloads-not-realistic-states-probation-officers-without-funds/.

Severson, M., & Pettus-Davis, C. (2013). Parole officers' experiences of the symptoms of secondary trauma in the supervision of sex offenders. *International Journal of Offender Therapy and Comparative Criminology, 57*(1), 5–24. doi: 10.1177/0306624X11422696.

Stelter, L. (2013, May 16). Tennessee joins growing number of states arming probation and parole officers. *In Public Safety.* Retrieved from http://inpublicsafety.com/2013/05/tennessee-joins-growing-number-of-states-arming-probation-and-parole-officers/.

Stinchcomb, J. B., McCampbell, S. W. & Layman, E. P. (2006). Future force: A guide to building the 21st century community corrections workforce. Washington, DC: U.S. Department of Justice, National Institute of Corrections.

USA Jobs. (2016). *United States Court: Probation officer.* Retrieved from https://www.usajobs.gov/GetJob/ViewDetails/423611100.

U.S. Bureau of Labor Statistics. (2015). Probation officers and correctional treatment specialists. *Occupational Outlook Handbook, 2016–2017.* Washington, DC: U.S. Department of Labor. Retrieved from http://www.bls.gov/ooh/community-and-social-service/probation-officers-and-correctional-treatment-specialists.htm#tab-2.

Vogel, E. (2012, January 24). Now hiring: State corrections department has 200 openings. *Las Vegas Review Journal.* Retrieved from www.reviewjournal.com/news/nevada-and-west/now-hiring-state-corrections-department-has-200-openings.

Vogelvang, B., Clarke, J., Weiland, A. S., Vosters, N., & Button, L. (2014). Resilience of Dutch probation officers: A critical need for a critical profession. *European Journal of Probation, 6*(2), 126–146. doi: 10.1177/2066220314540570.

von Zielbauer, P. (2003, August 7). Probation dept. is now arming officers supervising criminals. *New York Times.* Retrieved from http://www.nytimes.com/2003/08/07/nyregion/probation-dept-is-now-arming-officers-supervising-criminals.html.

Washington State Criminal Justice Training Academy. (2016). *Corrections officer academy.* Retrieved from https://fortress.wa.gov/cjtc/www/index.php?option=com_content&view=article&id=259&Itemid=208.

Yaniv, O. (2013, April 2). Remorseless thug flips off courtroom before being hauled to prison for shooting parole officer. *New York Daily News.* Retrieved from http://

Chapter 12

Finding Their Place: Ex-Offenders Fight to Regain a Place in Society

Student Learning Outcomes

After reading this chapter, you should be able to:

- Identify the many invisible punishments or collateral consequences of a conviction status.

- Explain the collateral consequences in terms of civil and political rights that are inhibited due to conviction status.

- Summarize if, how, and whether ex-offenders can possibly restore their lost civil rights.

Introduction

As humans, we all make mistakes with some mistakes being larger in magnitude than others. Reflect on some of the mistakes that you have made in your life—both big and small. Depending on what mistake you made, it may have had longer-term consequences in your life. Now, imagine if that mistake followed you for the rest of your life. For many ex-offenders, their mere conviction status is a mistake that can haunt them for years to come. Even after serving time in prison or successfully completing a community corrections sentence, their conviction status can block them from many opportunities in the United States. Michael Mirsky of New Jersey, was, for all intents and purposes, living the American dream. He was working at Verizon and pulling in a six-figure annual salary (Appelbaum, 2015). However, he lost his job and work was hard to find, therefore, he enrolled in a community college as a heating and air-conditioning specialist to increase his chances of obtaining gainful employment (Appelbaum, 2015). Unfortunately, jobs were sparse and Mirsky could not locate work and soon found himself in deeper in debt, including being in foreclosure on his home and owing child support (Appelbaum, 2015). It was his back child support that led to a warrant for his arrest. For whatever reason, when officers arrived to arrest Mirsky, he struggled, thus, he was charged with resisting arrest (Appelbaum, 2015). This was the first time Mirsky was arrested, and he pled guilty,

Image 24. © iStockphoto.com/RichLegg.

which resulted in a conviction status (Appelbaum, 2015). As if things in life were not already tough for Mirsky, he soon encountered additional hardships. With his conviction status, Mirsky had even greater difficulty in finding legal employment and his church no longer accepted his assistance as an usher (Appelbaum, 2015). When things were finally looking up for Mirsky as he landed a new temporary job, he was arrested a second time for back child support (Appelbaum, 2015). It seems that Mirsky's difficulties will likely continue in the future, and perhaps compound, until he can land a better paying job—that is, if employers give him a chance with his conviction record.

Sometimes it is not even your own mistake that can have serious implications and consequences on your life. Wait, how can that be?! Well, it may depend on who you associate with or even marry. In 2005, Melissa WolfHawk, a Pennsylvania resident with no conviction record, quickly discovered that the mistakes of others could severely impact her life (Scolforo, 2005). WolfHawk's husband was a convicted sex offender, and she was pregnant with their baby boy (Scolforo, 2005). The County Children and Youth Services learned about her pregnancy, and their position was that the child would not be safe in the custody of WolfHawk's husband (Scolforo, 2005). Ultimately, the county seized the three-day-old newborn after birth and placed the infant in foster care (Parker, 2005; 2006). Despite fighting this outcome in the courts, WolfHawk was not successful, and the courts ruled that her son would remain in custody of the state indefinitely; however, WolfHawk has visitation rights with her son (Parker, 2006).

As mentioned earlier in this text, successful offender reentry is no easy plight. It can be even more complex for ex-offenders as they struggle to regain custody of their children or the restoration of their rights (e.g., voting). This chapter devotes attention to the invisible punishments and collateral consequences of being convicted, such as barriers to employment, housing, and financial assistance, as well as the civil and political barriers convicted offenders face and the impact their status has on others. Additionally, this chapter describes the process of how ex-offenders can begin to restore some of their rights.

Consequences of Conviction

In the United States, those citizens who have a conviction record endure more than just the blemish of their conviction status attributed to their name. Those with conviction records encounter many collateral consequences due to their record. **Collateral consequences** refer to "laws and policies […] being enacted to restrict persons with a felony conviction (particularly convictions for drug offenses) from employment, receipt of welfare benefits, access to public housing, and eligibility for student loans for higher education" (The Sentencing Project, 2016). Such laws and policies severely impact the ability of the ex-offender to reintegrate successfully into society. More often than not, these collateral consequences impact the ex-offender directly, however, these draconian laws and policies definitely impact those around the offender as well, such as their children. When you think about it, how could such policies not impact family members? If the ex-offender is denied housing or employment options, then surely those vulnerable family members (i.e., children) who rely on the ex-offender for support are also impacted. The following sections outline many of the collateral consequences that offenders encounter.

Personal Barriers

Employment

As mentioned in an earlier chapter, ex-offenders struggle to gain employment. This is not a small problem as approximately 70 million offenders have either an arrest or conviction record (DePillis, 2015). While some in society may argue that ex-offenders should not get jobs ahead of law-abiding citizens, it should be of concern for all citizens as those without jobs are likely to recidivate. Clearly, one aspect of their lack of employability is stigmatization, as many employers do not want to hire those with records for fear of theft or liability. However, ex-offenders' hardships in getting employed go much deeper than stigmatization, as other factors are at play. Often what complicates their ability to land a job is the actual job application itself, which requires applicants to check a box as to whether they have any criminal convictions—particularly felony convictions. The disclosure of prior offending for all open positions in a given company is of great concern to the U.S. Equal Employment Opportunity Commission (EEOC) as it views such policies as paving the way for discrimination in hiring, and such disclosure can impact minorities disproportionately compared to other ex-offender groups, resulting in them having even further difficulties in being hired (Pettinato, 2014; Smialek, 2014). In 2012, the EEOC updated its guidelines to "encourage employers who use criminal records in employment decisions to review the seriousness of the crime, to consider how long ago the crime occurred, and to consider how relevant the crime is to the specific job in question. They also discourage bright-line criminal records policies and instead call for an 'individualized assessment' of applicants and employees" (Pettinato, 2014, p. 776).

Concern over the disclosure of criminal records on job applications has prompted approximately one dozen states to remove the check box on applications and has also led to some major retailers, such as Wal-Mart and Target, to remove the box from their job applications regardless of whether their store is operating in a state that has issued removal of the box on job applications (Smialek, 2014). In those states where removal of the check box on applications is not mandated, cities within those states have led efforts to "ban the box" in their own jurisdictions. For instance, in 2009, the city of Seattle removed this question from city job applications, but in 2013, the city enacted a "Ban the Box Ordinance" that also disallows private employers from asking about criminal history on job applications (see Text Box 12.1) (Weisenfeld, 2013).

Text Box 12.1: Seattle's Ban the Box Ordinance

14.17.020 Prohibited Use of Arrest and Conviction Records

A. No employer shall advertise, publicize, or implement any policy or practice that automatically or categorically excludes all individuals with any arrest or conviction record from any employment position that will be performed in whole or in substantial part (at least 50% of the time) within the City.

B. An employer may perform a criminal background check on a job applicant or require a job applicant to provide criminal history information, but only after the employer has completed an initial screening of applications or resumes to eliminate unqualified applicants.

C. An arrest is not proof that a person has engaged in unlawful conduct. Employers shall not carry out a tangible adverse employment action solely based on an employee's or applicant's arrest record.

D. Employers may inquire about the conduct related to an arrest record. Employers shall not carry out a tangible adverse employment action solely based on the conduct relating to an arrest unless the employer has a legitimate business reason for taking such action.

E. Employers shall not carry out a tangible adverse employment action solely based on an employee's or applicant's criminal conviction record or pending criminal charge, unless the employer has a legitimate business reason for taking such action.

F. Before taking any tangible adverse employment action solely based on an applicant's or employee's criminal conviction record, the conduct relating to an arrest record, or pending criminal charge, the employer shall identify to the applicant or employee the record(s) or information on which they are relying and give the applicant or employee a reasonable opportunity to explain or correct that information.

G. Employers shall hold open a position for a minimum of two business days after notifying an applicant or employee that they will be making an adverse employment decision solely based on their criminal conviction record, the conduct relating to an arrest record, or pending charge in order to provide an applicant or employee a reasonable opportunity to respond to, correct, or explain that information. After two business days, employers may, but are not required, to hold open a position until a pending charge is resolved or adjudicated or questions about an applicant's criminal conviction history or conduct relating to an arrest are resolved.

Source: Office of County Clerk. (2013, June 20). City of Seattle legislative information service. *Seattle.gov*. Retrieved from http://clerk.ci.seattle.wa.us/~scripts/nphbrs.exe?s3=117796+&s4=&s5=&s1=&s2=&S6=&Sect4=AND&l=0&Sect2=THESON&Sect3=PLURON&Sect5=CBORY&Sect6=HITOFF&d=ORDF&p=1&u=%2F~public%2Fcbor1.htm&r=1&f=G.

In other cities and states across the nation, other employment initiatives have been implemented to assist ex-offenders in obtaining employment. Several cities, such as San Francisco, Cleveland, Des Moines, and Indianapolis hold job fairs for ex-offenders. In fact, the Northern California Service League (NCSL) has been hosting an annual job fair for ex-offenders in San Francisco since 1996 (Center on Juvenile and Criminal Justice, 2016). These job fairs directly link ex-offenders with employers willing to hire them. The NCSL has served approximately 400 ex-offenders at each of these annual fairs and has had great success at helping these ex-offenders secure employment. The National H.I.R.E. network is a national advocacy group that strives to increase employment opportunities for those with criminal records through improving employment practices and educating the public (National Legal Center, 2015). Other organizations such as Fair Shake, an online reentry resource center, aims to connect employers, property managers, families of ex-offenders, and community members together to enhance opportunities for ex-offenders (Fair Shake Reentry Resource Center, 2016). This organization has a stated mission of "belief in success" for ex-offenders. It is with such city initiatives and organizational support that ex-offenders may find themselves in a better position to obtain employment.

Food

Without obtaining employment, ex-offenders will find it difficult to nourish themselves. Thus, they are often in need of food (Gunnison & Helfgott, 2013). For some ex-offenders, the ability to satisfy the basic need of sustenance is a great challenge, and the lack of ability to properly maintain their bodies is yet another collateral consequence. Mukamal (2000) explains that the **Federal Welfare Law of 1996** permanently prohibits states from permitting ex-offenders with drug-related felony convictions to receive any form of welfare benefits, including food assistance with the Supplemental Nutrition Assistance Program (SNAP). When implementing this law, the Court reasoned that such a ban would reduce fraud as there was great concern that ex-offenders would exchange food stamps for drugs (Archer & Williams, 2006). This ban is not merely for a few years, but rather a lifetime ban (Cohen, 2014; Gunnison & Helfgott, 2013; Mukamal, 2000). This policy impacts not only ex-offenders but also their families. Mohan and Lower-Basch (2014, p. 2) explain the impact by describing the hardships experienced by one ex-offender, "Christine McDonald, a single mother who was rapidly losing her vision, could not apply for SNAP benefits due to a drug conviction from long ago. Since her prior conviction, Christine had turned her life around, having written a book, bought a house, and

Text Box 12.2: State SNAP Drug Felon Bans as of July 2015

Full Ban	Modified Ban		No Ban	
AK	AR	MN	AL	NY
AZ	CO	MO	CA	OH
GA	CT	MT	DE	OK
MS	FL	NE	IL	PA
ND	HI	NV	IA	RI
SC	ID	NC	KS	SD
WV	IN	OR	ME	UT
	KY	TN	MA	VT
	LA	TX	NH	WA
	MD	VA	NJ	WY
	MI	WI	NM	

Source: Mohan, L., & Lower-Basch, E. (2014). *No more double punishments: Lifting the ban on basic human needs help for people with a prior drug felony conviction.* Washington, DC: CLASP.

currently running a nonprofit agency. As she puts it, 'If I would've killed someone I could've gotten food stamps.'"

While many states have since reversed their lifetime ban for such offenders, seven states still adhere to this ban while other states have modified their policies (see Text Box 12.2) (Mohan & Lower-Basch, 2014). For example, in Colorado and Connecticut, ex-offenders can regain their benefits if they successfully complete a drug education or treatment program (Mohan & Lower-Basch, 2014). In other states, such as Arkansas, Florida, and North Dakota, only those ex-offenders whose drug convictions were based on possession are eligible for benefit reinstatement, as those ex-offenders whose convictions were due to the manufacturing or distributions of drugs still endure a lifetime ban on food assistance (Mohan & Lower-Basch, 2014). Without a doubt, the lifetime bans, as well as the modified bans, have greatly impacted women, children of ex-offenders, and African Americans and other minority groups (Finzen, 2005; Mauer & McCalmont, 2013). Some ex-offenders may become desperate to obtain food and may resort to committing crimes, including prostitution, to earn income. For those ex-offenders turning to prostitution to meet their basic needs, they are putting themselves at greater risk of acquiring health problems such as sexually transmitted diseases or HIV/AIDS. Other ex-offenders who are hungry may numb their hunger pains through the use of drugs, which may impair their judgement regarding safe sex practices and put them at a greater risk of contracting HIV/AIDS. Wang and colleagues (2013), examined 100 male and female prisoners recently released from prisons in Texas, California, and Connecticut to explore the relationship between hunger and risky HIV-related behaviors. The researchers found that those ex-offenders who did not eat for an entire day were more likely to use alcohol, heroin, and cocaine prior to sex and engage in prostitution.

Text Box 12.3: State TANF Drug Felon Bans as of July 2015

Full Ban	Modified Ban		No Ban	
AK	AR	MA	AL	VT
AZ	CO	MI	CA	WA
DE	CT	MN	KS	WY
GA	FL	MT	ME	
MS	HI	NV	NH	
MO	ID	NC	NJ	
NE	IL	ND	NM	
SC	IN	OR	NY	
SD	IA	TN	OH	
TX	KY	UT	OK	
VA	LA	WI	PA	
WV	MD		RI	

Source: Mohan, L., & Lower-Basch, E. (2014). *No more double punishments: Lifting the ban on basic human needs help for people with a prior drug felony conviction.* Washington, DC: CLASP.

Cash Assistance

With the passage of the **Personal Responsibility and Work Opportunity Act** in 1996, a revised cash assistance program for those in need, known as Temporary Assistance to Needy Families (TANF) was instituted (Mauer & McCalmont, 2013). Approximately 16 billion dollars is earmarked each year by the federal government and given to states to distribute cash assistance to those in need, such as individuals that are unemployed (Center on Budget and Policy Priorities, 2015). An integral component of the act was the banning of TANF benefits for those individuals only with a felony drug conviction—those convicted of violent felonies against another person are not barred from receiving benefits. Additionally, those offenders who violate their conditions of probation or parole can have their TANF benefits rescinded (McCarty et al., 2015). Depending on the state the ex-offender resides in, the banned TANF benefits could be for a lifetime or it may be a partial ban. Currently, 12 states have imposed lifetime bans on TANF benefits for ex-drug offenders while many other states have allowed former drug offenders to regain TANF benefits after a specified period of time or after successful completion of a drug treatment program (see Text Box 12.3) (Mohan & Lower-Basch, 2014). Many of the states that have implemented modified bans require ex-offenders to be drug-tested (McCarty et al., 2015). Those who fail the drug test may receive a partial suspension of TANF benefits (e.g., six months to one year). In order for the ex-offender to gain benefits back, he/she has to test negative—otherwise, they could face a lifetime ban.

Not surprisingly, the permanent and modified TANF bans have had a disproportionate impact on persons of color, particularly African Americans (Finzen, 2005; Mauer & McCalmont, 2013; Mohan & Lower-Basch, 2014). Once again, female ex-

Text Box 12.4: Estimated Number of Women
Affected by the TANF Ban, 1996–2011

States with Full Ban	
State	Women
Alabama	9,600
Arkansas	1,200
Delaware	2,000
Georgia	56,100
Illinois	18,800
Mississippi	10,500
Missouri	5,200
Nebraska	2,200
South Carolina	5,400
South Dakota	1,400
Texas	65,900
West Virginia	1,800

Source: Mauer, M., & McCalmont, V. (2013). *A lifetime of punishment: The impact of the felony drug ban on welfare.* Washington, DC: The Sentencing Project.

offenders, and their children, are greatly impacted by the TANF bans (Mauer & McCalmont, 2013). Mauer and McCalmont (2013) report that between 1996–2011, approximately 180,000 women were impacted by TANF bans, with women in the states of Texas and Georgia being the hardest hit (see Text Box 12.4). In regards to the children of women ex-offenders, Mauer and McCalmont (2013, p. 4) explain, "Under the terms of the law, in a TANF-eligible household the monthly grant allotment is reduced for the ineligible parent, but is still allowed for that person's children. For example, if a single mother with two dependent children has a felony drug conviction the TANF benefit will be reduced from the three-person level to that of a two person household." Since the monetary allotments dispersed by states are rather low, the additional restriction in benefits the family of convicted women endure only serves to further harm her family.

Housing

For any community corrections offender reintegrating into society, obtaining housing can be difficult. While part of the difficulty stems from gaining employment to pay for the housing, a more significant aspect to their acquisition of housing is the barrier put into place due to their criminal conviction. With a criminal record, many landlords are reluctant to rent to ex-offenders due to their status and/or out of concern of liability (Clark, 2007; Harding & Harding, 2006; Helfgott, 1997). Apart from the stigmatization that blocks housing access, federal legislation has made it increasingly difficult for ex-offenders to find suitable housing (see Text Box 12.5). The blocked access to housing that ex-offenders encounter today is rooted in laws and policies that were implemented during the "War on Drugs" campaign, which took place in the 1980s and 1990s (Silva, 2015). For instance, the passage of the **Anti-Drug Abuse Act of 1988** resulted in federally funded housing being more restrictive as to who was allowed to live in these housing options and also permitted state public housing authorities to further refine their admission policies (Silva, 2015). The end result of this act was that ex-offenders with drug convictions were denied admission (Silva, 2015). Additional federal legislation was passed that further blocked housing for former offenders, including the Cranston-Gonzalez National Affordable Housing Act of 1990, the Housing Opportunity Program Extension Act of 1996, the Quality Housing and Work Responsibility Act of 1998, and the Independent Agencies Appropriations Act of 1999 (Silva, 2015).

The **Cranston-Gonzalez National Affordable Housing Act of 1990** permitted public housing authorities to utilize criminal records when making admission decisions (Silva, 2015). With this provision, those with criminal convictions, not for just drug offenses, found their housing options further limited. Additionally, the **Housing Opportunity Program Extension Act of 1996** further restricted housing options for convicted felons as those ex-offenders who were juveniles at the time of their offense but were charged as adults could be denied housing (Silva, 2015). Further, in 1998, the **Quality Housing and Work Responsibility Act** was passed, which stated that those with one felony conviction, specifically a drug, sex, or violent conviction, would be banned from public housing—this mandate is often referred to as the "one strike" policy for offenders (Hunt, Schulhof, Holmquist, & Solomon, 1998; Mock, 2015). Under the law, states could further refine public housing authority restrictions for residents. Sex offenders, for example, are not welcome in federally public funded housing. McCarty and colleagues (2015, p. 18) explain that all state public housing authorities and property owners that offer "public housing, Section 8 vouchers, and project-based Section 8 are required under federal law to deny admission to the programs to persons subject to lifetime registration on a sex offender registry under a state program" (see Text Box 12.5). The passage of the **Independent Agencies Appropriations Act of 1999** prevents ex-offenders who were involved in methamphetamine production or their family members from being admitted into public housing (Silva, 2015).

Curtis, Garlington, and Schottenfeld (2013) investigated individual state public housing policies in the U.S. and found that for drug-related convictions states have either imposed: (1) no time length ban; (2) a 1–2 year ban; (3) a 3–5 year ban; (4) a 6–10 year ban; (5) or a lifetime ban. The researchers also discovered that for violent crime convictions, state public housing policies followed the same bans imposed as for drug convictions with the addition of a six-month ban as well. It should be noted

Text Box 12.5: Summary of Restrictions

Summary of Federal Drug- and Other Crime-Related Restrictions in Federal Housing Assistance Programs

(denial=denial of admission to applications; termination=termination of assistance and/or tenancy)

Activity	Public Housing	Section 8 Vouchers	Project-Based Section 8
Drug-related criminal activity	Grounds for denial; grounds for termination	Grounds for denial; grounds for termination	Grounds for denial; grounds for termination
Violent criminal activity	Grounds for denial	Grounds for denial; grounds for termination	Grounds for denial
Criminal activity that interferes with health, safety, peaceful enjoyment of other residents	Grounds for denial; grounds for termination	Grounds for denial; grounds for termination	Grounds for denial; grounds for termination
Determined to be currently using illegal drugs	Mandatory denial; grounds for termination	Mandatory denial; grounds for termination	Mandatory denial; grounds for termination
Abuse of drugs or alcohol that interferes with health, safety, peaceful enjoyment of other residents	Grounds for denial; grounds for termination	Grounds for denial; grounds for termination	Grounds for denial; grounds for termination
Subject to lifetime registration on a state sex-offender registry	Mandatory denial	Mandatory denial	Mandatory denial
Convicted of producing methamphetamines on federally assisted property	Mandatory denial; mandatory termination	Mandatory denial; mandatory termination	No provision
Fugitive felon	Grounds for termination	Grounds for termination	Grounds for termination
Drug testing	No provision	No provision	No provision

Source: Table prepared by CRS.

Note: This table summarizes only federal policies. While there may be no federal policies in a given category, local administrators may have adopted a policy in that category using their discretionary authority.

Source: McCarty, M., Falk, G., Aussenberg, R. A., & Carpenter, D. H. (2015). Drug testing and crime-related restrictions in TANF, SNAP, and housing assistance. Retrieved from https://www.fas.org/sgp/crs/misc/R42394.pdf.

that in those states without lifetime bans on housing access, it is really next to impossible for them to actually obtain housing in federally funded facilities. With long waiting lists, often several years-long waiting lists, with those on the lists not having criminal records, ex-offenders are at the very bottom on these lists. Thus, their chances of actually being able to gain access to such housing are very slim.

For individuals residing in public housing who acquire a felony (i.e., drug, sex, violent) conviction, they can expect to be evicted within 30 days and are not entitled to any due process or grievance hearings (Hunt et al., 1998). Additionally, the family of the convicted offender could face eviction from public housing—as if they are somehow culpable by association. If the convicted offender returns to his/her family who are residing in public housing after serving a sentence for that conviction, the family is also at risk of eviction (Mock, 2015). In fact, state public housing authorities can even evict an individual or his/her family based on *suspected* criminal involvement, thus, an arrest or conviction is not necessary (Curtis et al., 2013). DeVuono-Powell, Schweidler, Walters, and Zohrabi (2015) investigated housing barriers for formerly incarcerated individuals and found that 79% of their sample were denied housing and 18% of their families either faced eviction or were denied housing, if they were on a waiting list, when their convicted loved one returned home. Because of the impact the ex-offender's return to home may have on their family, many decide to avoid returning home altogether and seek out other affordable housing options. However, both the denial of housing options mandated by legislation as well as fears of the impact that residing with loved ones may have on them, results in many ex-offenders being left to "choose" undesirable housing options due to the lack of availability of affordable housing and landlords willing to rent to them. For instance, DeVuono-Powell and colleagues (2015, p. 27) report that one of their focus group participants reported, "All of the places that I wanted to live—that were nice and where I could raise kids told me 'no.' So I ended up where I am now, in a rundown four-plex that's a slum with moldy walls." Without suitable housing, ex-offenders must resort to being homeless or residing in an environment (i.e., a high-crime community) that undermines their likelihood of successful rehabilitation and reintegration (Bradley, Oliver, Richardson, & Slayter, 2001; Clear, 2007; 2008; Gunnison & Helfgott, 2013; Kirk, 2009, 2012). Not surprisingly, the ex-offender group hit the hardest by such housing restrictions, particularly drug offenses, are African Americans (Finzen, 2005; Mock, 2015). Thus, restrictive housing policies greatly inhibit this group of ex-offenders from finding suitable housing. It is difficult to obtain an exact figure as to how many African American ex-offenders are impacted by such housing policies, but it definitely has resulted in thousands being denied housing and being pushed into residing in criminogenic neighborhoods (Clear, 2007; United States Government Accountability Office, 2005).

Education

Many ex-offenders have a substantial need for funding for education and failure to receive it makes their ability to successfully reenter society much more difficult. Unfortunately, those with felony convictions, specifically drug convictions, can expect that their access to education will be blocked. In 1965, Congress passed the 1965 **Higher Education Act**, which provided access to higher education to those who could not afford it (ACLU, 2003). However, in 1998, Congress amended the act with the passage of the **Drug Free Student Loans Act** (ACLU, 2003; Finzen, 2005). The act stated that "any person convicted of a federal or state offense involving the possession or sale of drugs is ineligible to receive any grant, loan, or work assistance" to pursue higher education (Finzen 2005, p. 318). Depending on the drug offense, the ban to access for funding may range from a one-year period (e.g., for a first conviction for drug possession) to a lifetime ban (e.g., for a second drug sale conviction or for a third conviction for drug possession) (Finzen, 2005). This law also applies to those drug offenders who were convicted before the enactment of the 1998 act (ACLU, 2003). It should be noted that it is possible for some ex-offenders to regain eligibility to access to funding if they complete a drug treatment program—even if they are not addicted to drugs (ACLU, 2003). Essentially, ex-offenders are screened and then blocked from financial assistance upon filling out the Free Application for Federal Student Aid (FAFSA) form. A question on the form asks the applicants to disclose if they have been convicted of any drug offense (ACLU, 2003). If applicants answer "yes" or fail to answer the question on the application, they are automatically denied financial aid (ACLU, 2003).

While an exact figure as to how many ex-offenders have been impacted by this law is not known, it has been reported that approximately 88,000 individuals have been denied funding due to this act (ACLU, 2003). Once again, this law has dispro- portionately impacted minorities—specifically, African Americans (ACLU, 2003; Finzen, 2005). Since African Americans are more likely to be arrested, due to en- forcement, and ultimately convicted for drug offenses, this group is significantly being blocked from educational advancement, which further hinders their ability to secure employment. Apart from the disparate impact the law has on racial mi- norities, the ACLU (2003) points out that the law is also not fair, as those who have money and a drug conviction can still pursue higher education as they can pay for their education. Thus, ex-offenders' socioeconomic status can play a significant role in whether the door to education can be widened or shut closed. However, ex-of- fenders having the financial means to pay for their education does not automatically result in their ability to pursue higher education. Over 500 colleges and universities in the nation ask applicants about their criminal histories, and this information is used in the admission decision process (Rosenthal et al., 2010). For some ex-offend- ers, just seeing the question on the application is enough to discourage them from even finishing the application. In an examination of criminal history and the college application process, one ex-offender reported, "I felt like it was a waste of time to try to apply when that was one of the first questions asked in the application process" (Rosenthal et al., 2010, p. 16). If ex-offenders answer "yes" to the box about whether they have a criminal history, they will be required to explain their background and provide additional documentation. Sometimes the burden of having to obtain ad- ditional documentation, such as a letter of recommendation from a probation officer or official list of charges filed, often results in ex-offenders giving up on completing their college application altogether (Rosenthal et al., 2010). If ex-offenders hang in there and submit all additional supplemental information as required by the uni- versity, their chances of acceptance to the university is often very low. Because of this reality, many have called for a "ban the box" campaign for college applications as well. For example, in 2015 in New York, the state proposed a Fair Access to Ed- ucation Act, which would disallow colleges from asking applicants about their crim- inal histories and would only allow them to ask applicants about their criminal histories after admission (Blakinger, 2015).

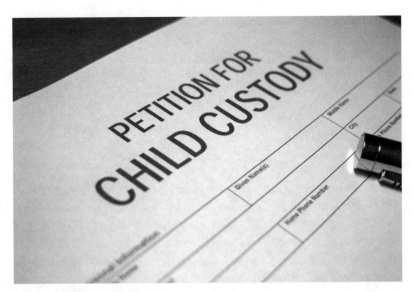

Image 25. © iStockphoto.com/Hailshadow.

Custody

Many ex-offenders lose custody of their children when they are convicted, regardless of whether their punishment is a prison term or a community corrections sentence. Whether ex-offenders are trying to obtain custody of their children after completing a prison sentence or while serving a community corrections sentence, the regaining of custody is another uphill personal battle for ex-offenders. During the 1970s, the courts began to make child custody decisions based on the "best interest of the child" standard (Ahrens, 2000). While there is no legislation preventing ex-offenders from obtaining custody of their children, except for sex offenders, the courts do not necessarily favor awarding custody to the parent who has a criminal record. Citing the "best interest of the child" standard, some courts have assumed that those who have engaged in illegal behavior are also poor parents and have used the parents' criminal record as a way to remove children from their custody or refuse to grant them custody (Ahrens, 2000). For those convicted of non-serious offenses, such as drug possession, they can face difficulties in retaining custody of their children. Ahrens (2000, pp. 771–772) explains, "Drug activity and convictions carry express moral taint. Such activity, standing alone, without other evidence of poor parental skills or any evidence that children have been exposed to drug use or trade, may terminate all parental rights. The mere fact of conviction even in the absence of physical incarceration has also been determined to constitute the sort of 'change of circumstance' requiring review of custody arrangements." Thus, ex-offenders may be denied custody, not based on how they treated their children, but because they are viewed as somehow unsuitable due to their conviction status.

In sum, ex-offenders face a wide range of barriers that directly impede their ability to successfully reintegrate back into their communities. These personal barriers experienced by ex-offenders, such as no food or cash assistance, blocked employment opportunities, and lack of access to higher education, are substantial and severe enough to further make the task of reentry more difficult. All too often, the barriers put in place for ex-offenders ultimately end up not just harming them but also their families. Unfortunately, such personal difficulties are just the tip of the iceberg as ex-offenders will also find that they lose valuable civic rights as well due to their conviction status.

Civic Consequences

Voting

Imagine not being able to vote. It is one of those fundamental rights that we don't think about too often unless we are unable or not permitted to do so. The push for extending the right to vote for all citizens has occurred in the United States for over 100 years. One of the first major challenges to voting laws occurred in the early 1900s when women pressed for the right to vote. It was not until the passage of the Nineteenth Amendment in 1920 that women were provided with a constitutional right to vote (Baker, 2002). However, it took longer for other marginalized groups in society to be afforded this right. The passage of the **Voting Rights Act of 1965** resulted in granting minorities, particularly African Americans, the right to vote (Manza, Brooks, & Uggen, 2004). Prior to the passage of this law, African Americans were not allowed to vote in state and local elections. On the surface, it would seem that the implementation of the act would eliminate the disparity experienced by African Americans in regards to their ability to exercise their civil rights. Still, this act did not grant ex-felons the opportunity to vote as the act extended to only law-abiding citizens who did not have prior records. This omission of granting ex-felons the right to vote severely impacted

Image 26. © Burlingham/Fotolia.

African Americans who at the time, and still today, are overrepresented in the criminal justice system. Essentially, the disallowing of ex-felons the opportunity to vote further marginalized an already disenfranchised group in U.S. society (Wheelock, 2005).

Felon disenfranchisement refers to barriers placed on the ability of individuals to participate in the democratic process due to their felony convictions (Chung, 2014). Such disenfranchisement has not gone unnoticed in society, and there have been legal challenges to barring ex-felons from voting. For instance, in *Richardson v. Ramirez* in 1974, three ex-felons from California sued for their right to vote, noting that their rights under the Fourteenth Amendment were violated (Chung, 2014). Chung (2014, p. 3) explains that "Under Section 1 of the Fourteenth Amendment, a state cannot restrict voting rights unless it shows a compelling state interest." Despite the constitutional challenge, the Supreme Court upheld the denial for ex-felons to vote.

Today, just under 6 million U.S. citizens, who have been convicted of felonies, are denied the opportunity to vote (Chung, 2014). According to Chung (2014), there are 12 states that do not permit ex-felons to vote even after they have served their prison sentence and are no longer under the custody of community corrections sanctions, such as probation and parole (see Figure 12.6). In fact, Chung (2014, p. 1) states that "individuals in those states make up approximately 45 percent of the entire disenfranchised population." The impact of such laws on African Americans cannot be overstated, as such laws result in 1 in every 13 African Americans being denied the right to vote (Chung, 2014). A few states, such as Florida, Kentucky, and Virginia, impose a lifetime ban on voting for ex-felons (see Figure 12.6) (Chung, 2014). Uggen, Shannon, and Manza (2012) report that such bans result in the following African American disenfranchisement rates: Florida (23%), Kentucky, (22%), and Virginia (20%). For Hispanic American ex-offenders, Martinez (2004) explains that the exact rates of voting disenfranchisement for this group cannot be determined, however, he states that not allowing these ex-offenders to vote sends a message to them that they are "second-class citizens" and further inhibit their ability to successfully reenter society. Miller and Spillane (2012a) investigated the impact of the loss of voting to ex-offender reintegration. One subject in their study stated, "I still consider myself an American citizen even though the Government doesn't feel that way. I still believe in hope and prosperity although it's getting thinner and thinner. I start to wonder if all I am trying to do is for nothing … not being able to vote at all you might as well be stuck at the back of the class" (Miller & Spillane, 2012a, p. 415).

Given the racial inequality that exists in the criminal justice system, questions have been raised as to whether such bans could be instituted in an equitable manner (Munn, 2011). Currently, Chung (2014) reports that only two states, Maine and Vermont, have not placed any restrictions on voting for ex-offenders—even those is prison (see Figure 12.6).

Despite such laws, the American public does not appear to be supportive of such policies (Manza et al., 2004). Because of this, many states have modified their voting laws to allow for more ex-felons to be granted the right to vote. Chung (2014) reports that since 1997, 23 states have modified their voting laws, resulting in approximately

Figure 12.6: Felony Disenfranchisement by State, 2014

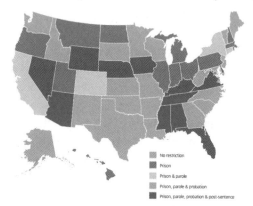

Source: Chung, J. (2014). *Felony disenfranchisement: A primer.* Washington, DC: The Sentencing Project.

800,000 ex-offenders, who once were ineligible to vote, being granted the opportunity to vote. Most recently, in 2015, the state of Wyoming modified their voting laws to allow ex-offenders who have been convicted of a first-time non-violent felony offense, to automatically be able to have their voting rights restored (Chung, 2014). Each state and country differs in regards to if, when, and how ex-offenders are able to restore their voting rights (see Text Box 12.7).

Text Box 12.7: Barriers Experienced by Ex-Offenders: An International Glance

The experiences of ex-offenders being blocked access to rights is not unique to U.S. ex-offenders. Rather, ex-offenders in other countries also face barriers due to their conviction status. For instance, in Ireland, ex-offenders face much employment discrimination as a result of their criminal record (O'Reilly, 2014). Without laws preventing employer discrimination of ex-offenders in Ireland, these former offenders face increased difficulties in obtaining jobs and reintegrating back into their communities. Additionally, in many European countries, ex-offenders also lose their rights to participate in the civic process. However, the policies vary between countries, with some allowing access to voting and others restricting such rights. Home and White (2015) report that prisoners are denied the opportunity to vote in Belgium for a period of time ranging anywhere from permanently (e.g., for those serving life sentences) to 5–30 years, and those ex-offenders who are not sentenced to imprisonment can also lose access to voting for 5–10 years. Decisions regarding voting restrictions are determined by a judge. For ex-offenders in Italy, anyone serving a life sentence is permanently banned from voting while other ex-felons, after release, can be banned from voting for a specified period of time (Home & White, 2015). On the other hand, prisoners and ex-offenders can participate in the voting process unless the crime they committed was against the government, such as terrorism (Home & White, 2015).

Jury Service

With restrictions on ex-offenders in place to stymie their participation in the voting process, it should probably come as no surprise that ex-offenders are excluded from participation in other civil processes, such as serving on a jury (Finzen, 2005; Kalt, 2003; Roberts, 2013). Although ex-felon exclusion from jury duty has been challenged in the courts as being unconstitutional or as a violation of the **Equal Protection Clause** of the Fourteenth Amendment, the denial of this civil service opportunity has been upheld for this group (Kalt, 2003). Depending on the state in which ex-offenders reside, they may endure a lifetime ban on being able to serve on a jury (see Text Box 12.8) (Kalt, 2003; Roberts, 2013). At the federal level, ex-offenders are barred for life from jury duty (Kalt, 2003; Roberts, 2013).

There have been several arguments or rationales proposed for the exclusion of ex-offenders from participating in jury duty, including (1) the ex-offenders would be biased jury members; (2) since ex-offenders broke the law, they should be excluded from participation in the law process; and (3) ex-offenders would not be impartial and perhaps be more "pro-defense" (Binnall, 2014; Kalt, 2003). On the other hand, many argue that the exclusion of ex-offenders from jury duty results in a potential jury pool that is not representative of the actual community (Kalt, 2003). That is, a jury pool without ex-offenders does not reflect the community or jurisdiction that it is serving. Regardless of the arguments, Roberts (2013) asserts that ex-offender exclusion from jury duty results in three harms: (1) racial disparity, (2) loss of experience, and (3) non-adherence to reintegrative goals. In regards to racial disparity, Kalt (2003) reports that lifetime bans on jury service result in approximately 30% of African American men being excluded from this civic duty. Wheelock (2011), in an investigation of ex-felon jury exclusion in the state of Georgia, found that African Americans were disproportionately impacted. Other scholars have also uncovered that such bans have resulted in a disproportionate number of Latinos and Latinas being excluded from jury duty service (see Johnson, 2005). Roberts (2013) explains that the exclusion of minorities on jury duty has further ramifications. With fewer potential persons of color to serve on juries for defendants of color, convictions for minority defendants may increase due to discrimination. As Roberts (2013) points out, studies have found that the "whiter" the jury, the more likely the jury is to convict defendants of color.

The second harm, the loss of experience, refers to the fact that exclusion of ex-offenders from jury service denies the opportunity of a differing perspective, or voice, to be considered. After all, an ex-offender who has journeyed through the criminal justice system can put forth ideas and concepts not perhaps considered by the average citizen. For example, Roberts (2013) explains that a citizen may not understand how an innocent person could confess to a crime—perhaps erroneously thinking that he/she would never confess to crime that he/she did not do. However, a former offender could enlighten the citizen of the jury about police interrogation practices and how it is indeed possible for this to occur. Finally, the third harm caused by ex-offender exclusion from jury duty is that such exclusionary policies can undermine reentry. Ex-offenders are instructed to assimilate or reintegrate into society and become law-abiding citizens. Yet, ex-offenders are also sent the message that, even if they are successfully reintegrating into society, they aren't really accepted back into society fully as there are limitations placed on their participation in their civic communities. Roberts (2013, p. 612) states that such exclusions send the message to ex-offenders that " 'you do not belong'—and in many instances 'you will never belong.' "

Text Box 12.8: State Policies on Jury Duty

State	Ban	State	Ban
Alabama	Life	Montana	Life
Alaska	During supervision	Nebraska	Life
Arizona	Life (repeat offenders) or during sentence (first offenders)	Nevada	Life
Arkansas	Life	New Hampshire	Life
California	Life	New Jersey	Life
Colorado	No exclusion for petit juries; life for grand juries	New Mexico	Life
Connecticut	During incarceration or seven years from conviction, whichever is longer	New York	Life
Delaware	Life	North Carolina	During supervision
Florida	Life	North Dakota	During incarceration
Georgia	Life	Ohio	Life
Hawaii	Life	Oklahoma	Life
Idaho	During supervision	Oregon	During incarceration plus fifteen years (criminal and grand juries) or during in- carceration (civil juries)
Illinois	Life	Pennsylvania	Life
Indiana	During sentence	Rhode Island	During supervision
Iowa	Challengeable for cause (for life)	South Carolina	Life
Kansas	During supervision or ten years from conviction, whichever is longer	South Dakota	During supervision
Kentucky	Life	Tennessee	Life
Louisiana	Life	Texas	Life
Maine	No exclusion	Utah	Life
Maryland	Life	Vermont	Life
Massachusetts	During incarceration or seven years from conviction, whichever is longer; removable for cause for life	Virginia	Life
Michigan	Life	Washington	During supervision (life if committed before July 1984)
Minnesota	During sentence	West Virginia	Life
Mississippi	Life	Wisconsin	During sentence
Missouri	Life	Wyoming	Life

Source: Kalt, B. C. (2003). The exclusion of felons from jury service. *American University Law Review, 53*(1), 65–189.

Political Office

With bans on voting and serving on juries for formerly convicted felony offenders, it will likely come as no surprise that ex-offenders are also blocked from holding positions in the political arena (Hull, 2009). Steinacker (2003) explains that the ability of ex-offenders convicted of a felony to hold a particular political office position varies by state law. In fact, Steinacker (2003) explains that the laws can be categorized as follows: (1) states that have no bans; (2) states that require that an offender must have completed his/her sentence before running for office; (3) states that allow an offender to run for an office if he/she has received a pardon or has had his/her civil rights restored; (4) states that require voter qualification in order to run for office; (5) states with a waiting period; (6) states that automatically disallow an ex-offender running for office; and (7) states that will disallow an ex-offender from pursuing a political office depending on their conviction (e.g., those convicted of bribery would be excluded). At the constitutional level, Steinacker (2003) explains that the Supreme Court has upheld that state bans and restrictions regarding running for political office is allowed and, thus, not unconstitutional. Such bans and restrictions at the state level have had a disproportionate impact on minority ex-offenders (Hull, 2009).

At the federal level, there are only three constitutional qualifications that need to be met in order for a citizen to run for office: (1) age, (2) residency, and (3) citizenship (Steinacker, 2003). While there have been Supreme Court challenges at the federal level to impose restrictions on ex-offenders running for Congress, the court has maintained that "Congress has no power to alter the qualifications in the text of the Constitution" (Steinacker, 2003, p. 801). Therefore, the three original qualifications for serving in a political office at the federal level stand and no modifications of requirements can be made without an amendment to the Constitution.

In sum, those convicted of felonies in the United States are blocked from participating in many fundamental civil activities such as voting, participating in jury duty, and even running for, or holding, a political office. Other obstacles include barriers to owning a firearm, serving in the Armed Forces, operating a private aircraft, and even traveling (Smith & Kramer, 2012). The chief problem with such barriers is that formerly convicted felony offenders are enduring additional layers of punishment after successfully serving their sentences. Even more importantly, such laws disproportionately impact minorities, resulting in segments of U.S. society, whom are directly impacted by the criminal justice system, being powerless to affect and implement changes.

Restoration of Rights

Those ex-offenders who have lost their civil rights (i.e., voting, jury duty, or eligibility to run for a political office) due to their felony conviction, can go through a **rights restoration process** which will result in the reestablishment of their formerly stripped rights. Each state may differ in regards to the restoration of rights policies and procedures. In the state of Florida, for example, depending on the felony offense, the process for rights restoration differs and depends on the level of seriousness of the offense committed (i.e., Level 1, 2, or 3) (Miller & Spillane, 2012b). For those ex-offenders convicted of Level 1, or non-serious felonies, such as non-violent offenses, the Florida Department of Corrections automatically sends a list of their names to the Probation and Parole Commission, who then investigates whether the sentence was completed in full (including all of the probation or parole sentence), if there are any outstanding criminal charges pending, and whether all restitution orders have been paid in full (Miller & Spillane, 2012b). If Level 1 ex-offenders are cleared by the commission, their rights are automatically restored, and, if, for some reason, their names are not cleared, then they have to seek restoration of their rights on their own. These ex-offenders; Level 2 ex-offenders, those convicted or serious felonies except murder or rape; and Level 3 ex-offenders, those convicted of murder or rape, in Florida, are required to first complete an application in order for the civil rights restoration process to begin (Miller & Spillane, 2012b). Once ex-offenders have filed the paperwork, the restoration of rights process may proceed with or without a formal hearing (Miller & Spillane, 2012b). Text Box 12.9 outlines the two processes in Florida in detail.

Text Box 12.9: Civil Rights Restoration Process in Florida

<u>RESTORATION OF CIVIL RIGHTS *WITHOUT* A HEARING CASES:</u> This type of investigation is designed to process less serious offenses and requires <u>that 5 years have passed since the date of completion of all sentences and conditions of supervision imposed for all felony convictions, and you must remain crime and arrest free for 5 years prior to being reviewed by the Florida Commission on Offender Review</u>. You are also required to <u>provide certified court documents for EACH felony conviction</u> with the application before it will be entered into our system. A certified court document is a copy of the original document on file with the applicable agency (Clerk of Court, State Attorney's Office, Law Enforcement Agency, etc.) which bears the Clerk's original signature and seal attesting that the document is a true and correct copy of the original. The court documents can be obtained from the Clerk of Court in the county where the offense occurred and consist of the charging document (often referred to as the State Attorney Information or Indictment); Judgment; and Sentence/Community Control/Probation Order.

<u>RESTORATION OF CIVIL RIGHTS *WITH* A HEARING CASES:</u> This type of investigation is designed to process the more serious offenses and requires that <u>7 years have passed since the date of completion of all sentences and conditions of supervision imposed for all felony convictions.</u> You are also required to <u>provide certified court documents for EACH felony conviction</u> with the application before it will be entered into our system. The court documents can be obtained from the Clerk of Court in the county where the offense occurred as stated above.

During the investigative phase, the Executive Clemency Board will consider, but not be limited to, the following factors when determining whether to grant an applicant restoration of civil rights or other form of clemency.

- The nature and circumstances of the offense
- Prior and subsequent criminal record, including traffic offenses
- Employment history
- Mental health, drug, or alcohol issues
- Domestic violence issues
- Letters submitted in support of, or in opposition to, the granting of executive clemency

The information this agency requests from you is necessary to provide the basic facts needed by the Clemency Board to make an informed judgment as to whether or not you should be granted Restoration of Civil Rights or any other form of clemency.

Source: Florida Department of Corrections. (2011). Restoration of civil rights. *Office of Executive Clemency.* Retrieved from http://www.dc.state.fl.us/restoration.html.

For Level 2 ex-offenders in Florida, their files are reviewed by the Probation and Parole Commission. If their files require a case review, then their file is sent to the Executive Clemency Board (ECB) for formal review, hearing, and decision (Miller & Spillane, 2012b). Miller and Spillane (2012b) further explain that such hearings are closed to the public. In their investigation of the rights restoration process in Florida, Miller and Spillane (2012b) found that an ex-offender's parole recommendation, attendance at the hearing, and victim representation at the hearing had a significant impact as to whether rights were restored. Further, the researchers found that the victim representation had the largest impact as to whether civil rights were restored for ex-offenders, suggesting that the victim representation during this process can perhaps have a prejudicial impact on the ECB's final decision (Miller & Spillane, 2012b).

Perhaps the best solution to restore civil rights for all ex-offenders is the implementation of laws that will no longer disenfranchise them. Rather than restricting ex-offenders to civic participation or requiring them to jump through enormous hoops to restore their rights, laws that can be implemented that can eliminate this disenfranchisement. In 2015, the **Democracy Restoration Act** was introduced into Congress with the aims of: (1) restoring federal voting rights to ex-offenders; (2) making sure probationers can vote in federal elections; and (3) ensuring that all ex-offenders are notified about their right to vote in federal elections when leaving prison or when sentenced to a community corrections sanction (ACLU, 2015). If this law is enacted, this is one step to reducing the disenfranchisement of ex-offenders. As this law addresses federal voting, more work would need to be done at the state level to ensure that ex-offenders are able to vote within the states in which they reside. With substantial media coverage of disenfranchisement impacting ex-offenders, it is possible for the public to become aware of policies that harm ex-offenders and perhaps prompt them to join scholars in the fight to remove these barriers for ex-offenders (Campbell, 2007; Crutchfield, 2007; Uggen, Manza & Thompson, 2006). Finally, restoring voting rights is just one aspect of the rights that ex-offenders have lost due to their conviction status. Therefore, more work needs to be done to restore *all* of their civic rights that have been lost.

Conclusion

In sum, this chapter devoted attention to the invisible punishments and collateral consequences of being convicted, such as barriers to employment, housing, and financial assistance as well as the civil and political barriers convicted offenders face and the impact their status has on others. Additionally, this chapter discussed some of the steps that ex-offenders can take to begin to restore their rights. With successful reentry a focus for the public and policymakers alike, laws and policies at both the state and federal levels must be revised to remove the continued punishments as well as disenfranchisement that is being experienced by ex-offenders after they complete their punishments and to assist them in reintegrating back into society (Pinard, 2010).

Key Terms

Anti-Drug Abuse Act of 1988

Collateral Consequences

Cranston-Gonzalez National Affordable Housing Act of 1990

Democracy Restoration Act

Drug Free Student Loans Act

Equal Protection Clause

Federal Welfare Law of 1996

Felon disenfranchisement

Higher Education Act

Housing Opportunity Program Extension Act of 1996

Independent Agencies Appropriations Act of 1999

Personal Responsibility and Work Opportunity Act

Quality Housing and Work Responsibility Act

Rights restoration process

Voting Rights Act of 1965

Discussion Questions

1. Research the personal and civil barriers for ex-offenders in your state. What laws exist in your state that may limit ex-offender reintegration?

2. Develop suggested policy recommendations to present to legislators in your state to remove the personal and civil barriers for ex-offenders. Be clear on your ideas and explain how initial small steps may result in large gains for ex-offenders, their families, and their communities.

3. How to you feel about lifetime bans on engagement in the civic process? Think about such bans and discuss your thoughts on the topic with another classmate.

4. Research the policies and procedures for the restoration of civil rights in the state in which you reside. What recommendations do you have for policymakers about the process that may better assist ex-offenders in restoring their civil rights?

References

ACLU. (2003). *Collateral consequences of the war on drugs.* New Haven, CT: Drug Policy Litigation Project.

ACLU. (2015). *ACLU factsheet on the Democracy Restoration Act of 2015.* Retrieved from https://www.aclu.org/fact-sheet/aclu-factsheet-democracy-restoration-act-2015.

Ahrens, D. (2000). Not in front of the children: Prohibition on child custody as civil branding for criminal activity. *New York University Law Review, 75*(3), 737–774.

Appelbaum, B. (2015, February 28). Out of trouble, but criminal records keep men out of work. *The New York Times.* Retrieved from http://www.nytimes.com/2015/03/01/business/out-of-trouble-but-criminal-records-keep-men-out-of-work.html?_r=0.

Archer, D. N., & Williams, K. S. (2006). Making America "the land of second chances": Restoring economic rights for ex-offenders. *NYU Review of Law & Social Change, 30*, 527–536.

Baker, J. H. (2002). *Votes for women: The struggle for suffrage revisited.* New York, NY: Oxford University Press.

Binnall, J. M. (2014). A field study of the presumptively biased: Is there empirical support for excluding convicted felons from jury service? *Law & Policy, 36*(1), 1–34. doi: 10.1111/lapo.12015.

Blakinger, K. (2015, June 21). Why colleges should admit more ex-felons. *Washington Post.* Retrieved from https://www.washingtonpost.com/posteverything/wp/2015/06/21/why-colleges-should-admit-more-ex-felons/.

Bradley, K. H., Oliver, R. B. M., Richardson, N. C., & Slayter, E. (2001). *No place like home: Housing and the ex-prisoner.* Boston, MA: Community Resources for Justice.

Bushway, S. D., & Sweeten, G. (2007). Abolish lifetime bans for ex-felons. *Criminology & Public Policy, 6*(4), 697–706. doi: 10.1111/j.1745-9133.2007.00466.x.

Campbell, M. C. (2007). Criminal disenfranchisement reform in California: A deviant case study. *Punishment & Society, 9*(2), 177–199. doi: 10.1177/1462474507074748.

Center on Budget and Policy Priorities. (2015). *Policy basics: An introduction to TANF.* Retrieved from http://www.cbpp.org/research/policy-basics-an-introduction-to-tanf Center on Juvenile and Criminal Justice. (2016). *Northern California service league.* Retrieved from http://www.cjcj.org/about/northern-california-service-league.html.

Chung, J. (2014). *Felony disenfranchisement: A primer.* Washington, DC: The Sentencing Project.

Clark, L. M. (2007). Landlord attitudes toward renting to released offenders. *Federal Probation, 71*(1), 20–30.

Clear, T. R. (2007). *Imprisoning communities: How mass incarceration makes disadvantaged neighborhoods worse.* New York, NY: Oxford University Press.

Clear, T. R. (2008). The effects of high imprisonment rates on communities. *Crime & Justice, 37*(1), 97–132. doi: 10.1086/522360.

Cohen, R. (2014, April 10). 10 states enforce lifetime food stamp bans for drug-related felonies. *Nonprofit Quarterly.* Retrieved from https://nonprofitquarterly.org/2014/04/10/10-states-enforce-lifetime-food-stamp-bans-for-drug-related-felonies/.

Crutchfield, R. D. (2007). Abandon felon disenfranchisement policies. *Criminology & Public Policy, 6*(4), 707–715. doi: 10.1111/j.1745-9133.2007.00483.x.

Curtis, M. A., Garlington, S., & Schottenfeld, L. S. (2013). Alcohol, drug, and criminal history restrictions in public housing. *Cityscape: A Journal of Policy Development and Research, 37*(3), 37–52.

DePillis, L. (2015, January 22). Millions of ex-cons still can't get jobs. Here's how the White House could help fix that. *The Washington Post.* Retrieved from https://www.washingtonpost.com/news/storyline/wp/2015/01/22/millions-of-ex-cons-still-cant-get-jobs-heres-how-the-white-house-could-help-fix-that/.

DeVuono-Powell, S., Schweidler, C., Walters, A., & Zohrabi, A. (2015). *Who pays? The true cost of incarceration on families.* Oakland, CA: Ella Baker Center, Forward Together, Research Action Design.

Fair Shake Reentry Resource Center. (2016). *Formerly and currently incarcerated people.* Retrieved from https://www.fairshake.net/formerfelons/.

Finzen, M. E. (2005). Systems of oppression: The collateral consequences of incarceration and their effects on Black communities. *Georgetown Journal on Poverty Law & Policy, 12*(2), 299–324.

Florida Department of Corrections. (2011). Restoration of civil rights. *Office of Executive Clemency.* Retrieved from http://www.dc.state.fl.us/restoration.html.

Gunnison, E., & Helfgott, J. B. (2013). *Offender reentry: Beyond crime and punishment.* Boulder, CO: Lynne Rienner.

Harding, A., & Harding, J. (2006). Inclusion and exclusion in the re-housing of former prisoners. *Probation Journal, 53*(2), 137–153. doi: 10.1177/0264550506063566.

Helfgott, J. B. (1997). Ex-offender needs versus criminal opportunity in Seattle, Washington. *Federal Probation, 61,* 12–24. doi: 10.1177/0264550506063566.

Home, A., & White, I. (2015). *Prisoners' voting rights (2005 to May 2015).* Parliament: U.K. Retrieved from http://researchbriefings.parliament.uk/ResearchBriefing/Summary/SN01764.

Hull, E. (2009). *The disenfranchisement of ex-felons.* Philadelphia, PA: Temple University Press.

Hunt, L., Schulhof, M., Holmquist, S., & Solomon, R. (1998). *Summary of the Quality Housing and Work Responsibility Act of 1998.* Retrieved from https://portal.hud.gov/hudportal/documents/huddoc?id=DOC_8927.pdf.

Johnson, K. R. (2005). *Hernandez v. Texas*: Legacies of justice and injustice. *Chicano-Latino Law Review, 25,* 153–200. doi: 10.2139/ssrn.625403.

Kalt, B. C. (2003). The exclusion of felons from jury service. *American University Law Review, 53*(1), 65–189.

Kirk, D. S. (2009). A natural experiment on residential change and recidivism: Lessons from Hurricane Katrina. *American Sociological Review, 74*(3), 484–505. doi: 10.1177/000312240907400308.

Kirk, D. S. (2012). Residential change as a turning point in the life course of crime: Desistance or temporary cessation. *Criminology, 50*(2), 329–358. doi: 10.1111/j.1745-9125.2011.00262.x.

Manza, J., Brooks, C., & Uggen, C. (2004). Public attitudes toward felon disenfranchisement in the United States. *Public Opinion Quarterly, 68*(2), 275–286.

Martinez, D. J. (2004). Felony disenfranchisement and voting participation: Considerations in Latino ex-prisoner reentry. *Columbia Human Rights Law Review, 36*(1), 217–240.

Mauer, M., & McCalmont, V. (2013). *A lifetime of punishment: The impact of the felony drug ban on welfare.* Washington, DC: The Sentencing Project.

McCarty, M., Falk, G., Aussenberg, R. A., & Carpenter, D. H. (2015). Drug testing and crime-related restrictions in TANF, SNAP, and housing assistance. Retrieved from https://www.fas.org/sgp/crs/misc/R42394.pdf.

Miller, B. L., & Spillane, J. F. (2012a). Civil death: An examination of ex-felon disenfranchisement and reintegration. *Punishment & Society, 14*(4), 402–428. doi: 10.1177/1462474512452513.

Miller, B. L., & Spillane, J. F. (2012b). Governing the restoration of civil rights for ex-felons: An evaluation of the Executive Clemency Board in Florida. *Contemporary Justice Review, 15*(4), 414–434. doi: 10.1080/10282580.2012.734568.

Mock, B. (2015, September 18). Should people with criminal histories be banned from public housing? *The Atlantic City Lab.* Retrieved from http://www.citylab.com/crime/2015/09/should-people-with-criminal-histories-be-banned-from-public-housing/406015/.

Mohan, L., & Lower-Basch, E. (2014). *No more double punishments: Lifting theban on basic human needs help for people with a prior drug felony conviction.* Washington, DC: CLASP.

Mukamal, D. A. (2000). Confronting the employment barriers of criminal records: Effective legal and practical strategies. *Journal of Poverty Law and Policy, (January–February),* 597–606.

Munn, N. (2011). The limits of criminal disenfranchisement. *Criminal Justice Ethics, 30*(3), 223–239. doi: 10.1080/0731129X.2011.628826.

National Legal Center. (2015). *Helping individuals with criminal records reenter through employment.* Retrieved from http://www.hirenetwork.org/.

Office of County Clerk. (2013, June 20). City of Seattle legislative information service. *Seattle.gov*. Retrieved from http://clerk.ci.seattle.wa.us/~scripts/nphbrs.exe?s3= 117796+&s4=&s5=&s1=&s2=&S6=&Sect4=AND&l=0&Sect2=THESON&Sect3= PLURON&Sect5=CBORY&Sect6=HITOFF&d=ORDF&p=1&u=%2F~public%2 Fcbor1.htm&r=1&f=G.

O'Reilly, M. F. (2014). Opening doors or closing them?: The impact of incarceration on the education and employability of ex-offenders in Ireland. *The Howard Journal of Criminal Justice, 53*(5), 468–486. doi: 10.1111/hojo.12086.

Parker, C. (2005, October 22). Schuylkill takes WolfHawk baby boy. *The Morning Call*. Retrieved from http://articles.mcall.com/2005-10-22/news/3641722_1_ daishin-wolfhawk-custody-county-s-child-welfare-agency.

Parker, C. (2006, October 19). Boy turns 1 as court battle of parents, Schuylkill lingers. *The Morning Call*. Retrieved from http://articles.mcall.com/2006-10-19/ news/3704774_1_custody-case-baby-schuylkill-county-s-children.

Pettinato, T. R. (2014). Defying "common sense"?: The legitimacy of applying Title VII to employer criminal records policies. *Nevada Law Journal, 14*(3), 770–784.

Pinard, M. (2010). Reflections and perspectives on reentry and collateral consequences. *Journal of Criminal Law & Criminology, 100*(3), 1213–1224.

Roberts, A. (2013). Casual ostracism: Jury exclusion on the basis of criminal convictions. *Minnesota Law Review, 98*, 592–647.

Rosenthal, A., Warth, P., Wolf, E., & Messina-Yauchzy, M. (2010). *The use of criminal history records in college admissions*. Syracuse, NY: Center for Community Alternatives.

Scolforo, M. (2005, October 11). Sex offender's wife in child custody fight. *The Free Republic*. Retrieved from http://www.freerepublic.com/focus/f-news/1500580/posts.

The Sentencing Project. (2016). *Collateral consequences*. Retrieved from http://www. sentencingproject.org/template/page.cfm?id=143.

Silva, L. (2015). Criminal histories in public housing. *Wisconsin Law Review, 2*, 375–397.

Smialek, J. (2014, January 30). Ex-convict hire hurdle draws U.S. suits against employers. *Bloomberg Business*. Retrieved from http://www.bloomberg.com/news/ articles/2014-01-31/ex-convict-hire-hurdle-draws-u-s-suits-against-employers.

Smith, W. S., & Kramer, J. M. (2012). *Consequences of a federal felony conviction*. Retrieved from http://www.smithkramerlaw.com/Article_Consequences-of-a-Federal-Felony-Conviction.asp.

Steinacker, A. (2003). The prisoner's campaign: Felony disenfranchisement laws and the right to hold public office. *Brigham Young Law Review, 2*, 801–828.

Uggen, C., Manza, J., & Thompson, M. (2006). Citizenship, democracy, and the civic reintegration of criminal offenders. *Annals of the American Academy of Political & Social Science, 605*, 281–310. doi: 10.1177/0002716206286898.

Uggen, C., Shannon, S., & Manza, J. (2012). *State-level estimates of felon disenfranchisement in the United States.* Washington, DC: The Sentencing Project.

United States Government Accountability Office. (2005). *Drug offenders: Various factors may limit the impacts of federal laws that provide for denial of selected benefits.* Washington, DC: U.S. Government Accountability Office.

Wang, E. A., Zhu, G. A., Evans, L., Carroll-Scott, A., Desai, R., & Fiellin, L. E. (2013). A pilot study examining food insecurity and HIV risk behaviors among individuals recently released from prison. *AIDS Education and Prevention, 25*(2), 112–123.

Weisenfeld, D. B. (2013, November 5). Seattle ban the box law expanded to include private employers. *XpertHR.* Retrieved from http://www.xperthr.com/news/seattle-ban-the-box-law-expanded-to-include-private-employers/11760/.

Wheelock, D. (2005). Collateral consequences and racial inequality: Felon status restrictions as a system of disadvantage. *Journal of Contemporary Criminal Justice, 21*(1), 82–90. doi: 10.1177/1043986204271702.

Wheelock, D. (2011). A jury of one's "peers": The racial impact of felon jury exclusion in Georgia. *Justice System Journal, 32*(3), 335–359.

Chapter 13

Looking Ahead:
The Future Trends in
Community Corrections

Student Learning Outcomes

After reading this chapter, you should be able to:

- Identify future trends in community corrections.
- Describe the various forms of technology that are being utilized in community corrections today to monitor and manage ex-offenders.
- Summarize the principle needs of community corrections offenders.

Introduction

Believe it or not, there once was a time when social media did not exist. Yes, there was life before *The Kardashians*! How did people of the pre-social media era survive? For those of us who grew up without it, we are often pretty thankful that we did not have it during our adolescence and early adulthood years. While many of us were able to avoid social media earlier in our lives, today, we have embraced it. Think about the social media sites that you subscribe to. While college students today may be less likely to use Facebook, many still have accounts and are active users. Other students may be more likely to maintain Twitter, Instagram, or Snapchat accounts. Of course, additional students may have LinkedIn, Pinterest, Yik Yak, Vine, Tumblr, and even Tinder accounts. Should we expect that ex-offenders don't have these accounts? Probably not, and community corrections officers are now primed and ready to "mine" the accounts of their clients' social media sites to determine if they are maintaining compliance with court-ordered conditions. For instance, probation officers in Boston are actively conducting "virtual home visits" by reviewing their clients' social media postings (Sweeney, 2012). Oftentimes, the probation officers are unable to review the social media postings on their work computers as access to such sites are typically blocked by the office networks. Thus, these officers are reviewing the postings after office hours on their own home computers, or in some cases, officers bring their own personal laptops or tablets to the office and scour the postings on their personal devices (Sweeney, 2012). 50 Cent, while not on probation, recently got into hot water with the courts when he began posting pictures of himself with large stacks of money on Instagram (Jagannathan, 2016). Certainly, that is not a crime, but the problem that the courts had with his postings is that he had filed for bankruptcy. His social media postings required him to report to court and explain why, if he was broke and indeed $53 million dollars in debt, he had stacks of money picture postings on his social media account (Jagannathan, 2016).

Reflect, for a moment, on what information probationers may post online that might be useful to probation officers. As one probation officer states, "Juveniles have a tendency not to be bright about what they post. Many times I've gotten kids posting pictures of themselves using drugs, pictures of themselves with alcohol.... Kids are tweeting all the time, 'I just got high'" (Sweeney, 2012). The juvenile probationers are postings such images or making such statements on their social media accounts despite the fact that they *know* their probation officer is monitoring their accounts (Sweeney, 2012). In other cases, the probationer may abscond and the officer can review various social media accounts to get clues about his/her whereabouts in hopes of bringing the probationer back into custody (Sweeney, 2012). Boston probationer officers are not alone in their use of social media, as such monitoring is being used by community corrections agencies across the nation (Russo & Matz, 2014). In fact, results of an American Probation and Parole Association survey of members revealed that agencies were using social media in the following ways: (1) viewing public pages to look for clients, (2) requiring clients to open his/her accounts at meetings so that the officer can review them, (3) creating a pseudo identity to monitor their clients covertly, and (4) sending "friend" requests to their clients in order to be able to effectively monitor their private postings (Russo & Matz, 2014). Thus, social media has greatly assisted community corrections officers in their supervision efforts of clients.

Community corrections has burgeoned over the past several decades and will continue to do so over the next several decades, thus, its place in the correctional system has a firm foothold. The final chapter in the text provides a glimpse into the future trends in community corrections, including into the role of technology and its use within community corrections. Additionally, discussion regarding the steps that are currently being taken or need to be implemented to assist both offenders and practitioners within community corrections will be addressed. Finally, a discussion of what is needed to help ex-offenders succeed while under community corrections sentences and thereafter will be presented.

Role of Technology

Can you think of any ways in which technology has transformed community corrections over its history? Perhaps you thought of the role of blood testing or the use of computers and cellphones/smartphones. Without question, technology has played a significant role in community corrections. Technology has enabled community corrections agencies to more effectively monitor their clients and to ensure that court-ordered conditions are being abided by. As technology has advanced in society, the tools utilized by community corrections agencies have also advanced. As discussed

Image 27. © iStockphoto.com/cybrain.

earlier in the book, global positioning systems (GPS) have enabled community corrections agencies to better track higher risk offenders, such as sex offenders, gang offenders, and offenders who perpetrated intimate partner violence. Evaluations of GPS use for higher risk parolees, for example, have yielded favorable results, whereby researchers have found lower recidivism rates for these offender groups (Erez et al., 2012; Gies et al., 2012; 2013).

While improved outcomes in recidivism measures as well as compliance to conditions of release are promising, GPS is not without its drawbacks. Of course, there is a risk that offenders could still commit a crime even though they are being monitored more closely, and merely wearing the GPS device does not stop offenders from engaging in crime if they want to. The media is quick to publicize such instances and label offenders on GPS devices who commit crimes as running "amok" (Byrd, 2014). For instance, in Indianapolis, Justin Cherry, a probationer convicted of robbery, was required to wear a GPS ankle bracelet. However, the device did not deter him from committing 11 robberies over eight days in 2014 (Byrd 2014; Mack 2014). Another drawback of GPS is the cost. Across the board, GPS devices cost community corrections agencies more per offender to utilize than supervision without such devices (Erez et al., 2012; Gies et al., 2012; 2013). Although, with more costs of supervision being passed on to offenders, it may be less of a burden to the budgets of community corrections agencies (Diller, Greene, & Jacobs, 2009).

More recently, applications or "apps" have been developed for smartphones that utilize GPS technology to assist community corrections agencies in monitoring offenders and officers, improving officer safety, and offering the ability to reduce the normally higher costs for GPS monitoring. For instance, in 2012, a community corrections agency in Indiana began using the Telenav Track application installed on twelve iPhones that the agency purchased primarily to track officers' movements in the field as a way of increasing accountability and enhancing officer safety (Coppola, 2013). The Telenav app can be likened to having a supervisor watching an officer during the day without the supervisor being physically present, as the app reports when, where, and how long an officer is at a particular location (Coppola, 2013). Information logged by the app can be cross-referenced with case logs prepared by the officers that state what they were doing, when, where, and with whom — in this sense, the app keeps officers accountable (Coppola, 2013). As for the safety aspect, if an officer goes missing or is in crisis, the Telenav app can immediately signal to supervisors where the officer is located (Coppla, 2013).

In 2015, Telmate, a corrections technology provider, announced it was launching the Telmate Guardian, touted as "the most innovative, smartphone-based, GPS monitoring solution for community corrections, including parole, probation, pre-trial, and work release" (PRWeb, 2015). Unlike the Telenav app that is more officer focused, the Telmate Guardian app is used by both offenders and officers. The Telmate Guardian app requires officers to "set up a new user online and provide a unique PIN to the enrollee. Enrollees download the app and sign up. Based on their program, enrollees are prompted to check in by reading a random series of numbers. Voice and facial detection then confirm the check-in as successful.... Telmate Guardian offers case managers real-time monitoring, reports, and check-in controls, along with features like voice and facial detection, and geo zones (inclusion and exclusion zones), making it simple to actively pinpoint and supervise enrollees" (PRWeb, 2015). Additionally, the Telmate Guardian app reduces costs for community corrections agencies as agencies do not need to invest in extra equipment for officers or offenders and the cost is passed down to the clients. Since offenders have to own a smartphone to install the app, the agency is not paying the bill for it. Of course, requiring offenders to obtain a smartphone can be burdensome for many due to the cost of such devices as well as subscribing to costly service plans, which may be necessary to establish an Internet connection. Thus, for many offenders, having to obtain a more expensive mobile phone is a significant hardship, as many are struggling to obtain jobs and take care of themselves and their families. Some agencies, such as Pioneer Human Services (PHS) in Washington State, that offer transition housing to released offenders in the forms of work release centers, halfway houses, and even apartments, have recently adopted the Telmate system. PHS recognizes that obtaining a smartphone may be a hardship for ex-offenders, thus, the agency offers loaner phones to those in need.

Geographic information systems (GIS) are also playing a significant role in community corrections today. According to Russo (2001, p. 140), "GIS combines traditional database systems with a graphic component that allows visual representation and analysis of tabular data on a map, helping agencies use geography to observe, analyze and provide solutions to challenges they face." GIS are not a newcomer in the criminal justice system, as it has been utilized quite heavily by police departments since the 1990s (Russo, 2001). Community corrections agencies soon recognized the value of utilizing GIS. For instance, GIS can assist agencies in "assigning probation and parole officers by geographic location; directing probationers and parolees to services and treatment centers; and making site selection decisions for the placement of new facilities within a community" (Karuppannan, 2005). For instance, agencies can assign officers clients that reside in close proximity to one another, thus reducing the likelihood that the officers will have to drive all over town to perform residence checks of their clients. Additionally, with community corrections officers already overwhelmed with high caseloads, GIS allow officers the ability to plan out their routes for making residence checks, particularly if the residences are dispersed, which will save the officers much pre-planning and route preparation (Karuppannan, 2005). The efficiency benefit is also reaped by the agency, which will save money on gas and maintenance costs of their vehicles that otherwise may have been driven longer and on less direct routes (Karuppannan, 2005). Further, GIS allow agencies to increase officer safety as it can be utilized to provide estimates as to how many officers should report for a residence check at a specific offender's home based its location as well as risk level of offender (Karuppannan, 2005).

Similar to GPS, GIS also can have its drawbacks. Russo (2001) reported on the potential barriers to GIS being implemented in a corrections environment based on a corrections group meeting held in the late 1990s. Specifically, Russo (2001, p. 146) stated the group identified the following barriers:

- Institutional Barriers. Resistance to data-sharing, problems integrating with existing systems, questions of data ownership, locating funding, lack of infrastructure and securing "buy-in."
- Ideological Barriers. The reluctance to move outside of "fortress corrections" and into community-based corrections.
- Community Barriers. Communities may fear being identified as having a high number of probationers for fear of declining property values.
- Geocoding Barriers. Missing data, difficult addresses and confidentiality issues associated with juvenile offenders raise issues when implementing a GIS system.

Thus, GIS is not a simple system for correctional agencies to pick up today and implement tomorrow. It does require a team approach with top administrators working together, with line staff, with community partners, and with IT personnel to obtain the necessary "buy-in" for GIS to be effective. For instance, if line staff are not trained and don't understand the importance of entering all data correctly into the system, or if they don't care, then GIS will be essentially rendered an ineffective tool.

Since many community corrections offenders are prohibited from using alcohol while under supervision, several devices have been developed to assist community corrections officers in ensuring that their clients are adhering to this condition (DeMichele & Payne, 2009). Some devices are designed to require an offender to submit to a test when prompted while other devices offer continuous, around-the-clock alcohol monitoring. For instance, the SCRAM Remote Breath is a handheld wireless GPS unit that will require an offender to submit to a breathalyzer test when prompted (SCRAM, 2016a). It also has facial recognition intelligence as one of its features to ensure that the individual who is taking the test is indeed the client (SCRAM,

2016a). DeMichele and Payne (2009, p. 43–44) explain that the continuous alcohol monitoring device, "… utilizes a lightweight ankle bracelet that captures alcohol readings from continuous samples of vaporous or insensible perspiration collected from the air above the skin. These alcohol readings are non-invasive and determine if an offender has consumed alcohol and, if so, approximately how much alcohol was consumed. This technology enables for a near-instantaneous detection of court ordered abstinence violations, and provides continuous remote alcohol readings." The SCRAM Cam System is an example of such a device that is utilized in many agencies. This tamper-proof device acquires perspiration readings every 30 minutes and uploads the readings via wireless, Ethernet, or a landline to a computer at designated times (SCRAM, 2016b). Officers can also access reports on demand (SCRAM, 2016b).

In 2014, a corrections advisory panel comprised of 25 community and institutional practitioners was assembled to discuss the top needs for community corrections (Jackson et al., 2015). Not surprisingly, some of the recommendations focused on technology. For instance, the group recommended the development of "affordable, portable, accurate, real-time, multilanguage speech-to-speech translators" (Jackson et al., 2015, p. 57). While the group noted that these technologies exist, they are often inaccurate and, thus, need to be improved. Additionally, the panel recommended technologies that can assist officers in determining whether a client is being deceptive, such as tools that can recognize microfacial expressions or even the ability to utilize biometric sensory tools remotely (Jackson et al., 2015). Although not ranked as a top need, the panel also recommended the development of a device to monitor the time that officers are investing in specific clients—an application, perhaps, may be the solution to this problem (Jackson et al., 2015). With technology continuing to advance, it may not be too far into the future until the suggestions made by the Corrections Advisory Panel are implemented and become mainstay tools for community corrections agencies.

As technology advances, community corrections agencies will be presented with new options, or tools, to monitor their clients. DeMichele and Payne (2009) caution that agencies should not adopt every tool that they may be presented with. Rather, the researchers suggest that agencies conduct their own organizational analysis of needs to determine if the new tools will enhance supervision and will be cost effective.

Steps Needed

With budget woes faced by many corrections agencies across the nation, more state policymakers are looking to divert offenders from incarceration terms, which has resulted in an increase in the use of community corrections sanctions. Additionally, the fiscal restraints have resulted in several states passing legislation that requires corrections agencies to utilize **evidence-based programming** or to utilize other sanctions besides re-incarceration for probation and parole violations (Vera Institute of Justice, 2013). The Vera Institute of Justice (2013, pp. 29–31) outlines what is needed for community corrections to be effective as follows:

Collaboration with key stakeholders. Securing the outcomes sought by policy makers — in public safety, dollars saved, communities improved — is more likely if key stakeholders are part of the process. Corrections agencies cannot affect desired outcomes on their own; police, judges, prosecutors, paroling authorities, and others play an important role as well. Legislators and executive branch policymakers can provide needed outreach to these constituencies to build their understanding of why change is needed and to encourage their cooperation. They can also convene forums through which corrections agencies and other stakeholders can discuss the progress and impact of change.

Realistic expectations. Elected officials must not expect anticipated outcomes, such as a reduction in prison population, to happen overnight. For some agencies, the kinds of changes needed to achieve the outcomes envisioned may take a long time. Changes in hiring, training, case classifications, caseload assignments, staff reward structures, and so on all require extended, focused effort on the part of agency leadership.

Skilled, bold leaders. Effective community supervision requires agency leaders who have the support of policymakers to produce systemic change. Leaders need vision, freedom to create an executive team of their own choosing, support from above, and the ability to withstand the pressure to maintain the status quo. Governors and county executives also need help: corrections should warrant the same kind of professional recruiting guidance that most executives would look for in hiring an education or health official. Once hired, these agency heads need ongoing support to implement fully mission, policy, and practice changes throughout their agencies.

Culture change. Changing supervision practices within agencies includes changing the ethos of the entire operation: mission, vision, values — everything from policies to job descriptions and staff promotion criteria. This process is long and arduous: not only is there predictable resistance to changes to the way things have always been done, but recalibrating an agency toward the success of probationers and parolees (as opposed to just avoiding or catching failure) can be a fundamental challenge to the way an agency's employees see themselves, their work, and their purpose. There are many proven ways to make these changes successfully, from using vertical implementation task groups drawn from different levels of staff and different divisions within an agency to providing rewards and incentives to employees, but the process must be carefully thought out.

An additional challenge may be frequent changes in leadership and, hence, approach. Staff may resist change in anticipation that this new person and his or her team will not be in place for very long. This attitude makes it all the more imperative that hiring and promotion criteria be overhauled quickly, and policy changes be developed with input from line staff and institutionalized as rapidly as possible. Support from outside experts is usually helpful in identifying and managing the many different aspects of the change process — from coaching leaders and framing messages to staff to creating new hiring and promotion criteria and developing policies that reflect new goals.

Training for staff. Training that provides staff with the knowledge and skills they need to meet new job expectations is critical: research findings, motivational interviewing, communication skills, and risk and needs assessments are just some of the needed training areas. Training, however, is resource intensive and takes staff away from their regular duties. Agency leaders must make its value clear across the agency, particularly to its mid-level managers.

Available programming that meets evidence-based standards. Evidence-based programming is key to producing positive public safety outcomes and simply may not be available in certain jurisdictions. Especially in rural and smaller metropolitan areas, choices in providers may be extremely limited. Agencies must have the resources to assess providers and to seek either training for their own staff or to create incentives for providers to acquire needed skills and assets to fill program gaps.

The Vera Institute of Justice's (2013) recommendation of collaboration did not fall on deaf ears. As a matter of fact, in 2016, the U.S. Department of Justice officially designated the week of April 24–30 as National Reentry Week (Lynch, 2016). As the nation's first ever official reentry week kicked off in jurisdictions across the United States, the U.S. Department of Justice (DOJ) requested that the Bureau of Prisons coordinate reentry events within their facilities. Additionally, the DOJ requested "each U.S. Attorney's Office to coordinate reentry events, including meetings between local reentry stakeholders, reentry court proceedings, employer roundtables or other events designed to raise awareness about the importance of reentry work. We are encouraging federal partners and grantees to work closely with stakeholders like federal defenders, legal aid providers, and other partners across the country to increase the impact of this effort" (Lynch, 2016). The reentry week is an important step in not only raising national awareness about reentry, but it also demonstrates a further commitment by the federal government to reentry and stresses collaboration as the key to assisting ex-offenders in the reintegration back into society.

The 2014 Corrections Advisory Panel also echoed some of the Vera Institute's suggestions (Jackson et al., 2015). In regard to staffing, the panel noted that many agencies experience difficulties recruiting, hiring, and even retaining corrections staff, thus, "the panel recommended that agencies devote more time and attention to further refining this aspect of their organization" (Jackson et al., 2015). For instance, the panel noted that outdated agency materials, including training materials, are problematic and recommended the updating of these materials so that they are current. In particular, given the pervasive drug and/or mental health issues experienced by clients, the panel suggested that community corrections officer training should include components that inform officers about techniques for assisting their clients with drug and/or mental health problems (Jackson et al., 2015). Additionally, since caseload sizes can impede officers' ability to effectively help their clients, the panel suggested that procedures be developed to assist officers in assessing the amount of time that they should invest in a single case (Jackson et al., 2015). Similarly, supervisors should have clear methods developed to help them determine the relationship between case-load size and the actual amount of time and work that officers are investing in their assigned cases.

Apart from staffing recommendations, the panel also recognized that enhancement of risk and needs assessment tools are needed in community corrections (Jackson et al., 2015). Specifically, the panel noted that many current assessment tools utilized either lacked dynamic factor components entirely or contain very few dynamic factors, therefore, assessment instruments should be updated to include, or expand, such measures. Additionally, the panel suggested the development of "tools or components of case management systems that can dynamically update risk assessments and automatically validate and update risk assessment models. The tool should also identify anomalies in case management, such as signs of riskscore manipulation and anomalous churn" (Jackson et al., 2015, p. 57). Along similar lines, the panel also recommended a tool that can assist officers in meting out the best type of sanction for violations of conditions based on the clients' violation and needs (Jackson et al., 2015). The panel also suggested that such a tool should not be just developed, but that it should be researched as to its effectiveness over time. With the "proper" sanction applied to clients, permanent behavioral changes may occur as well as reduced recidivism rates. Finally, the panel identified the lack of data sharing between community corrections agencies and other criminal justice agencies or stakeholder agencies (e.g., mental healthcare providers) to be problematic (Jackson et al., 2015). Without proper data sharing between federal, state, and local corrections and other agencies, gaps in addressing client needs can occur resulting in unsuccessful reentry.

It is clear that in order for community corrections agencies to increase public safety, assist ex-offenders, and take a step forward toward the future, they must begin working in partnership with other service agencies and fostering a commitment to utilizing empirically based assessment tools by providing programming based on empirically based standards (see Text Box 13.1). Additionally, it is important to recognize that change will not occur overnight, strong leadership must be instilled in agencies, and these leaders must prepare for organizational barriers such as staff resistance to instituted changes. Leadership must take a central role in fostering cultural change within the agency and hiring staff that are committed to the values of the agency and carrying out its goals. Further, high standards of training must be developed to instill the skills that officers will need on the job.

Text Box 13.1: International Trends in Community Corrections

The use of incarceration has increased not only in the United States, but all around the world (Byrne, Pattavina, & Taxman, 2015). Byrne and colleagues (2015), however, note that the Russian Federation, South Africa, and Pakistan have actually reduced their use of incarceration, while at the same time actually reducing their crime rates. The reductions in incarceration in the Russian Federation is likely due to the increased use of community-based correctional sentences (Penal Reform, 2015). As other countries feel the squeeze of increased prison usage and shrinking budgets, they will likely begin to seek other alterative sentences. In China, for instance, the use of electronic monitoring has been offered as a method for increasing community corrections (Penal Reform, 2015). In some countries, a lack of sentencing alternatives besides prison stymies their efforts. Therefore, according to Penal Reform (2015, p. 36), one recommendation that should be set forth to increase the use of community corrections sentences at the international level is that "Work should be undertaken to strengthen the availability and implementation of alternative sentences for minor offenders, to promote the United Nations Standard Minimum Rules for Non-custodial Measures (the Tokyo Rules), and to increase public awareness of and involvement in their use." At the international level, there is a commitment to the use and expansion of community corrections sentences with organizations such as the International Community Corrections Association leading the charge with awareness and suggested solutions. The future of community corrections internationally looks bright as there is a greater commitment to the use and expansion of such sentences as well as the recognition that evidence-based programming, such as cognitive behavioral treatment, for community corrections offenders may promote future desistance from crime.

Ex-Offender Success

As mentioned throughout the book, if we are to expect community corrections offenders to refrain from future criminal involvement they must have their needs met. Much research has been published on the importance of proper assessment of the static and dynamic risk factors for offenders in order to ensure their needs are met (Andrews & Bonta, 2015). Risk-needs assessments assist correctional administrators and probation and parole officers in orienting clients to appropriate interventions tailored specifically to them (Bonta & Andrews, 2007). Additionally, these new tools assist corrections personnel in determining whether various programs and interventions that the offender was participating in were effective for that offender and can further assist officers in the creation of strategic supervision plans for the offender (Bonta & Andrews, 2007).

Researchers have determined that, at a minimum level, community corrections offenders must be able to have food and acquire access to affordable housing (Gunnison & Helfgott, 2013). In the case of housing, simply ensuring that ex-offenders obtain housing is not sufficient. Ex-offenders must also receive access to treatment services that target their fundamental risk factors. Thus, simply providing a bed or access to shelter for ex-offenders does not equate to reentry success unless the needs and risk factors of ex-offenders are being addressed. Beyond that, offenders need assistance with securing employment, meeting their financial obligations (both civil and personal), and, oftentimes, reunification with their children and families (Gunnison & Helfgott, 2013). The importance of employment cannot be overstated as Sampson and Laub (1993) posit that individuals who build social capital in areas such as employment are more likely to desist from crime. Thus, the ability of ex-offenders to obtain employment is a huge factor that sets the stage for their potential success during reentry. However, finding employment is often fraught with difficulties. Kelly and Fader (2012) state that many employment applications are online, and therefore ex-offenders not only need access to computers but also need training in the use of computers, including Internet navigation. It is important to not assume that all ex-offenders are able to access a computer or know how to operate one.

In general, ex-offenders are less likely to obtain jobs than those without criminal records. The stigma of a conviction often hinders employment success. For minority ex-offenders, their quest for employment is often fraught with increased difficulties. Unfortunately, many persons of color, without criminal records, are discriminated against for employment in U.S. society due to the bias of some employers. This issue can be further compounded when minority ex-offenders attempt to obtain jobs as they often experience "**double discrimination**," whereby they experience discrimination due to their minority status and their ex-offender status (Gunnison & Helfgott, 2013). Thus, minority ex-offenders may need more support in their quest for employment. Community corrections agencies should be aware of the unique difficulties that minority ex-offenders face when seeking employment and be willing to perhaps give minority ex-offenders more leniency (e.g., time in securing a job) and training (e.g., techniques that ex-offenders could utilize to combat discrimination). Additionally, Apel (2011) cautions that giving ex-offenders jobs or helping them find jobs is not enough, but rather a clear need exists for the enhancement of employability of ex-offenders. That is, ex-offenders need job skill enhancements in order to reduce their chances of job termination and recidivism. Moreover, Latessa (2012) stresses the importance of targeting offenders' attitudes and values about work. Without forming a connection to work, ex-offenders are not likely to hang onto their jobs for the long term.

As reported in earlier chapters, both male and female offenders can suffer from drug and alcohol addictions. Thus, addiction is a risk factor that many offenders experience which inhibits successful reentry and often leads to recidivism. For those offenders being released from prison to serve parole sentences or who are released to halfway houses, the following few months post-release is the critical time period that ex-offenders are most at risk for relapse and recidivism (Visher, Yahner, & La Vigne, 2010). For other community corrections offenders, getting a handle on their addiction(s) is critical. One form of programming that may be helpful for those ex-offenders suffering from addictions is therapeutic communities, or long-term residential treatment programs that are embedded in communities (Petersilia, 2005). This treatment modality is one of the more widely used treatment styles for helping drug offenders both within and outside of prison (Zhang, Roberts, & McCollister, 2011). Numerous researchers have found support for therapeutic programming to assist drug offenders even for offenders who suffer from co-occurring problems such as mental illness (Inciardi, Martin, & Butzin, 2004; Martin, Butzin, & Inciardi, 1995; McKendrick et al., 2006; Pearson & Lipton, 1999; Van Stelle & Moberg, 2004). In particular, those therapeutic community programs that assist offenders both within prison and in the community upon release have been linked to lower rates of drug relapse and criminal recidivism (Vanderplasschen et al., 2013).

For female community corrections offenders, Herrschaft and colleagues (2009) note that reentry programs need to be designed with them specifically in mind, not just modeled after reentry programs that have been designed for men. Thus, programming that addresses the needs for women, such as coming to terms with prior sexual abuse, is critical both for those within prison and those serving community corrections sentences of all races and ethnicities (Belknap, 2007; Chesney-Lind, 1989). In 2016, the Helen B. Ratcliff Work Release Center, located in Seattle, began offering female residents a "trauma-informed" yoga program (Pioneer Human Services, 2016). As described by Pioneer Human Services (2016), "The goal of a trauma-informed yoga practice is to build resiliency and establish greater self-regulation. It is about helping a person to feel safe and at-home in her body so that she can feel stable, have good self-esteem, and healthy relationships. A trauma-informed yoga practice is sensitive to the needs of a participant with trauma symptoms and offers them tools to feel safe, empowered, and self-regulated." Such a program provides another avenue beyond individual or group therapies for women offenders to cope with prior traumas in a healthy manner. Additionally, fostering the ability of female offenders to set realistic expectations when reentering their communities (rural or urban) is also needed (Kellett & Willging, 2011). Further, any program serving community corrections offenders must be sensitive to cultural differences. Thus, a one-size-fits-all approach to reforming ex-offenders is not likely providing the opportunity for all ex-offenders to succeed, but rather just a select few (Vigesaa, 2013).

Oftentimes the focus is on the ex-offender and his/her needs as being the linchpin for successful reentry. However, it is important to remember that the community corrections agency and officer also play an important role in successful reentry. At the organizational level, if there is not a commitment to providing access to quality evidence-based programming, then ex-offenders are unlikely to succeed. Agencies must also look beyond their own doors and be willing to build and foster relationships with other partners in the communities that may also be able to support their clients. Thus, any development of transition programs that may begin in prisons and continue seamlessly in the community when ex-offenders are released is a terrific way to bridge the gap between prison and parole agency programming. Many prisons may already be offering programming, but Petersilia (2003) notes that existing programs are often in need of enhancement in order to best assist ex-offenders transitioning into their communities. For those offenders sentenced directly to community corrections sentences, programs that are being offered to them must target their specific needs.

Conclusion

In conclusion, community corrections has held an important place in the correctional systems in the United States for hundreds of years and will continue to do so in the future. Community corrections is indeed a fundamental branch of the correctional system. Over the last several decades, the use of community corrections sentences has burgeoned and future trends indicate that it will do so over the next few decades as well. Thus, employment trends in community corrections over the next decade are strong. This is an exciting era for community corrections as the field continues to innovate. Today, community corrections agencies and officers are much more aware of the needs and challenges that their clients have, and they are devoted to assisting them with getting their needs met through the adoption of various assessment tools and the use of evidence-based programming. Additionally, community corrections agencies have embraced technology to carry out their surveillance of offenders and to ensure community safety. As technology continues to advance, agencies will likely adopt new gadgets or apps to carry out their duties. The knowledge you have acquired will assist you in enhancing the functioning of community corrections if you choose to pursue a career in it. If you enter the profession, you will find that there are often knowledge gaps in agencies and a thirst for those employed in those agencies to institute changes to better serve clients. You can definitely be part of the solution in corrections and help to avert the longstanding revolving door phenomenon that is commonly associated with corrections. It is possible to successfully divert offenders from returning back to the system—assuming their needs are met through innovative programming.

Key Terms

Evidence-based programming

Double-discrimination

Discussion Questions

1. Research community corrections in your county or state. What trends do you observe?

2. With technology playing a more integral part of corrections that it did in the past, what role is technology having in community corrections in your jurisdiction? Are there any discussions to use new devices or apps? If so, what is being considered and what are their strengths and weaknesses?

3. Research community corrections hiring trends either in your current county or state or a county or state in which you want to reside. Do hiring trends appear to be increasing? If so, are there desired skills that employers are looking for in applicants?

4. What do you think is needed for the future of community corrections? What steps should policymakers be taking to assist ex-offenders while ensuring community safety?

References

Andrews, D. A., & Bonta, J. (2015). *The psychology of criminal conduct* (5th ed.). Cincinnati, OH: Anderson Publishing Co.

Apel, R. (2011). Transitional jobs program: Putting employment-based reentry into context. *Criminology and Public Policy, 10*(4), 939–942. doi: 10.1111/j.1745-9133.2011.00781.x.

Belknap, J. (2007). *The invisible woman: Gender, crime, and justice.* Belmont, CA: Thomson, Wadsworth.

Bonta, J., & Andrews, D. A. (2007). *Risk-need-responsivity model for offender assessment and rehabilitation 2007–06.* Retrieved from http://www.pbpp.pa.gov/Information/Documents/Research/EBP7.pdf.

Byrd, R. (2014, April 24). Criminals on GPS 'run amok' in Marion County. *Wishtv.com.* Retrieved from http://wishtv.com/2014/04/24/criminals-on-gps-run-amok-in-marion-county/.

Byrne, J. M., Pattavina, A., & Taxman, F. S. (2015). International trends in prison upsizing and downsizing: In search of evidence of a global rehabilitation revolution. *Victims & Offenders, 10*(4), 420–451. doi: 10.1080/15564886.2015.1078186.

Chesney-Lind, M. (1989). Girl's crime and woman's place: Toward a feminist model of female delinquency. *Crime and Delinquency, 35*(1), 8–10. doi: 10.1177/001 1128789035001002.

Coppola, M. (2013). App tracks probation and community corrections officers. *Tech Beat.* Retrieved from https://www.justnet.org/pdf/App-Tracks.pdf.

DeMichele, M., & Payne, B. (2009). *Offender supervision with electronic technology: A community corrections resource* (2nd ed.). Washington, DC: Bureau of Justice Administration.

Diller, R., Greene, J., & Jacobs, M. (2009). *Maryland's parole supervision fee: A barrier to reentry.* New York: New York University School of Law, Brennan Center for Justice.

Erez, E., Ibarra, P. R., Bales, W. D., & Gur, O. M. (2012). *GPS monitoring technologies and domestic violence: An evaluation study.* Washington, DC: National Institute of Justice.

Gies, S. V., Gaine, R., Cohen, M. I., Healy, E., Duplantier, D., Yeide, M., Bekelman, A., Bobnis, A., & Hopps, M. (2012). *Monitoring high-risk sex offenders with GPS technology: An evaluation of the California supervision program, final report.* Washington, DC: National Institute of Justice.

Gies, S. V., Gaine, R., Cohen, M. I., Healy, E., Yeide, M., Bekelman, A., & Bobnis, A. (2013). *Monitoring high-risk gang offenders with GPS technology: An evaluation of the California supervision program, final report.* Washington, DC: National Institute of Justice.

Gunnison, E., & Helfgott, J. B. (2013). *Offender reentry: Beyond crime and Punishment.* Boulder, CO: Lynne Rienner.

Herrschaft, B. A., Veysey, B. M., Tubman-Carbone, H. R., & Christian, J. (2009). Gender differences in the transformation narrative: Implications for revised reentry strategies for female offenders. *Journal of Offender Rehabilitation, 48*(6), 463–482. doi: 10.1080/10509670903081250

Inciardi, J. A., Martin, S. S., & Butzin, C. A. (2004). Five-year outcomes of therapeutic community treatment of drug-involved offenders after release from prison. *Crime and Delinquency, 50*(1), 88–107. doi: 10.1177/0011128703258874.

Jackson, B. A., Russo, J., Hollywood, J. S., Woods, D., Silberglitt, R., Drake, G. B., Shaffer, J. S., Zaydman, M., & Chow, B. G. (2015). *Fostering innovation in community and institutional corrections: Identifying high-priority technology and other needs for the U.S. corrections sector.* Santa Monica, CA: RAND.

Jagannathan, M. (2016, February 21). Judge orders 50 Cent to explain Instagram cash stacks in bankruptcy court. *New York Daily News*. Retrieved from http://www.ny dailynews.com/entertainment/gossip/judge-orders-bankrupt-50-cent-explain-instagram-cash-pics-article-1.2538553.

Karuppannan, J. (2005). Mapping and corrections: Management of offenders with geographic information systems. *Corrections Compendium, 30*(1), 7–9, 31–33.

Kelly, C. E., & Fader, J. J. (2012). Computer-based employment applications: Implications for offenders and supervising officers. *Federal Probation, 76*(1), 14–18.

Kellett, N., & Willging, C. E. (2011). Pedagogy of individual choice and female inmate reentry in the U.S. Southwest. *International Journal of Law and Psychiatry, 34*(4), 256–63. doi: 10.1016/j.ijlp.2011.07.003.

Latessa, E. J. (2012). Why work is important and how to improve the effectiveness of correctional reentry programs that target employment. *Criminology and Public Policy, 11*(1), 87–91.

Lynch, L. (2016, March 21). National reentry week: An essential part of our mission. *Huffington Post*. Retrieved from http://www.huffingtonpost.com/loretta-lynch/national-reentry-week_b_9513312.html.

Mack, J. L. (2014, February 24). GPS monitor leads police to Indy robbery suspect on probation. *Indy Star*. Retrieved from http://www.indystar.com/story/news/crime/2014/02/24/-gps-monitor-leads-police-to-indy-robbery-suspect-on-probation/5786045/.

Martin, S. S., Butzin, C. A., & Inciardi, J. A. (1995). Assessment of a multistage therapeutic community for drug-involved offenders. *Journal of Psychoactive Drugs, 27*(1), 109–116. doi: 10.1080/02791072.1995.10471679.

McKendrick, K., Sullivan, C., Banks, S., & Sacks, S. (2006). Modified therapeutic community treatment for offenders with MICA disorders: Antisocial personality disorder and treatment outcomes. *Journal of Offender Rehabilitation, 44*(2/3), 133–159. doi: 10.1080/00952990701653800.

Pearson, F. S., & Lipton, D. S. (1999). A meta-analytic review of the effectiveness of corrections-based treatments for drug abuse. *Prison Journal, 79*(4), 384–410. doi: 10.1177/0032885599079004003.

Penal Reform. (2015). *Global prison trends 2015*. Retrieved from http://www.penalreform.org/wp-content/uploads/2015/04/PRI-Prisons-global-trends-report-LR.pdf.

Petersilia, J. (2003). *When prisoners come home: Parole and prisoner reentry*. New York: Oxford University Press.

Petersilia, J. (2005). Meeting the challenges of prisoner reentry. In American Correctional Association (Ed.), *What works and why: Effective approaches to reentry* (pp. 175–192). East Peoria, IL: Versa Press.

Pioneer Human Services. (2016, April 27). *Volunteer teaches women trauma-informed yoga at reentry facility*. Retrieved from http://pioneerhumanservices.org/2016/04/volunteer-teaches-women-trauma-informed-yoga-at-reentry-facility/.

PRWeb. (2015, April 20). *Telmate guardian offers innovative smartphone-based, GPS monitoring solution for community corrections.* Retrieved from www.prweb.com/releases/2015/04/prweb12658452.htm.

Russo, J. (2001). Helping corrections inside and outside prison walls. *Corrections Today, 63*(7), 140–144.

Russo, J., & Matz, A. K. (2014). The use of social media for monitoring defendants, probationers and parolees: Results of a survey of the APPA Membership. *Perspectives, 38*(1), 22–33.

Sampson, R. J., & Laub, J. H. (1993). *Crime in the making: Pathways and turning points through life.* Cambridge, MA: Harvard University Press.

SCRAM. (2016a). *SCRAM Remote Breath.* Retrieved from https://www.scramsystems.com/images/uploads/general/downloads/scram-remote-breath-product-brochure.pdf.

SCRAM. (2016b). *SCRAM Continuous Alcohol Monitoring.* Retrieved from https://www.scramsystems.com/images/uploads/general/downloads/scram-cam-product-brochure.pdf.

Sweeney, E. (2012, November 29). Probation 2.0: How technology is changing probation work. *The Boston Globe.* Retrieved from https://www.bostonglobe.com/metro/regionals/south/2012/11/29/probation-how-technology-changing-probation-work-probation-officers-tap-social-media/Qtv52cQffcVbkAsJqcg6lK/story.html.

Vanderplasschen, W., Colpaert, K., Autrique, M., Rapp, R. C., Pearce, S., Broekaert, E., & Vandevelde, S. (2013). Therapeutic communities for addictions: A review of their effectiveness from a recovery-oriented perspective. *The Scientific World Journal, 2013,* 1–22. doi: 10.1155/2013/427817.

Van Stelle, K. R., & Moberg, D. P. (2004). Outcome data for MICA clients after participation in an institutional therapeutic community. *Journal of Offender Rehabilitation, 39*(1), 37–62. doi: 10.1300/J076v39n01_03.

Vera Institute of Justice. (2013). *The potential of community corrections to improve safety and reduce incarceration.* New York, NY: Vera Institute of Justice.

Vigesaa, L. E. (2013). Abuse as a form of strain among Native American and white female prisoners: Predictors of substance-related offenses and recidivism. *Journal of Ethnicity in Criminal Justice, 11,* 1–21. doi: 10.1080/15377938.2013.739384.

Visher, C., Yahner, J., & La Vigne, N. (2010). *Life after prison: Tracking the experiences of male prisoners returning to Chicago, Cleveland, and Houston.* Washington, DC: Urban Institute.

Zhang, S., Roberts, R. E. L., & McCollister, K. E. (2011). Therapeutic community in a California prison: Treatment outcomes after 5 years. *Crime and Delinquency, 57*(1), 82–101. doi: 10.1177/0011128708327035.

Glossary

A

Active GPS monitoring—An active electronic monitoring system whereby the device transmits offender location information to a monitoring center in near-real time.

Adam Walsh Child Protection and Safety Act—Legislation that created a national federal sex offender registry.

Adoption and Safe Families Act—Legislation designed to protect children, but it resulted in making it difficult for female offenders to regain custody of their children upon release from prison.

Alexander Maconochie—Considered the founder of parole.

Alford plea—No contest, or silent guilty plea.

Anti-Drug Abuse Act of 1988—Resulted in federally funded housing being more restrictive as to who was allowed to live in these housing options and also permitted state public housing authorities to further refine their admission policies.

B

Boot camps—A correctional sanction that is aimed at non-violent, young, and first-time offenders that is rooted in militaristic principles.

C

Caseloads—The number of clients that community corrections officers supervise at one time.

Charles L. Chute—Prominent advocate for the establishment of probation at the federal level in the United States.

Child-saving movement—Refers to educated middle-class reformers, mostly women, who fought for reforms for delinquent youth in the late 1800s and early 1900s.

Civil death—Refers to the loss of civil rights experienced by those individuals who have been convicted of crimes.

Classification—Refers to the procedure whereby the risk and needs factors of the offender are identified and an appropriate supervision plan is recommended.

Collateral consequences—Refers to laws or policies that place restrictions on persons with felony convictions.

Community corrections—Refers to the range of formal criminal justice punishments that are carried out in the community.

Community corrections officer—A correctional employee who works with offenders serving a community corrections sentence.

Community Mental Health Centers Act—Legislation that required the deinstitutionalization of the mentally ill from mental health hospitals.

Conditionary probation—Offenders released from custody without a formal probation sentence but having to abide by conditions placed on probationers.

Contract—A formal agreement between two parties, in corrections, usually between the offender and the state/federal government.

Corrections—The study of correctional systems, practices, and policy.

Cranston-Gonzalez National Affordable Housing Act of 1990—Permitted public housing authorities to utilize criminal records when making admission decisions.

Criminogenic needs—Factors that are empirically associated with criminal behavior and recidivism.

D

Day fines—A fine that is assessed based on an individual's normal pay for one day of work.

Day reporting center—A facility that offenders report to during business hours for treatment services and for monitoring.

Democracy Restoration Act—Proposed in 2015 in an effort to restore federal voting rights for all ex-offenders.

Deterrence theory—A criminological theory which states that punishment should be certain, swift, and severe to prevent the offender from committing crime again.

Double discrimination—A form of discrimination on two levels, such as race and conviction status.

Drug Free Student Loans Act—Enacted in 1998 and prohibited those with a federal or state drug conviction from receiving any assistance for higher education.

Dynamic factors—Factors that are changeable through some form of intervention, such as alcohol and drug use, marital problems, education level, skills level, or moral reasoning.

E

Electronic monitoring—A technological device that is adhered to the offender that tracks his/her movements to ensure that he/she is in compliance with release terms.

Equal Protection Clause—A clause of the Fourteenth Amendment which stipulates that all citizens should be protected equally by laws.

Evidence-based practices—Utilizing research principles and empirical assessments to determine whether treatment or programming is effective.

Evidence-based programming—Utilizing research principles and empirical assessments to design, develop, and deliver intervention programming.

Exclusionary rule—Evidence not obtained legally may not be used in criminal court proceedings.

F

Federal Welfare Law of 1996—Permanently prohibits states from permitting ex-offenders with drug-related felony convictions to receive any form of welfare benefits, including food stamps.

Felon disenfranchisement—Refers to barriers placed on the ability of individuals to participate in the democratic process due to their felony convictions

Final revocation hearing—A formal due process proceeding that is carried out by a judge or the probation and/or parole authority whereby the offender has an opportunity to testify and even present witnesses regarding the alleged violation.

G

General conditions—Rules that apply to all offenders regardless of their offense.

Good time law—A law where offenders received a slight deduction in their sentence for good behavior while incarcerated.

H

Halfway houses—Residential reentry centers that assist ex-offenders in their transition from prison to the community or are used as an alternative to an incarceration term.

Higher Education Act—Enacted in 1965 and provided access to higher education to those who could not afford it.

House arrest—A soft form of incarceration whereby the offender serves a confinement sentence in his/her own home.

Housing Opportunity Program Extension Act of 1996—Restricted housing options for convicted felons, as those ex-offenders who were juveniles at the time of their offense but were charged as adults could be denied housing.

Hybrid systems—A new type of electronic monitoring system that are a combination of active and passive GPS systems.

I

Independent Agencies Appropriations Act of 1999—Resulted in ex-offenders who were involved in methamphetamine production or their family members from being admitted in public housing.

Indeterminate sentences—A sentence that is given on a range from minimum to maximum.

Intensive supervision parole—A parole sanction that is designed to be more intense than traditional parole.

Intensive supervision probation—A probation sanction that is designed to be more intense than a traditional probation sentence.

Intermediate sanctions—Community corrections sentences that are alternatives to probation.

Irish system—A prison system whereby offenders were first placed in solitary confinement, followed by placement in a prison to work alongside others, and then transferred to another prison facility where they could earn early release.

J

Jacob Wetterling Crimes Against Children and Sexually Violent Offender Act—Legislation that required sex offenders to register and be tracked for specified periods of time.

John Augustus—The founder of probation in the United States.

L

Legal financial obligations—Refers to financial obligations that defendants and convicted offenders must pay, such as court fees and fees for community supervision.

M

Manhattan Bail Project—A research study that sought to determine which offenders should be released, pre-trial, from jail without the use of monetary bail based on a point scale.

Marks system—An incentive system for prisoners whereby they were granted credits for good behavior and these credits were taken away when they behaved poorly.

Matthew Davenport Hill—A key contributor to modern-day probation who developed a form of probation in England.

Megan's Law—Required community notification of registered sex offenders residing in neighborhoods.

N

National Probation Act—Formally established probation in the United States in 1925.

Net widening—An administrative practice that resulted in a greater number of persons being under the control of the criminal justice system.

O

Offender Accountability Act—Provides legal recourse for victims of crime committed by an offender.

P

Parole—The granting of early release of an inmate from prison that occurs in the community whereby the offender must abide by conditions and meet with a parole officer.

Parole actuarial tool—A predictive tool comprised of various risk factors that assist parole boards in identifying which offenders would be successful on parole.

Parole board—A group of criminal justice professionals that make a decision about whether an offender will be released from prison early on parole.

Parole d'honneur—French term meaning "word of honor" given to prisoners of war who were released early if they gave their word not to rejoin the war efforts.

Passive GPS monitoring—An electronic monitoring device where the location and time data of an offender's whereabouts are stored in a device and this information is later transferred to a monitoring center.

Pennsylvania Model—Early penitentiary model developed in Pennsylvania whereby inmates were housed in single cells and also received religious instruction in their cells.

Personal Responsibility and Work Opportunity Act—Enacted in 1996 and revised the cash assistance program for those in need.

Policy implications—Refer to policies that can be implemented to combat a social problem.

Preliminary hearing—A hearing where it is decided whether there is probable cause that a violation occurred.

Preponderance of evidence—Sufficient evidence is provided regarding the alleged violation.

Presentence investigation reports—Reports that contain a history of information on an offender, including information on his/her case, criminal history, prior arrests, prior convictions, employment status and history, residency status, mental health status, financial status, family history and relationships, victim impact, and a recommended sentence.

Prisoner Rehabilitation Act of 1965—This legislation expanded the use of community correctional alternatives that were rehabilitative for federal offenders.

Probation—A court-ordered punishment that occurs in the community in lieu of incarceration, whereby the offender must abide by conditions and meet with a probation officer.

Q

Quality Housing and Work Responsibility Act—Passed in 1998 and stated that those with one felony conviction, specifically a drug, sex, or violent conviction, would be banned from public housing.

R

Recidivate—Re-offending, or committing a new crime.

Release on Recognizance (ROR)—Releasing an offender on their own word that he/she would appear in court.

Responsivity—The utilization of programming, preferably cognitive-behavioral and social learning approaches, that are individually tailored to the needs and abilities of the offender.

Revoked—Terminated.

Rights restoration process — Process whereby ex-offenders can reestablish their formerly stripped rights.

Risk assessments — Attempt to determine the offender's risk, or propensity, to re-offend.

S

School-based probation — Probation whereby the probation officer manages the juvenile probationers from inside school walls rather than at a traditional program agency.

Second Chance Act — Federal legislation implemented in 2008 to assist states in creating, managing, or expanding programs to assist offenders in making a successful transition from prison or jails and to reduce recidivism rates.

Secondary traumatic stress — Occurs when CCOs are exposed to the suffering that their clients have inflicted on others and they then begin to develop traumatic stress symptoms as a result of their exposure.

Sex Offender Registration and Notification Act — Legislation that reclassified the tiers of sex offenders and specified the length of time that sex offenders were to be kept on the registry.

Shock Incarceration — This form of punishment, also known as boot camps, requires a period of confinement and then in many cases, release to supervised probation.

Sir Walter Crofton — The director of the Irish prison system in the 1850s.

Social distance — The perceived social distance or barrier between community corrections officers and their clients.

Specific conditions — Rules that apply specifically to an offender based on their offense.

Static factors — Unchangeable factors such as the number of arrests or convictions.

Status offenses — Crimes that only apply to juveniles due to their age.

T

Technical violations — Violations of conditions of a probation or parole sentence.

Temperance Movement — A social movement that advocated for moderate consumption of alcohol and the reformation of alcoholics.

"Three strikes law" — Offenders convicted of a third felony would receive a prison sentence for life without the possibility of parole.

Ticket-of-leave system — Offenders who were transported from England to other countries could return to England after their sentences were completed.

Treatment communities — Residential facilities that offer drug and/or alcohol abuse assistance via trained staff.

Truth-in-sentencing laws — Laws that require violent offenders to serve a greater percentage of their sentences, typically 85% or more, in order to be considered for parole.

V

Voting Rights Act of 1965—Granted minorities the right to vote.

W

Work release—A community based treatment correctional program where an offender, after serving most of his/her prison sentence, resides in a work release facility to assist him/her in reintegrating back into society.

Z

Zebulon Brockway—An American penologist who pushed for the implementation of a parole system in the United States.

Index

Note: Page numbers followed by *f* designate figures; *b*, text box